Cases in
Global Marketing
Strategies:
2005 Annual Update

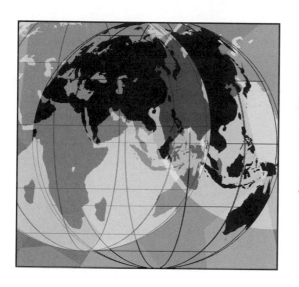

Cases in Global Marketing Strategies: 2005 Annual Update

Sixth Edition

Jean-Pierre Jeannet

F. W. Olin Distinguished Professor of Global Business
Babson College, Wellesley, Massachusetts

Professor of Global Marketing and Strategy
International Institute for Management Development (IMD)
Lausanne, Switzerland

H. David Hennessey

Associate Professor of Marketing and International Business
Babson College, Wellesley, Massachusetts

Associate, Ashridge Management College
Berkhamsted, United Kingdom

Houghton Mifflin Company   **Boston**   New York

V.P., Editor-in-Chief: *George Hoffman*
Technology Manager/Development Editor: *Damaris Curran*
Project Editor: *Kristin A. Penta*
Editorial Assistant: *Sage Anderson*
Senior Composition Buyer: *Sarah Ambrose*
Senior Art and Design Coordinator: *Jill Haber*
Senior Manufacturing Coordinator: *Priscilla Bailey*
Senior Marketing Manager: *Steven W. Mikels*
Marketing Associate: *Lisa E. Boden*

Cover image: *Jun Yamashita / Photonica*

Printed in the U.S.A.

Library of Congress Control Number: 2004105478

ISBN: 0-618-310614

123456789-QWF-08 07 06 05 04

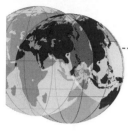

Contents

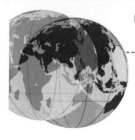

Preface

This 2005 casebook update has been designed to accompany *Global Marketing Strategies, Sixth Edition.* By combining the cases in a separate book, we are able to provide regular annual updates rather than be limited to the revision cycles of the main text.

In choosing the collection of cases provided here, our aim has been to provide ample opportunity for both students and instructors to apply the concepts and principles appropriate to global marketing in a changing world and across a variety of industry and geographic settings.

The case collection has undergone substantial additions from the previous version (© 2004). Three new copyright 2003 cases have been added. The new cases reflect our drive toward more global marketing issues, and an attempt to include more strategically oriented cases.

Here is a brief description of the four new cases for this casebook update:

- "Toyota: Repositioning the Brand in Europe (A)" deals with the positioning of the Toyota brand in Europe. Considered are three options: (1) positioning as a Japanese brand, (2) as a European brand, and/or (3) as a global brand.
- "Manchester United PLC" is considered one of the strongest global sports or team brands. The case deals with the global approach taken by Manchester United, ranging from sponsorships and marketing or team kits, to player and media strategies.
- "Real Madrid Club De Fútbol" is a football club with a long tradition and the major challenger for global dominance to Manchester United. Real Madrid has chosen a different pathway to develop its brand globally. The case allows students to pose the question as to which club has a better approach in the long run.
- "Football Club Ajax," the third case in a new series, highlights a club from a small country (Netherlands) competing against clubs globally who come from large markets (UK, or Spain).

Cases that have been eliminated from the previous edition include the following:

- "Make Yourself Heard: Ericsson's Global Brand Campaign"
- "ABB Flexible Automation (A): Global Strategy for the Millennium"
- "ABB Flexible Automation (B): Global Strategy for the Millennium"
- "A Note on the Robotics and Flexible Automation Industry (1999)"

All cases remain available through ECCH sources in Europe or the United States.

Cases that have been retained from the previous edition include the following:

- A group of four cases, "Note on the World Over-the-Counter (OTC) Drug Industry," "Note on the Competitors in the OTC Drug Industry," "Note on OTC Brands," and "Ciba Self Medication," describe the situation in the over-the-counter drug industry prior to the merger of Ciba with Sandoz to form Novartis Consumer Health.

- "Interactive Computer Systems Corp." deals with the issues of pricing, parallel imports, and gray markets.

- "ICI Paints (B): Considering a Global Product Organization" focuses on global strategy and global organizations.

- "Gillette International's TRAC II" highlights competitive strategies within the global marketplace.

- "Delissa in Japan (Revised)" deals with a European food company in the process of entering the Japanese market.

- A group of cases dealing with global account management and its managerial challenges, consisting of "Marriott International," "Hewlett-Packard," and "Xerox Corporation."

- "tonernow.com: A Dot-Com goes Global" deals with an existing small and entrepreneurial bricks and mortar business that wants to change into clicks and mortar by taking advantage of e-business opportunities.

- "Euro RSCG Worldwide: Global Brand Management in Advertising" deals with the global branding and account management practice of one of the largest advertising agencies.

Acknowledgments

The content of the cases would not have been possible without the generous participation of a number of companies and executives: Herman Scopes and John Thompson (ICI paints); Roland Jeannet (Novartis Consumer Health and OTC Series), Henry Kasindorf and Richard Katz (Tonernow.Com), and Bob Schmetterer (Euro RSCG). These executives, and others who prefer to remain anonymous, gave generously of their time so that other current and future managers could learn from their experiences. We would like to thank our colleagues Kamran Kashani (Ericsson), Dominique Turpin (Delissa Japan, Toyota Repositioning the Brand in Europe), Sean Meehan (Toyota), and Bob Collins (co-author of Manchester United, Real Madrid, and Ajax Amsterdam cases) from IMD for their willingness to have those cases reprinted in our new casebook version. We would also like to thank Persita Egeli, head of Case Administration at IMD, who provided us with crucial support in guiding our cases through the approval, release, and copyright process.

   To turn the collected material and data into readable form, we counted on a number of students, graduate assistants, and research associates. We wish to thank former Babson College students Peter Mark, Christine Detweiler, and Shauna Pettit, who wrote parts of the cases used in this text. We are grateful to Barbara Priovolos, Susan Nye, Robert Howard, Martha Lanning, and Caleb McCann, who in their roles as research associates wrote several of the cases at IMD and Babson College.

J.P.J.   H.D.H.

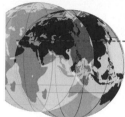

CASE 1

Note on the World Over-the-Counter (OTC) Drug Industry

In early December of 1994, Roland M. Jeannet, recently appointed to head Ciba's global Self Medication (OTC) business, convened a three-day strategy meeting near Geneva Airport.

By next spring we need to develop a complete road map of how we want to compete in this industry. Before we do this, however, we need to answer some fundamental questions about our industry. The questions foremost on my mind include how any company, to be successful, will have to compete in this industry, now and in the future. Will past industry practices be applicable as we move into the 21st century? Is this a global industry, run on a global scale, that will lend itself to global marketing approaches, or is this a regional or even local industry that will have to be directed accordingly? Unless we can come to some understanding of the rules of this industry, we cannot make real progress towards a strategy that will secure an important place for Ciba in Self-Medication.[1]

OTC INDUSTRY OVERVIEW

Over-the-counter (OTC) pharmaceutical products were consumer health care products approved but nonprescription bound. In 1995, the global market was estimated at US$51 billion. The pharmaceutical industry

●

This case was written by Kristi Menz and Shauna Pettit, MBA candidates at the F. W. Olin Graduate School of Business at Babson College, under the direction of Professor Jean-Pierre Jeannet. Copyright © 1997 by IMD—International Institute for Management Development, Lausanne, Switzerland. All rights reserved. Not to be used or reproduced without written permission directly from IMD.

1. Ciba prefers to use the term *self-medication* instead of *over-the-counter* (OTC).

and, specifically, the OTC sector, was characterized by fragmentation. The entire industry was changing rapidly. There were changes in ownership of the players, growing consumer awareness, and new government regulations. Realizing that marketing OTC products to consumers required a different skill set than the one needed for ethical pharmaceuticals aimed at health care professionals, many international pharmaceutical companies were developing separate self-medication divisions or forming relationships with experienced OTC companies to market OTC products and switches based upon prescription products.

In broad terms, user segments were categorized as Self-Medicators, Doctor Seekers, Home Remedy Users, Non-treaters, and Don't Knows (refer to Exhibit 1). However, users often changed from one category to another depending on the type and severity of the ailment.

Not only was it difficult to lump consumers into consistent market segments, but their demographics and attitudes were changing (refer to Exhibit 2). Top OTC markets, such as Europe, Japan, and the United States, had to adapt to aging populations. Consumers and government alike tended to turn to self-medication to fight rising health care costs. Consumers in most markets were also moving toward more alternative, natural remedies.

OTC INDUSTRY SIZE AND STRUCTURE

It was estimated that the world market for OTCs would reach U.S.$53 billion in 1996 and sustain a compound annual growth rate (CAGR) of over 7 percent through the year 2004. The United States was estimated to have the majority of the 1996 sales in the world OTC market at 31 percent, with Europe following closely behind at 29 percent.[2] Japan's share of the revenues was estimated at 17 percent (refer to Exhibit 3).

2. Excluding sales of most eastern European countries.

Exhibit 1 ● Analysis of Consumer Segments by Source of Treatment: % of Adult Populations Suffering Minor Ailments

	Self-medicators	*Doctor Seekers*	*Home Remedy Users*	*Non-treaters*	*DK*
FRANCE	26%	48%	4%	19%	3%
GERMANY	25	55	4	14	2
SPAIN	26	54	5	11	4
UNITED KINGDOM	30	22	3	45	0

Self-medicators—Those who usually or always buy OTCs instead of visiting a doctor.
Doctor seekers—Those who usually or always go to the doctor for advice and a prescription.
Home remedy users—Those who often use something they have at home rather than seeking a prescription or buying an OTC.
This category has some overlap with doctor seekers and self-medicators.
Non-treaters—Those who usually or always do not treat an ailment.
DK—Those who don't know.

Historically, the United States had experienced the highest growth of any country or region. By the year 2004, growth rates of Asian countries were expected to surpass all other regions (refer to Exhibit 4).

The top ten OTC companies accounted for almost 35 percent of worldwide industry sales in 1995 (Exhibit 5). Mergers and acquisitions were common in the industry. With that trend expected to continue, market analysts predicted the top ten companies would command more than 50 percent of global OTC revenues by the year 2005 (see Exhibits 6 and 7).

RELATIONSHIP TO PHARMACEUTICAL INDUSTRY

An important relationship existed between OTCs and the pharmaceutical industry as a whole, since OTCs accounted for 17 percent of total 1995 pharmaceutical industry sales. Of sixty-six new OTC brands introduced over a seventeen-year period by fourteen leading United States marketers, 30 percent were switches.[3] In the United States, the ten top-selling switched products since 1975 accounted for sales of U.S.$1047 million in 1994 compared to only U.S.$316 million for the ten top-selling new OTC brands introduced during the same period. Increasingly, pharmaceutical companies

3. Switches were pharmaceutical products approved for OTC status.

found OTC switches an important means of justifying the heavy R&D costs associated with developing new prescription drugs. As an executive at Ciba Self Medication stated, "We think that with investment in consumer advertising and some changes to a drug (i.e., taste, delivery system, etc.) we can extend the life cycle of a prescription drug significantly" (Exhibit 8).

There were two ways to develop new OTC products. The first, and most common, was to reformulate a prescription-bound product for use as an OTC. This usually meant lowering the dosage and/or strength and perhaps changing the drug delivery system. In the industry, this was referred to as a switch. The other way was to scan the world market for ingredients that had already been tested and approved. Often by introducing a new combination of ingredients, companies had been able to make innovations in the OTC market without developing new substances from scratch. For example, Procter & Gamble was awaiting final patent approval of a new cold remedy which combined ibuprofen and an antihistamine, both commonly available ingredients used in other products, but never before used together.

If a company did not have its own products moving through its research and development pipeline, there were several other ways of adding a new product: licensing, acquisitions, joint ventures, and comarketing.

Exhibit 2 ● Changing Consumer Demographics

% of Population by Age 1994						
Age	France	Germany	Italy	United Kingdom	United States	Japan
0–14	9.9%	17.1%	15.7%	19.6%	21.9%	17.1%
15–64	65.4	68.2	69.0	64.8	65.5	69.5
65–79	10.8	10.8	12.0	11.8	9.7	10.9
80+	3.9	3.8	3.4	3.6	2.9	2.5

Estimated % of Population by Age 1998						
Age	France	Germany	Italy	United Kingdom	United States	Japan
0–14	19.5%	17.1%	15.1%	20.0%	21.8%	16.5%
15–64	65.1	67.8	67.3	64.6	65.7	68.2
65–79	11.6	11.7	13.1	11.6	9.4	12.4
80+	3.8	3.4	3.4	3.8	3.0	2.9

Growth in Self-medicators			
	% Adult Pop. 1993	% Adult Pop. 2000	% Growth
USA	38%	45%	18%
FRANCE	26	33	30
GERMANY	25	45	80
SPAIN	26	32	23
UK	30	45	50

Annual OTC Consumption per Capita (US$ ex-manu. sales)		
	1990	1995
US	27	55
GERMANY	20	85
FRANCE	16	80
UK	13	23
ITALY	8	23
JAPAN	36	67

Source: Scrip Reports & OTC Review 1996.

Exhibit 3 ● World Self-medication Market by Volume, 1996 (estimated)

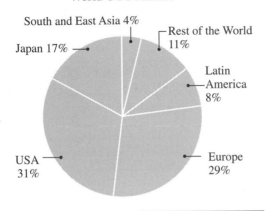

World OTC Market

- South and East Asia 4%
- Japan 17%
- Rest of the World 11%
- Latin America 8%
- USA 31%
- Europe 29%

Source: James Dudley International Ltd. trade estimates 1996; from *Self-Medication in Europe,* vol. 1, *The European Market,* p. 1-1.

Exhibit 4 ● Historic and Forecast Growth Rates in the World OTC Market

	Average Growth	
	1989–1993	1993–2004
Europe	4.3%	5.8%
USA	6.0	5.9
Japan	3.4	5.2
Others[a]	4.7	6.7

a. Historic estimate based on average IMS Asia growth rate.
Source: OTC Insight (IMS), Kline, 1994; from Zyma.

American Home Products and Warner-Lambert each chose different strategies for developing their product portfolio. American Home Products often used licensing and acquisition. To develop the brand Advil, AHP licensed the U.S. distribution rights for the active ingredient, ibuprofen, from Boots, a British company. To enter the vitamin, mineral, and supplement (VMS) market, on the other hand, AHP acquired American Cyanamid.

Warner-Lambert was well known for entering into joint venture agreements. It had two major joint venture agreements with pharmaceutical companies Glaxo and Wellcome. Since the merger of Glaxo and Wellcome in 1995, Warner-Lambert had pledged to repurchase its share of the OTC Warner Wellcome Consumer Healthcare joint venture.

Another frequently used strategy was comarketing agreements with other companies. In this case, a company would sell its brand to another OTC company to be marketed under a different brand name in the same geographic market. This strategy was used when it was not in the strategic interest of a company to employ a larger sales force in a secondary market.

OTC INDUSTRY PARTICIPANTS

The lines between participants in the OTC industry were fuzzy at best. The level of vertical integration varied greatly among the players. In general, however, they could be classified as chemical intermediate suppliers, OTC manufacturers distributors, and retailers (refer to Exhibit 9). In addition, consumers, doctors, governments, and managed care organizations had an important impact on the industry.

Chemical Intermediate Suppliers

Fine chemical companies produced the active ingredients which were the building blocks of OTCs. They started with base chemicals of natural origins or made from petrochemicals. These base chemicals were then combined to form the intermediates or active ingredients. OTC companies could either source the active ingredients from the fine chemicals industry or produce them internally.

OTC Manufacturers

OTC manufacturers provided the critical link from active ingredient to the pharmacy shelf. Most of the major international competitors were divisions of larger companies.

OTC manufacturers were generally responsible for developing, registering, manufacturing, packaging, and marketing OTC products. This varied greatly according to the level of integration of the company and the specifics of the product involved. Manufacturers began their part of the process by either switching a product from prescription status or by reformulating commonly available active ingredients. They performed efficacy and safety tests in an effort to get the

Exhibit 5 ● OTC Company Rank, 1995

	World			Europe		
Rank	Company	Home Country	Share of Market	Company	Home Country	Share of Market
1	J&J	US	6.9%	Rhone	France	4.1%
2	AHP	US	4.8	Bayer	Germany	3.2
3	Bayer	Germany	3.9	SmithKline	UK	3.0
4	P&G	US	3.8	Roche	Switz.	2.7
5	SmithKline	UK	3.2	AHP	US	2.5
6	W-L	US	3.0	Boehringer	Germany	2.4
7	Rhone	France	2.6	Ciba	Switz.	2.2
8	BMS	US	2.5	Pierre Fabre	France	2.0
9	Ciba	Switz.	2.3	Servier	France	2.0
10	Roche	Switz.	1.6	Sanofi	France	1.9
Top 10 Share of Market			34.6%			26.0%

	United States			Japan		
Rank	Company	Home Country	Share of Market	Company	Home Country	Share of Market
1	J&J	US	14.3%	Taisho	Japan	19.2%
2	AHP	US	9.1	Takeda	Japan	8.1
3	P&G	US	7.2	Sato	Japan	7.5
4	W-L	US	5.8	SS Pharma	Japan	7.0
5	Bayer	Germany	5.3	Kowa	Japan	5.1
6	SmithKline	UK	3.9	Chugai	Japan	4.1
7	BMS	US	3.7	Sankyo	Japan	3.4
8	Abbott	US	3.7	Eisai	Japan	3.1
9	Schering	US	2.8	Zevia	Japan	2.9
10	Ciba	Switz.	2.7	Zenyaku	Japan	2.8
Top 10 Share of Market			58.5%			63.2%

Source: OTC Review 1996.

product registered for sale as an OTC. Once the product received regulatory approval, full-scale manufacturing started. Manufacturers packaged the products themselves and then either distributed them to a wholesaler or directly to a retailer. Their final responsibility was to market the product to health care professionals, retailers, and consumers.

Distributors

Distributors were responsible for the transportation of OTC products from the manufacturer to the retailer, or in some cases, directly to the consumer. Manufacturers had the choice of either distributing the products themselves, distributing their products

Exhibit 6 ● Share of World OTC Market (%) Held by Top Ten Players

	World	*USA*	*Europe*	*Japan*
1991 SOM[a] by top 10 Players	30%	47.7%	27.3%	55.1%[b]
1995 SOM by top 10 Players	34.6	58.4	25.7[c]	63.2
2005 SOM by top 10 Players	50+		54.0	

a. SOM=Share of market
b. 1990 for Japan.
c. If self-medication sales only are included, the percentage goes up to 28.7.

Source: Scrip Reports: *Rx to OTC Report* (p. 6), *OTC Review 1995, OTC Bulletin,* January 25, 1996.

Exhibit 7 ● Merger and Acquisition in the OTC Industry, 1993–1995

Business	*Buyer*	*Seller*	*Price (millions)*	*Sales (millions)*	*Pretax profit (millions)*	*Price/profit ratio*	*Price/sales ratio*
JV to market OTC products	Warner-Lambert	Wellcome	n/a	—	—	—	—
License agreement for WW to market Glaxo's switches	Glaxo	Warner Wellcome	n/a	—	—	—	—
Sterling Health	SmithKline Beecham	Eastman Kodak	U.S.$2,900	U.S.$1,006	—	—	2.9
Sterling Health North American business	Bayer AG	SmithKline Beecham	U.S.$1,000	U.S.$346	—	—	2.9
American Cyanamid	American Home Products	Takeover	U.S.$9,600	U.S.$4,277	—	—	2.2
North American OTC business	Ciba	Rhône-Poulenc Rorer	U.S.$407[a]	U.S.$154	—	—	2.6
43.57% stake in Lipha of France (took holding over 96%)	E Merk	Coopération Pharmaceutique Française	Undisclosed	FF 2,820	FF 306	—	—
Wellcome	Glaxo	Takeover	£9,000	£2,280	£738	12.2	3.9
Planta-Subtil of Germany	Boeringer Ingelheim	Takeover	Undisclosed	DM 22	—	—	—
Soekami Lefrancq of France	Roche	Roussel Uclaf	Undisclosed	FF 200	—	—	—
Marion Merrell Dow	Hoechst	Dow/Takeover	U.S.$7,150	U.S.$3,060	U.S.$438[b]	16.3	2.3

Exhibit 7 ● Merger and Acquisition in the OTC Industry, 1993–1995 (*Continued*)

Business	Buyer	Seller	Price (millions)	Sales (millions)	Pretax profit (millions)	Price/profit ratio	Price/sales ratio
Gastrocote brand[c]	Seton Healthcare	Boeringer Mannheim	£10.0	£2.6	£1.8 gross	—	3.8
Pharmacia & Upjohn	Merger	Merger	—	U.S.$6,800	—	—	—
Milupa of Germany	Nutricia	Atlanta Group	DM 820	DM1,000	DM 25	36.9	0.9
Fisons	Rhône-Poulenc Rorer	Takeover	£1,830	£500[d]	£100[d]	—	3.7[d]
Ferrosan of Denmark (70% stake)	Management buyout	Novo Nordisk	DKK 400	DKK 600 app.	—	—	—
Woodward's brand	Seton Healthcare	London International	£4.8	£2.2	£1.0 gross	—	2.2
Biogal of Hungary (78% stake)	Teva of Israel	—	U.S.$26	U.S. $102	U.S.$5.4 net	—	0.3
Setlers Brand	Stafford-Miller	SmithKline Beecham	Undisclosed	—	—	—	—
Pharmavit of Hungary	Bristol-Myers Squibb	Takeover	U.S.$110	U.S. $39.6	U.S.$6.05	18.2	2.8
Diocalm and Ralgex brands	Seton Healthcare	SmithKline Beecham	£7.85	£2.16	£1.4 gross	—	3.3
Abtei Pharma of Germany	SmithKline Beecham	Private owner	DM 203	DM 110	—	—	1.8
Warner Wellcome (acquisition)	Warner-Lambert	Glaxo Wellcome	U.S.$1,050	U.S.$360	—	—	2.9

a. Estimated net value of transaction over seven years, Ciba has U.S.$143 million option to purchase intellectual property rights after seven years.

b. Net income 1994.

c. Worldwide rights excluding Austria, Slovakia, and Portugal in Europe. Most U.K. sales on prescription.

d. Fisons' pharmaceutical operation had sales of £254 million in the six months to June 20, 1995. Operating profit was £47.6 million.

Source: OTC Bulletin, January 25, 1996, p. 18.

through wholesalers, or using an agency distribution system.

Wholesalers bought in volume from the manufacturer and then resold the inventory to retailers. Often, carriers acted as middlemen between manufacturers and wholesalers to physically transport the product from one to another. However, ownership of the inventory went directly from the manufacturer to the wholesaler.

Agency distribution differed from wholesaling only in the ownership of the products. With an agency, the manufacturer retained ownership of the products until they were distributed to retailers. The agency was responsible for distributing the products and re-

Exhibit 8 ● Product Life Cycle Extension Through a Prescription-to-OTC Switch

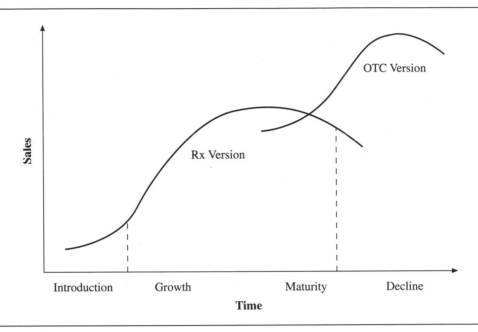

Exhibit 9 ● The Generalized Distribution Channel for OTC Products (Manufacturers, Wholesalers, Retailers, Consumers)

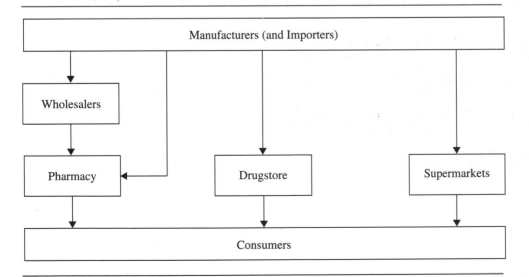

Source: Datamonitor; from *European Pharmaceuticals,* "Switching to OTC Status," p. 26.

Exhibit 10 ● Possible Distribution Channels for OTC Products

Country	Pharmacy	Chain Pharmacy	Drugstore	Chain Drugstores	Grocery
France	X				
Germany	X		X[a]	X[a]	X[a]
Italy	X	n/a			
United Kingdom	X	X	X[a]	X[a]	X[a]
United States	X	X	X	X	X
Japan	X	X	X	X	

n/a = data not available

a. Limited to OTC products that have been available for a long time and are frequently purchased by consumers (e.g., confectionery cough drops and chewable antacids).

ceived a management fee for its services. The manufacturer still had the ultimate control over the price of its products to retailers. Glaxo used this system extensively and with much success. Because of this, other pharmaceutical and OTC manufacturers were considering a switch to agency distributors.

Retailers

The most common retail outlet varied from one geographic region to the next. In part, government regulation was to blame, but consumer lifestyles and retail preferences were also important determinants. Pharmacies were the most common distribution outlet in Europe, Japan, and to a lesser extent in the United States. Other retailers included food stores, drugstores,[4] mass merchandisers, and mail order companies (refer to Exhibit 10).

Europe   In 1993, OTC sales through pharmacies accounted for 85 percent of the total market in Europe, which made them the most important OTC distribution channel for all countries except the Netherlands (refer to Exhibit 11). In the future, sales in pharmacies were expected to fall as governments deregulated the

4. Drugstores differed from pharmacies in that the former did not require a pharmacist to be on staff. In addition, pharmacies could dispense prescription-only medicines, whereas drugstores could not.

retail sector. Several EU countries were beginning to discuss legislation which would allow distribution of OTCs in outlets other than pharmacies. In the United Kingdom and Germany, for instance, some categories of OTCs were frequently sold in drugstores and supermarkets.

United States   Thirty-eight percent of all OTC sales in the United States came from pharmacies. Combination stores made up an additional 25 percent of sales (refer to Exhibit 12). The growth of mass merchandisers and in-store pharmacies in the United States caused a continuing decline of sales through independent pharmacies. More and more "mom and pop" stores closed down. Distributing OTC products through the mail represented a very small portion of the industry but was a growing trend in the United States, especially to care facilities that required products in bulk. This trend was most evident in the sale of vitamins and nutritional supplements. It was attractive for consumers and governments who wanted to cut health care costs since it was often cheaper than other distribution and retailing methods. In 1990, more than half of the pharmaceutically-oriented mail order companies carried OTCs.

Japan   Japan had five categories of pharmaceutical retailers. At each level, there were more and more restrictions on the activities retailers could perform.

Exhibit 11 ● European Consumer Purchases of OTC Medicines in Pharmacy Compared to Nonpharmacy Outlets, 1993

	% Purchases by Value		
Country	*Pharmacy Purchases*	*Nonpharmacy Purchases*	*Commentary*
France	100%	<1%	Restricted to limited vitamin products only
Germany	87	13	Excludes analgesics, antacids, and cough, cold, and flu medicines
Hungary	65	35	Herbal medicines largely sold through herbalists
Netherlands	36	64	Druggists licensed to sell OTC brands in limited pack sizes
United Kingdom	69	31	General sale list for nonpharmacy outlets

Source: James Dudley International Ltd. Trade.

Pharmacies were at the top level and were allowed to both sell and dispense drugs. Drugstores usually fell into the first-class retailer category, which was one step below pharmacies. First-class retailers could not dispense drugs and were only allowed to sell them. Traditionally, most OTCs were sold through pharmacies. However, drugstores were becoming a popular channel for OTC sales in Japan, as the government continued its effort to separate the prescribing and dispensing activities traditionally taking place at the doctor level.

Consumers

Rising health care costs, delisting of reimbursable drugs, and increasing health-conscienceness caused a growing number of consumers to turn to OTCs. Unlike the prescription pharmaceutical industry, consumers had the ultimate choice over brands and products.

This was less the case in Europe, where 36 percent of the overall OTC sales came from doctors "prescribing" non–prescription-bound products (commonly known as semi-ethicals). In many European countries, semi-ethicals were used by the government as a stepping stone to a product becoming a completely nonreimbursable OTC.[5] Consumers often sought

5. In many European countries, governments reimbursed consumers for prescription drugs through government-controlled health insurance.

prescriptions for OTCs, knowing that medicines purchased on prescription were government-reimbursable. This practice was especially prevalent in Germany and France with 41.8 percent and 46.1 percent of their respective OTC sales in 1994 generated through these semi-ethical products. Both British and German law allowed advertising of reimbursable OTCs directly to consumers, which continued to drive sales of semi-ethical products. In France, consumers shied away from self-medicating and preferred to get prescriptions from doctors. Other European markets had similar characteristics.

Doctors

Other than prescribing semi-ethicals in Europe, doctors did not impact the OTC industry in the same manner as for Rx products. OTC manufacturers sometimes found it difficult to persuade doctors to recommend OTCs. This was partly because they lacked sufficient information about OTCs and their efficacy and partly because doing so effectively cut them out of the payment loop. Doctors in the United Kingdom were the exception, and they had a reputation for being in favor of OTC medicines.

Doctor recommendations were not critical, but they did significantly impact a product's sales in some cases. A good example was the marketing of Advil and Nuprin in their launch year (1984). Advil spent

Exhibit 12 ● U.S. OTC Distribution by Outlet, 1993

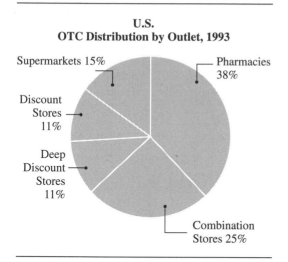

**U.S.
OTC Distribution by Outlet, 1993**

Supermarkets 15%

Pharmacies 38%

Discount Stores 11%

Deep Discount Stores 11%

Combination Stores 25%

Source: Contributors/James Dudley International Ltd/Calc JDI.

U.S.$1 million on advertising to professionals with a dedicated sales team, while Nuprin completely neglected advertising to this segment. After one year, Advil achieved sales of U.S.$79 million, compared to only U.S.$15 million for Nuprin. This and other examples proved to manufacturers that, at the very least, they needed passive support from doctors. If a consumer asked for a recommendation on a particular product, the worst possible situation from the manufacturer's standpoint was for a doctor to dissuade the consumer from buying that product.

Government and Managed Care Organizations

Governments, insurance companies, managed care organizations (e.g., HMOs and PPOs), and pharmacy benefit managers (PBMs) played an important role in the OTC industry. By delisting drugs from reimbursement, or adding OTCs to their formularies, or purchasing OTC products for distribution to consumers, these institutions had a direct impact on the industry. Rising health care costs forced a growing number of consumers and governments to look for help from OTCs. The United States set the trend in

this area, mostly due to its privatized health care system.

Experts estimated that some 18 percent of U.S. managed care organizations offered reimbursement for some OTC products. Furthermore, future sales and marketing strategies were affected, as OTC manufacturers began lobbying HMOs to add OTCs to their lists of reimbursable drugs. Products with the highest chance of being added to HMO or PBM formularies were those that could possibly reduce future costs to the organization through prevention or substitution. SmithKline Beecham (SB), for example, lobbied HMOs to reimburse its OTC smoking cessation aid, Nicorette. SB's main selling point was that the relatively inexpensive Nicorette would reduce future, expensive-to-treat degenerative diseases. Similar advantages were touted for home diagnostic products, which could curtail costs due to doctor visits and unnecessary surgery.

In the United States, the drive to lower costs came from consumers. In other countries, governments shouldered most of the burden for health care; thus, HMOs were not as prevalent. Rather than privatize their health care systems through HMOs, governments preferred to contain costs in other ways (e.g., with price controls for OTCs or pressure on doctors to prescribe fewer reimbursable drugs). Still, the state health care systems operating in many European countries were similar to managed care organizations, since they, too, bought in volume and had considerable leverage with a full range of health care suppliers. As U.S. managed care organizations looked to expand, it was possible for them to become advisors to foreign organizations.

Regulators

Regulators played an integral role in the OTC industry. They governed which products could be switched from Rx to OTC status, determined manufacturing guidelines to be followed, had an impact on where products could be sold, and how the marketing could be done. This was especially true for the European and Japanese markets. Each country had its own set of rules regarding OTC products. However, as the member countries of the European Union worked toward harmonization, adapting to the local countries' regulations was expected to become easier.

OTC COMPANY OPERATIONS

Research & Development

R&D for OTCs differed from prescription-bound products. With OTCs, the active ingredients had already been developed, causing most research to center on new delivery systems, flavors, and product stability. Typically, products only incurred 2–5 percent of their final retail cost at this stage (refer to Exhibit 13). In the case of switched products, OTC firms benefited from the basic clinical and safety work done by the pharma division of its parent company or the licensor. Increasing price pressure in the industry further caused many companies to focus their attention on new formulations of existing compounds as opposed to searching for new ones.

The Registration Process

OTC manufacturers were responsible for conducting clinical trials before being granted regulatory approval to market. In the case of a switch, this was less extensive than for the original Rx approval. Many of the required trials were completed by the pharma company which had initially developed the drug. The main element of this process was to prove effectiveness at the OTC dose and a side effect profile safe enough for consumers to use without doctor supervision. In cases where the product in question utilized a new drug delivery system, the company had to prove to regulators that it did not dramatically alter the effects of the drug compared to its original prescription form.

Production Processes

Production centered around active ingredients. The trend was for OTC and pharma firms to divest themselves of this task, however, preferring instead to spend their investment dollars on R&D and marketing. Some of the larger companies had their own chemical divisions, which perhaps also did synthesis

---

Exhibit 13 ● Cost Structure of the OTC Industry, by Percentage of Total Cost

The cost structure of the industry varied depending on the country, the size of the players, and the level of integration. The general trends can be observed with the following breakdown:

MANUFACTURERS			60–70%
Cost of Goods Sold		17–23%	
Raw Materials	2–4%		
Packaging	5–9		
Direct Labour	2–4		
Equipment	1–2		
Quality Control	1–2		
Manufacturing Overhead	5–8		
Transportation		2–5	
Research & Development		2–5	
General & Administrative		2–5	
Marketing & Sales		17–23	
Profit		7–12	
WHOLESALERS			7–12
RETAILERS			15–25
CONSUMERS			100%

for smaller OTC companies to gain economies of scale. Rhone-Poulenc Rorer, for instance, had a fine chemicals division generating between U.S.$400–U.S.$500 million per year on overall company sales of about U.S.$4.2 billion (10–12 percent).

Dosage manufacturing began after the production of the active ingredients. There were several guidelines which had been adopted first by the United States and then by Europe to regulate the manufacturing process. Good Manufacturing Practices (GMPs) were followed by all international companies, since most of the major markets required it for products that were sold in their countries.

Packaging Operations

Unlike prescription pharmaceuticals, OTCs packaging was an extremely important part of the manufacturing process. Packaging had to be eye-catching and appealing to consumers. Safety, as in the case of child-resistant packaging, was also a major concern. Thus, packaging accounted for almost twice as much of the cost of a product as the active ingredients themselves. Manufacturers generally packaged the product themselves, mostly in small packages ready for resale to consumers. Specific guidelines governing the required information for the inside and outside packages were stipulated by each country. All countries required that labeling be printed in the native language of the country where the product was marketed (which was another reason that packaging absorbed a large part of product cost). The EU, in working toward harmonization, hoped to specify one set of packaging guidelines for all member countries.

As with packaging, labeling was regulated by individual countries. Labeling requirements were relatively stringent in most countries; however, it was up to manufacturers to decide how much warning information to include on the package in excess of the requirements. In the case of Europe, EC Directive 92/27/EEC identified sixteen standard OTC labeling requirements for all member countries. The United States did not have a similar labeling procedure, although it hoped to adopt stricter regulation in the future.

Distribution of OTCs

There were several distribution alternatives available to manufacturers. These alternatives included whole-saling, direct and self-distribution, parallel importing, and direct-to-consumer. The preferred method of distribution varied widely, depending on the geographic region. In the United States and Japan, the distributors tended to be the manufacturers themselves, perhaps hiring a carrier to physically transport the goods. As with the chemical synthesis process, manufacturers tended to stick to their core competencies rather than concentrating on distribution.

In Europe, a bulk of the distributing was done through independent wholesalers. The distributors added little value; however, in the case of wholesalers, they had a fair amount of leverage. The wholesaling trend toward large-scale operations and quantity discounts meant eroded profit margins for manufacturers. A growing trend in wholesaling was to develop business on an international level. This allowed wholesalers to buy in greater volume and at lower prices. In Europe, wholesalers tried to gain the needed critical mass by integrating in all directions: vertically, horizontally, forward, and backward (refer to Exhibit 14). For example, Gehe, Germany's leading pharmaceutical wholesaler, began producing branded generic and nonprescription-bound products. These products, while accounting for less than 10 percent of 1994 sales, contributed to over 25 percent of the profits.

Exhibit 14 ● Vertical Integration of OTC Wholesalers

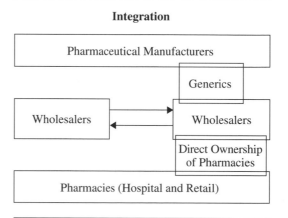

Integration

Source: Datamonitor; from *European Pharmaceutical,* "Switching to OTS Status," p. 29.

Direct distribution and self-distribution cut the middlemen out of the process. OTCs went directly from the manufacturer to the retailer. Direct distribution differed from self-distribution with respect to transportation. The manufacturer transported OTCs under direct distribution, and the retailer performed the task under self-distribution. Fewer OTCs in Europe were distributed through these channels, since retailers preferred delivery several times in one day due to a lack of storage space. Shelf space was divided among an increasing number of products, and it was difficult to stock in significant quantities.

In the United States direct distribution played a more significant role, since the trend in the United States was away from the independent pharmacies. The larger outlets that distributed OTCs in the United States did not need the frequent deliveries required by smaller pharmacies. Japanese manufacturers also preferred direct distribution to doing business with wholesalers. This was especially true of the major manufacturers such as Taisho, SS Pharmaceutical, and Sato (refer to Exhibit 15). The Japanese trend was furthered by government initiatives toward separation of prescribing and dispensing activities. As the main prescriber role shifted from doctor to pharmacist, it became much more economical to distribute in this fashion. Direct-to-consumer distribution was unique to the Japanese market and was only allowed for herbals and first-aid kit replenishing supplies.

Parallel importing, which involved the buying of OTCs in one country and selling them in another, was a factor in Europe. Distributors took advantage of regulated prices to buy products much cheaper in one country than they could be sold in another. Generally, distributors required a price differential of 20–25 percent between the same product in different countries

Exhibit 15 ● Taisho Pharmaceutical Company Direct Marketing System for OTC Drugs

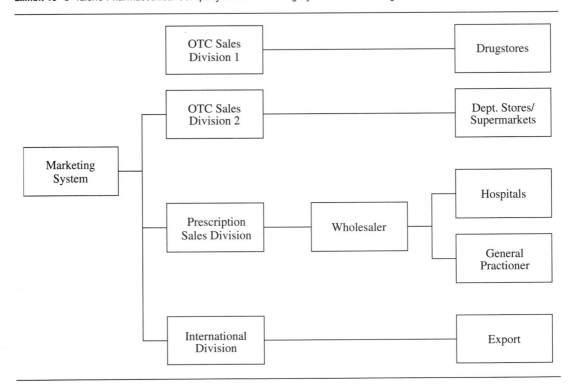

Source: MarketLine Annual Report.

for parallel importing to be lucrative. Parallel importing affected the prescription portion of the pharma industry much more than the OTC sector due to higher margins on the former.

Sales and Marketing Activities

The main role of a manufacturer in the marketing process was to create and maintain brand awareness. The OTC industry was increasingly competitive, so marketing and education were vital at all levels: consumers, retailers, distributors, and the medical community. Manufacturers used a combination of push and pull strategies, which included brand awareness advertising, keeping retailers shelves stocked with products, and detailing medical professionals.

Approximately one-fifth of the final cost of an OTC product (at consumer level) was spent on marketing and sales at the manufacturer level. Various activities contributed, the most common being customer service, brand management, sales, advertising, and promotion. Exhibit 16 shows a typical allocation of an OTC manufacturer's marketing budget.

There were essentially three types of product introductions that took place in the OTC industry, each with different launch costs. The most expensive launch was the introduction of a new brand (refer to Exhibit 17). The advertising-to-sales (A/S) ratio in the first year was almost always over 100 percent. The cheapest product introduction was to extend an existing brand. This required much less effort and money, since consumers were already familiar with other OTC products of the same brand name. Switching a prescription product to OTC status using the same name fell in between the two extremes.

Exhibit 16 ● Typical Marketing Budget for an OTC Manufacturer

Marketing Activity	Proportion of Budget
Customer service	6–9%
Brand management	10–14
Sales force	15–20
Advertising & promotion	65–75
Advertising	30–40
Consumer promotion	7–10
Trade promotion	15–20
Medical promotion	10–13
Total marketing & sales	100%

Consumer marketing programs relied primarily on television advertising and points-of-purchase displays. Supporting ads were sometimes placed in print media and billboards. Consumer education was an important part of the advertising campaign. For the consumer to understand the scientific message, a different level of advertising and education was needed. Pamphlets produced by manufacturers played an important part in the education process. They were given to retailers who then distributed them to the consumer. The pamphlets could specifically advertise the brand or could simply provide information on health care subjects. Furthermore, information contained on the packaging was an important educating tool, since most self-medicators did not have contact with informed health professionals.

Exhibit 17 ● New Product Launch Costs

	New OTC Product Launch Using New Brand Name	New OTC Product Launch Using Rx Brand Name	OTC Line Extension Using Existing Brand Name
Advertising $/year (millions)	U.S.$40–45	U.S.$25	U.S.$20
AS ratio after 3 or 4 years	40–50%	40%	30–40%
Breakeven point	5–7 years	3–5 years	3–4 years

Consumer education was even more important in Asian countries, such as Japan, where there was less differentiation between prescription and OTC medicines. Also, Asian consumers were very company and brand loyal, which made it difficult for new entrants.

Another source of information for consumers came from pharmacists and doctor recommendations. As such, a strong relationship with these groups was invaluable. It was the manufacturer and/or the distributor who educated the retailer on the use of the OTC product. Companies such as SmithKline Beecham, Glaxo, and others even started including training packages complete with reference manuals and videos in their professional and trade promotional campaigns for new OTCs.

OTC companies also marketed their products to the various managed care organizations. They positioned their products as preventive tools and/or an alternative to the higher-cost prescription drugs. However, since there was a fine line between being cost-conscious and providing quality care, there was a limit to how far this relationship could go. Managed care organizations needed to ensure to their subscribers that they were receiving as good, if not better, benefits than from competing providers.

GEOGRAPHIC SEGMENTS & TRENDS

There were four basic geographic regions that were important markets for the OTC industry: Europe, North America, the Pacific Rim, and the developing regions (the Far East and Latin America). These markets were grouped together because they had a similar infrastructure, and in some cases, harmonization efforts were underway via free trade pacts and other trade alliances. Exhibit 18 describes each region and its OTC sales.

The European Market and Trends

The European market was comprised of the fifteen European Union (EU) members, the associated countries of the European Free Trade Area (EFTA), eastern Europe, and the Community of Independent States (CIS).[6] This market accounted for 32 percent of in-

6. The Community of Independent States replaced the Soviet Union in 1990 and comprises Russia, Ukraine, and other former Soviet republics.

Exhibit 18A ● OTC Sales by Region, 1995

Country	OTC Sales (U.S.$bn)	% of World Total
Europe (including eastern Europe and CIS)	16.45	32%
North America	15.10	29
Pacific Rim	8.78	17
Latin America	4.14	8
Far East and China	4.55	9
Others	2.43	5
Total World	51.45	100%

dustry sales. Germany, France, and the United Kingdom were the dominant markets in this region (refer to Exhibit 18). Most European countries had a semi-ethical category for OTC products, and therefore, it was not uncommon for a consumer to receive partial reimbursement for a purchase.[7]

As a region, Europe was developing into a unified market, similar to the United States in size and scope. However, there were many aspects that made it more difficult to compete in this market. For one thing, there were as many different languages as countries. In the United States, there was one primary language. Furthermore, in all countries, governments played a strong role in the health care system, be it through compulsory health insurance programs, such as in France, or through administration of health funds, as in the case of Germany. In contrast, the majority of U.S. residents had private insurance policies which were administered by corporations. There was increasing pressure by governments to reduce health care expenditures, and since most medical plans included the reimbursement of pharmaceutical products, health authorities were more eager than before to see some pharmaceuticals switched to OTC status and/or taken off the reimbursement list.

European consumers had strong relationships with pharmacists and often relied on them as a source of information. This was especially true in countries where consumer advertising was either strictly controlled or altogether banned (refer to Exhibit 19).

7. Exceptions were the Netherlands and Finland.

Exhibit 18B ● OTC Sales Breakdowns by Region, 1995

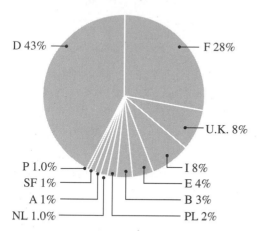

**Europe
Share of Total Sales of Non Rx-Bound Products
by Country, 1995**

D 43%
F 28%
U.K. 8%
P 1.0%
SF 1%
A 1%
NL 1.0%
I 8%
E 4%
B 3%
PL 2%

Total Sales in U.S.$ 16.45 billion
Ex-Manufacturer Sales in U.S.$

Source: OTC Review 1996, pp. 2-19, 3-1, 5-1.

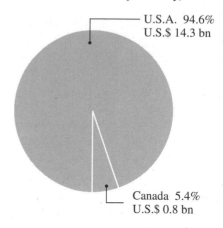

**North America
Self-Medication Sales by Country, 1995**

U.S.A. 94.6%
U.S.$ 14.3 bn

Canada 5.4%
U.S.$ 0.8 bn

Total Sales in U.S.$ 15.1 billion
Ex-Manufacturer Sales in U.S.$

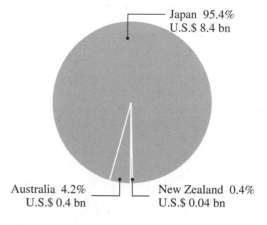

**Pacific Rim
Self-Medication Sales by Country, 1995**

Japan 95.4%
U.S.$ 8.4 bn

Australia 4.2%
U.S.$ 0.4 bn

New Zealand 0.4%
U.S.$ 0.04 bn

Total Sales in U.S.$ 8.8 billion
Ex-Manufacturer Sales in U.S.$

Consumer differences were subtle but nevertheless existed. Of all the European countries, the British were the least likely to treat ailments, but when they did, they were most likely to use OTCs. Germans were noted for their interest in using OTCs as preventative treatments. The French consumed the highest level of pharmaceuticals in the EU; however, they were culturally attached to reimbursable products. In general, reimbursement was less for OTCs and the French preferred the advice of doctors rather than reliance on self-diagnosis.

Government regulations differed from country to country as well. Price controls on ethical and semi-ethical pharmaceuticals existed in some countries, such as France, but not as much in others, such as the United Kingdom. Likewise advertising restrictions varied from one country to another, making some populations easier to reach than others.

Eastern Europe was rapidly developing as governments restructured their health care and reimburse-

Latin America
Self-Medication Sales by Country, 1995

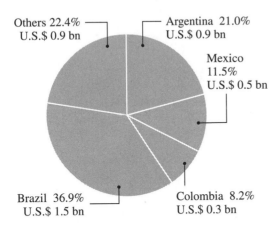

Total Sales in U.S.$ 4.1 billion
Ex-Manufacturer Sales in U.S.$

Far East and China
Self-Medication Sales by Country, 1995

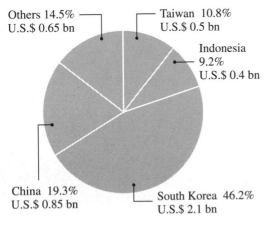

Total Sales in U.S.$ 4.5 billion
Ex-Manufacturer Sales in U.S.$

ment policies came more in line with those of the European Union. As a result, countries such as Hungary and the Czech Republic were aggressively developing the necessary marketing infrastructure for OTC products. Significant opportunities for expansion of OTC sales were predicted (refer to Exhibit 20).

Harmonization efforts were underway, and governments realized that open borders and cable television limited their ability to maintain the same kind of control. Furthermore, the propensity for consumers to self-medicate was increasing at a very fast pace. By the year 2000, Germany, France and the United Kingdom expected to have 45 percent of the population self-medicating, the same proportion as the United States.

The North American Segment and Trends

North America included Canada and the United States. The United States dominated the region with 95 percent of the sales (refer to Exhibit 18). The North America OTC market was well developed in comparison with the other regions of the world.

North America was an attractive market for OTCs not only because of its large, relatively homogeneous population, but due to its relatively loose advertising regulations. Both OTCs and prescription pharmaceuticals could be promoted directly to the public. However, these liberalized laws meant that regulatory bodies, such as the FTC, and other OTC competitors kept a close eye on advertising claims. Unsupported claims of safety and efficacy in Rx-to-OTC switches resulted in numerous lawsuits.

U.S. consumers were considered to be the most advanced in the world in terms of propensity to self-medicate. In 1993, 38 percent of the adult population were self-medicators. This was expected to grow to 45 percent by the year 2000. This was in part due to their history of privatized medicine, and the fact that American consumers were accustomed to taking both financial and personal responsibility for their health care.

Prescription products played an important role in the U.S. OTC industry. The driving forces behind new product introductions were the recent switches from prescription to OTC status. One reason was the threat of patent expiry on pharmaceutical products. Once a nonprescription product's patent expired, generic pro-

Exhibit 19 ● Advertising Regulation Differences Between Major Countries

Market	OTC Versions of Rx Brands Permitted	Advertising Reimbursed Brands Permitted	Advertising Limited to OTC Status Only	Media Permitted
France	Yes	No	Yes	All
Germany	Yes	Yes	No	All
Netherlands	Yes	Yes	No	All
UK	Yes	Yes	No	All
Italy	No	No	Yes	All
USA	Yes	Yes	No	All
Japan	Yes	n/a	n/a	All

n/a = not available

Source: James Dudley Self-Medication in Europe Volume 1, pages 1-39.

Exhibit 20 ● Eastern Europe OTC Growth

Region Totals		
1995 Sales in $US mn	*% Growth in 1994/1995*	
$737	34.7	

Sample Country Breakdowns		
	Industry Activity[a]	*Number of OTCs 1995*	*Recent Developments*
--------	--------	--------	--------
HUNGARY	100+ Switches in 1994/5	348	Non-Prescription Pharmaceutical Manufacturers and Wholesalers Association created
CZECH REPUBLIC	638 Switches 1994/5	1660	Gov't encouraging OTC switching and liberating prices

a. In 1994, Italy had approximately 190 switches, Germany had 5 switches, and France had 3 switches.

ducts inevitably appeared on the market, stealing profits from the original manufacturer. Also, a growing number of managed care organizations began adding OTCs to their formularies of approved medications. This gave added incentive to pharmaceutical companies to switch their products to OTC status. Finally, as mentioned above, the United States was the most liberal country with respect to the advertising of pharmaceutical products directly to consumers. Thus, Americans tended to be much more aware of a switch product's prescription and medical heritage.

Influential organizations in the United States, aside from the FDA, included the American Medical Association, and various specialty organizations such as the American Heart Foundation and the Arthritis Foundation. The FDA was the only organization which played a role in getting products approved. The other organizations were involved in independent research and their buy-in was very important to gaining the trust of the public. OTC companies had begun to pursue relationships with these organizations to help market their products. For example, Johnson & Johnson and the Arthritis Foundation partnered to introduce an anti-inflammatory product which carried the organization's name instead of a Johnson & Johnson brand name.

Canada, unlike the United States, was under a socialized health care system. Still, consumers in that market were much the same as their southern neighbors, since the socialized system did not cover pharmaceuticals. Only those people with private health insurance policies or those qualifying for social assistance received partial or full reimbursement for prescription and nonprescription products (much like Medicare, SSI, and Medicaid in the United States). To further development of the Canadian pharmaceutical market, regulators began to standardize pharma categories across provinces. A new registration system for OTCs was developed, which legislators hoped would result in faster registration times and a more efficient switching procedure. Additionally, more governmental resources were allocated for processing switch applications.

The Pacific Rim Segment and Trends

The Pacific Rim, comprising Japan, New Zealand, and Australia (refer to Exhibit 18), were separated from the other Far East countries primarily because they shared a similar level of sophistication regarding their consumers and their health care systems. All three were advanced economies with significant consumer purchasing power. Though all three countries were under socialized health care systems, private insurance plans were encouraged by the governments and were on the rise.

Japan was the dominant player in this area, accounting for approximately 17 percent of world OTC sales. Public health care was provided to all citizens through one of two ways: Employee Health Insurance (EHI) and National Health Insurance (NHI). Approximately two-thirds were provided for by EHI. Pre-

scription drugs were reimbursed, under both policies. EHI members contributed 10 percent of prescription drugs' cost whereas NHI members and EHI dependents contributed 30 percent.

Historically, it was difficult for western OTC companies to achieve critical mass in the Japanese market. First there were significant philosophical differences between Eastern and Western medical heritage. Eastern medicine was based on herbal remedies and acupuncture. The Japanese viewed OTCs as products for prevention rather than for treatment. Evidence of this was found in both the overwhelming popularity of tonics and vitamins and mineral supplements in Japan (the tonics segment was virtually nonexistent anywhere else with the exception of Germany) and the low usage of pain relief products compared to other countries (refer to Exhibit 21).

Second, there was a reluctance by the Japanese companies to expand internationally. This was illustrated by the fact that the industry structure in Japan had been unaffected by the wave of mergers and acquisitions taking place in North America and Europe. None of the Japanese companies consolidated to gain critical mass nor did they appear interested in buying any of the big OTC divisions that were up for sale (e.g., Sterling in 1994) in the United States or Europe.

Finally, retail prices for OTC products were unusually high in Japan (up to six times the ex-factory price). Thus, consumers still tended to seek medical advice for a majority of ailments. The high cost of OTCs was mostly due to Japan's resale price maintenance (RPM) scheme, which the government planned to dismantle by 1999. The disappearance of the RPM system was expected to lead to increased price cutting and discounting of OTC products. Margins for retailers ranged from 15–20 percent for tonics to 35–60 percent for other OTCs.

New Zealand experienced the highest growth rates in the region, but accounted for only .4 percent of sales in 1995. It was considered to be one of the most progressive OTC markets in the world. Switching was common, and regulators had an open attitude on advertising aimed at consumers.

Emerging Regions

Emerging regions included countries in Latin America, the Far East, and China (refer to Exhibit 18). Although

Exhibit 21 ● Market Segment Sales Breakdown for Non–Prescription-based Products, by Region and Major Country, 1995

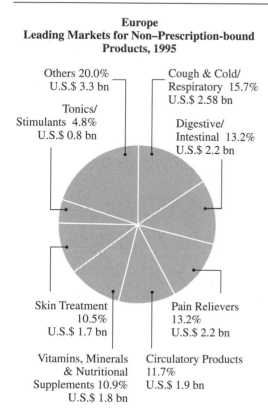

Europe
Leading Markets for Non–Prescription-bound Products, 1995

Others 20.0%
U.S.$ 3.3 bn

Cough & Cold/
Respiratory 15.7%
U.S.$ 2.58 bn

Tonics/
Stimulants 4.8%
U.S.$ 0.8 bn

Digestive/
Intestinal 13.2%
U.S.$ 2.2 bn

Skin Treatment
10.5%
U.S.$ 1.7 bn

Pain Relievers
13.2%
U.S.$ 2.2 bn

Vitamins, Minerals
& Nutritional
Supplements 10.9%
U.S.$ 1.8 bn

Circulatory Products
11.7%
U.S.$ 1.9 bn

Self-Medication Sales in U.S.$ 16.45 billion
Ex-Manufacturer Sales in U.S.$

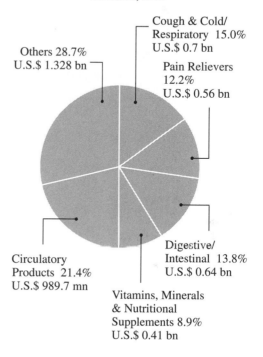

France
Leading Markets for Non–Prescription-bound Products, 1995

Others 28.7%
U.S.$ 1.328 bn

Cough & Cold/
Respiratory 15.0%
U.S.$ 0.7 bn

Pain Relievers
12.2%
U.S.$ 0.56 bn

Circulatory
Products 21.4%
U.S.$ 989.7 mn

Digestive/
Intestinal 13.8%
U.S.$ 0.64 bn

Vitamins, Minerals
& Nutritional
Supplements 8.9%
U.S.$ 0.41 bn

Self-Medication Sales in U.S.$ 4.62 billion
Ex-Manufacturer Sales in U.S.$

there were many cultural and geographic differences between emerging markets, there were also many similarities in the way they were viewed in the context of the OTC industry. For instance, their economies were still developing and, in some cases, governments were going through major restructuring. This impacted the OTC industry because historically there was less of a distinction between prescription-bound and non–prescription-bound products.

Most emerging markets showed a high incidence of illegal distribution of prescription-bound products. This suggested that part of the population was self-medicating. Because there was no infrastructure to encourage the introduction of new OTC drugs, distributors were doing so illegally.

Rapidly developing economies such as those in Southeast Asia, China, and Latin America were developing a more formalized health care system which included a more official place for OTC products. As this progressed, opportunities for OTC companies would increase.

MARKET SEGMENTS AND TRENDS

The OTC market was divided into eighteen different market segments followed by various therapeutic segments. The leading market segments varied somewhat

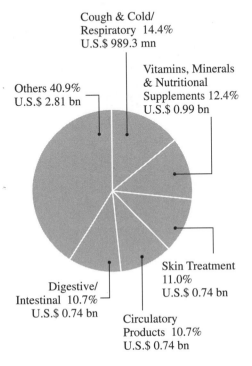

**Germany
Leading Markets for Non–Prescription-bound
Products, 1995**

Cough & Cold/
Respiratory 14.4%
U.S.$ 989.3 mn

Vitamins, Minerals
& Nutritional
Supplements 12.4%
U.S.$ 0.99 bn

Others 40.9%
U.S.$ 2.81 bn

Skin Treatment
11.0%
U.S.$ 0.74 bn

Digestive/
Intestinal 10.7%
U.S.$ 0.74 bn

Circulatory
Products 10.7%
U.S.$ 0.74 bn

Self-Medication Sales in U.S.$ 6.88 billion
Ex-Manufacturer Sales in U.S.$

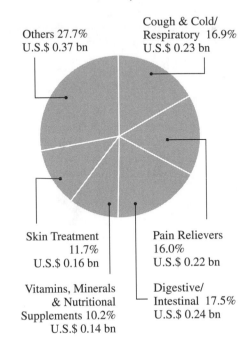

**Italy
Leading Markets for Non–Prescription-bound
Products, 1995**

Others 27.7%
U.S.$ 0.37 bn

Cough & Cold/
Respiratory 16.9%
U.S.$ 0.23 bn

Pain Relievers
16.0%
U.S.$ 0.22 bn

Digestive/
Intestinal 17.5%
U.S.$ 0.24 bn

Skin Treatment
11.7%
U.S.$ 0.16 bn

Vitamins, Minerals
& Nutritional
Supplements 10.2%
U.S.$ 0.14 bn

Self-Medication Sales in U.S.$ 1.36 billion
Ex-Manufacturer Sales in U.S.$

by geographic region, but in general, the majority of the volume was concentrated on six main categories: cough, cold, and other respiratory; pain relief; digestive and other intestinal remedies; vitamins, minerals, and nutritional supplements; tonics and other stimulants; and skin treatments (refer to Exhibits 21 and 22).

The highest growth segments were diagnostic tests, habit treatment, and herbal and homeopathic remedies. Growth in these segments represented the changing attitudes of consumers in favor of more preventative medicating and healthier lifestyles. This move toward overall wellness was also evident within existing top segments. For example, products were introduced to *prevent* heartburn, cold sores, and other

ailments rather than just to treat them once they happened. Growth in market segments also occurred because borders were becoming more open. The world was, in effect, becoming a smaller place. Thus, consumers contracted new strains of viruses from other cultures and were more likely to pass them on to others. OTC manufacturers addressed this issue by introducing a wider variety of antiviral and antifungal products.

Major OTC Categories

Pain Relief Sales for the pain relief segment were U.S.$7.3 billion in 1994, making it the largest in the industry. Growth was predicted to reach U.S.$9 billion in 1999. Pain relief was one of the first market

**UK
Leading Markets for Non–Prescription-bound
Products, 1995**

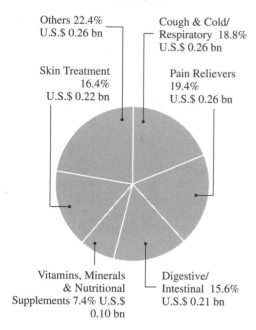

Others 22.4%
U.S.$ 0.26 bn

Cough & Cold/
Respiratory 18.8%
U.S.$ 0.26 bn

Skin Treatment
16.4%
U.S.$ 0.22 bn

Pain Relievers
19.4%
U.S.$ 0.26 bn

Vitamins, Minerals
& Nutritional
Supplements 7.4% U.S.$
0.10 bn

Digestive/
Intestinal 15.6%
U.S.$ 0.21 bn

Self-Medication Sales in U.S.$ 1.35 billion
Ex-Manufacturer Sales in U.S.$

segments to be developed by pharmaceutical companies. Even so, the segment was very dynamic. The sheer size and sales opportunity enticed new entrants and made the segment very competitive. Most segment growth came both from switches of new nonsteroidal anti-inflammatory drugs (NSAIDs) and the proliferation of niche products aimed at taking some category business away from entrenched leaders, such as Tylenol and Bayer.

The major therapeutic categories are illustrated in Exhibit 22. Note that the general pain relief category accounted for close to 70 percent of the entire segment. Higher than average growth was expected from the second largest segment, muscular pain relief, between the years 1995 and 2000. In general, environmental factors that contributed to the use of pain relief included lifestyle, stress, the pressure to "keep

going," and an aging population. Users of pain relief products covered most of the population segments. For example, in Europe, 75 percent of the population used analgesics in any one year.

The global market leader was Johnson & Johnson with its Tylenol brand, although Tylenol was not a global brand. It had gained its rank due to its success in the large U.S. market. The leading brands in Europe and Asia were different from those in the United States. For example, Bayer Aspirin was the only analgesic with a European-wide presence. In Japan, Bufferin was the number one pain relief product.

Products in the pain relief category were differentiated based on their efficacy in treating specific types of pain. The oldest and most common form of pain relief product was analgesics, which treated pain caused by headaches, cold/flu, and fever. In the 1980s and 1990s, significant activity was observed when a new treatment was introduced to the OTC market in the form of nonsteroidal anti-inflammation drugs (NSAIDs). Much of the success of this OTC treatment was attributed to its prior success and efficacy reputation in the prescription market. Another form of differentiation was based on the delivery system, as in the case of topical pain remedies which usually contained analgesics or NSAIDs. This was useful to some consumers because it tended to have a lower incidence of side effects.

Finally, a growing trend in the pain relief segment was the use of these products for prevention rather than for treatment of a specific ailment. For example, in the United States and the United Kingdom medical professionals began recommending a daily dose of aspirin to prevent cardiovascular problems. This trend had a positive impact on sales of lower-dose aspirin products.

Cough, Cold and Other Respiratory Remedies

Sales for this category reached U.S.$7.1 billion in 1994 and were expected to grow between 7.7 percent and 10.2 percent from 1995 to 2000. Key therapeutic categories included cough remedies, cold remedies, sore throat, hay fever, and asthma. Growth in this segment came from new switches from the prescription-only segment. The worldwide market leader for this category was Procter & Gamble with the Vicks brand franchise. Product offerings were differentiated based

**USA
Leading Markets for Non–Prescription-bound
Products, 1995**

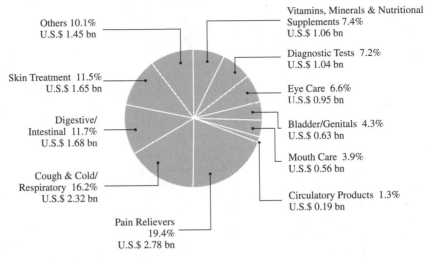

Others 10.1%
U.S.$ 1.45 bn

Vitamins, Minerals & Nutritional
Supplements 7.4%
U.S.$ 1.06 bn

Skin Treatment 11.5%
U.S.$ 1.65 bn

Diagnostic Tests 7.2%
U.S.$ 1.04 bn

Digestive/
Intestinal 11.7%
U.S.$ 1.68 bn

Eye Care 6.6%
U.S.$ 0.95 bn

Bladder/Genitals 4.3%
U.S.$ 0.63 bn

Cough & Cold/
Respiratory 16.2%
U.S.$ 2.32 bn

Mouth Care 3.9%
U.S.$ 0.56 bn

Circulatory Products 1.3%
U.S.$ 0.19 bn

Pain Relievers
19.4%
U.S.$ 2.78 bn

Self-Medication Sales in U.S.$ 14.30 billion
Ex-Manufacturer Sales in U.S.$

**Japan
Leading Markets for Non–Prescription-bound
Products, 1995**

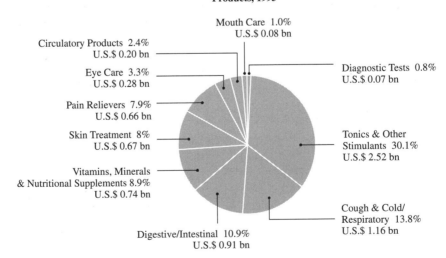

Mouth Care 1.0%
U.S.$ 0.08 bn

Circulatory Products 2.4%
U.S.$ 0.20 bn

Diagnostic Tests 0.8%
U.S.$ 0.07 bn

Eye Care 3.3%
U.S.$ 0.28 bn

Pain Relievers 7.9%
U.S.$ 0.66 bn

Skin Treatment 8%
U.S.$ 0.67 bn

Tonics & Other
Stimulants 30.1%
U.S.$ 2.52 bn

Vitamins, Minerals
& Nutritional Supplements 8.9%
U.S.$ 0.74 bn

Cough & Cold/
Respiratory 13.8%
U.S.$ 1.16 bn

Digestive/Intestinal 10.9%
U.S.$ 0.91 bn

Self-Medication Sales in U.S.$ 8.37 billion
Ex-Manufacturer Sales in U.S.$

Exhibit 22 ● 1995 OTC Industry Product Classification and Sales Figures

Category	Major Therapeutic Segments	Share of Segment Sales[a]	% Growth 1995–1998	Top U.S. Brands
World OTC	Total Sales: U.S.$51.45 Billion			
Pain relief	Percent of Total Sales: 17%		4.6%	
	General pain relievers	69.5%	4.2	Tylenol, Advil, Aleve
	Muscular pain	26.4	6.1	Ibuprofen (PL), Ben-Gay
	Migraine remedies	.25	5.8	Migraclear
	Mouth pain relief	1.97	3.9	Anbesol, Orajel
Cough, cold, and respiratory	Percent of Total Sales: 17%			
	Cough remedies	29.0	5.9	Halls, Robitussin DM
	Cold remedies	44.0	8.1	NyQuil, Alka Seltzer Plus C
	Sore throat	12.9	8.5	Chloraseptic, Sucrets
	Hayfever	11.5	9.4	Benadryl OTC, Tavist-D
	Asthma	2.6	9.2	Bronkaid, Primatene Mist
Digestive preparations	Percent of Total Sales: 12%		3.4	
	Stomach remedies	53.0	4.1	Pepcid AC, Pepto Bismol
	Laxatives	28.1	2.7	Metamucil, Milk of Magnesia
	Antidiarrheals	14.1	2.0	Imodium-AD, Pedialyte
	Liver remedies	4.2	2.1	Lipoflavonoid, Decholin
	Worm treatment	0.6	2.0	Combantrin, Pin-X
Skin treatments	Percent of Total Sales: 12%		7.6	
	Skin protection	28.3	8.7	Coppertone
	Skin irritation relief	18.2	8.8	Campho Phenique
	Antiseptics	11.2	8.2	Alcohol (PL), Campho Phenique
	Antifungals	11.0	9.2	Lotrimin AF, Desenex
	Spot and blemish care	8.2	4.5	Clearasil, Oxy
	Antidandruff	5.7	7.7	Head & Shoulders
	Antiparasites	3.1	2.2	Lice Treatment Kit
	Cold sore remedies	1.3	31.3	Zovirax, Blistex
	Antibaldness	0.7	17.3	Rogaine
Vitamins, minerals, and nutritional supplements	Percent of Total Sales: 10%		8.1	Centrum, One-A-Day, Ensure
Diagnostic tests	Percent of Total Sales: 5%		15.5	One Touch, E.P.T
Tonics and stimulants	Percent of Total Sales: 4%		6.5	Vivarin, No Doz, Ginseng
Eye care	Percent of Total Sales: 4		4	Renu, Opti-Free, Aosept
Oral care	Percent of Total Sales: 4%		1.2	Listerine, Polident, Fixodent
Circulatory remedies	Percent of Total Sales: 4%		5.5	Preparation H, Tucks
Ear care	Percent of Total Sales: .5%		7.3	Murine Ear Drops
Bladder and genitals	Percent of Total Sales: 2.5%		-1.6	Monistat-7, Trojans
Habit control	Percent of Total Sales: .3%		21	Nicorette, Nicotinell
Other	Percent of Total Sales: 7.7%			

a. 1995 sales for ten countries: Belgium, France, Germany, Italy, the Netherlands, Spain, United Kingdom, Canada, United States, and Japan.

on whether or not they were a single- or multiple-symptom–relieving product, or a time-release product. Further differentiation came from alternative delivery systems such as capsules, liquids, nasal sprays, and topical treatments.

Most of the sales in this category were generated by the population aged twenty-five to forty-four. This segment of the population had the greatest concentration of workers who, for convenience sake, opted to use OTC products rather than visit a doctor. It was important to note that these preferences differed from region to region. For example, in the United Kingdom, 50 percent of allergy and hay fever sufferers purchased OTCs as a first line of treatment. In Italy, most of the sufferers preferred to treat hay fever with doctor prescribed formulas.

There were several external factors that affected sales of this category. Mild winters or unusually high pollen counts in spring could significantly impact sales for that year. In addition, consumer misdiagnoses and confusion between cold, flu, hay fever, and sinus ailments distorted segment sales to some degree in the United States and the United Kingdom. There was evidence that this segment was somewhat price sensitive, especially in Japan, where there seemed to be significant correlation between raising the price of a product and the sales volume decrease. Finally, the recent availability of allergy and flu vaccinations in some markets also impacted sales.

Digestive and Other Intestinal Remedies This category had sales of U.S.$5.8 billion in 1994 and was expected to reach U.S.$6.75 billion in 1999. The United States commanded the largest share of the market with 39 percent, followed by Japan (32 percent). The number one subcategory was stomach remedies which accounted for approximately 53 percent of all category sales. Users purchased digestive remedies to treat a range of ailments including: colic, constipation, diarrhea, flatulence, heartburn, and indigestion.

Prescription-to-OTC switches in the United States, Europe, and Japan had the most impact on this segment. The first switch of this kind was loperamide, a derivative of opium, which was known as a very effective treatment for diarrhea. Until this ingredient was made available for OTCs, consumers had not been able to effectively treat the symptoms. Additionally, the switch of H_2 antagonists, such as Tagamet 100, Pepcid AC, and Zantac 75, known for the treatment for ulcers, received considerable attention. Having received approval to be marketed as a heartburn prevention, H_2 was introduced to the OTC market and brought indigestion remedies to a new level. As a result, several companies had to expand the market segments to maintain their competitive position. This meant either extending the existing product line or developing new attributes for existing products.

Vitamins, Minerals, and Nutritional Supplements
This market segment experienced sales in 1995 of U.S.$5 billion and was expected to reach U.S.$6.4 billion in 1999. This category was broadly defined and encompassed many different therapeutic categories. Unlike the other segments, vitamins, minerals, and nutritional supplements (VMS) was highly fragmented. For example, in Germany, the top ten brands accounted for no more than 22 percent of self-medication sales. Furthermore, user trends regarding the most sought-after substances and delivery systems varied from country to country. For example, fish oil supplements was one of the most popular categories in the United Kingdom, vitamin E in Germany, and bottled nutritive drinks in Japan.

Despite these differences, there were a few common characteristics of the category. First, there was a reliance on science to lend credibility to this market segment. Since dietary supplements could not be patented, there was no incentive for pharmaceutical companies to conduct independent studies. As a result, much of the research for this segment was done by government agencies. Second, to a certain extent, these items were considered commodities. In some markets, such as the United States and the United Kingdom, private labels dominated and branded products had to rely on heavy consumer advertising. Some companies tried to differentiate themselves from the competition by offering products that were highly targeted to specific groups, or to package them in easy-to-use containers (like vitamin packs or calendar packs). Finally, in part due to the characteristics listed above, this industry was predisposed to fads, which made predicting growth and sales opportunities very difficult. Nevertheless, the sheer size of the market and the increasing interest in preventive measures meant that this segment had the potential to be very profitable for those players who entered at the right time.

The trend for VMS in the future was in the creation of new forms of dietary supplements called medico-foods, functional foods, or nutraceuticals.[8] With this new market segment. the line between food and OTCs became less distinct.

Tonics and Other Stimulants   Sales for tonics and other stimulants were $2.46 billion in 1993.[9] The market was expected to grow to U.S.$3.3 billion by 1998, with most sales generated in Japan (80 percent) and Germany (14 percent). Similar to the VMS segment, this segment was broadly defined and meant different things in different markets. For example, in Japan, tonics were the largest OTC segment. One of the most common applications there was to consume tonics containing caffeine to combat fatigue. In fact, caffeine was the second most commonly used molecule in this segment. On the other hand, in Germany, tonics accounted for a fairly small portion of the country's OTC sales, and consumers there used tonics more as "health" drinks. Caffeine did not even make the country's top twenty list of most commonly used ingredients.

The most notable trend in Japan was a line of "mini-drinks" that were similar to the bottled nutritive drinks of the VMS segment. These products were positioned as both energy boosters and nutritional supplements. Mini-drinks were targeted primarily at the young and fashionable. Industry analysts believed this market had matured by the late 1990s, and while still a strong presence in the Japanese OTCs, it was not going to be an area of growth and opportunity for other areas. The strongest players in this segment were national companies like Chugai Seiyaku and Kowa Shinyaku in Japan and Klosterfrau in Germany.

Skin Treatment   Worldwide OTC sales for this segment were $5.4 billion in 1995 and were anticipated to grow to $6.8 billion in 1999 (compound annual growth rate [CAGR] of 7.6 percent). Historically, OTC skin treatments were defined as products that offered a medicinal benefit such as treating excessively dry skin, dandruff, or protecting skin from sun damage. However, a trend was emerging where more and more pharmaceutical applications were aimed at creating cosmetic improvements rather than treating an ailment. The industry buzz word for products such as these was "cosmeceuticals."

The dominant therapeutic segment was general skin protectors, followed by skin irritation treatments, such as lotions and lip balms. The highest growth was anticipated from two new segments which were created from prescription-only switches: cold sore prevention and antibaldness. For cold sore prevention, acyclovir, marketed under the brand name of Zovirax, was anticipated to attract new users based on its capability to stop cold sores from developing. The antibaldness category was created by the switch of minoxidil and tested the barriers of whether or not an image-enhancing product should be considered an OTC.

Growth Areas   The diagnostics, habit treatment, and herbals/homeopathic segments were emerging categories in the OTC industry. With increasing emphasis placed on prevention and wellness, they offered the most interesting growth opportunities.

Diagnostics   The OTC diagnostics segment was defined as products that enabled consumers to obtain information about their health by performing a test, similar to those done in clinics, but at home and without the supervision of health care professionals. Sales in this segment were $872 million in 1993.[10] While relatively small, this market was considered to be in the growth stage with potential as technology improved and retail prices declined. Examples of self-diagnostic kits were pregnancy tests, ovulation kits, blood glucose tests for diabetics, and cholesterol tests. Expected to move through the pipeline were home HIV test kits and some types of cancer screening tests.

As consumers everywhere were forced to take more and more responsibility for their health care, in-

8. Medico-foods, functional foods, and nutraceuticals refer to the cross-classification of traditional food products that had proven therapeutic benefits and were therefore used as therapeutic or preventative remedies.

9. Figures for ten countries only: Belgium, France, Germany, Italy, the Netherlands, Spain, the United Kingdom, Canada, the United States, and Japan.

10. Figures for ten countries only: Belgium, France, Germany, Italy, the Netherlands, Spain, the United Kingdom, Canada, United States, and Japan. *OTCforesight*, Vol. 1, London: SelfMedication International, 1995, pp. 11–177.

dustry analysts believed diagnostics would become more popular. In the United Kingdom, the government started charging for pregnancy tests, creating the market for at home pregnancy tests. However, the ultimate success of self-diagnostic kits depended on affordability, ease of use, accuracy, and consumer awareness.

Habit Treatment   A newly created segment, habit treatment amounted to $64 million in 1993 and was expected to grow to $166 million in 1998. This segment was brought to life by the prescription switch of nicotine replacement therapies. The driving force behind this category's increasing popularity was the growing interest from governments, managed care organizations, and employers who had a financial stake in the future health of their constituents. Furthermore, in the United States, antismoking campaigns succeeded in the prohibition of smoking at work and many public places. The antismoking movement developed at a much slower pace elsewhere in the world.

Herbal Remedies and Homeopathic Treatments   Natural remedies did not have OTC classification. They were often considered alternatives to the chemically-based products produced by OTC companies. Herbals and homeopathics were not required to be registered. As such, it was difficult to value the market. Industry analysts suggested, however, that the total worldwide market for these products was around U.S.$2 billion in 1994. However, because these products were distributed in so many different outlets and defined in so many different ways, an accurate estimate was difficult to obtain. More than 75 percent of the herbal and homeopathic market was in China, Japan, and other Far Eastern countries. The U.S. share of the market was estimated at about 1 percent.

The main attraction of natural remedies was the medicinal benefit (with fewer side effects) received by consumers. Also, as rising health care costs in many countries caused consumers to take more personal responsibility for their health, the relatively inexpensive natural remedies looked more attractive. Even though, traditionally, OTC producers did not offer products that fit the natural remedies definition, many began to seriously consider this emerging market. Initially, OTC producers seemed to test the market by offering herbal and homeopathic line ex-

tensions of their current products. For example, Bayer marketed a One-A-Day Extra garlic line extension.

TECHNOLOGY TRENDS

The driving forces behind technology were changes in consumer demographics, dissatisfaction with taste, form of dosage, the desire for fast-acting therapies, and changing consumer attitudes. A technology breakthrough potentially gave a company a significant competitive advantage. One of the most important decisions was how a product was going to interact with the human body. This was referred to as the delivery system, or "galenics," of a drug.

A drug could be introduced to the body a number of ways, and once there, it chose from a variety of transportation systems to reach its final destination. The most common dosage forms of OTCs were tablets, capsules, and liquids.

Advancements were made whereby the different modes of the drug delivery system offered consumers a more desirable form of treatment. Companies who wanted to maximize their growth potential in a mature market needed to look for ways to differentiate themselves from the competition. Technological breakthroughs played an important role.

Gelatin capsules and effervescent tablets were two examples of new delivery systems that changed the competitive landscape by offering consumers new benefits in terms of taste, improved efficacy, and convenience. More recent developments included transdermal patches for delivering a substance through the skin, time-release capsules which decreased the frequency of dosages, and topical creams which made the need to swallow pills (difficult for some people, especially the elderly) unnecessary.

REGULATORY ISSUES

The regulatory process for getting OTCs approved differed in every country and, in the case of some developing countries, was nonexistent. However, most countries had government-chosen regulatory bodies composed of health care professionals and academics. The role of these organizations was to classify OTCs according to their characteristics and potential impact on the welfare of the public. The following list describes the questions most commonly asked when evaluating whether or not a product was safe for OTC use.

- Was the medicine likely to present a danger, either directly or indirectly, if utilized without medical supervision?

- How likely was it that the medicine was going to be used incorrectly and, as a result, was it likely to present a direct or indirect danger to human health?

- Had the medicine been fully proven to be safe and effective with the target population?

- Was the substance addictive?

All pharmaceuticals and most OTCs had to be registered. The registration application needed to prove two things: the proposed product was safe and effective. However, each country had its own definition of safety and efficacy, requiring specific dossiers to be prepared for each country.[11]

The time required to pass the application procedure depended on the quality of the document, the potential impact on the public health, the efficiency of the health authority, and whether or not the product was a new drug or a copy of an existing product. The average time spent in the OTC registration process was two to three years, but there was an economic incentive for some countries, especially in Europe, to improve on this process. For example, in 1995, the United Kingdom streamlined its procedure so that it could process OTC registrations in less than a year.

The differences in regulatory practices made it difficult for companies to initiate global product launches. Inevitably, some products were OTC-registered in one country and still prescription-bound in another (refer to Exhibits 23 and 24). However, with the breakdown of trade barriers, European, American, and Japanese regulatory authorities initiated the International Conference on Harmonization. This organization was to establish a consensus for all pharmaceutical regulatory practices, including OTCs.

The U.S. Experience

The regulation and registration process was controlled by the Food and Drug Administration (FDA). In the 1970s, the FDA realized the value of enabling consumers to purchase medical products on their own. There was a flood of applications for switches. To streamline the process, the FDA established the monograph system. A monograph was a public standard spelled out by the FDA, which aimed at standardizing labeling, indications, and dosages for very common products generally recognized as effective and safe. Once a monograph for a substance was established, products using a monograph could quickly pass through the approval process.

Products introduced to the market were classified as either a new OTC or a monograph. If a product was considered a new OTC, the company had to get labeling approved from the FDA and then undergo postmarketing surveillance. It generally took longer for a new drug application (NDA) to pass through the

11. "Dossier" referred to an application which was prepared and included all the necessary documentation and proof the company thought necessary to submit for regulatory approval.

Exhibit 23 ● Comparison of OTC Regulation Between Regions

Regulated Activity	United States	Europe	Japan
New OTC drug approval	1–3 years	1–3 years	4 years
Advertising and promotion restrictions	No	Yes	Yes
Monography system	Yes	No	Yes
Postmarketing surveillance of new substance	3 years	2 years	6–10 years
Banned dosage forms	No	No	Yes[a]
Resale price maintenance	No	Yes[b]	Yes

a. Includes chewable tablets, effervescent powders, and chewing gum.

b. Only in Germany, Italy, Spain, Switzerland, and the United Kingdom.

Exhibit 24 ● Regulatory Differences by Country for R-to-OTC Candidates

			Country	
Substance	*Product Segment*	*Sample Brand Name*	*Austria*	*Belgium*
Loperamide	Antidiarrheals	Imodium	Rx	OTC
Hydrocortisone	Anti-itch treatment	Hydrocortisone cream	Rx	OTC
Clotrimazole	Antifungal	Gyne-Lotrimin	OTC	OTC
Miconazole	Antifungal	Monistat 7	Rx	OTC
Nicotine	Smoke cessation	Nicorette	OTC	OTC
Acyclovir	Cold sore/herpes treatment	Zovirax	OTC	OTC
Ketoprofen	Analgesic	Oruvail gel	Rx	OTC
Cimetidine	H_2 antagonist	Tagament	Rx	(OTC)
Loratidine	Antihistamine	Clarityn	Rx	OTC
Ranitidine	H_2 antagonist	Zantac	Rx	(OTC)
Famotidine	H_2 antagonist	Pepcid AC	Rx	Rx

a. Previously OTC, but switched back to Rx status.

b. As of 1993.

registration process than for an application based on a monograph (refer to Exhibit 25).

OTC companies often chose to submit an NDA because this path offered many benefits. A private license was granted to the new drug holder or sponsor. In addition, it was possible to secure exclusivity for up to three years, which, if granted, offered companies high profit potential.

In general, it was more difficult to get prescription products switched in the United States than in some European countries, such as the United Kingdom. This was due to the fact that once a product has been granted OTC status, there were no other safety nets in place (in terms of advertising and distribution restrictions) to protect the consumers.

The European Experience

Historically, companies had to register each new product in each country. This meant up to fifteen different registration applications and fees to market a product throughout western Europe.

In order to harmonize the process for registering and regulating OTC products, the EU developed directives[12] relating to the registration, classification, labeling, and advertising of OTC medicines. Effective January 1, 1995, companies that wished to register a nonprescription medicine in more than one EU country had three options:

- **National Procedure:** Prepare separate applications for each country (until 1998 only).

- **Decentralized System:** Apply for registration in one country and, if approved, application was circulated to other member states. There was a specified process for resolving disputes, and final decision was legally binding for all member states.

- **Centralized System:** The applicant submitted one dossier to the European Medicines Evaluation Agency (EMEA). The EMEA coordinated the process, but evaluation of the dossier was done by the Committee for Proprietary

12. A directive was legally binding legislation passed by the European Union. Member states needed to put the directive into effect through national laws by a specified date.

Exhibit 24 ● Regulatory Differences by Country for R-to-OTC Candidates (*Continued*)

			Country				
France	Germany	Italy	Netherlands	Spain	UK	Japan	US
OTC	OTC	Rx[a]	OTC	Rx	OTC	OTC	OTC
OTC	Rx	OTC	Rx	OTC	OTC	OTC	OTC
OTC	OTC	OTC	OTC	OTC	OTC	OTC	OTC
OTC	OTC	OTC	OTC	Rx	OTC	OTC	OTC
(OTC)	OTC	OTC	OTC	OTC	OTC	(OTC)	OTC
OTC	OTC	Rx	OTC	Rx	OTC	Rx	(OTC)
Rx	Rx	Rx[a]	(OTC)	Rx	OTC	Rx[b]	OTC
(OTC)	Rx	OTC	Rx	Rx	OTC	(OTC)	OTC
Rx	OTC	Rx	Rx	Rx	OTC	Rx[b]	(OTC)
Rx	(OTC)	OTC	(OTC)	Rx	OTC	(OTC)	OTC
Rx	Rx	OTC	(OTC)	Rx	OTC	(OTC)	OTC

a. Previously OTC, but switched back to Rx status.
b. As of 1993.

Medicinal Products (CPMP). If approved, a single marketing authorization was granted, and it was valid for all member countries.

Reimbursement status was also subject to regulatory control. OTC producers determined whether it was in their strategic interest for the product to be reimbursed. If the product was approved for reimbursement, the product was subject to price controls and advertising restrictions. Products for easily self-diagnosed ailments, such as the common cold, rarely applied for reimbursement status.

A major difference from the U.S. process was that European regulatory restrictions went a step further and controlled the distribution and advertising activities of the products as well. Some countries were more stringent than others, with the United Kingdom and the Netherlands on the liberal end and France and Italy on the conservative side (refer to Exhibit 19). With harmonization efforts under way, these differences were expected to become less distinct.

Most OTCs had to be distributed in pharmacies owned by a licensed pharmacist. The only products that could be sold in the mass market were those that were considered general health and beauty aids such as cough drops, skin care, and general antiseptics.

The Japanese Experience

Japan imposed the tightest regulations of all the developed regions. The registration process was similar to other countries, except that in most cases the health authority did not accept western clinical trials. If a company wanted to register a product in Japan but the substance was not a registered prescription product, it had to first register the product as a prescription substance. The cost for a new product registration was approximately $5 million dollars and required about six years of surveillance as a prescription substance before it could be available OTC.

There were no advertising restrictions applied to different product classifications. However, OTC companies were not allowed to make references to medical endorsements or previous ethical use in public advertisements. Finally, some dosage forms were not allowed if they resembled a food product too closely.

Exhibit 25 ● OTC Registration/New Product Development Process

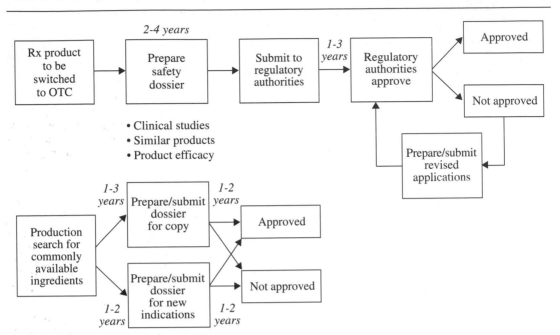

Previously banned delivery forms were chewable tablets, effervescent powders, and chewing gum.

CONCLUSION

As the strategy meeting drew to a close, Roland M. Jeannet spoke to the group:

In the past, most traditional OTC companies operated based on their individual core competencies and tried to apply these strengths to the regions and markets to which they were best suited. A pharma approach was applied to the OTC market and OTCs were often a by-product of the pharma business. As such, OTCs were not usually differentiated from their other businesses. For us at Ciba, we need to think about the evolving self-medication industry and reflect on whether these traditional practices still apply, and if not, what specific changes any firm needs to adopt if it wants to remain or become a world-class player in this industry.

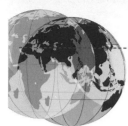

CASE 2

Note on Competitors in the OTC Drug Industry

INDUSTRY OVERVIEW

Over-the-counter (OTC) pharmaceutical products were consumer health care products that were approved and nonprescription bound. In 1995, this was a U.S.$51 billion industry and was growing at more than 7 percent per year. OTC products covered a broad array of consumer health products ranging from vitamins and minerals to self-diagnostic kits (refer to Exhibits 1 and 2.)

The industry was rapidly growing and changing as both ends of the spectrum expanded. On one end, the lines between consumer products such as beauty aids and food products were becoming fuzzier. On the other end, a growing number of prescription-bound products were being switched to over-the-counter products. This was in response to consumers looking for alternatives to the oftentimes higher-priced prescription drugs, governments trying to reduce health care expenditures, and pharmaceutical companies trying to expand the product life cycle of key products.

What started as a fragmented industry became a rapidly changing one with mergers and acquisitions (M&A) the order of the day. Many OTC companies used M&A to grow a product portfolio, gain econ- omies of scale, and boost their traditionally lower profit margins.[1]

COMPETITOR OVERVIEW

Strategies among OTC companies varied, but competitors could generally be grouped into one of the following categories: Global OTC, Global Pharma, Regional OTC, National OTC, Niche Player, and Pharmaceutical Only (see Exhibit 3).

Global OTC companies were those that generated the majority of their pharmaceutical sales from nonprescription products. Typically, these companies competed in a majority of the top market segments and geographic regions. Global OTCs generally offered products that were closer to being consumer products than to prescription pharmaceuticals.

The opposite of a Global OTC company was a Global Pharma company, whose products were oftentimes more technically-oriented and innovative. Prescription-bound pharmaceutical sales exceeded OTC sales for these companies. As with Global OTC companies, Global Pharma companies offered OTC products in a broad range of market segments and geographic regions.

The core strengths for a Regional OTC company lay in one particular geography, such as Europe or North America. A regional player usually chose to attack each geography on a country by country basis and did not generally market brands on a regional basis. This was less true for companies in North Amer-

This case was written by Kristi Menz and Shauna Pettit, MBA candidates at the F. W. Olin Graduate School of Business at Babson College, under the direction of Professor Jean-Pierre Jeannet. This case is to be used in conjunction with Cases 2 and 4. Copyright © 1997 by IMD—International Institute for Management Development, Lausanne, Switzerland. All rights reserved. Not to be used or reproduced without written permission directly from IMD.

1. An OTC company earned lower profits on average than a pharmaceutical company, since the former usually had a lower retail selling price for its products and spent money on consumer advertising (although in the United States, even prescription-bound drugs could be advertised to consumers.)

Exhibit 1 ● OTC Industry Market Segment Share and Growth

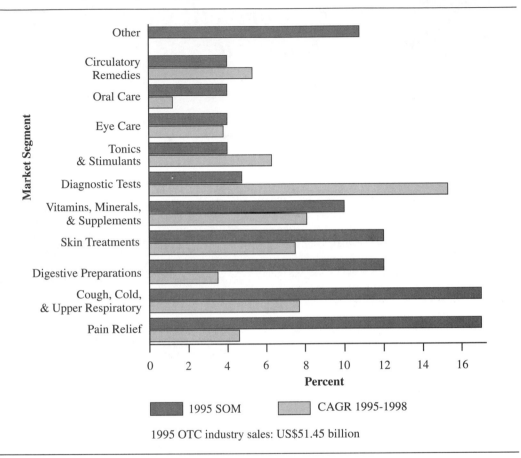

1995 OTC industry sales: US$51.45 billion

Source: OTC Review 1996, OTC Foresight 1995.

ica, since consumers in the United States and Canada shared many common attitudes.

National OTC companies realized the majority of their annual turnover in one country. The Japanese market, for example, spawned many companies that did not cross national borders with their products. In some cases, the intricacies of the individual country made it hard to apply the same principles elsewhere. This could be caused by peculiar government practices or consumer attitudes.

In contrast to companies with core competencies in a particular geography, Niche Players specialized in a specific nongeographical segment of the OTC industry. Some niche companies focused on a particular market segment such as eye care in the case of Bausch and Lomb or vitamins in the case of Pharmavite. Other niche companies, like Perrigo, followed a "me too" strategy and concentrated their efforts on private label versions of popular nonprescription products.

The final competitor category contained companies that chose not to directly compete in the OTC industry, but were important players due to their

Exhibit 2 ● 1995 Split of OTC Sales by Geography

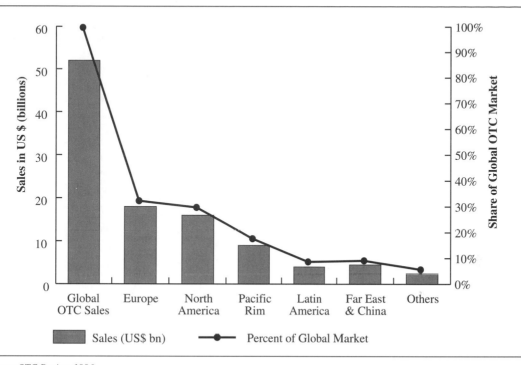

Source: OTC Review 1996

pipelines of potential Rx-to-OTC switches. Prescription Only companies generally signed licensing agreements and formed joint ventures to market Rx-to-OTC switches. Glaxo and Marion Merrell Dow both used this strategy and were significant suppliers of products to the OTC industry.

Exhibits 4 through 10 show the major players in these categories and their competive advantages in different makets, as discussed below.

COMPETITORS

Procter & Gamble

In 1995, the United States-based Procter & Gamble (P&G) reached sales of U.S.$33,434 million (Exhibit 11). Nonprescription sales accounted for just under 6 percent of that total, making it the fourth-largest OTC company in the world. Unlike some of its OTC competitors, P&G had no significant presence in the prescription pharmaceutical industry. P&G divided its operations into six categories: Laundry & Cleaning, Paper, Beauty Care, Food & Beverage, Health Care, and Corporate (refer to Exhibit 12). Most of its corporate sales came from North America and Europe, although it had a growing presence in Asia and Latin America (Exhibit 13). P&G employed 99,200 people worldwide.

The company entered the health care market in 1982, when it acquired Norwich Eaton and its OTC products, the most notable of which were Pepto-Bismol and Chloraseptic. Following this trend, Vicks and Clearasil were added to P&G's portfolio in 1985 through the purchase of Richardson-Vicks. Metamucil,

Exhibit 3 ● Strategic Groupings of OTC Competitors

Global OTC	Global Pharma	Regional OTC	National OTC	Niche Player	Rx Only
Procter & Gamble	SmithKline Beecham	Rhône-Poulenc Rorer	Taisho	Pharmavite/ Otsuka	Glaxo Wellcome
Warner-Lambert	Bayer	Schering-Plough	Angelini	Perrigo	Merck
	American Home Products	Boots PLC	Takeda	Ross/Abbott Laboratories	Eli Lilly
	Roche	Boehringer Ingelheim	SS Pharmaceutical	Bausch and Lomb	Tanebe
	Johnson & Johnson		Sato Pharmaceutical	Seton	
	Bristol-Myers Squibb		Gehe	Thompson Medical	
	Sandoz		Kowa	Rexall	
	Ciba-Geigy		Klosterfrau	Allergan	
			Sanofi	Vitamex	
			Pierre Fabre	Boiron	
			Servier	Standard Homeopathic	
			Synthelabo	Boericke and Tafel	

Blendax (a German oral hygiene product), and Noxzema were acquired in a similar fashion by the end of the 1980s.

P&G competed in all major market segments except vitamins, minerals, and supplements. Most of P&G's OTC sales came in the cough and cold and skin treatment segments through the Vicks, NyQuil, and Clearasil brands. It also had strong brands in the gastrointestinal segment in the United States with Metamucil and Pepto-Bismol (see Exhibit 14). In its domestic market. P&G entered the pain relief segment with Aleve in 1994 through a joint venture agreement with Syntex. It also announced an agreement with Cygnus Therapeutic to launch an OTC version of its smoking cessation skin patch. Neither of these joint venture agreements carried into any other geographies, however.

Part of P&G's success came from its ability to extend global brands such as Vicks and Clearasil into

new products. For example, Vicks was a company name whose first product was a vaporub. When P&G purchased the company and its products, Vicks remained as an umbrella brand name. P&G expanded the Vicks line through new delivery systems such as liquid gel caps and other product segments such as cough drops. Clearasil had a similar success story. What started as only an acne treatment evolved into a full line of facial cleaning products.

P&G's product portfolio aimed at treating ailments that required little doctor intervention, such as cold and cough, acne treatment, and mild indigestion. Thus, P&G was able to focus its attention on what it did best: winning over retailers and consumers. P&G also concentrated on a value pricing strategy with many of its products. It relied on fast-moving consumer goods with low prices and high volumes for much of its turnover.

Geographically, P&G was dependent on its home

Exhibit 4 ● Competitive Positioning Map

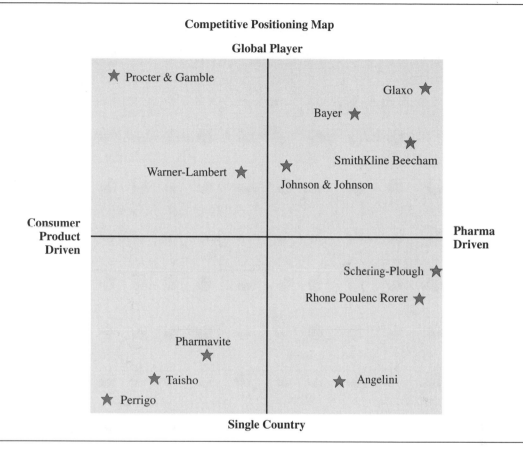

Competitive Positioning Map

Global Player

Procter & Gamble

Glaxo

Bayer

SmithKline Beecham

Warner-Lambert

Johnson & Johnson

Consumer Product Driven

Pharma Driven

Schering-Plough

Rhone Poulenc Rorer

Pharmavite

Taisho

Angelini

Perrigo

Single Country

market in the United States for 64 percent of self-medication sales (refer to Exhibit 14).[2] While Japan did not account for a great percentage of annual turnover, P&G was the largest overseas manufacturer there, with 1993 sales of U.S.$70 million. In the European market, self-medication sales were concentrated in Germany, France, and Italy. P&G's strategy for entering new markets was to first introduce fast-moving consumer goods that were not regulated, such as cleaning products and paper goods, and follow with OTCs.

Warner-Lambert

Warner-Lambert (W-L) was another strong U.S.-based competitor, with a 3 percent share of the world OTC market. W-L's 36,000 employees generated sales in 1995 of U.S.$7,040 million. Sales and earnings growth were positive from 1993–1995, but somewhat less stable in prior years (refer to Exhibit 15). The Consumer Health Care division accounted for nearly

2. The total sales figure that this percentage was based upon does not include semi-ethicals in Europe.

Exhibit 5 ● Relative Competitive Position of OTC Competitors

Legend: ● Very Strong　◕ Strong　◐ Good　◔ Moderate　○ Weak

	Relationship with Retailers	Relationship with Healthcare Professionals	Willingness to Form Partnerships	Presence in Growth Segments/ Geographies	Presence in Key Market Segments	Rx-to OTC Switch Experience	Protection from Generics/ Private Labels	Consumer Brand Awareness	Innovation	Financial Position	Relationship with Pharma Industry	Rx-to-OTC Pipeline	Global Presence
Procter & Gamble	●	○	◐	◐	◕	◔	◐	●	◐	◐	◔	◔	●
Warner-Lambert	●	◐	◐	◐	◐	◐	◐	◕	◕	◔	◕	◕	◕
Bayer	◐	◔	◐	◔	◔	◐	◔	◐	◐	◔	◐	○	◔
Johnson & Johnson	◐	●	◔	◐	◕	◐	◐	●	●	◔	◔	◕	◐
SmithKline Beecham	◐	●	◐	●	●	◔	◐	◐	◔	◔	●	●	◔
Rhone Poulenc Rorer	◔	●	◔	◕	◕	◐	●	◐	◐	◔	◐	○	◔
Schering-Plough	◐	●	◐	◐	◔	◐	◔	◐	●	●	◔	◔	◐
Angelini	◔	N/A	◐	◔	○	◔	●	◔	○	○	◔	◔	○
Taisho	N/A	N/A	◐	◔	●	●	●	●	◐	●	◐	◔	○
Perrigo	●	○	◔	●	●	○	N/A	○	○	◐	○	◔	○
Pharmavite	●	○	◔	◔	○	N/A	○	○	○	N/A	○	○	◔
Glaxo	N/A	●	●	◐	◔	N/A	◔	◔	◔	●	N/A	◔	●

Exhibit 6 ● Geographic and Market Segment Strength of OTC Competitors: *Overview*

	France	Germany	Italy	United Kingdom	United States	Japan	Latin America	Far East
PAIN RELIEF	Rhône Bayer	J&J Bayer	Bayer Angelini	Rhône Bayer	P&G J&J SB Bayer Perrigo	Bayer Taisho	SB Bayer	SB
COUGH/COLD	P&G J&J S-P W-L Rhône	P&G J&J W-L Rhône SB Bayer	P&G S-P W-L Rhône SB Bayer	P&G J&J S-P W-L SB	P&G J&J S-P W-L SB Bayer Perrigo	SB Taisho		S-P W-L SB
DIGESTIVE	P&G J&J W-L Rhône SB	J&J W-L Rhône Bayer	Rhône Bayer Angelini	J&J Rhône SB Bayer	P&G J&J S-P W-L SB Bayer Perrigo	P&G Taisho	Bayer	W-L
SKIN TREATMENT	P&G	P&G W-L	P&G S-P W-L SB	P&G J&J S-P W-L Rhône SB	P&G J&J S-P W-L SB Bayer Perrigo	Bayer Taisho		W-L
VITAMINS	Rhône	Rhône SB	Bayer	SB	J&J SB Bayer Perrigo Pharma	Taisho Pharma		

Exhibit 6 ● Geographic and Market Segment Strength of OTC Competitors: *Overview (Continued)*

	France	Germany	Italy	United Kingdom	United States	Japan	Latin America	Far East
DIAGNOSTICS					J&J			
					W-L			
					Bayer			
						Taisho		
TONICS	Rhône	Rhône						
						Taisho		
					Perrigo			
CIRCULATORY			W-L		W-L			
	Rhône	S-P						
				SB				
					Perrigo			
GENERAL PRESENCE						P&G		
			J&J					
						W-L	W-L	
	SB							
								Taisho
			Angelini					

half of the company's sales (refer to Exhibit 16) and the percentage was growing. W-L split itself geographically into the United States; Europe, Middle East and Africa; and Americas and Far East. Sales were relatively even between the segments, but the United States accounted for slightly more than the other regions at 43 percent (refer to Exhibit 16).

Even though W-L did have a pharmaceutical division, most of its products came through joint venture agreements with other companies.[3] In general, its prescription products focused on more chronic ailments such as angina and epilepsy, not on products that were conducive to OTC sales.

W-L's most notable joint venture agreement was with Glaxo Wellcome. Through this arrangement, W-L received the OTC marketing rights to two important

products: Zovirax and Zantac 75. In the prescription world, Zovirax was a genital herpes treatment that also proved to be effective for the prevention and treatment of cold sores. In the United Kingdom and Germany, Zovirax was switched to OTC as a cold sore treatment. Glaxo Wellcome delayed the U.S. launch in an effort to get it approved as an OTC treatment for genital herpes. However, there was some doubt as to whether or not it was going to get FDA approval.

Zantac 75 was an H_2 antagonist, an often prescribed anti-ulcer medicine. The switch of H_2 antagonists received a lot of attention. By adding Zantac to its product mix, W-L was increasing its interest in the gastrointestinal market. Heavy competition existed from two products: SmithKline's Tagamet and Johnson & Johnson's Pepcid AC, both hitting the market before Zantac 75.

Cough and cold was W-L's dominant market

---

3. The most notable exception to this strategy was the Halls brand franchise, one of W-L's most successful brands.

Exhibit 7 ● Geographic and Market Segment Strength of OTC Competitors: *Individual*

	France	Germany	Italy	United Kingdom	United States	Japan	Latin America	Far East
PROCTER & GAMBLE								
Pain relief					X			
Cough/cold	X	X	X	X	X			
Digestive	X				X	X		
Skin treatment	X	X	X	X	X			
Vitamins								
Diagnostics								
Tonics								
Circulatory								
General presence						X		
WARNER-LAMBERT								
Pain relief								
Cough/cold	X	X	X	X	X			X
Digestive	X	X			X			X
Skin treatment		X	X	X	X			X
Vitamins								
Diagnostics					X			
Tonics								
Circulatory			X		X			
General presence						X	X	
BAYER								
Pain relief	X	X	X	X	X	X	X	
Cough/cold		X	X		X			
Digestive		X	X	X	X		X	
Skin treatment					X	X		
Vitamins			X		X			
Diagnostics					X			
Tonics								
Circulatory								
General presence								
JOHNSON & JOHNSON								
Pain relief		X			X			
Cough/cold	X	X		X	X			
Digestive	X	X		X	X			
Skin treatment				X	X			
Vitamins					X			
Diagnostics					X			
Tonics								
Circulatory								
General presence			X					

Exhibit 7 ● Geographic and Market Segment Strength of OTC Competitors: *Individual* (*Continued*)

	France	Germany	Italy	United Kingdom	United States	Japan	Latin America	Far East
SMITHKLINE BEECHAM								
Pain relief					X		X	X
Cough/cold		X	X	X	X	X		X
Digestive	X			X	X			
Skin treatment			X	X	X			
Vitamins		X		X	X			
Diagnostics								
Tonics								
Circulatory				X				
General presence	X							
RHÔNE-POULENC RORER								
Pain relief	X			X				
Cough/cold	X	X	X					
Digestive	X	X	X	X				
Skin treatment				X				
Vitamins	X	X						
Diagnostics								
Tonics	X	X						
Circulatory	X							
General presence								
SCHERING-PLOUGH								
Pain relief								
Cough/cold	X		X	X	X			X
Digestive					X			
Skin treatment			X	X	X			
Vitamins								
Diagnostics								
Tonics								
Circulatory	X							
General presence								
ANGELINI								
Pain relief			X					
Cough/cold								
Digestive			X					
Skin treatment								
Vitamins								

Exhibit 7 ● Geographic and Market Segment Strength of OTC Competitors: *Individual (Continued)*

	France	Germany	Italy	United Kingdom	United States	Japan	Latin America	Far East
ANGELINI								
Diagnostics								
Tonics								
Circulatory								
General presence			X					
TAISHO								
Pain relief						X		
Cough/cold						X		
Digestive						X		
Skin treatment						X		
Vitamins						X		
Diagnostics						X		
Tonics						X		
Circulatory								
General presence								X
PERRIGO								
Pain relief					X			
Cough/cold					X			
Digestive					X			
Skin treatment					X			
Vitamins					X			
Diagnostics								
Tonics					X			
Circulatory					X			
General presence								
PHARMAVITE								
Pain relief								
Cough/cold								
Digestive								
Skin treatment								
Vitamins					X	X		
Diagnostics								
Tonics								
Circulatory								
General presence								

Exhibit 8 ● OTC Competitor Overview

	Procter & Gamble	Warner-Lambert	Bayer	Johnson & Johnson	SmithKline Beecham[d]
Home country	USA	USA	Germany	USA	UK
Type of company	Global OTC	Global OTC	Global Pharma	Global Pharma	Global Pharma
1995 corporate sales ($mn)	$33,434	$7,040	$31,110	$18,842	$11,077
Corporate profit margin	7.9%	10.5%	5.4%	12.8%	14.7%
Corporate ROE	25.0%	32.9%	13.1%	26.6%	58.3%
1995 # of employees	99,200	36,000	142,900	82,300	52,400
OTC divisional sales ($mn)[a]	$3,025	$3,293	$7,746	$5,831	$3,171
Div. operating profit	$360	$858	$1,273	$298	$526
Div. net assets[b]	$2,882	$1,759	$5,236	$4,334	$2,209
Div. RONA	12.5%	48.8%	24.3%	6.9%	23.8%
1995 est. global OTC sales ($mn)	$1,955	$1,540	$2,007	$3,550	$1,646
1995 U.S. OTC sales ($mn)	$702	$760	$662	$1,555	$602
1995 % TME of sales[c]	26.4%	17.2%	22.2%	38.2%	19.8%
World rank	4	6	3	1	5
World SOM	3.8%	3.0%	3.9%	6.9%	3.2%
USA rank	3	4	5	1	6
USA SOM	7.2%	5.8%	5.3%	14.3%	3.9%
Europe rank	—	—	2	—	3
Europe SOM	—	—	3.2%	—	3.0%
Japan rank	—	—	—	—	—
Japan SOM	—	—	—	—	—

n/a=not available.
a. Sales of the corporate division handling OTC sales.
b. Identifiable assets less capital expenditures and depreciation & amortization.
c. U.S. nonprescription drug advertising expenditures as a percentage of U.S. OTC sales.
d. 1994 figures instead of 1995.

segment, due to the success of the Halls brand of products (refer to Exhibit 17). Oral care and skin treatments were also important segments for the company. Lacking in the company's product portfolio was a pain relief product.

Within the self-medication sector, W-L derived 76 percent of its 1994 sales in the United States. Sales in Europe were far behind at 18 percent, and the rest of the world accounted for only 6 percent.[4] Thus, W-L was heavily dependent on its domestic market for its revenues and profits. Its major markets in Europe were the United Kingdom, Germany, and France, which accounted for 84 percent of sales in that region.

4. Does not include sales of semi-ethical products in Europe.

Rhône-Poulenc Rorer	Schering-Plough	Angelini[d]	Taisho	Perrigo	Pharmavite[d]	Glaxo
France	USA	Italy	Japan	USA	Japan	USA
Regional	Regional	National	National	Niche	Niche	Pharma Only
$5,142	$5,104	$173	Est $2,400	$717	Est $140	$11,247
6.9%	17.4%	0.3%	13.1%	6.2%	n/a	9.4%
15.1%	54.6%	0.8%	9.6%	13.0%	n/a	13.6%
28,000	20,100	750	4,816	4,410	650	52,419
$1,557	$633	$67	$1,605	$517	$140	$—
N/A	$154	n/a	n/a	n/a	n/a	$—
N/A	$373	n/a	n/a	n/a	n/a	$—
—	41.2%	—	—	—	—	—
$1,338	$545	$67	$1,605	$517	$140	$—
$—	$436	$—	$—	$517	$140	$—
—	12.2%	—	—	—	n/a	—
7	—	—	—	—	—	—
2.6%	—	—	—	—	—	—
—	9	—	—	—	—	—
—	2.8%	—	—	—	—	—
1	—	—	—	—	—	—
4.1%	—	—	—	—	—	—
—	—	—	1	—	—	—
—	—	—	19.2%	—	—	—

Bayer

The German corporation, Bayer, was a significant player in both the United States and Europe, holding the number five and number two positions in those respective markets. Bayer's 1995 corporate sales of about U.S.$31,110 million and OTC sales of U.S.$2,000 million ranked them as the third-largest OTC company worldwide. Bayer was the largest chemical conglomerate in the world, which explains the fact that almost half of the company's annual turnover came from chemical products (refer to Ex-

hibit 18). This made the company somewhat vulnerable to the cycles of the chemical industry, as can be seen by the variability in sales and profits (refer to Exhibit 19). In contrast, the Health Care division accounted for 51 percent of Bayer's profits while generating only 25 percent of sales. Not surprisingly, the bulk of Bayer's sales came from Europe, its home continent (refer to Exhibit 18).

In general, Bayer's product portfolio was old and lacked innovation. The company's strongest market segment was analgesics, with its Aspirin brand. As recently as 1994, Bayer recovered the use of its own

Exhibit 9 ● Common Size 1994 Income Statements: Parent Corporations

	Procter & Gamble	Warner-Lambert	Bayer	Johnson & Johnson	Smithkline Beecham
1994 Sales	100.0%	100.0%	100.0%	100.0%	100.0%
COGS	57.3%	33.6%	56.6%	33.7%	37.7%
Gross margin	42.7%	66.4%	43.4%	66.3%	62.3%
SG&A	30.9%	43.5%	26.4%	40.4%	41.1%
R&D		7.1%		8.1%	9.8%
Other			9.4%		
EBIT	11.8%	15.8%	7.6%	17.8%	11.4%
Interest	1.6%		-0.2%	0.5%	0.8%
Other	-0.8%	1.4%	0.2%	0.3%	-0.1%
EBT	11.0%	14.4%	7.6%	17.0%	10.7%
Taxes	3.7%	3.4%	3.0%	4.3%	8.8%
Profit margin	7.3%	11.0%	4.6%	12.7%	1.9%
DUPONT MODEL					
Financial Leverage	2.9	3.0	1.6	2.2	2.9
Asset Turnover	1.2	1.2	1.6	1.0	1.9
Profit Margin	7.3%	11.0%	4.6%	12.7%	1.9%
ROA	8.7%	12.5%	7.2%	12.8%	3.5%
ROE	25.0%	38.2%	11.5%	28.2%	10.4%

a. Used Otsuka numbers for Pharmavite since Pharmavite's were not available.

name and trademark in North America by purchasing it from Sterling Health. During World War II, the U.S. government confiscated Bayer's U.S. assets, causing Bayer to operate under the name of Miles in the United States.

The Alka Seltzer family performed well in both the cough and cold and digestive categories. Other strong Bayer brands included Mycelex 7, Phillips' Milk of Magnesia,[5] Campho-Phenique, and Flintstones vitamins. In addition, Bayer had significant presence in the emerging diagnostic market with its blood glucose self-test kits.

Within the Consumer Care division, Bayer's annual sales were split more evenly between geogra-

5. Originally a Sterling Health product.

phies. Europe still retained the lead with 36 percent, followed by North America with 33 percent, Latin America with 19 percent, and Asia Pacific with 12 percent. Most European business was generated in Germany, Spain, and Italy. Bayer showed its commitment to growing business in other parts of the world by building a manufacturing facility in Japan. In addition, its strong presence in Europe gave Bayer a strong foothold in the emerging eastern European markets.

Johnson & Johnson

Johnson & Johnson's (J&J) top rank in its home country, the United States, also made it the largest OTC company in the world. J&J had 1995 sales of U.S.$18,842 million, of which U.S.$3,550 million

Rhône-Poulenc Rorer	Schering-Plough	Angelini	Taisho	Perrigo	Otsuka[a] (Pharmavite)	Glaxo
100.0%	100.0%	100.0%	100.0%	100.0%	100.0%	100.0%
34.7%	20.0%	62.3%	28.0%	71.0%	56.5%	
65.3%	80.0%	37.7%	72.0%	29.0%	43.5%	100.0%
35.8%	38.7%	36.5%	14.2%	14.6%	35.5%	34.9%
13.5%	13.4%		8.9%	0.9%		15.2%
2.7%	0.8%		25.3%			17.8%
13.3%	27.1%	1.2%	23.6%	13.5%	8.0%	32.1%
1.0%		0.6%	-2.5%	0.5%	0.3%	-0.4%
0.9%					0.1%	
11.4%	27.1%	0.6%	26.1%	13.0%	7.6%	32.5%
3.2%	6.6%	0.3%	13.0%	4.8%	4.1%	9.5%
8.2%	20.5%	0.3%	13.1%	8.2%	3.6%	23.0%
2.2	2.8	2.0	1.3	1.6	1.9	1.5
1.0	1.1	1.2	0.6	1.4	1.5	1.1
8.2%	20.5%	0.3%	13.1%	8.2%	3.6%	23.0%
7.9%	21.3%	0.4%	7.4%	6.1%	5.2%	24.6%
17.4%	58.6%	0.8%	10.1%	18.5%	9.9%	36.9%

came from OTC products. Sales and profits enjoyed especially strong growth from 1994 to 1995 (refer to Exhibit 20). J&J's three divisions, Consumer, Pharmaceutical, and Professional, accounted for roughly one-third each of the corporation's sales. As with many other global competitors, J&J relied on the United States for critical mass, generating almost 50 percent of its sales in that market (refer to Exhibit 21).

With the exception of a joint venture agreement with Merck, J&J's primary means of growing its OTC portfolio was through innovative developments from its 150+ autonomous operating units. These units were decentralized such that it was easy to get rid of those that were unprofitable. J&J's main OTC operating units were McNeil Consumer Products in the United States and Janssen-Cilag in Europe.

Tylenol was the highest revenue generator in J&J's OTC portfolio. This was due to its great success in the United States, where Tylenol sales accounted for almost 36 percent of company turnover. The Tylenol brand franchise was particularly successful in leveraging its brand name in the pain relief segment to other segments such as cough and cold and pediatrics.

Besides the analgesics segment, J&J had significant presence in all key segments and played a strong role in growing new segments. For example, it competed in gastrointestinals, diagnostics, cough and cold, skin treatments, habit control, and wound care (refer to Exhibit 22). Mylanta brought in half of gastro-intestinal sales, with Imodium accounting for another third. Pepcid AC, an H_2 antagonist, was the rising star in the GI segment.

Exhibit 10 ● Main Product Offerings of OTC Companies

Company	Top Brands	Indication	Future Switches	Indication
P&G	Aleve	Pain relief	smoking cessation patch	Habit control
	Clearasil	Acne treatment		
	Lactulose	Laxative		
	Metamucil	Fiber laxative		
	NyQuil	Cough/cold		
	Pepto-Bismol	Stomach remedy		
	Vicks	Cough/cold		
W-L	Anusol	Hemorrhoid treatment	Zovirax (in the US)	Genital herpes treatment
	Benadryl	Allergy relief & cold/flu		
	Caladryl	Anti-itch treatment		
	e.p.t.	Pregnancy test		
	Halls	Cough/cold		
	Listerine	Mouthwash		
	Neosporin	Topical antibiotic		
	Rolaids	Antacid		
	Sudafed	Cold/flu & sinus relief		
	Zantac	Antacid		
Bayer	Alka-Seltzer	Cough/cold, antacid	bone resorption and formation	Diagnostic kits
	Aspirin	Pain relief		
	Bactine	Antiseptic		
	Bayer Select	Pain relief		
	Campho-Phenique	Antiseptic		
	Flintstones	Multivitamin		
	Midol	Pain relief		
	Milk of Magnesia	Laxative		
	Mycelex	Vaginal yeast infection		
	One-A-Day	Multivitamin		
	Stri-Dex	Acne treatment		
J&J	Children's Motrin	Pain relief	Confide	HIV Test Kit
	Fact Plus	Pregnancy test	Hismanal	Allergy relief
	Imodium	Antidiarrheal	Nizoral	Dandruff shampoo
	Micatin	Athlete's foot	Renova	Protocamage
	Monistat 7	Vaginal yeast infection	Retin-A	Acne treatment
	Mylanta	Antacid	Spectazole	Athlete's foot
	Nicotrol	Habit control		
	One Touch	Glucometer test		
	Pepcid AC	Antacid		
	Tylenol	Pain relief, cough/cold		

Exhibit 10 ● Main Product Offerings of OTC Companies (*Continued*)

Company	Top Brands	Indication	Future Switches	Indication
SmithKline	Citrucel	Fiber laxative	Bactroban	Topical antibiotic
	Contac	Cough/cold	Nicoderm	Habit control
	Ecotrin	Pain relief	Relafen	Pain relief
	Gaviscon	Antacid	Seldane	Allergy relief
	Geritol	Dietary supplement		
	Nicorette	Habit control		
	Oxy	Acne treatment		
	Panadol	Pain relief		
	Sucrets	Cough/cold		
	Tagamet	Antacid		
	Tums	Antacid		
Rhône	Anthisan	Insect bites and stings		
	Brol-eze	Eye drops		
	Bronchicum	Cough/cold		
	Doliprane	Pain relief		
	Maalox (Europe)	Antacid		
	Oruvail	Topical pain relief		
	Resiston One	Allergy remedy		
Schering	Afrin	Cough/cold	Carafate	Antiulcerent
	Chlor-Trimeton	Cough/cold	Claritin	Allergy relief
	Correctol	Laxative	Proventil	Asthma treatment
	Drixoral	Cough/cold		
	Gyne-Lotrimin	Vaginal yeast infection		
	Lotrimin	Athlete's foot		
	Polaramin	Allergy relief		
	Tinactin	Athlete's foot		
Angelini	Moment	Pain relief		
	Tachipinna	Pain relief		
	Tantum Verde	Sore throat relief		
Taisho	Dermarin	Athlete's foot	Minoxidil	Hair loss
	Kanpo Ichoyaku	Stomach remedy	Zantac	Antacid
	Lipovitan	Bottled nutritive drinks		
	Pabron	Cough/cold		
	Preser	Antihemorrhoidal		
Perrigo	N/A			
Pharmavite	Nature Made	Vitamin		
	Nature's Resource	Herbal remedy		
Glaxo			Beconase	Allergy treatment
			Flonase	Allergy treatment
			Zovirax (in the US)	Genital herpes treatment

Exhibit 11 ● Procter & Gamble Sales and Earnings Growth

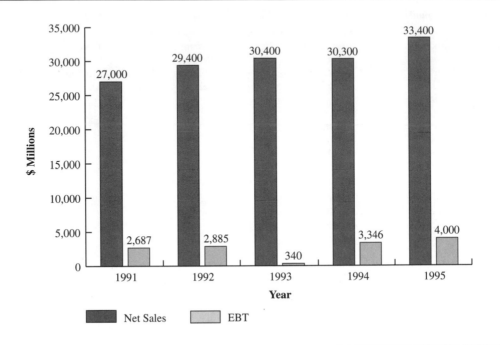

Source: Company reports.

Closely aligning itself with the medical community, J&J tried to create a feeling of reassurance with its self-medicating customers. For example, the slogan for Tylenol had always been "Hospitals use it," and with Mylanta, the slogan was ". . . my doctor said 'Mylanta.'" In addition, J&J had an entire sales force in the United States that was dedicated to health care professionals.

SmithKline Beecham

SmithKline Beecham (SB), head-quartered in the United Kingdom, generated 1995 sales of U.S. $11,077 million. SB was ranked number five worldwide for its OTC sales, number four in Europe, and number six in the United States. Before tax earnings showed solid growth in 1995, rebounding from lower-than-usual profits in 1994 (refer to Exhibit 23). The company was

organized into three divisions: Pharmaceuticals, Consumer Health, and Clinical Laboratories. Pharmaceuticals was the highest revenue-generating division, accounting for almost 60 percent of 1995 sales. Consumer Health, which contained mostly OTC products, accounted for 29 percent of total sales (refer to Exhibit 24). While SB as a corporation derived almost half of its sales from the United States, OTCs were more evenly divided among geographic regions (Refer to Exhibit 25).

SB, in its effort to be a truly global company, participated in numerous marker segments. It had a strong presence in gastrointestinals with its Tums and Gaviscon[6] products. Tums had a 45 percent share of the United States antacid market. In skin care, SB's

6. Gaviscon was marketed by SmithKline in the US only. Reckitt & Coleman sold it in Europe.

Exhibit 12 ● Procter & Gamble 1995 Sales Breakdowns by Geography and Activity

Geography

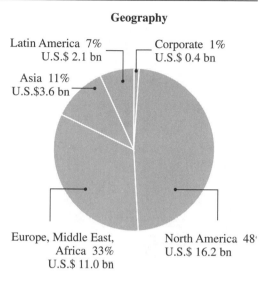

Latin America 7%
U.S.$ 2.1 bn

Corporate 1%
U.S.$ 0.4 bn

Asia 11%
U.S.$3.6 bn

Europe, Middle East, Africa 33%
U.S.$ 11.0 bn

North America 48ᵃ
U.S.$ 16.2 bn

Total Sales in U.S.$ 33.43 billion

Activity

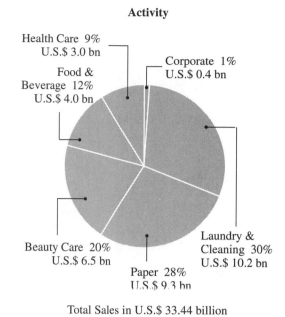

Health Care 9%
U.S.$ 3.0 bn

Corporate 1%
U.S.$ 0.4 bn

Food & Beverage 12%
U.S.$ 4.0 bn

Beauty Care 20%
U.S.$ 6.5 bn

Paper 28%
U.S.$ 9.3 bn

Laundry & Cleaning 30%
U.S.$ 10.2 bn

Total Sales in U.S.$ 33.44 billion

a. Includes OTC sales.

Source: Company reports.

Oxy ranked only behind Clearasil in the United States. Contac, for coughs and colds, had a truly global reach and was particularly strong in Japan and China. Geritol was the company's main product in the dietary supplements category. SB entered the analgesic market with its purchase of Sterling Healthcare, who brought along the Panadol brand.

SB was among the first to market with two newsworthy products: Tagamet, an H_2 antagonist, and Nicorette, a smoking cessation aid.[7] Both technologies were expected to grow their market segments, but SB faced stiff competition from other OTC competitors.

SB grew its OTC portfolio through acquisition of other companies, joint ventures with pharmaceutical companies such as Marion Merrell Dow, and Rx-to-

7. Nicorette was first to market for SB in the U.S. market only. It was licensed from Pharmacia & Upjohn, who marketed the product outside the U.S.

Exhibit 13 ● Split of Procter & Gamble's Self-Medication Sales, 1992–1993

Procter & Gamble
Split of Global Self-Medication Sales, 1992-1993

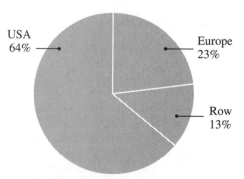

USA
64%

Europe
23%

Row
13%

Source: James Dudley International Ltd. Trade Estimates 1996; © *James Dudley Management.*

Exhibit 14 ● Procter & Gamble's Top 5 OTC Brands (U.S. Sales)

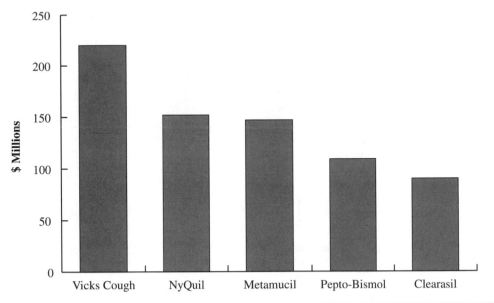

Source: Nicholas Hall & Company estimates.

OTC switches from its own pharmaceutical division. SB closely aligned itself with managed care organizations in the United States for both its pharmaceutical and OTC divisions. SB's goal was to position its products, particularly Nicorette, as wellness and prevention tools for managed care organizations.

Rhône-Poulenc Rorer

Rhône-Poulenc Rorer (RPR) was the leading OTC company in Europe, commanding a 4.1 percent share of the market in 1995. The French company employed 22,100 people who generated U.S.$5,142 million in sales. Around 26 percent of those sales were self-medication, making RPR the seventh-ranked OTC company in the world. Similar to Bayer, RPR was dependent upon the cyclical chemical industry for much of its sales, which caused its sales and earnings to fluctuate from one year to the next (refer to Exhibit 26). RPR's health sector accounted for around 37 percent of sales and consisted of human pharmaceuticals,

veterinary pharmaceuticals, and animal nutrition. Thirty-five percent of the company's overall sales came from France and another 23 percent from the rest of Europe (refer to Exhibit 27).

RPR had many joint venture agreements within its pharmaceutical operations; however, the OTC portfolio was built up mostly by acquisition. Furthermore, even though the type of research and products coming through its pharmaceutical division was revolutionary, RPR's Rx-to-OTC pipeline was empty.

RPR's key market segments were cough and cold, pain relief, and gastrointestinals. It also had strengths in vitamins and tonics (refer to Exhibit 28). The Maalox line was a particularly strong global brand for the company, except in the United States. RPR no longer controlled Maalox in that market since it sold its North American OTC business to Ciba at the end of 1994. Within France, Germany, and the other European countries, RPR approached each country individually. As a result, the leading brands in each country differed dramatically, with the exception of

Exhibit 15 ● Warner-Lambert Sales and Earnings Growth

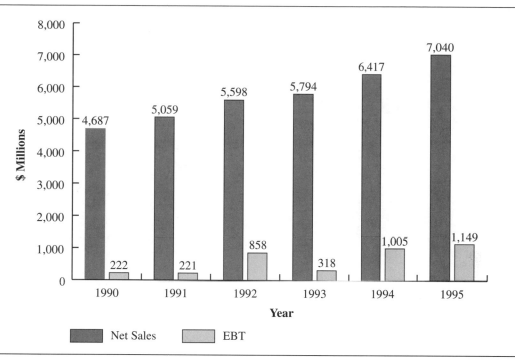

Source: Company reports.

Maalox. For example, one of RPR's most successful products was its analgesic, Doliprane. However, this product was only a top seller in France. Likewise, the innovative Oruvail, a gel-based topical analgesic, was launched only in the United Kingdom.

In the self-medication sector, RPR was even more reliant on France for its sales. Sixty percent of its European self-medication sales came from that market and another 25 percent from Germany. The North American OTC business contributed 35 percent of annual turnover before it was divested. That segment was mostly dependent upon Maalox, whose sales were consistently falling over time. In an attempt to become less reliant on France and Germany, RPR acquired the United Kingdom pharmaceutical company, Fisons, in 1995. Fisons brought with it mostly prescription-bound products, especially in the

asthma category, but also a couple of OTC hay fever remedies.

Schering-Plough

Schering-Plough (S-P) generated about 10 percent of its overall corporate sales of U.S.$5,104 million with OTC products.[8] This was enough to rank them number nine in the United States, but S-P did not make the top ten in any other market. The OTC division's share of the overall corporate sales fell from 7 percent in 1993 down to 5 percent in 1995. S-P had one of the highest earnings before taxes of the companies stud-

8. The OTC division only accounted for 5 percent of sales. However, some OTC products were accounted for in the foot care and sun care divisions.

Exhibit 16 ● Warner-Lambert Sales Breakdowns by Geography and Activity, 1995

Exhibit 17 ● Warner-Lambert OTC Sales by Category and Brand, 1994*

Geography

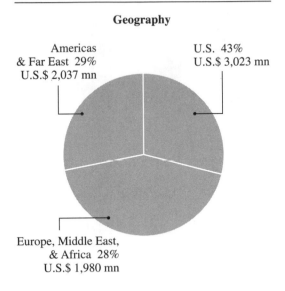

Americas & Far East 29%
U.S.$ 2,037 mn

U.S. 43%
U.S.$ 3,023 mn

Europe, Middle East, & Africa 28%
U.S.$ 1,980 mn

Total Sales in U.S.$ 7,040 million

*Includes OTC sales, shaving products, and pet care products.
Source: Company reports.

**Warner Lambert
OTC Sales by Category, 1994* (RSP)**

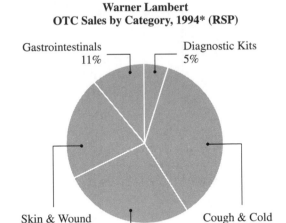

Gastrointestinals 11%

Diagnostic Kits 5%

Skin & Wound Care 21%

Oral Care 27%

Cough & Cold 36%

* Including Warner Wellcome brands

Source: UPDATE U.S.A. based on trade estimates.

Activity

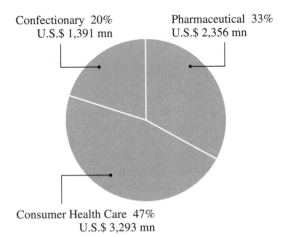

Confectionary 20%
U.S.$ 1,391 mn

Pharmaceutical 33%
U.S.$ 2,356 mn

Consumer Health Care 47%
U.S.$ 3,293 mn

Total Sales in U.S.$ 7,040 million

**Warner Lambert
Cough & Cold Sales by Brand, 1994* (RSP)**

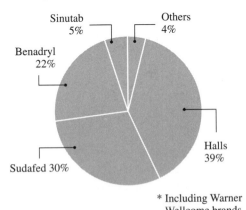

Sinutab 5%

Others 4%

Benadryl 22%

Halls 39%

Sudafed 30%

* Including Warner Wellcome brands

**Warner Lambert
Skin & Wound Care Sales by Brand, 1994* (RSP)**

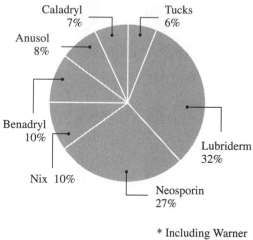

* Including Warner
Wellcome brands

Exhibit 18 ● Bayer Group Sale Breakdowns by
Geography and Activity, 1995

Activity

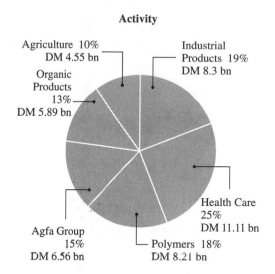

Total Sales in DM 44.6 billion

*Includes OTCs, diagnostics, pharmaceuticals.

Source: Company reports; *Nonprescription Drugs USA
1995.*

Geography

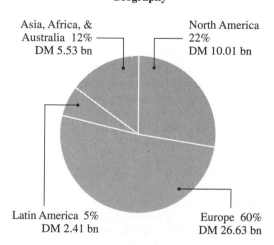

Total Sales in DM 44.6 billion

ied (refer to Exhibit 29). S-P generated 55 percent of
its sales in the United States, followed by 25 percent
in Europe, the Middle East, and Africa (refer to Exhibit 30).

In the OTC industry, S-P concentrated in a few
selected product markets: skin treatments, cough and
cold, and gastrointestinals. Most of the products in its
OTC portfolio were the result of switches. Of eight
successful switches in the United States between
1951 and 1991 (refer to Exhibit 31) seven went on to
become top-selling brands. Skin treatments were its
top category in the United States. S-P held the top two
spots in antifungals with Lotrimin and Tinactin.
Afrin, Drixoral, and Chlor-Trimeton were S-P's top
products in cough and cold. Correctol rounded out the
top products in the gastrointestinals market in the
United States. Europe was a much smaller OTC market for S-P, generating only 5 percent of sales, com-

Exhibit 19 ● Bayer Group Sales & Earnings Growth

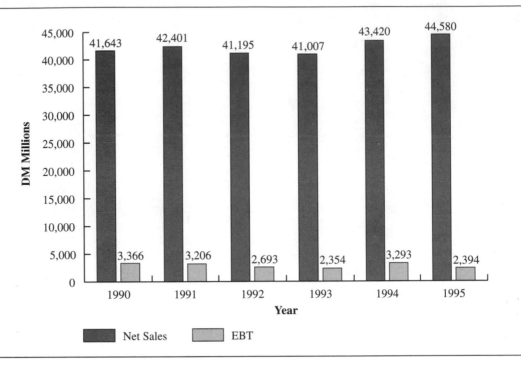

Source: company reports.

pared to the United States' 80 percent. Allergy and hay fever remedies were the strongest products for S-P in that region (refer to Exhibit 31).

S-P held the patent for Clarityn, the number one prescription for allergies. The company had already switched this product to OTC status in the United Kingdom and was gearing up for a U.S. switch with a consumer advertising campaign.

Two of S-P's consumer divisions, foot care and sun care, had OTC products in its mix. S-P was able to create several OTC products by leveraging the brand name of its two biggest franchises: Dr. Scholl's and Coppertone.

Angelini

Angelini, an Italian pharmaceutical company, generated 1994 sales of about U.S.$174 million. Over one-

third of the company's sales came from OTCs, making Angelini the third-largest OTC company in its domestic market. This was also enough to rank them first among the local players in Europe in 1994. Angelini was mostly an Italian company, although two wholly owned subsidiaries, one in Spain and one in Venezuela, generated U.S.$16–18 million and U.S.$14–16 million of pharmaceutical sales in their respective countries. The four divisions of the company included, Dispecial (ethicals), Area "C" (OTC, hospital, and veterinary). Pharma International (export), and Materie Prime (fine chemicals). Angelini had negative sales and earnings growth from 1991–1993, but began to rebound in 1994 (refer to Exhibit 32).

Pain relief was Angelini's biggest market segment (refer to Exhibit 33). Two analgesic products, Moment and Tachipirina, accounted for a majority of sales in this category. In fact. Tachipirina was a top-

Exhibit 20 ● Johnson & Johnson Sales and Earnings Growth

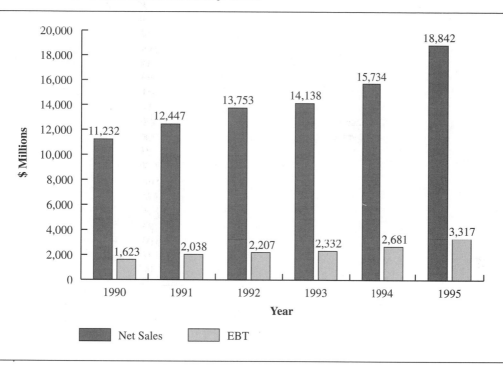

Source: Company reports.

selling product in the Italian OTC industry. It shared the second-place position with Halls (by W-L) in 1994. Moment ranked fourth in 1994. The throat preparation, Tantum Verde, generated the majority of sales in Angelini's second-biggest category, oral care. Angelini also competed in the gynecological segment with another Tantum product, Tantum Rosa P.

In Italy, the pharmaceutical market was changing rapidly. For example, pressures from the government to reduce health care expenditures and changing consumer attitudes enabled OTC companies to expand. Angelini was a well-known Italian company and had a strong foundation in its home country.

An example of how Angelini was able to leverage its nationally known name happened with the launch of Moment. There was a battle in the analgesics market between Moment and the British company Boots' Nurofen. Being the home country paid

off for Angelini as it was able to ward off the market penetration of Nurofen to take the number two spot in the Analgesics market behind Bayer's Aspirin.

Taisho

Japan's number one OTC company, Taisho, generated 1995 sales of approximately U.S.$2,400 million. Exhibit 34 shows Taisho's steady sales growth from 1990–1994. Roughly two-thirds of its sales were generated from OTC products (refer to Exhibit 35). The remaining sales came primarily from other pharmaceuticals (25 percent) and consumer products (5 percent). The main market segments for Taisho were cough and cold, gastrointestinals, pain relief, diagnostics, skin treatments, and tonics. Taisho had a strong OTC Drug Research Division and planned to diversify into other OTC product segments in the future. While Japan was

Exhibit 21 ● Johnson & Johnson Sales Breakdowns by Geography and Activity, 1995

Exhibit 22 ● Johnson & Johnson U.S. OTC Sales by Category and Brand, 1994–1995

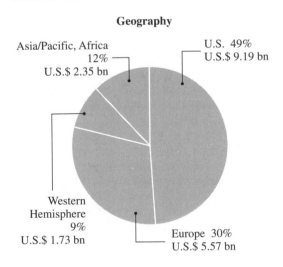

Geography

Total Sales in U.S.$ 18.84 billion

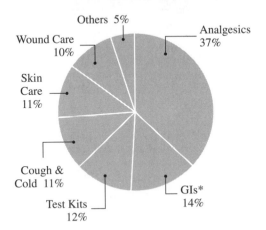

Johnson & Johnson
U.S. OTC Sales by Category, 1994-95 (RSP)

* Includes first few months of Pepcid AC sales

Source: UPDATE U*S*A based on Towne-Oller data from 1994–1995.

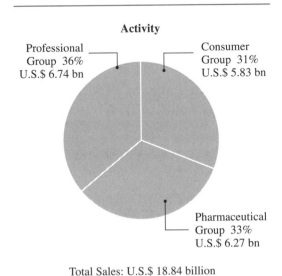

Activity

Total Sales: U.S.$ 18.84 billion

*Includes OTCs and personal care products.
Source: Company reports.

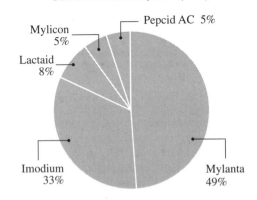

Johnson & Johnson
GI Portfolio Shares, 1995 (RSP)

Source: Based on Towne-Aller food and drugstore tracking service, 12 months to 7/95.

Exhibit 23 ● SmithKline Beecham Sales and Earnings Growth

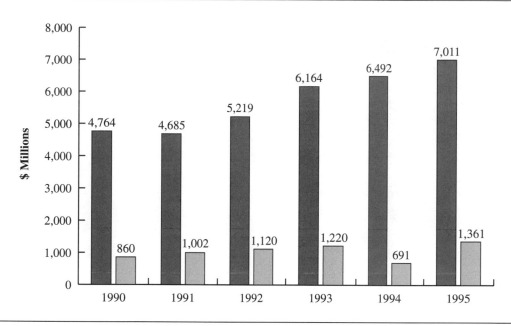

Source: Company reports.

its main geographic market, it also had sales in the Far East, Latin America, and the United States.

Almost half of Taisho's self-medication sales came from the Lipovitan line of mini-drinks. In fact, one particular product, Lipovitan D, accounted for almost 7 percent of sales in the entire Japanese OTC market. Taisho had the top or one of the top products in all categories in which it competed. Pabron, a cough and cold remedy, was another strong product for the company. Taisho was a leader in Rx-to-OTC switching in Japan, having done over eighteen switches in its history. Most of the switches were the result of agreements with other companies. Future possible switch ventures included the H_2 antagonist Zantac and a minoxidil product for hair loss treatment.

Perrigo

Perrigo was the leading private label manufacturer of nonprescription drugs in the United States. Sales in 1995 reached U.S.$717 million. Sales and profit growth were historically solid, although earnings dipped a bit in 1995 (refer to Exhibit 36). Unlike the other competitors profiled previously, Perrigo did not generate any sales in the prescription sector. That, coupled with the fact that its products could not command a premium price for being national brands, meant lower gross margins for the company. Still, Perrigo saved immensely on R&D and selling costs, which made its bottom line competitive with other industry players. Its sales were split between OTC, personal care, and vitamins (refer to Exhibit 37). Perrigo stuck to its core competency of selling its products in the U.S. market.

Perrigo's main products were in the analgesics, cough and cold, gastrointestinals, skin treatments, and vitamins markets, although it had a presence in almost every category (refer to Exhibit 38). Access to new products depended on whether or not companies still had a patent or if it had been granted an exclusivity by the FDA. In some cases Perrigo was offered licensing

Exhibit 24 ● SmithKline Beecham Sales Breakdowns by Geography and Activity, 1995

Exhibit 25 ● SB/Sterling OTC Sales by Region, 1993

Geography

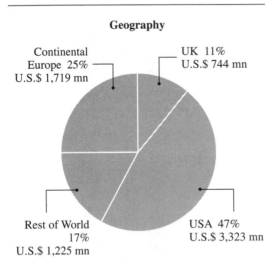

Continental Europe 25% U.S.$ 1,719 mn

UK 11% U.S.$ 744 mn

Rest of World 17% U.S.$ 1,225 mn

USA 47% U.S.$ 3,323 mn

Total Sales in U.S.$ 7,011 million

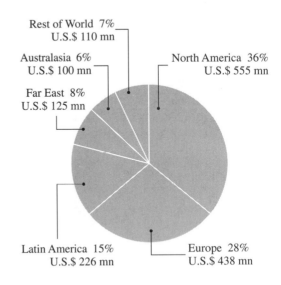

Rest of World 7% U.S.$ 110 mn

Australasia 6% U.S.$ 100 mn

Far East 8% U.S.$ 125 mn

North America 36% U.S.$ 555 mn

Latin America 15% U.S.$ 226 mn

Europe 28% U.S.$ 438 mn

Source: Nicholas Hall & Co. estimates.

Activity

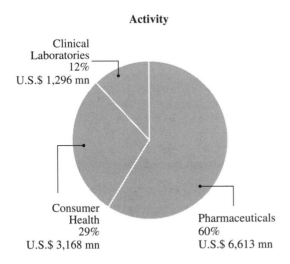

Clinical Laboratories 12% U.S.$ 1,296 mn

Consumer Health 29% U.S.$ 3,168 mn

Pharmaceuticals 60% U.S.$ 6,613 mn

Total Sales in U.S.$ 11,077 million

*Includes OTCs, nutritional health care, and oral health care.
Source: Company reports; *Nonprescription Drugs USA 1995.*

arrangements from other pharmaceutical companies. A good example of this was the marketing agreement Perrigo had with Sandoz to market a private-label version of Tavist and the future promise to market Aleve in 1997.

In the United States, private labels were taking more and more market share away from branded products. This was in part due to the increased education of consumers about health care. In 1994, U.S. private label OTCs grew 10.2 percent over the previous year, compared to only 3.4 percent growth for the overall OTC industry. Private labels accounted for 18.2 percent of all OTC sales, up from 16.8 percent in 1993. This trend was expected to continue.

Pharmavite

Pharmavite was a wholly owned subsidiary of Otsuka America, which was, in turn, a wholly owned sub-

Exhibit 26 ● Rhône-Poulenc Rorer Sales and Earnings Growth

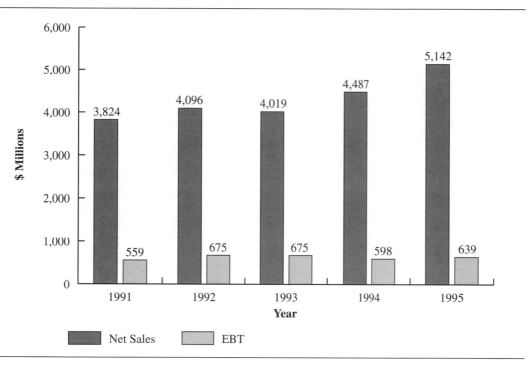

Source: Company reports.

sidiary of Otsuka Pharmaceutical of Japan. It was acquired by Otsuka in 1989. Estimated 1994 sales of U.S.$140 million made it the smallest of the competitors analyzed. Roughly 96 percent of the company's sales came from vitamins and minerals, with personal care products making up the difference. The United States was Pharmavite's primary market, although through the parent corporation, access to Japan and other markets was possible.

Nature Made was Pharmavite's most-well-known product line, accounting for 10–12 percent of company turnover in 1994. Nature Made was the leading brand in most individual vitamin categories in the United States, and was also sold in Japan. Pharmavite introduced a line of homeopathic products in May 1994 called Nature's Resource. The herbal line had U.S.$3.6 million in sales during its first year. In addi-

tion to its own lines, Pharmavite manufactured some private label products for other companies.

Pharmavite's strategy was to develop a strong relationship with retailers and support it with magazine advertising. The company would go into retail outlets and set up full displays and train the sales forces. Traceable media expenditures in 1993 were $3.1 million, or roughly 2 percent of total OTC sales. This was a much lower figure than for other companies (e.g., P&G at 26.4 percent in 1995). However, the average for the vitamins, minerals, and nutritional supplements market segment in the United States was only 3.5 percent in 1993. Thus, Pharmavite was only a little below average. Advertising and promotional spending in the category was dominated by big brands such as Centrum (American Home Products) and One-A-Day (Bayer).

Exhibit 27 ● Rhône-Poulenc Rorer Sales Breakdowns by Geography and Activity, 1995

Geography

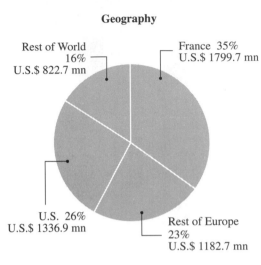

Rest of World
16%
U.S.$ 822.7 mn

France 35%
U.S.$ 1799.7 mn

U.S. 26%
U.S.$ 1336.9 mn

Rest of Europe
23%
U.S.$ 1182.7 mn

Total Sales in U.S.$ 5,142 million

Source: Datamonitor, Company report.

Activity

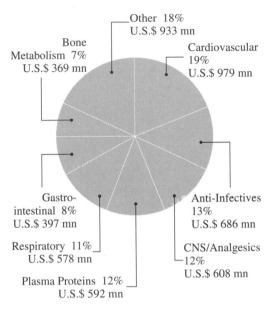

Other 18%
U.S.$ 933 mn

Bone
Metabolism 7%
U.S.$ 369 mn

Cardiovascular
19%
U.S.$ 979 mn

Gastro-
intestinal 8%
U.S.$ 397 mn

Anti-Infectives
13%
U.S.$ 686 mn

Respiratory 11%
U.S.$ 578 mn

CNS/Analgesics
12%
U.S.$ 608 mn

Plasma Proteins 12%
U.S.$ 592 mn

Total Sales in U.S.$ 5,142 million

Glaxo Wellcome

Glaxo Wellcome (Glaxo) was not an OTC company in the traditional sense of the word; however, it had strong ties to the OTC industry. Sales in 1995 were U.S.$11,264 million, mostly generated by pharmaceutical products. Glaxo used joint ventures and licensing agreements to market its products in the OTC market. Due to its prescription product portfolio, Glaxo had the highest profit margin of any of the competitors (refer to Exhibit 39). The company's sales were relatively evenly split between the United States, Europe, and the rest of the world (refer to Exhibit 40). Glaxo reinforced its relationship with Warner-Lambert by purchasing Wellcome in 1995. Warner-Lambert already had a joint venture with Wellcome (Warner-Welcome) dating back to 1993. Glaxo used this relationship to market its Rx-to-OTC switches.

Gastrointestinals played a major role in annual turnover, generating 43 percent of corporate-wide sales in 1994 (refer to Exhibit 40). Zantac was Glaxo's main product in this segment, and a global switch to

OTC was in process. The cold sore treatment, Zovirax, had much OTC potential in the skin treatment segment, although it was only available OTC in Europe. Regulators in the United States had not approved it for sale in their nonprescription market. Beconase, which was an allergy remedy, was launched in Europe, but had not hit the U.S. market yet. It was not expected to be introduced in the United States until the patent neared expiration in 1999.

Glaxo decided to focus on its core competencies: bringing new drugs through the pharmaceutical process and selling them to professionals. As a result, the company relied on relationships with other companies for both development and OTC marketing. Unlike many of its competitors, Glaxo resisted the merger craze in the pharmaceutical industry for many years. Glaxo's deviation from this policy to purchase Wellcome was an effort to protect its competitive position through improved synergies and clout with customers. Glaxo was the number one pharmaceutical company in the world.

Exhibit 28 ● RPR's Leading European OTC Brands, 1994–1995

Country	Category	Brand	Rank	% share	Market ($mn)
France	Internal analgesics	Doliprane	1	25	260
	Sore throat pastilles	Solutricine	3	14	72
	Indigestion remedies	Maalox	4	9	117
	Vitamin C	Vitascorbol	3	18	21
	Antiseptics/disinfectants (pharmacy)	Hexomédine	1	10	119
	Hay fever remedies	Phénergan	5	7	6
		Théralène Sirop	7	6	
Germany	Cold remedies	Contramutan	4	6	52
	Cough remedies	Bronchicum	1	8	156
	Indigestion remedies	Maaloxan	2	19	57
	Tonics	Biovital	2	19	74
	Garlic	Ilja Rogoff	2	23	89
Italy	Chest rubs & inhalants	Calyptol Inalante	2	22	8
	Varicose vein remedies	Essaven gel	2	35	8
	Topical antihistamines	Calmogel	4	9	11
Netherlands	Cough remedies (syrups)	Bronchicum	2	16	13
	Indigestion remedies	Maalox	2	10	7
Spain	Antacids	Maalox Concentrado	6	8	18
United Kingdom	Topical analgesics	Oruvail Gel	5	6	21
	Antidiarrheals/ORT	Dioralyte	1	70	5
	Insect bites & stings	Anthisan	1	60	2
	SCG eye drops	Brol-eze	1	32	2
		Opticrom	2	31	

Source: OTC News based on trade estimates (MSP).

Exhibit 29 ● Schering-Plough Sales and Earnings Growth

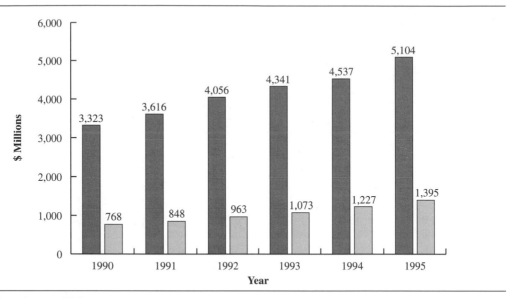

Source: Annual report, 1995.

Exhibit 30 ● Shering Plough Sales Breakdowns by Geography and Activity, 1995

Activity

Geography

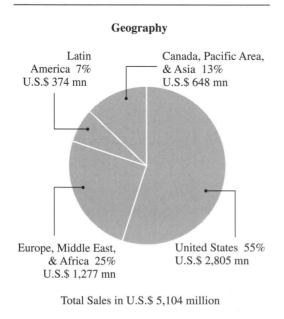

Latin America 7%
U.S.$ 374 mn

Canada, Pacific Area, & Asia 13%
U.S.$ 648 mn

Europe, Middle East, & Africa 25%
U.S.$ 1,277 mn

United States 55%
U.S.$ 2,805 mn

Total Sales in U.S.$ 5,104 million

Source: S-P Annual Report, 1995.

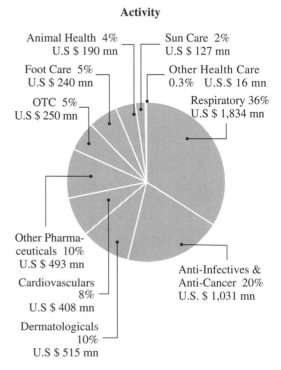

Animal Health 4%
U.S $ 190 mn

Sun Care 2%
U.S $ 127 mn

Foot Care 5%
U.S.$ 240 mn

Other Health Care
0.3%   U.S.$ 16 mn

OTC 5%
U.S $ 250 mn

Respiratory 36%
U.S $ 1,834 mn

Other Pharmaceuticals 10%
U.S $ 493 mn

Cardiovasculars 8%
U.S $ 408 mn

Dermatologicals 10%
U.S $ 515 mn

Anti-Infectives & Anti-Cancer 20%
U.S $ 1,031 mn

Total Sales in U.S.$ 5,104 million

Exhibit 31 ● Schering-Plough U.S. and European Brands

U.S. Rx-to-OTC Switches, 1951–1991

Brand	Category	Year
Coricidin	Cough & cold	1951
Tinactin	Topical antifungals	1971
Afrin	Nasal decongestants	1976
Chlor-Trimeton	Anti-allergy	1976
Drixoral	Cough & cold	1982
Lotrimin AF	Topical antifungals	1989
Gyne-Lotrimin	Vaginal thrush treatments	1990
DuoFilm	Wart treatments	1991

Source: Schering-Plough.

Leading European OTC Brands, 1994

Country	Category	Brand	Rank	% Share	Market ($mn)
France	Hay fever remedies	Polaramine	1	30	6
Italy	Topical antihistamines	Polaramin	1	35	10
	Hay fever remedies	Polaramin	1	57	4
	Antifungals	Tinaderm	4	19	1
Portugal	Cold remedies	Antigripe Asclepi	1	30	4
	Nasal decongestants	Constipal	4	9	5
Spain	Cold & flu remedies	Desenfriol	3	6	32
	Nasal decongestants	Respir	6	9	11
	Anti-itching products	Polaramine	4	7	1
	Antifungals	Tinaderm	3	3	2
United Kingdom	Hay fever remedies	Clarityn	5	8	12
	Athlete's foot treatments	Tinaderm	5	4	6

Source: OTC News based on trade estimates (MSP).

Exhibit 32 ● Angelini Sales and Earnings Growth

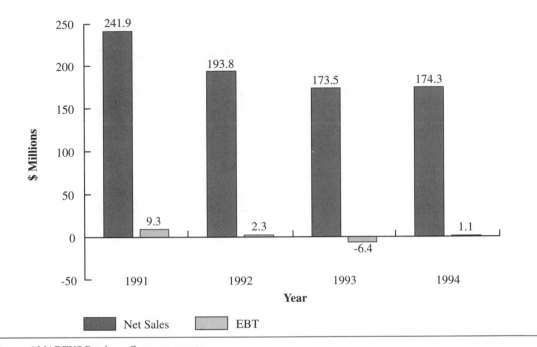

Source: AMADEUS Database, Company reports.

Exhibit 33 ● Angelini OTC Sales Breakdown by Product Category, 1995

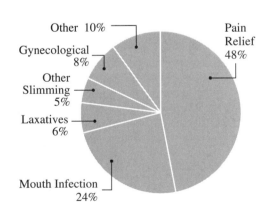

Source: OTC Review 1996.

Exhibit 34 ● Taisho Sales and Earnings Growth

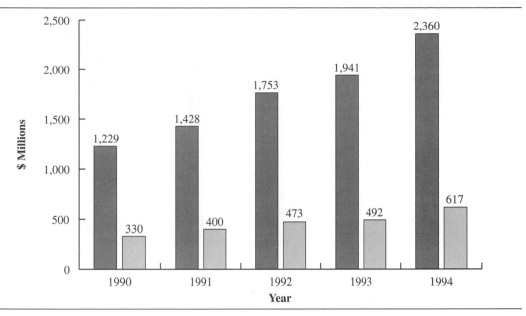

Source: Company reports.

Exhibit 35 ● Taisho Sales Breakdowns by Activity, 1994

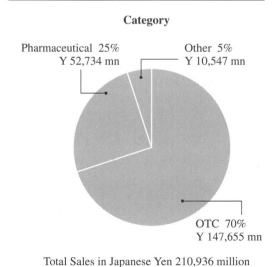

Category

Pharmaceutical 25%
Y 52,734 mn

Other 5%
Y 10,547 mn

OTC 70%
Y 147,655 mn

Total Sales in Japanese Yen 210,936 million

Source: Far East Focus, Company reports.

Product Line

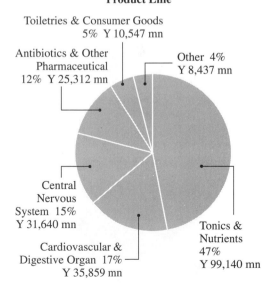

Toiletries & Consumer Goods
5% Y 10,547 mn

Antibiotics & Other
Pharmaceutical
12% Y 25,312 mn

Other 4%
Y 8,437 mn

Central
Nervous
System 15%
Y 31,640 mn

Cardiovascular &
Digestive Organ 17%
Y 35,859 mn

Tonics &
Nutrients
47%
Y 99,140 mn

Total Sales in Japanese Yen: 210,936 million

Exhibit 36 ● Perrigo Sales and Earnings Growth

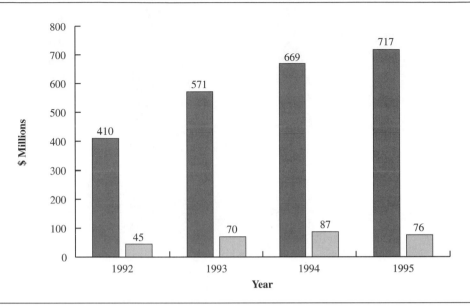

Source: Merrill Lynch Capital Markets Report.

Exhibit 37 ● Perrigo Sales Breakdown by Division, 1995

Perrigo
Sales Breakdown by Division, 1995

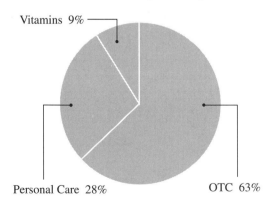

Source: Nonprescription Drugs USA 1995.

Exhibit 38 ● Sampling of Perrigo Nonprescription Drugs and Their National Brand Equivalents

Perringo Product	*National Brand Equivalent*
ACNE AIDS	
Medicated Skin Cream	Noxzema (Procter & Gamble)
ANALGESICS	
Aspirin	Bayer Aspirin (Bayer Group)
Extra Strength Pain Releiver	Tylenol Gelcaps (Johnson & Johnson)
Pain Reliever & Sleep Aid PM	Tylenol PM (Johnson & Johnson)
Ibuprofen Tablets and Caplets	Advil (American Home Products)
ANTACIDS AND ANTI-GAS	
Antacids Gelatin Caps	Mylanta Gelcaps (J&J/Merck)
Flavored Antacid Tablets	Tums (SmithKline Beecham)
Maldroxal	Maalox (Ciba)
ANTIDIARRHEALS	
Loperamide Hydrochloride	Imodium A-D Caplets &
Caplets & Liquid	Liquid (Johnson & Johnson)
ANTI-ITCH PRODUCTS	
Calamine Lotion	Caladryl (Warner-Lambert)
COUGH/COLD REMEDIES	
Dailyhist-1	Tavist-1 (Sandoz)
Diphedryl	Benadryl (Warner-Lambert)
Effervescent Cold Relief	Alka-Seltzer Plus (Bayer Group)
Nite Time Cough Syrup	NyQuil (Procter & Gamble)
Pseudoephedrine	Sudafed (Warner-Lambert)
DIET AIDS	
Diet Caplets	Dexatrim (Thompson Medical)
FEMININE YEAST INFECTION REMEDIES	
Miconazole-7 Cream	Monistat 7 (Johnson & Johnson)
HEMORRHOIDAL PREPARATIONS	
Hemorrhoidal Ointment	Preparation H (American Home Products)
LAXATIVES	
Milk of Magnesia U.S.P.	Phillips' Milk of Magnesia (Bayer Group)
Natural Fiber Laxative	Metamucil (Procter & Gamble)
VITAMIN AND NUTRITIONAL SUPPLEMENTS	
A-Shapes Chewables	Flintstones (Bayer Group)
Century IV vitamins	Centrum (American Home Products)
Multiple vitamins	One-A-Day (Bayer Group)
Ginseng	Ginsana (Sunsource)

Source: Nonprescription Drugs USA 1995.

Exhibit 39 ● Glaxo Sales and Earnings Growth

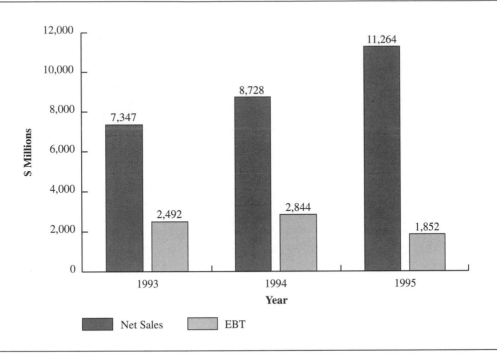

Source: Company reports.

Exhibit 40 ● Glaxo Sales Breakdowns by Geography and Activity, 1995

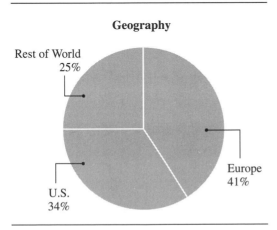

Source: Company reports.

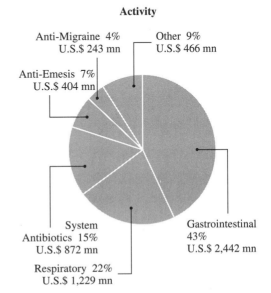

Total Sales in U.S.$ 5,656 million

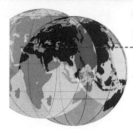

CASE 3
Note on OTC Brands

OTC INDUSTRY BACKGROUND

The world market for OTC pharmaceutical products was estimated at $51.45 billion in 1995 and was expected to sustain a compound annual growth rate (CAGR) of 7 percent through the year 2004. Many factors were driving this growth: more educated consumers taking control of their health care, governments and managed care organizations trying to reduce health care expenditures, and pharmaceutical companies trying to expand the product life cycle of key brands.

Typically, the market was divided by geography and product segment. The biggest markets were the United States, Japan, Germany, the United Kingdom, and France. The largest product segments were cough/cold and upper respiratory, skin treatments, digestive remedies, vitamins, minerals, and nutritional supplements, and tonics and stimulants. Two growth categories were habit control and diagnostic kits. Exhibit 1 details the size of these segments and their respective growth rates.

The behavior of OTC consumers changed according to the particular medical situation: when suffering from an ailment, consumers either self-medicated, visited a doctor, applied a home remedy, or did nothing at all. Most people either self-medicated or visited a doctor. The choice depended on the ailment and how comfortable the consumer

was with self-diagnosis. Consider two common ailments in the United Kingdom with OTC remedies available: headaches and vaginal yeast infections. For headaches, 86 percent of sufferers chose to self-medicate, compared to only 34 percent for vaginal yeast infections.

One could observe a development pattern in the OTC industry. In the early stages of the industry life cycle, consumer choice was limited to general purpose products. As the segment evolved, new competitors entered, niche products emerged, and new product segments were created. As a result, growth in developed countries with largely mature OTC markets came from introducing new products, or line extensions. At the same time, product life cycles of old products were extended by entry into developing countries. The drivers for this evolution were a combination of new medical technologies making their way to the OTC market and existing products needing to redefine the segment in order to remain competitive. Also, changes were happening with consumer products in general that created an atmosphere of more extensive segmentation and product specialization.

The most important demographic trends affecting the OTC industry were the aging populations of the United States, Japan, and Europe and the increasing buying power of consumers in developing countries due to rapidly advancing economies.

There were many participants in the OTC industry. The following were main players: chemicals suppliers, OTC manufacturers, distributors, retailers, consumers, medical professionals, governments and regulators, and managed care organisations. Exhibit 2 describes the forces in the industry.[1]

This case was written by Kristi Menz and Shauna Pettit, MBA candidates at the F. W. Olin Graduate School of Business at Babson College, under the direction of Professor Jean-Pierre Jeannet. To be used in conjunction with Cases 2, 3, and 5. Copyright © 1997 by IMD—International Institute for Management Development, Lausanne, Switzerland. All rights reserved. Not to be used or reproduced without written permission from IMD.

1. For more information on the OTC industry and competitors, see Case 3 and Case 5.

Exhibit 1 ● OTC Industry Product Classification and Sales Figures, 1995

Category	Major Therapeutic Segments	Share of Segment Sales[a]	Growth 1995–1998	Top U.S. Brands
World OTC	*Total Sales: U.S.$51.45 Billion*			
Pain relief	*Percent of total sales: 17%*		4.6%	
	General pain relievers	69.5%	4.2	Tylenol, Advil, Aleve
	Muscular pain	26.4	6.1	Ibuprofen (PL), Ben-Gay
	Migraine remedies	.25	5.8	Migraclear
	Mouth pain relief	1.97	3.9	Anbesol, Orajel
Cough, cold, and respiratory	*Percent of total sales: 17%*		7.7	
	Cough remedies	29.0	5.9	Halls, Robitussin DM
	Cold remedies	44.0	8.1	NyQuil, Alka Seltzer Plus C
	Sore throat	12.9	8.5	Chloraseptic, Sucrets
	Hay fever	11.5	9.4	Benadryl OTC, Tavist-D
	Asthma	2.6	9.2	Bronkaid, Primatene Mist
Digestive preparations	*Percent of total sales: 12%*		3.4	
	Stomach remedies	53.0	4.1	Pepcid AC, Pepto Bismol
	Laxatives	28.1	2.7	Metamucil, Milk of Magnesia
	Antidiarrheals	14.1	2.0	Imodium-AD, Pedialyte
	Liver remedies	4.2	2.1	Lipoflavonoid, Decholin
	Worm treatment	0.6	2.0	Combantrin, Pin-X
Skin treatments	*Percent of total sales: 12%*		7.6	
	Skin protection	28.3	8.7	Coppertone
	Skin irritation	18.2	8.8	Campho Phenique
	Antiseptics	11.2	8.2	Alcohol (PL), Campho-Phenique
	Antifungals	11.0	9.2	Lotrimin AF, Desenex
	Spot and blemish care	8.2	4.5	Clearasil, Oxy
	Antidandruff	5.7	7.7	Head & Shoulders
	Antiparasitics	3.1	2.2	Lice Treatment Kit
	Cold sore remedies	1.3	31.3	Zovirax, Blistex
	Antibaldness	0.7	17.3	Rogaine
Vitamins, minerals and nutritional supplements	*Percent of Total Sales: 10%*		8.1	Centrum, One-A-Day, Ensure
Diagnostic tests	*Percent of total sales: 5%*	–	15.5	One Touch, E.P.T.
Tonics and stimulants	*Percent of total sales: 4%*	–	6.5	Vivarin, No Doz, Ginseng
Eye care	*Percent of total sales: 4%*		4	Renu, Opti-Free, Aosept
Oral care	*Percent of total sales: 4%*		1.2	Listerine, Polident, Fixodent
Circulatory remedies	*Percent of total sales: 4%*		5.5	Preparation H, Tucks
Ear care	*Percent of total sales: 5%*	0.5	7.3	Murine Ear Drops
Bladder and genitals	*Percent of total sales: 2.5%*		–1.6	Monistat-7, Trojans
Habit control	*Percent of total sales: .3%*		21	Nicorette, Nicotinell
Other	*Percent of total sales: 7.7%*			

a. 1995 sales for ten countries: Belgium, France, Germany, Italy, Netherlands, Spain, United Kingdom, Canada, United States, and Japan.

Exhibit 2 ● OTC Industry's Five Forces

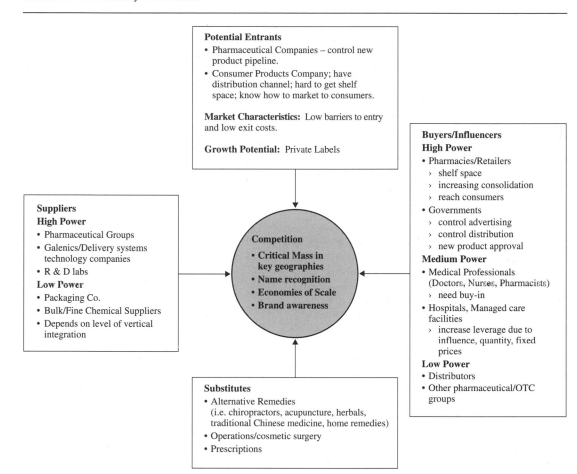

Potential Entrants
- Pharmaceutical Companies – control new product pipeline.
- Consumer Products Company; have distribution channel; hard to get shelf space; know how to market to consumers.

Market Characteristics: Low barriers to entry and low exit costs.

Growth Potential: Private Labels

Suppliers
High Power
- Pharmaceutical Groups
- Galenics/Delivery systems technology companies
- R & D labs

Low Power
- Packaging Co.
- Bulk/Fine Chemical Suppliers
- Depends on level of vertical integration

Competition
- **Critical Mass in key geographies**
- **Name recognition**
- **Economies of Scale**
- **Brand awareness**

Buyers/Influencers
High Power
- Pharmacies/Retailers
  - › shelf space
  - › increasing consolidation
  - › reach consumers
- Governments
  - › control advertising
  - › control distribution
  - › new product approval

Medium Power
- Medical Professionals (Doctors, Nurses, Pharmacists)
  - › need buy-in
- Hospitals, Managed care facilities
  - › increase leverage due to influence, quantity, fixed prices

Low Power
- Distributors
- Other pharmaceutical/OTC groups

Substitutes
- Alternative Remedies (i.e. chiropractors, acupuncture, herbals, traditional Chinese medicine, home remedies)
- Operations/cosmetic surgery
- Prescriptions

BRANDING IN THE OTC INDUSTRY

As mentioned above, the OTC industry evolved from a generalist market to a specialist-oriented market with an abundance of choices. Companies tried to grow in the OTC market through product differentiation based on product form (e.g., liquid versus tablets) and new product advancements (e.g., 24-hour relief, extra strength, improved taste, etc.).

New products were introduced as a result of new product or brand developments or through product line extensions. New products were created either from an existing substance from the prescription pharmaceutical market or from commonly available ingredients. Factors that influenced product rollout decisions included: prescription brand heritage, advertising regulation by governments and protection of other businesses such as prescription and/or semi-ethical business. Furthermore, if an OTC company obtained access to a new substance from another company, the licensing agreement may have contained limitations either on branding or geographic distribution.

Another strategy often used by OTC companies to grow product portfolios was to extend product lines by leveraging strong brand names across different therapeutic categories within existing segments or completely different product segments (e.g., a cold medicine brand migrating to include a cough medicine or a cold medicine brand migrating into the stomach remedies category).

As a product moved from the prescription arena to OTC, the target customer also changed. With prescription products, doctors and other medical professionals were targeted. With an OTC product, the consumers were the final decision makers. Therefore, it was not uncommon to see a change in presentation when the product switched from prescription to OTC (e.g., changing tablets to liquids, improvement in taste, etc.).

There was no uniform description of an OTC company. Likewise, there was no uniform method of competing. However, like most industries, there were classic examples of strategies that enabled companies to achieve their goals and strategies that did not.

SUCCESSFUL NEW BRAND LAUNCHES

Advil

Advil was first introduced in 1984 in the U.S. pain relief market segment by American Home Products (AHP). At the time, the pain relief segment was dominated by two brands, Bayer Aspirin and Tylenol, an acetaminophen.

Advil was the first ibuprofen switch in the United States. Six weeks after the launch of Advil, Bristol-Myers Squibb launched its own version of ibuprofen, Nuprin. Both products had a two-year patent protection.

As a prescription product, ibuprofen was sold under many brand names. In the United States, the best known was Motrin. Considered a breakthrough in pain relief, ibuprofen was in many ways superior to aspirin and acetaminophen. It was known to be more potent and exhibited fewer side effects than the other products. It was easier on the stomach than aspirin and, in the event of an overdose, safer than acetaminophen.

AHP had a ten-year licensing agreement for the ibuprofen substance with a U.K. pharmaceutical group, Boots. Production was initially carried out by Boots in its U.K. factories. This enabled AHP to launch the new brand more quickly and without the need for a production commitment. The company could instead focus on educating consumers and gaining support from the medical community.

The brand name Advil was completely new. It had neither a prescription nor consumer brand heritage. However, due to clever marketing it was able to create both by association. Advil was positioned as a new standard for the treatment of pain that was "the same as the prescription drug, Motrin."

To support its positioning, AHP implemented an integrated marketing campaign, investing significantly in consumer advertising and also launching an extensive professional campaign. This included dedicating an entire sales force of 650 people to call on doctors and hospitals. In addition, AHP unleashed an intensive pharmacist campaign lasting over six months and offering pharmacists education and training programs. Exhibit 3 shows a snapshot of Advil's advertising and promotion investment for the first three years of launch as well as its position in 1994.

Exhibit 3 ● Advil and Nuprin Advertising Expenditures at Launch

Indicator	1984		1985		1986		1994	
	ADVIL	*NUPRIN*	*ADVIL*	*NUPRIN*	*ADVIL*	*NUPRIN*	*ADVIL*	*NUPRIN*
Advertising ($mn)	$26	$20	$37	$29	$52	$37	$90	$0
A:S^a ratio (%)	119	138	48	76	37	66	25	0
Share of voice (%)	13	10	16	13	21	16	24	0
Budget for professional campaign ($mn)	$1	$0	$2	$1	$5	$1	n/a	n/a

Note: n/a = not available

a. A:S = advertising-to-sales

As a result of this effort, AHP was able to gather medical testimonials for future advertisements.

In 1995, Advil was ranked behind Tylenol as the second-leading brand in the U.S. pain relief segment. (See Exhibit 4 for comparative shares of U.S. pain relief market.) Furthermore, it was the largest-selling OTC ibuprofen product in the United States, Canada, and France. This position was expected to be challenged as significant activity continued in the pain relief segment (Exhibit 5). New active ingredients, such as ketoprofen and naproxen, were beginning to be introduced to the market.

Aleve

In 1994, Procter & Gamble (P&G) launched Aleve as a new brand to the U.S. pain relief market. The active

Exhibit 4 ● Share of U.S. Pain Relief Market

	1984	1994
Acetaminophens	45%	44%
Ibuprofen-based	2	29
Aspirin	53	27

Source: James Dudley, *Winning Strategies*, pp. 1–2.

ingredient in Aleve was naproxen sodium. Aleve was originally a prescription product named Anaprox. Anaprox closely resembled the best-selling prescription brand, Naprosyn, which also contained naproxen sodium. Both Anaprox and Naprosyn were nonsteroidal anti-inflammatory drugs (NSAIDs), which were known as effective treatment for chronic pain such as arthritis. Like ibuprofen ten years earlier, naproxen sodium was a new substance to the OTC market. P&G licensed the U.S. marketing rights for the product from Syntex, a pharmaceutical company.

Aleve's major competitors were Advil, Tylenol, and Bayer. P&G invested in clinical studies to show that Aleve provided stronger relief than Advil and Extra-Strength Tylenol. In addition, the cost for a full day of pain relief was about half that of Advil and Tylenol. The product targeted heavy users of pain relief, for example, consumers with arthritic or muscular pain. Its slogan was "All Day Strong. All Day Long." Its position as a value-oriented product was supported by the 150- and 250-unit packages, compared to many other analgesics which came in units of less than 100. The image of Aleve as new and different was reinforced through the introduction of a new Safety Squeeze cap which was easier for adults to use than the traditional child-resistant packaging.

In 1994, Aleve reached $65 million in sales and surpassed the first year results of Advil in terms of sales, market share, trial, and brand awareness (refer to Exhibit 6). By 1995, Aleve accounted for 5.2 per-

Exhibit 5 ● U.S. Market Share (%) and Advertising Expenditures for Major Analgesic Brands

Brand	Market Share		Measured Advertising ($mn)	
	1993	*1992*	*1993*	*1992*
Tylenol	24.5%	25.2%	$74.9	$56.9
Private label	19.0	17.3	0	0
Advil	13.7	13.5	74.7	68.2
Extra Strength Excedrin	3.8	4.1	15.9	4.3
Motrin IB	3.7	3.6	27.2	28.5
Tylenol PM	3.7	3.2	15.4	13.1
Genuine Bayer	2.9	3.3	8.2	1.6
Anacin	2.4	2.8	13.2	38.0
Nuprin	2.0	2.6	6.0	11.5
Ecotrin	2.0	2.2	0.1	5.5

Source: Advertising Age, September 1994.

cent of the highly competitive internal analgesics market. Company officials credited Aleve's success to the growing analgesics category and said 45 percent of Aleve's volume came from increased usage and new analgesic consumers. To help prevent retailer stockouts, P&G established a "Fast Start" program which guaranteed customer delivery on day one for any orders placed three weeks prior to the start of shipments. More than 1 million cases were shipped within the first two weeks.

P&G was able to leverage its joint venture rela-

tionship with Syntex to fill in for its weak position in the prescription pharmaceutical industry. While P&G focused on its strength, marketing to consumers, Syntex targeted doctors and other health care professionals.

Imodium

Johnson & Johnson's (J&J) Imodium was first switched to OTC status from prescription-only in the United Kingdom in 1983 and in other major markets over the following eight years (refer to Exhibit 7). Based on the active ingredient loperamide, Imodium was the prescription leader for antidiarrheal treatments (refer to Exhibit 8A). J&J achieved sales with Imodium of U.S.$92.4 million in the twelve months to July 1995. The biggest market for Imodium was the United States with a 53 percent share of the antidiarrhea remedies market in 1994. Kaopectate was ranked second with a 30 percent share. Other competitors were Pepto-Bismol from P&G and Maalox A-D from Ciba.

As a prescription product, Imodium was sold in tablet form. Studies showed that consumers preferred liquid formulas. J&J changed the dosage at switch

Exhibit 6 ● Sales and Advertising Expenditures for Aleve

	1994	*1995*
Sales ($mn)	$65	$125
Advertising ($mn)	$37	$69
A:S ratio (%)	57	55
Share of voice (%)	9.7	14.5

Exhibit 7 ● National Brand Names and Market Share for Imodium

Country	Brand Name	Year of Switch	1993 Market Share (%)
United Kingdom	Arret, Imodium	1983	33%
United States	Imodium A-D	1988	62[a]
Belgium	Imodium	c. 1988	n/a
France	Imossel	1992	10
Germany	Imodium Akut	1993	6
Netherlands[b]	Diacure	1986	n/a
Japan	Marupi Geridome	1990	n/a

a. In the twelve months ended 8/93.

b. Comarketing venture with Taxandria.

time. Later in 1990, caplets were introduced as a convenience for travelers' diarrhea. A big campaign accompanied this new product formulation, with the tag line "When all you've got is one week, even a morning of diarrhea is too much." This campaign helped grow the category significantly for J&J.

J&J launched the product in many major markets with a strategy that best fit each market. In the United States, J&J adopted a three-pronged marketing strategy which included consumer advertising, a professional campaign, and a pharmacist campaign. In some European markets, J&J opted for a dual brand strategy, enabling them to target both consumers and medical professionals. In Japan, the company chose to license loperamide to Dainippon

In the United States, campaign budgets for the first three years of launch are listed in Exhibit 8B. Twelve months after launch, Imodium A-D was the most highly recommended antidiarrhea brand by pharmacists. It received a pharmacist recommendation 88 out of 100 times, whereas its challenger, Kaopectate, only received 7 out of 100 recommendations. In general, the product was positioned as "Imodium A-D. The original prescription for one dose relief." This tag line helped J&J to leverage its prescription heritage.

In the United Kingdom, Imodium was a semi-

Exhibit 8A ● Prescription Heritage of Imodium in the Global Market

Country	Market Share (%)	Rank
United States	44%	1
France	86	1
Germany	87	1
Italy	35	1

Exhibit 8B ● U.S. Imodium Promotional Spending

	1988	1989	1990
CONSUMER CAMPAIGN			
Advertising (mn)	$9	$16	$17
A:S ratio %	144%	108%	52%
Share of voice	32%	46%	32%
PROFESSIONAL CAMPAIGN ($mn)			
Imodium A-D	1	1	2
Imodium Rx	3	2	1

ethical.[2] As a semi-ethical, sales were driven by doctors rather than consumers. Doctor prescriptions were considered an important driver for the brand's overall success. The reason for selecting a dual brand strategy in the United Kingdom was to avoid alienating health care professionals. In 1985, J&J launched Arret, an identical product, with an identical pricing structure and heavy consumer advertising. Arret directly targeted consumers and was positioned for travelers' diarrhea. At the same time, the Imodium brand continued to be marketed to doctors to treat general diarrhea throughout the year. Sales were disappointing and there was little brand awareness.

In 1994, Imodium had 24 percent of the U.K. market compared to Arret's 21 percent. J&J used this dual brand strategy to exploit the seasonality of the market.[3] Imodium gradually lost share to Arret, until J&J stopped advertising support for Arret in 1991. With the two brands combined, J&J's share of the U.K. market went from 41 percent in 1988 to 45 percent in 1994. After 1990, Arret trailed Imodium (the original switched brand) in sales volume. Virtually no consumer brand investment was ever expended on Imodium in the United Kingdom.

Nicotinell

Nicotinell was Ciba's smoking cessation product first switched to OTC in 1992 in Sweden, Denmark, and Italy. Approval was obtained for several other European countries in 1993 and 1994 (refer to Exhibit 9A).

Nicotinell's first major launch was in the United Kingdom, followed by Germany. In the United Kingdom, key OTC competitors with similar products were Nicorette by Pharmacia-Upjohn and Nicabate by Marion Merrell Dow.

It was government rather than industry which drove this OTC product launch. Pharmacia's Nicorette gum was first to market in the United Kingdom in 1991. The Nicorette patch went OTC in the United Kingdom in November 1992. However, its competitive advantage was nullified when the Depart-

---

2. "Semi-ethical" refers to a non–prescription-bound product that was reimbursed if prescribed by a doctor.

3. Travelers on vacation often suffered from diarrhea as a result of changes in diet. The sales were correlated with the cycles of the travel industry.

Exhibit 9A ● OTC Availability of Nicotinell

Country	Brand Name	Launch Date
Sweden	Nicotinell	1992
Denmark	Nicotinell	1992
Italy	Nicotinell	1992
United Kingdom	Nicotinell	late 1992
Germany	Nicotinell	1994
Austria	Nicotinell	1994
United States	Habitrol	1997[a]

a. Expected. Johnson & Johnson's Nicotrol patch was given approval in 1996.

ment of Health forced all transdermal patches into the OTC market. Pharmacia, Ciba, and Marion Merrell Dow were expecting to introduce their products as prescription-only medicines but ended up obtaining OTC status. Ciba was able to move in quickly and help establish the new sector by the end of 1992, although it had to use its prescription package for the first several months.

European OTC sales for smoking cessation products experienced a decline after the initial launch years. The concept of a transdermal nicotine patch was both new to consumers and considered to be scientifically advanced in comparison to the existing gum product. The newness of the product produced a high degree of interest and trial when first introduced. When the newness wore off, the sales for Nicotinell decreased with the market from $24.2 million in 1993 to $19.7 million in 1995. However, Nicotinell maintained its market share.

In 1993, European pharmaceutical sales for Nicotinell were $62 million. This gave the brand a number one rank and a 52 percent share of the European market. Of these sales, 60 percent came from doctor prescriptions. As a prescription product in the United States (brand name Habitrol), Germany, France and Italy, Nicotinell was one of the category leaders. Key competition came from Nicoderm in the United States and Nicorette in Europe (refer to Exhibits 9B and 11).

In the United Kingdom in July 1995, Ciba introduced a 2 mg nicotine gum that had been originally

Exhibit 9B ● Total Pharmaceutical SOM (%) for Smoking Cessation Products: Major Markets, 1993[a]

Brand	Company	United States	France	Germany	United Kingdom	Italy
Nicotinell Patch	Ciba-Geigy	—	37	54	42	32
Habitrol	Ciba-Geigy	32	—	—	—	—
Nicorette Patch	Pharmacia	—	—	—	27	4.6
Nicorette Gum	Pharmacia/SmithKline Beecham[b]	20	18	23	22	31
Nicoderm	Marion Merrell Dow/ SmithKline Beecham	31	—	—	—	—
Nicabate	Marion Merrell Dow	—	—	—	6.5	—
Nicotrans	Recordati	—	—	—	32	—
Nicotrol	Johnson & Johnson	9.5	—	—	—	—
Nicopatch	Pierre Fabre	—	39	—	—	—

a. Includes both prescription and nonprescription sales.

b. SmithKline Beecham had the license to market Nicorette Gum in the United States.

introduced as a transdermal nicotine patch.[4] One of the key differentiators for Nicotinell was that it was better tasting than the brand leader, Nicorette, and available in two flavors: original and mint.

Smoking cessation products were expected to support a price level similar to cigarettes. However, this resulted in a higher price level per purchase than for other OTCs. The average daily treatment cost for Nicotinell was competitive with Nicorette and Nicabate. The cost for the Nicotinell patch was $2.10. For Nicorette, the gum was $1.99 and the patch was $2.17. Nicabate's patch was $2.06. It was estimated to take three months to complete a full cycle of Nicotinell's smoking cessation schedule. In the United Kingdom, Ciba spent £4.1 million on consumer advertising, of which £1.5 million was for print. This was more than the promotional spending by both Nicorette and Nicabate (refer to Exhibit 10). In addition, in the United Kingdom, Ciba invested a large amount of resources into trade directed activity in comparison to the competitors. The Ciba U.K. office had a field force of over 200 people whereas Pharmacia and Marion Merrell Dow had fewer than 50 people each.

Ciba positioned Nicotinell as not just another

patch but a complete smoking cessation aid. One of Nicotinell's key competitive advantages was its twenty-four-hour effectiveness as opposed to sixteen hours for Nicorette. It was positioned as a product that would be able to help the consumer all day long. By lasting twenty-four hours, Nicotinell freed the consumer from having to suffer through hours when the product was ineffective. Hence the U.K. campaign slogan was "It needn't be hell with Nicotinell."

Ciba targeted heavy smokers with the patch and lighter smokers with the gum version. By segmenting the consumers, Ciba hoped to keep cannibalization to a minimum. By being offered both a patch and a gum, consumers had a choice and could change their smoking habits at their own pace.

Recognizing that consumer counseling was a very important aspect of product usage and success, Ciba used help lines, charts, audio tapes, and relaxation techniques as part of the program. To promote the product, heavy TV and point-of-sale advertising were used. Doctors were heavily detailed[5] since this was a new delivery system and since doctors had some responsibility for counseling patients. Educa-

4. Two mg of nicotine was the equivalent of one cigarette.

5. *Detailing* was an industry term which referred to the education and promotion of pharmaceutical products to medical professionals.

Exhibit 10 ● Smoking Cessation Promotional Spending in the United Kingdom (£mn)

Brand	1992	1993
Nicabate Patches	£0.0	£0.5
Nicorette Patches	0.3	0.6
Nicorette Gum	1.5	2.8
Nicotinell Patches	1.4	4.1
Nicotinell Gum[a]	n/a	n/a

a. Launch spending of Nicotinell Gum in the United Kingdom was £1.6 mn in 1995.

tional material was given to pharmacists and pharmacy sales assistants.

Despite being beaten to the market by Nicorette and Nicobate patches, Ciba won the battle for the pharmacists' support through higher levels of trade-directed activity and by capitalizing on the twenty-four-hour effectiveness. Not recognized by consumers as a benefit, the twenty-four-hour aspect was accepted by the trade. With all brands called "Nico-something," consumers had no brand affinity and asked pharmacists for recommendations.

Zantac 75

Zantac 75 competed in the stomach remedies product segment, which was a subcategory of the larger digestive remedies category. The global market for stomach remedies was $3.2 billion in 1995.

Originally a prescription product created and marketed by Glaxo Wellcome, the OTC version, Zantac 75, competed against Pepcid AC and Tagamet 100. Glaxo developed joint venture agreements to handle the OTC marketing of the product. Glaxo made this strategic decision so that it could focus on its prescription pharmaceuticals business. OTC partners were Warner-Lambert in Europe and the United States, and Taisho Pharmaceuticals in Japan.

One of the last H_2 antagonists to switch, Zantac 75 was introduced in the United Kingdom in January 1995, nearly a year later than competitors Pepcid AC and Tagamet. Final FDA approval for Zantac was not

granted for an OTC launch in the United States until 1996.

The three major H_2 antagonists were based on different active ingredients,[6] although the way they interacted with the body was similar. Consequently, each active ingredient had to go through its own approval process.

As a prescription product, Zantac was the world's biggest-selling drug and accounted for 45 percent of Glaxo's sales. The OTC version of Zantac was approximately half the strength of the prescription formula. Doctors typically prescribed Zantac as a general stomach remedy, or as a treatment for peptic ulcers. The U.S. patent for Zantac was expected to expire in 1997.

When Warner-Lambert launched Zantac in the United Kingdom, it targeted both consumers and medical professionals. The professional campaign included a support package with training materials for pharmacists and pharmacists assistants, reference manuals and a training video, and a suggested pharmacy prescription protocol. Zantac achieved approximately $2.2 million in sales in its first year. This was about twice as much as Pepcid AC and Tagamet 100 during the same time period (Exhibit 20). Although better than the competition, it was considered a marginal success.

Warner-Lambert targeted the larger market of antacid consumers, particularly Gaviscon users. J&J and SmithKline Beecham, owners of Pepcid and Tagamet, were more careful not to infringe upon the position of their other stomach remedy products, Mylanta and Tums.

To reaffirm Zantac's position as the number one prescription product, Glaxo advertised the brand name prior to launch in the United States. Because it was not yet an OTC product, it managed to escape the big marketing battle between Pepcid AC and Tagamet 100. Both J&J (Pepcid AC) and SmithKline Beecham (Tagamet 100) engaged in heavy comparison advertising and slightly exaggerated claims. The matters were eventually resolved in court. Glaxo focused on its prescription business and preparation for the OTC launch.

---

6. Zantac 75 was based on the active ingredient ranitidine; Pepcid AC was based on the active ingredient famotidine; and Tagamet 100 was based on the active ingredient cimetidine.

Exhibit 11 ● The Race for Smoking Cessation Leadership: OTC Market Share by Country

	1993	1994	1995
GERMAN SMOKING CESSATION MARKET SALES			
(U.S.$ THOUSANDS)	$899	$13,896	$19,836
Nicotinell	0%	23.5%	53.9%
Nicorette	0	63.1	32.2
Nicotin	0	5.7	8
Nikofrenon	0	2.4	3.2
Nicobrevin	87.9	4.6	2.3
U.K. SMOKING CESSATION MARKET SALES			
(U.S. $THOUSANDS)	$56,241	$33,756	$27,368
Nicorette	48.7%	54.4%	61.2%
Nicotinell	42.4	35.2	31.4
Nicotrol	.7	6.3	3.9
Stoppers	1.2	2	2.6
Logado	0	0	.5
Nicabate	>5	1.7	.01
FRENCH SMOKING CESSATION MARKET[a] SALES			
(U.S.$ THOUSANDS)	$275	$389	$290
Nicoprive	67.7%	56.6%	49.4%
Berthoit	0	14.2	35.8
Valerbe	18	10.2	7.4
Pastabe	13.7	17.4	5.9

a. In France, Nicotinell, Nicorette, and Nicopatch were not OTC products but were still prescription-bound.

Zovirax

The cold sore treatment Zovirax was a product of a joint venture between Glaxo Wellcome and Warner-Lambert. Zovirax was categorized as a skin treatment and created a new therapeutic category for cold sore prevention. It was estimated that the switch of Zovirax added a million new users to the market. Exhibit 12 shows the results of this category growth in the United Kingdom.

Zovirax was first introduced on an OTC basis in New Zealand in 1991. Its first major market was Germany in 1992, followed by the United Kingdom in

1993. At the end of 1995, Zovirax was available on an OTC basis in Europe (Germany, United Kingdom, Austria, Denmark, Finland, Ireland, Belgium) with OTC status pending for the United States and Japan. It was ranked number one in the United Kingdom and Germany with primary competition coming from Blisteze and Cymex in the United Kingdom, and Lomaherpin and Lipactin Gel in Germany. Both the U.K. and German markets saw similar growth and success with the switch of Zovirax, taking over half the market (refer to Exhibits 12 and 13).

Zovirax contained the active ingredient acyclovir

Exhibit 12 ● Growth of Cold Sore Market in United Kingdom after Launch of Zovirax

Before Zovirax, 1992		
Total Market	$1.9 mn/yr.	
Brand	*Market Share (%)*	*Sales (U.S.$mn)*
Blisteze	52%	$.99
Cymex	12	.23
Boots Cold Sore	12	.23
Lypsyl	9	.17
Brush Off	9	.17
Others	6	.11

After Zovirax, 1994		
Total Market	$7.1 mn/yr	
Brand	*Market Share %*	*Sales (U.S.$mn)*
Zovirax	78%	$5.54
Blisteze	11	0.78
Cymex	3	0.21
Boots	3	0.21
Others	5	0.36

Exhibit 13 ● Market Share (%) Before and After Launch of Zovirax in Germany

Before Zovirax	
Brand	*SOM*
Lipactin Gel	31%
Lomaherpin	35
Virudermin Gel	22
Others	12

After Zovirax	
Brand	*SOM*
Zovirax	49%
Lomaherpin	35
Lipactin	13
Others	11

and was available in cream, tablet, or liquid form. A top-selling prescription product, Zovirax was primarily used to treat genital herpes, shingles, and chicken pox. The OTC version had the same dosage as the prescription product but positioned itself as a treatment and preventative medicine for cold sores. As a result, there was little threat to the still important and existing prescription business.

As with many switches, Zovirax was introduced while it was still under patent. This allowed Glaxo Wellcome to establish an OTC market for the product under patent protection. When launched in the United Kingdom, it had three years left on the patent. In Germany, Glaxo Wellcome only had twelve months left to establish the OTC market. It comarketed Zovirax with the German pharmaceutical company, Hoechst. Germany's market was strongly semi-ethical, with several cold sore treatments that had a strong prescription heritage. Zovirax was initially marketed as a semi-ethical for six months.

Distribution of Zovirax was limited to pharmacies.[7] In Germany, the launch price was $15.70, but at the start of 1995, the retail price was cut in half to $7.80[8] for a 2 gm tube. Two generic manufacturers entered in 1994. They competed on consumer advertising and on price.

Zovirax held a unique position as the only really effective treatment for the prevention of cold sores. Warner-Lambert tried to move customer expectations from cold sore treatment to cold sore prevention. The campaign message was "Early use can stop a cold sore."

Warner-Lambert used the Zovirax name whenever possible throughout Europe. To promote the product to consumers, Warner-Lambert used TV advertising and print media with a "be kissable" catch line. Due to differences in regulatory procedures, Zovirax could not be launched at the same time in all European countries; however, Warner-Lambert tried to use a formula and to maintain the same look and feel in each country (i.e., used the same name, posi-

7. This was true of most medicines in Europe. In general, it was easier to get prescription products approved for OTC sale in Europe than in the United States, but distribution and merchandising were restricted, whereas they were not in the United States.

8. Prices were converted from DM at an exchange rate of U.S.$1 = .5186 DM.

Exhibit 14 ● Advertising Spending at Launch ($mn)

Brand	United Kingdom (1993)	Germany (1992)
Zovirax	$7	$3.5
Blisteze (United Kingdom)	0.36	n/a
Lypsyl (United Kingdom)	0.47	n/a
Lipactin (Germany)	n/a	0.4
Virudermin (Germany)	n/a	0.3

tioning, pack design, etc.). Consumer research indicated that consumer knowledge, awareness of, and attitudes toward cold sores and their treatment were fairly similar throughout Europe.

Zovirax ad spending was far beyond what was typical for that product category (refer to Exhibit 14). The high levels were expected to continue as pressure from generics played an important role. In addition to advertising, Warner-Lambert added an educational and merchandising program for pharmacists and pharmacy sales assistants.

However, not everything was kept the same. Some aspects, especially pricing and competition, were attacked on the national level, but as many common elements as possible were applied (with local adaptation to regulations, pharmacists, etc.). The launch for the U.S. market[9] began on a different course than in Europe. Warner-Lambert was trying to register an indication for genital herpes in the United States instead of for cold sores as in Europe. However, since final approval for this indication had not been granted yet, the final launch strategy was still unclear.

UNSUCCESSFUL OTC LAUNCHES

Efidac/24

Ciba's Efidac/24 was a nasal decongestant available in the United States. Sales reached $23 million and $17 million in 1994 and 1995, respectively. The product held a 1.6 percent market share in the U.S. cold remedies market (1995). Efidac's major competitors

were Sudafed and Contac, with 7.8 percent and 3.3 percent share of the market respectively.

Efidac was launched in 1993 as a breakthrough in cold relief by offering twenty-four hours of relief, compared to only four to six hours offered by competitors. Efidac used an osmotic delivery system which controlled the release of the medicine. Ciba obtained exclusive rights for the OROS delivery system developed by Alza. It had been difficult to obtain FDA approval because of the high dosage in each tablet and because the product was not based on an existing monograph. Consequently, Ciba could not change the product without undergoing a full review with the FDA.

Efidac was based on one single ingredient, not a combination of ingredients like most other products in its category. At the time, a majority of consumers preferred a combination product (e.g., a decongestant and analgesic or a decongestant and antihistamine).

Leveraging the time release technology, Efidac's marketing message was "Get consistent 24-hour cold symptom relief in just one tablet." The campaign was supported by a $27 million advertising budget in 1994. In addition, Efidac used extensive detailing and sampling programs, in-store displays, and mail-in rebates. However, studies showed that the majority of first-time users did not purchase the product again. Sales in the first two quarters were strong, but by the third quarter, sales began to drop. Exhibit 15 shows the sales and media spending for Efidac and two of its major competitors, Sudafed and Contac.

Gyne-Lotrimin

Schering-Plough's (S-P) Gyne-Lotrimin was a vaginal yeast infection product that was the first of its kind to be switched from prescription to OTC in the United States. Exhibit 16 illustrates the sales and market share of the brand from 1991 (the year of launch) to 1995. Gyne-Lotrimin's major competitors were Monistat 7 from J&J and Mycelex-7 from Bayer.

The prescription version entered the U.S. market in 1976 and achieved about 1 million prescriptions per year in 1990. However, the prescription version only had 6 percent market share[10] and was given little

---

9. The U.S. patent for Zovirax was expected to expire in 1997.

10. Compared to approximately 30 percent held by Johnson & Johnson's Monistat 7.

Exhibit 15 ● Sales and Advertising Spending for Efidac ($mn)

Brand	1993		1994		1995	
	Sales	TME[a]	Sales	TME	Sales	TME
Efidac/24	$10	$19	$23	$27	$17	$11.5
Contac	—	—	40	—	36	8.2
Sudafed	91	22.7	86	23.8	85	30.6
Cold Medication Category Total	1,085	283	1029	247	1,090	237

a. TME = Total marketing expenses.

marketing attention. Gyne-Lotrimin did not fit with S-P's focus on respiratory and derma products, which comprised the majority of the company's prescription pharmaceutical product mix.

When the FDA was reluctant to switch Gyne-Lotrimin, S-P agreed to make marketing and labeling concessions. It would only market the product to women with recurrent vaginal yeast infections, and it would use the term self-recognizable instead of self-diagnosable. To help with the application process, S-P sought support from women's groups and professional organizations. Finally, J&J, whose Monistat was also ready to go OTC, joined forces with S-P to lobby the FDA. Initially, J&J was reluctant to risk its highly profitable prescription version by coming to market with an OTC version, but acted quickly when it realized S-P might succeed with its switch of Gyne-Lotrimin.

Both Gyne-Lotrimin and Monistat were well-known prescription products, but Gyne-Lotrimin's brand heritage was weaker than that of Monistat. It only had about 20 percent of the prescriptions of Monistat. Despite this, when Gyne-Lotrimin was launched, S-P tried to leverage its prescription heritage with the consumer. When Monistat entered three months later, it capitalized on its stronger prescription heritage and quickly became the market leader.

Consumer promotion of Gyne-Lotrimin included heavy advertising, money-off coupons, and rebates. For retailers, S-P offered rapid shipment of stock directly to retailers via couriers. Detailing of medical professionals was also a part of the marketing

strategy. In fact, Schering-Plough's professional marketing campaign had a larger budget than J&J's Monistat (refer to Exhibit 17). Despite this difference in spending, Monistat received almost three times the doctor recommendations of Gyne-Lotrimin.

Nicabate

Nicabate was developed by Marion Merrell Dow as a smoking cessation product. Its only market was the United Kingdom, where it competed side by side with Pharmacia's Nicorette and Ciba's Nicotinell. Pharmaceutical sales[11] share for Nicabate accounted for 3.2 percent of the total European market for smoking cessation, compared with 52 percent for Nicotinell and 35 percent for Nicorette.

Similar to Nicotinell, Nicabate was marketed as a twenty-four-hour transdermal nicotine patch. However, Nicabate was the third product to enter the growing smoking cessation market.

Marion Merrell Dow put relatively more effort and resources on doctors than on pharmacies and less attention was given to consumer advertising. Press was the only medium used (refer to Exhibit 10).

Marion Merrell Dow was one of the major manufacturers of the nicotine patch but chose to license the technology to other companies for launch under their own brand names (i.e., Nicoderm in the United States, marketed by SmithKline Beecham). As a re-

11. Includes prescription-bound and non–prescription-bound products.

Exhibit 16 ● U.S. Sales of Vaginal Yeast Infection Products ($mn)

Brand	1991		1992		1993		1994		1995	
	Sales	SOM %	Sales	SOM %	Sales	SOM %	Sales	SOM %	Sales	SOM %
Gyne-Lotrimin	$57	—	$77	31%	$37	22%	$24	17%	$18	12.7%
Monistat 7	82	—	155	65	86	52	73	49	68	48.2
Mycelex-7	—	—	—	—	23	14	21	14	22	15.5
FemCare	—	—	—	—	12	7	7	5	2	1.4
Others	—	—	—	—	8	5	24	15	31	22

sult, the brand Nicabate had no prior prescription heritage, whereas its competitors, Nicotinell and Nicorette were the top-ranking prescription brands in Europe (refer to Exhibit 9B).

Nuprin

The second ibuprofen product (after Advil) to enter the analgesic market in 1984, Bristol Myers Squibb's (BMS) Nuprin failed to make inroads in the marketplace. As a joint venture between Bristol Myers Squibb and Motrin owners Upjohn, Nuprin should have been able to draw on the prescription heritage of Motrin, the original ethical drug, but AHP beat them to it in advertising Advil.

BMS allocated promotional dollars to a program targeted to health care professionals (Exhibit 3). In 1988, BMS changed the look of the product by coloring the pills yellow. This coincided with a new campaign whose tag line was "Little. Yellow. Different. Better."

The market for ibuprofen products grew and invited several other competitors (Exhibit 4). However, Nuprin was never able to capture enough market share to be considered a player (Exhibit 5). As sales continued to fall, BMS invested less and less in the brand. By 1994, there was no major media advertising support.

Nurofen

The ibuprofen product, Nurofen, was developed by Boots PLC of the United Kingdom, and launched by its consumer marketing group, Crookes. Boots held

Exhibit 17 ● Promotional Budgets: Gyne-Lotrimin and Monistat-7 ($mn)

	1991	1992	1993	1994	1995
GYNE-LOTRIMIN					
Ad spends	32	18	18	10	2
A:S ratio (%)	60	42	49	40	11
Professional campaign	3	2	n/a	n/a	n/a
MONISTAT-7					
Ad spends	n/a	n/a	36	31	27
A:S ratio (%)	n/a	n/a	42	42	40
Professional campaign	1	1	n/a	n/a	n/a

the original rights to the substance ibuprofen and used licensing agreements with other companies to develop the product in regions where it was weak.[12] Discovered in 1969 by Boots Research, ibuprofen was introduced to the prescription market under the brand name Brufen in most countries, and Motrin in the United States. It was one of the top three NSAIDs[13] prescribed around the world.

The only European markets where ibuprofen, as a prescription product, was unsuccessful were Germany and Spain. This carried over into the OTC market. For example, in Spain the total market share of all ibuprofen products in the pain relief segment was less than 2 percent from 1991 to 1995, compared with 17 percent in Italy and 14 percent in the United Kingdom.

The application for an OTC switch began in 1980 in the United Kingdom under the brand name Nurofen. Final approval was received in 1983. By 1990, Nurofen had achieved OTC analgesic leadership in the United Kingdom, among all pharmacy-only pain relievers.[14]

Distribution was limited to pharmacies only and Nurofen obtained 100 percent penetration of pharmacy outlets in the United Kingdom and benefited from the special relationship with Boots the Chemist.[15]

After initial success in the United Kingdom, Boots wanted to turn Nurofen into a pan-European brand. To accomplish this, Boots applied the same launch strategy to the Italian and Spanish markets. However, differences in each country as well as resistance from competitors such as Angelini and Bayer made this goal unachievable. Exhibit 18 illustrates these differences.

12. Boots licensed ibuprofen to other companies in the United States, Germany, and Japan all countries where it had limited market presence.

13. Nonsteroidal anti-inflammatory drugs (NSAIDs) were analgesics in the pain relief category They were considered a major scientific breakthrough since they provided powerful pain relief without the side effects of aspirin and acetaminophen.

14. In the United Kingdom, some aspirin-based analgesics were available mass market. New substances such as ibuprofen were limited to pharmacy-only distribution.

15. Boots the Chemist was the retailer division of Boots PLC and accounted for approximately 30 percent of all pharmaceutical sales in the United Kingdom.

In 1987, Boots launched Nurofen in Italy. A few weeks before launch, there was an advertising ban on NSAIDs. Boots went ahead and launched the product without any means of consumer education except through pharmacists who knew that the ban on advertising was due to speculation about NSAIDs safety.

When the ban was lifted, Angelini, a local Italian company, launched its ibuprofen brand, Moment. The campaign included heavy TV advertising and pharmacy promotion. Within two years, Moment took second place in the OTC general analgesic market. Boots failed to reassert Nurofen once the advertising ban was lifted (refer to Exhibit 19).

Nurofen was launched in Spain in 1989. Three years later, Bayer introduced its own ibuprofen, Dorval. Targeted to menstrual pain and supported by a strong brand name and heavy advertising and promotion dollars, Dorval outsold Nurofen. Boots had positioned Nurofen as a general pain relief product. Even though Dorval was the leader for ibuprofen products in Spain, the substance as a whole never captured more than 2 percent of the pain relief market. A focused position and a well-funded consumer and professional campaign would have been necessary to educate the consumer about the benefits of ibuprofen.

Tagamet 100/Tagamet HB

The H_2 antagonist Tagamet (SmithKline) was known in the prescription world as an anti-ulcerant treatment. In 1989, Denmark was the first market to issue OTC approval. Later, in April 1994, Tagamet 100 was switched to OTC in the larger U.K. market.[16] It was not until 1995 that it received approval from the FDA to be marketed as OTC in the United States.

Other H_2 antagonists were Pepcid AC (J&J) and Zantac 75 (Warner-Lambert). The entry of H_2 antagonists threatened the market position of existing heartburn remedies. Reckitt & Coleman launched a preemptive attack for Gaviscon declaring that Tagamet had a slower onset of action and more potential for dangerous interactions.

Post-launch sales of Tagamet met the company's expectations in the United States, but fell far short in Europe (refer to Exhibit 20). Worldwide sales of Tagamet were more than $74 million in 1995. The

16. In the U.S. the brand name was Tagamet HB.

Exhibit 18 ● Comparison of Nurofen Launch in Europe

	United Kingdom	Italy	Spain
Product position	General Analgesic	General Analgesic	General Analgesic
Competitive share of voice	Yes	No	No
Ibuprofen share of pain relief market	14%	17%	2%
Major competing brands	Anadin (American Home Products)	Bayer (Bayer AG) and Moment (Angelini)	Bayer (Bayer AG)
Primary source of distribution	Pharmacy chains	Independent pharmacies	Independent pharmacies
Sales and marketing infrastructure	Complete field force utilized, home country	Dependent on third-party relationships	Dependent on third-party relationships

U.S. sales for Pepcid AC were upward of $200 million in less than a year after its launch. Significant competition was expected to continue as Warner-Lambert prepared its launch of Zantac 75, another H_2 antagonist.

It took four years for Tagamet to receive final FDA approval in the United States. First, there was a question of efficacy as a heartburn treatment (Tagamet was primarily used as an anti-ulcer remedy prescription product). Second, there were concerns over negative drug interactions. Final approval was received in 1995. Again, as in Europe, Pepcid beat Tagamet to the U.S. market by several weeks.

Indigestion remedies fell under the broad umbrella of digestive remedies. Chalk-based tablets, such as Tums and Rolaids, were frequently used treatments for fast relief of mild indigestion and heartburn. For more serious cases, more powerful liquid remedies, such as Gaviscon, were used.

At the time Tagamet was launched, there were no obvious gaps in the indigestion market. Research in the United Kingdom showed that heartburn happened to a concentrated number of people. Those who did suffer exhibited a fairly high level of brand awareness and did not exhibit any dissatisfaction with their brands.

SmithKline's communications strategy leveraged Tagamet's successful prescription heritage and referred to the product as "superior" to the less potent remedies. It also differentiated itself as not only a heartburn treatment but also a heartburn preventative. J&J chose a different position for Pepcid. Coming from an inferior prescription heritage than both Tagamet and Zantac, it targeted a specific user group: the heavy and frequent heartburn sufferer. This strategy was supported by research that showed that 84 percent of all heartburn attacks were suffered by individuals who suffer heartburn once or more per week.

In comparison to other H_2 antagonists, Tagamet

Exhibit 19 ● Ibuprofen Market in Italy

	Launch of Ibuprofen in Italy		
Brand	Year of Launch	Entry Costs	1991 SOM
Nurofen	1987	$1 mn	15%
Moment	1989	$7 mn	43%

Ibuprofen Share of Pain Relief Market			
1991	1992	1993	1994
13%	15%	17%	13%

offered six hours of relief and Pepcid 9 hours. The product also came in either 16-, 32-, or 64-count packages. According to SmithKline, on a per dose basis, Tagamet was less expensive than Pepcid. For the consumer, it appeared more expensive than other H_2s available and far more expensive than the chalk brands, such as Rennie and Tums. Tagamet was four times more expensive than Rennie because the active ingredient was more expensive than chalk.

The U.K. launch included a professional campaign that targeted pharmacists and doctors. The pharmacist portion of the campaign included a support package with training materials for the pharmacists and their assistants, reference manuals, a training video, and a suggested pharmacy-counter–prescribing protocol. Despite this effort, pharmacists were four times more likely to recommend Pepcid AC than Tagamet.

H_2s were subject to restrictions on sale, contraindications, and side effect warnings, while no other competing brands, such as Rennie or Gaviscon, faced the same level of scrutiny. For example, Tagamet and Pepcid had to be displayed behind the sales counter. This restriction was put into effect to protect consumers from misusing the product. In contrast, all the other leading heartburn brands had approval to be displayed in self-select areas and were merchandised accordingly.

SUCCESSFUL PRODUCT LINE EXTENSIONS

Clearasil

Clearasil was a global brand created by Richardson-Vicks. In 1985, P&G acquired Richardson-Vicks and took over the marketing responsibility for the brand. It had a significant market presence in the United States, Europe, and Japan.[17] What started as an anti-acne product in the skin treatment category evolved into a franchise of products covering an entire skin care regime.

In 1995, US sales for Clearasil acne treatment products had reached $53 million (Exhibit 21A) resulting in a 23 percent market share. Key competitors

17. In Japan Clearasil was ranked eleventh in the entire skin treatment industry in 1995, and it was the only non-Japanese skin treatment product to be ranked.

were Oxy, Neutrogena, Sea Breeze, Stridex and private labels (refer to Exhibit 21B).

P&G often grew its products via line extensions, particularly with its major brands. Clearasil followed this pattern. The product was sold in many different forms: cream, stick, moisturizer, medicated pads, and lotion. It was also offered in many different strengths: regular, ultra, and Clearasil for sensitive skin (refer to Exhibit 22).

Although Clearasil was a global brand, P&G approached each country differently. In Germany, Ultra Clearasil was marketed only in pharmacies, whereas standard Clearasil was in the mass market. When the pharmacy market declined. P&G refocused its attention on the mass market and spent $8.2 million[18] on advertising in 1993. Also in 1993, P&G tried to improve Clearasil's performance in the French market by relaunching the product and introducing the Clearstick. Sales increased by 80 percent.

In addition, the product line was differently distributed depending on the country. In Germany, most of the product line competed in the mass market acne remedies category. Only Clearasil Ultra was restricted to pharmacies. In contrast, the entire product line was restricted to pharmacy-only in Italy. In the United Kingdom, the product line was sold equally through both pharmacy and grocery outlets. Mass market entries tended to have greater pressure to spend more on advertising than pharmacy products because they could not count on prescription driven sales (refer to Exhibit 23).

The traditional target for Clearasil products was teenage girls. However, when the teenage population began to decline, the company expanded its market by targeting teenage boys and adults. P&G created a product to treat adult acne. Advertising and promotional campaigns targeted both of these groups.

Gaviscon

Gaviscon was owned by Reckitt & Coleman and marketed in Europe. SmithKline Beecham marketed the product in the United States. Gaviscon was an antacid OTC product that provided-relief for acid-related stomach ailments such as heartburn, acid indigestion, and sour stomach.

18. Converted from DM using an exchange rate of U.S.$1 = .588 DM.

Gaviscon was launched as a prescription product in 1970. Slowly it evolved into an OTC product in Europe, although in some countries, it maintained a semi-ethical status. Gaviscon's primary market was Europe, with sales ranging from $67.3 million to $77.7 million from 1993 to 1995. The antacid category as a whole grew 5.9 percent in Europe during this time (Exhibit 20).

Traditionally, Gaviscon ranked as one of the most powerful OTC antacids available. As the product moved away from semi-ethical status, it faced severe competition from new OTC brands in the nonpharmacy sector (e.g., Tums). Furthermore, its position as the strongest available antacid was threatened with the switch of new H_2 antagonists. These were expected to enter the U.K. OTC market in early 1994 and target Gaviscon users.

As a semi-ethical, the product was sold in liquid form. As the product moved to OTC, it was apparent that some consumers preferred a tablet form. Reckitt & Coleman launched Gaviscon 250 in 1993 as a range of flavored tablets aimed at competing with the mass market antacids such as Tums.

By differentiating the dosage (tablet versus liquid) and modifying the brand name, Reckitt & Coleman was able to compete against both the mass market chalk-based tablets and the more potent, doctor-recommended, liquid formulas. Gaviscon 250 competed against mass market products. It was positioned as fast, effective, and long-lasting relief from heartburn and acid indigestion, which was safe enough for pregnant women to use. Flavor and merchandising support were competitive issues. The original Gaviscon formula maintained its position as a semi-ethical, doctor prescribed remedy.

Reckitt & Coleman launched a press campaign in 1991 to promote both to doctors and consumers. An unprecedented amount of advertising was spent at that time (refer to Exhibit 20). Unaided brand awareness increased from approximately 20 percent to 40 percent from 1990 to 1991. In Europe, the distribution of Gaviscon was kept to the self-select areas of pharmacies even though it had received approval to distribute in nonpharmacy outlets.

Prior to the switch of the H_2 antagonists, Gaviscon launched a preemptive trade campaign and pharmacy sales missions aimed at showing Gaviscon's strength in comparison to H_2 antagonists. This was executed ahead of H_2 launches in early 1994. Reckitt & Coleman subtly used the pharmacy displays of Gaviscon to remind pharmacists of H_2 antagonists' contraindications and warnings of side effects.

Tylenol

Johnson & Johnson's Tylenol line of pain relievers and cough/cold products were strong players in their market segments and achieved a top position in overall global sales. However, this success was attributed to the Tylenol line's strong position in the United States, since it was not very common in other parts of the world.

The original Tylenol was an acetaminophen product which was introduced to the OTC market in the 1970s as the first alternative to aspirin. By 1995, the brand franchise had grown to over $857 million in the United States with over twenty five line extensions. (Refer to Exhibit 24.)

The pain relief category had seen much activity through the years as new medical technologies made their way into the OTC sector.[19] To respond to these changes, J&J employed two different strategies. First, it strengthened the Tylenol product line through line extensions. Second, when it seemed that ibuprofen was going to be a strong therapeutic alternative in the pain relief category, J&J decided to introduce its own product, but not under the Tylenol brand name. Instead J&J adopted a multibranding strategy and introduced Medipren to the U.S. market.[20]

Product Line Extension   For product line extensions, Tylenol was introduced in new dosages, new delivery systems, and new combinations of ingredients. All major extensions attained leading positions in their respective subcategories (refer to Exhibit 25).

For new dosages, J&J introduced an extra strength formula (to compete with the ibuprofen products) and a children's formula. Both were leaders in their categories. As technology advancements in delivery systems[21] became available, Tylenol offered

---

19. The activity refers to the switch of NSAIDs such as ibuprofen in 1984 naproxen in 1995, and ketoprofen in 1996.

20. In contrast, Bristol Myers Squibb's extended its acetaminophen brand, Excedrin, to include an ibuprofen product which it called Excedrin IB.

21. Delivery systems, or galenics, referred to the way a drug was introduced into the body.

Exhibit 20 ● European Sales and Advertising Expenditures for Antacids, 1993–1995 (U.S. $mn)

Bramd	1993		1994		1995	
	Sales	Ad Spends	Sales	Ad Spends	Sales	Ad Spends
Gaviscon	$67.3	$3.0	$73.4	$3.6	$77.7	$3.2
Rennie	39.7	20.5	38.3	23.9	38.0	16.6
Tums[a]	2.2	0	2.1	1.9	2.0	1.8
Maalox	57.1	.6	59.5	6.3	63.1	9.3
Almax	36.2	.004	39.0	0	42.2	0
Talcid	18.7	2.1	19.9	2.6	19.6	4
Tagamet 100	0	0	1.1	3.6	1.0	3.7
Pepcid AC	—	—	—	7.0	.95	2.6
Zantac 75	—	—	—	—	2.2	n/a
Antacid Total	415.5	48.5	427.0	74.6	440.1	60

a. Tums a top player only in the United Kingdom and United States, not in France, Germany, Italy, Belgium, or Spain.

US Sales and Media Expenditures for Antacids and Antigas, 1993–1995 (U.S. $mn)

Brand	1993		1994		1995	
	Sales	Ad Spends	Sales	Ad Spends	Sales	Ad Spends
Gaviscon	$23	$0	$25	$3.9	$33	$10.7
Tums	135	28	143	22.8	144	27.8
Maalox	98	19	90	20	80	23.9
Mylanta	132	32	135	33	129	36.0
Tagamet HB	—	—	—	—	54	42.1
Pepcid AC	—	—	—	—	107	62.8
Zantac 75	—	—	—	—	—	—
Antacid Total	813	135	834	145	981	275

new options. For example, there were gelatin-coated capsules and tablets which made the product easier to swallow. Also, there was a liquid formula for those who could not swallow pills and, most recently, an extended release formula which offered a higher dosage that was released into the body slowly. This product was introduced as a direct response to the launch of Aleve, a new product offering all-day relief.

New combinations of active ingredients also added new products under the Tylenol umbrella. This allowed Tylenol to extend into new product segments. Tylenol introduced a line of cold and flu medicines,

Exhibit 21A ● Sales and Advertising Ratios for U.S. Acne Treatment Brands

Brand	1993 Sales ($mn)	A:S Ratio	1994 Sales ($mn)	A:S Ratio	1995 Sales ($mn)	A:S Ratio
Category Totals	$219	11%	$227	16%	$234	24%
Clearasil	56	14	54	16	53	25
Oxy	49	27	46	31	39	11
Stridex	14	2	17	5	17	20

cough formulas, and a nighttime product which combined acetaminophen with a sleep aid. Children's Tylenol was also expanded into the cough/cold segment. All of these line extensions achieved a top rank in their respective categories.

Advertising support for the different Tylenol products was not distributed evenly. Some products received more than others. Extra Strength Tylenol received the most (refer to Exhibit 24).

Multibranding Strategy   Medipren was launched in the United States in 1986 in an attempt to avoid cannibalizing the Tylenol brand. J&J positioned

Medipren for muscular aches and pains. It was launched only in the United States. Exhibit 26 illustrates sales for the product from 1986 to 1990, the year the product was discontinued.

Medipren's main competitors were other ibuprofen products that existed at the time (Advil, Nuprin, and Motrin). Exhibits 3 through 5 show sales and continued growth of each of the major pain relief brands and the ibuprofen market as a whole since ibuprofen was switched in 1984.

J&J was uncertain how to position the product so that it would benefit from the Tylenol heritage but not hurt Tylenol sales. J&J decided to position Medipren as a muscular aches and pain product and keep the headache and fever reduction indications for Tylenol.

Exhibit 21B ● U.S. Acne Treatment Shares (RSP), 1995

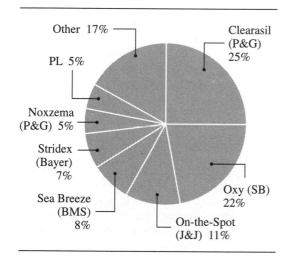

Other 17%
PL 5%
Noxzema (P&G) 5%
Stridex (Bayer) 7%
Sea Breeze (BMS) 8%
On-the-Spot (J&J) 11%
Oxy (SB) 22%
Clearasil (P&G) 25%

Exhibit 22 ● The Clearasil Brand in Europe, 1995[a]

Country	Sales (U.S. $mn)	SOM %	A:S Ratio
Germany	$27	44%	34%
France	6	20	7
Spain	2.5	32	59
Italy	3.1	31	35
United Kingdom	3.9	16	69

a. Sales figures and share of market figures used the following exchange rates: U.S.$1 = .64887367DM; U.S.$1 = .877 GHF (used for Italy sales figures); U.S.$1 = .00771861 pesetas; U.S.$1 = .1868633FF.

Exhibit 23 ● The Clearasil Brand Franchise in the United States

Segment	Brand	Sales ($mn)	% of Segment	% of Total Market
NONBENZOYL PEROXIDE CLEANSERS				
	Clearasil Daily Face Wash	$8	11.6%	3.4%
	Clearasil Moisturizer	2	2.9	.9
	Clearasil Moisturizer— Fragrance Free	—	—	—
NONBENZOYL PEROXIDE MEDICATED PADS				
	Clearasil Double Textured	4	6.9	1.7
BENZOYL PEROXIDE SPOT TREATMENTS				
	Clearasil Vanishing	15	28.8	6.4
	Clearasil Tinted	7	13.5	3.0
NON-PEROXIDE BAR SOAPS				
	Clearasil	4	16.7	1.7
NON-BENZOYL PEROXIDE SPOT TREATMENTS				
	Clearasil Clearstick	8	42.1	3.4
	Clearasil Adult Care	5	26.3	2.1

Introductory print advertising had the following copy: "Who makes Medipren? Medipren, brought to you by the makers of Tylenol products, so you know its a product you can trust. But Medipren is very different from Tylenol. Tylenol is widely used for headaches, fever reduction, and general pain. However, Medipren contains ibuprofen, ideal for relieving body aches and pains." But the TV ads, which could not go into much detail, only said "New Medipren. From the makers of Tylenol." Company officials later found this to be too confusing for consumers and discontinued the ads. Other advertising copy tried to position ibuprofen directly against aspirin. Meanwhile, the other ibuprofen products such as Advil, Motrin, and Nuprin were including a headache claim and were positioning the product against aspirin and Tylenol.

Medipren was subsequently launched in the United Kingdom and Germany under different brand names. In the United Kingdom, it was launched in 1990 as Inoven, and in Germany as Dolormin in 1992. Exhibit 27 illustrates sales and volumes from 1991 to 1995.

Tylenol was not known in Europe. When J&J decided to enter the European pain relief market, it started with a fresh slate. In the UK, the most opportunity in pain relief seemed to be with an ibuprofen product since that was the fastest-growing subcategory. The major U.K. competitor was Boots with Nurofen. In Germany, the market for ibuprofen was not large and, other than Dolormin, there were no strong entries. Germany was Bayer's home market, and so Bayer had an advantage over the classical pain relievers such as aspirin.

Exhibit 24 ● Traceable Media Expenditures for Tylenol Brands

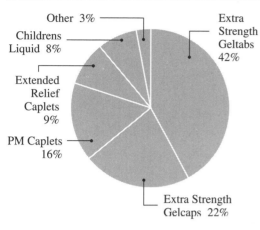

Other 3%
Childrens Liquid 8%
Extended Relief Caplets 9%
PM Caplets 16%
Extra Strength Gelcaps 22%
Extra Strength Geltabs 42%

Total Budget: $132.4 million

Vicks

The Vicks brand franchise had been managed by P&G since 1985.[22] The first product, Vicks VapoRub was introduced into the OTC market more than twenty-five years ago. All Vicks products were in the cough/cold and upper respiratory market segment.

Vicks was a global brand, with strong sales in the United States, France, Germany,[23] Italy, Spain, and the United Kingdom. In 1994, global sales of the Vicks range was $703 million, which made it the world's largest cough and cold brand. Exhibit 28 illustrates the brand's market share in these regions. Competitors tended to change with both the geographic market and the particular therapeutic category within the cough, cold, and upper respiratory segment. Major competition came from Tylenol, Alka Seltzer, Bayer Select, Afrin, Otrivine, Robitussin, and Sucrets.

Vicks was the leading cold remedies product in

22. In 1985, Procter & Gamble acquired Richardson-Vicks, founder of the Vicks brand.

23. For pronunciation reasons, Vicks was spelled Wicks in Germany.

the U.S. market. In Germany, it held 25 percent of the cold and flu market and approximately 30 percent of the medicated confectionery market. Vicks Sinex was the leading nasal decongestant in Italy and the United Kingdom. Vicks VapoRub dominated the chest rubs category in the United States, the United Kingdom, Italy, and Spain.

Through the years, the Vicks product line was extended with the introduction of new delivery systems and new combinations of products. For example, LiquiCaps was a major addition to the Vicks NyQuil cold medicine brand to improve the taste. With Liqui-Caps, the product could be administered orally without the need to taste it.

Vicks was considered to be a company name and, as a result, enabled P&G to use Vicks as an umbrella name for all products, regardless of ingredients used or product category. P&G focused on its core brand, Vicks VapoRub. Through a positive association with Vicks VapoRub, the customer would buy other Vicks products. Exhibit 29 illustrates the positioning of the major brands.

The latest introduction to the Vicks family was Vicks Action in the United Kingdom in 1994. This was a revolutionary multisymptom cold and flu remedy containing a combination of ibuprofen and the decongestant pseudoephedrine. It was available only in pharmacies and was priced at £2.29 for twelve tablets and £3.65 for twenty-four tablets. Its main competition in the market was Nurofen Cold & Flu. P&G intended to support this brand with £4 million in advertising.

In 1993, the Vicks Formula 44 brand extended its line and upgraded its packaging to create a megabrand look and feel. This was in direct response to extensions made by Robitussin.

OTC BRAND MANAGEMENT FAILURES

Bayer Select

Bayer Select was launched in the United States in 1992 by Sterling Health, then a division of Eastman Kodak, which had acquired the North American OTC business of Bayer during WWII.[24]

24. Bayer's U.S. assets were confiscated during World War II by the U.S. government and sold to U.S. companies.

Exhibit 25 ● Tylenol Products: U.S. Sales and Media Expenditures, 1995

Product	Market Share (%)	Sales ($mn)	TME ($mn)
TOTAL GENERAL PAIN RELIEVERS		*$2,245*	*$477*
Extra Strength Tylenol (Gelcaps, Caplets, Geltabs)	16.5%	$370	$91
Tylenol PM	3.7	84	25
Children's Tylenol (Elixir, Drops, Jr., and Chewable formulas)	6.3	140	12.4
Tylenol Extended Relief	1.6	35	28.5
Tylenol	1.5	33	
Tylenol Headache Plus	.3	6	.165
COLD MEDICATIONS		*$1,090*	*$237*
Tylenol Cold	3.6	39	1.8
Children's Tylenol Cold	3.2	35	2
Tylenol Flu Maximum Strength	2.5	21	13.6
Tylenol Cold & Flu	.3	3	—
ALLERGY MEDICATIONS		*$351*	*$82*
Tylenol Allergy Sinus and Tylenol Severe Allergy Caplets	11.7 •	41	18[a]
SINUS MEDICATIONS		*$159*	*$28*
Tylenol Sinus	29.6	47	11.3
COUGH SYRUPS		*$340*	*$40*
Tylenol Cough Maximum Strength	.9	3	—

a. $11.7 million was for Tylenol Severe Allergy Caplets.

Exhibit 26 ● Medipren Advertising Expenditures and Sales Figures, 1986–1989

	1986	1987	1988	1989
Market share (%)	1.5	2.1	NA	1.3
Advertising expenditures (U.S. $mn)	12	36	29	6

Bayer Select was intended as a remedy for every type of pain and every type of cold. In other words, "Not all pain is the same." Sterling envisioned that the consumer would see a display of all Bayer Select products and then "select" the best one for his or her ailment. The line was initially launched with five nonaspirin pain relievers. A year later, the company added six cold and flu products. The pain relievers addressed headache pain, back pain, period pain, night time, and sinus pain. The cold and flu remedies offered choices for treating head cold, a chest cold, head and chest cold, flu relief, nighttime cold, and allergy and sinus.

Unfortunately, the retailers did not envision the product layout the same way. First of all, not all products in the Bayer Select line were stocked. Second, those stocked were separated and placed with other brands with similar indications.

Consumers did not respond as favorably to the product as the company had expected. First of all, there was evidence that consumers misunderstood the concept and were combining products themselves and overdosing. Second, there was scepticism about the true differences between the versions. For example,

Exhibit 27 ● Sales and Advertising Expenditures for Medipren Brands in Europe, 1991–1995

(UK)	1991	1992	1993	1994	1995
INOVEN (U.K)					
Sales (U.S.$ thousands)	690	222	162	83	49
Market share (%)	—	—	0.1	almost 0	almost 0
Advertising expenditures (U.S.$ thousands)	—	—	—	—	—
A:S ratio	n/a	n/a	n/a	n/a	n/a
Share of voice (%)	n/a	n/a	n/a	n/a	n/a
Budget for professional campaign	0	0	0	0	0
DOLORMIN (GERMANY)					
Sales (U.S.$ thousands)	Product not available	741	7,402	8,282	10,100
Market share (%)	n/a	—	2.1	2.5	3.1
Advertising expenditures (U.S.$ thousands)	n/a	—	11,258	9,627	6,042
A:S ratio (%)	n/a	—	152	116	60
Share of voice (%)	n/a	—	12	9	8
Budget for professional campaign	n/a	—	0	0	0

Consumer Reports reported that ". . . with some of the products, one purportedly specific remedy differs from another only in packaging and price: Bayer Select Head Cold is identical to Bayer Select Sinus Pain, save for the colour of the caplet and the price. The lime-green head-cold caplets cost us 17 cents each; the dark green sinus-pain caplets 10 cents each." Finally, with a cold and flu, it was not uncommon for symptoms to start in one area and migrate to other areas as the ailment progressed. To expect that the consumer to be willing to purchase a different product for each stage of the cold required far more out of pocket expenditures than the consumer was accustomed to.

Unlike the Tylenol extensions, which always included their core ingredient acetaminophen, Bayer Select versions were not always aspirin-based.

For the allergy/sinus launch, Sterling used a direct mail campaign and radio during allergy season (July–September). Further support was given with a consumer rebate offer through three national free-standing inserts.

The entire Select line was advertised on national TV and print ads in women's magazines. Sterling announced that it would spend more than $100 million in advertising support. In reality, the only traceable media expenditures added up to approximately $50 million. Similarly, when the cold remedies line was launched a year later, the company announced that it had committed to a larger media investment than was actually the case.

Stridex

Stridex, created by Sterling Health, was an anti-acne treatment marketed in the United States. Sales in 1994 were $17 million, and the brand had a 7.3 percent market share, ranking fifth overall (refer to Exhibit 21B).

Stridex was best known for its unique packaging. It was the first to offer presoaked medicated pads for consumer convenience. This differentiation did not last because Clearasil and Oxy followed suit immediately. Stridex was still the leader in the medicated pads segment with a 29.3 percent share of the market.

Exhibit 28 ● Top Ranking Vicks Products Worldwide, 1993–1994 (MSP)

Country	Category	Brand	Total Marketing Expense ($ mn)	Rank	% MS	Market Size ($ mn)
Belgium	Chest rubs/inhalants	Vicks VapoRub	0.5	1	60	2
France	Chest rubs/inhalants	Vicks VapoRub	1.2	1	23	20
Germany	Cold & flu remedies	Wick MediNait	6.8	1	25	88
	Chest rubs/inhalants	Wick VapoRub	3.7	1	18	51
	Cough remedies	Wick	17.9	5	3.1	243
Italy	Cold & flu remedies	Vicks MediNait	1.9	2	12	21
	Nasal decongestants	Vicks Sinex	1.9	1	29	31.5
	Chest rubs/inhalants	Vicks VapoRub	1.6	1	58	9
Netherlands	Nasal decongestants	Vicks Sinex	n/a	2	13	7
	Chest rubs/inhalants	Vicks	n/a	1	24	3[a]
	Medicated confectionery	Vicks	n/a	1	40	21[a]
Spain	Nasal decongestants	Vicks Sinex	1.4	1	19	10
	Chest rubs/inhalants	Vicks VapoRub	8.7	1	77	3
United Kingdom	Chest rubs/inhalants	Vicks VapoRub	0.08	1	33	10
United States[b]	Cold remedies	Vicks NyQuil[c]	25	1	11	1029
		DayQuil	14[d]	12	2.7	1029
	Cough remedies	Vicks Formula 44	12.5	2	18	307
	Chest rubs/inhalants	Vicks VapoRub	10.9	1	65	44
	Sinus medications	DayQuil Sinus	—[e]	6	4	169
	Nasal decongestants	Sinex	1.7	2	8	207

a. 1992.
b. 1994 sales and advertising figures.
c. Includes all line extensions for NyQuil: liquid cold remedy, capsules, cold remedy, liquid children, liquid hot therapy, and cold formula for children.
d. Includes DayQuil line extensions which were: Liquid, LiquiCaps, and Cold & Sinus.
e. Most of advertising was done for all brands of DayQuil line: "More complete anytime relief from your cold, flu, sinus or allergy symptoms."

When the teenage population reached a low point in the 1980s and 1990s, players in the acne treatment category started to redefine the market to maintain sales. One trend was to enlarge the definition of a brand name beyond one product and redefine the brand to encompass an entire skin care regime. Another trend was to target adult women, a significant portion of whom suffered from acne. Neutrogena, Clearasil, and Oxy took significant steps in this direction.

The majority of Stridex's product line extensions focused on adding new versions of the pads (refer to Exhibit 30). The goal was to offer different pads to different members of the same household. The company eventually added an antibacterial soap and a gel formula to its product line. However, it was not nearly as extensive as offerings from Clearasil, Oxy, and Neutrogena.

Acne treatment consumers exhibited little brand loyalty. In 1994, Stridex's packaging was updated and a new logo was introduced to help the product stand

Exhibit 29 ● Product Positioning for Leading Vicks Products

Brand	Positioning	Product Forms
Vicks VapoRub	Targeted to parents for use on children. The medicated cream was applied directly to the skin, which helped to create a bond between parent and child.	Available in either a cream or ointment.
Vicks NyQuil (MediNait)	The all-inclusive medicine that relieves all cold and flu symptoms and enables the user to get a good night's sleep.	Available in liquid, liquid gel caps, and powder to make a hot therapy.
Vicks DayQuil	The all-inclusive medicine that relieves all cold & flu, sinus, and allergy symptoms but does not make you drowsy.	Available in liquid, liquid gel caps, multisymptom (cold, flu, & sinus), and allergy relief tablets, and allergy & sinus tablets and capsules.
Vicks Sinex	Nasal decongestant.	Available in nasal spray and a topical formula.
Vicks Formula 44	All-inclusive cough syrup that cures all kinds of coughs.	Available in regular strength, extra strength, pediatric, and combination cough & cold formulas.
Vicks Action	Revolutionary product combination to provide the most effective cold relief.	Available in tablets.

out on the shelf. In addition, the added versions Sensitive Skin, Super Scrub, and Dual-Textured used visible icons to convey added benefits.

Stridex spent about 2 percent of sales on advertising when under the management of Sterling. The average for the category was 11 percent (refer to Exhibit 21A).

Exhibit 30 ● Stridex Brand Franchise

NON-BENZOYL PEROXIDE MEDICATED PADS
    Stridex Medicated Pads Total
    Stridex Medicated Pads
    Stridex Big Pads
    Stridex Dual Textured Pads
    Stridex Maximum Strength
    Stridex Maximum Strength Big Pads
    Stridex Maximum Strength-Single
        Textured Pads
    Stridex Oil Fighting Formula
    Stridex with Aloe Vera for Sensitive Skin

NON-BENZOYL PEROXIDE BAR SOAPS
    Stridex Antibacterial Cleansing Bar

NON-BENZOYL PEROXIDE SPOT TREATMENTS
    Stridex Clear Gel Antiacne Treatment

NON-BENZOYL PEROXIDE CLEANSERS
    Stridex Anti-bacterial Face Wash

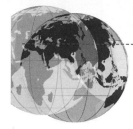

CASE 4
Ciba Self Medication

Roland M. Jeannet had been in his position as president of Ciba Self Medication for only six months when he arranged for a full strategy review in November of 1994. (In 1997, Ciba merged its health business with Sandoz to create Novartis. The Ciba self-medication operations are now under Novartis Consumer Health.)

Ciba Self Medication, although ranked tenth worldwide, is still a relatively small player compared with industry leaders. We need to think about a strategy that strengthens our global position in line with the realities of the industry. As a next step, the division needs to develop a strategy for presentation to the Ciba Group management. This strategy, among other issues, needs to articulate the type of global strategy we intend to pursue, where to place the emphasis both geographically and in segments, and how to structure our business organizationally.

COMPANY OVERVIEW

Ciba Self Medication was a division of Ciba-Geigy Limited, a Swiss-based chemical company. Formed in 1970 by the merger of two Swiss chemical companies, Ciba and Geigy, Ciba-Geigy had three operating segments: Healthcare, Agriculture, and Industry. Exhibit 1 shows the main business segments and their

●

This case was prepared by Kristi Menz and Shauna Pettit, MBA candidates at the F. W. Olin Graduate School of Business at Babson College, under the direction of Professor Jean-Pierre Jeannet. This case was written for class discussion purposes only. This case is to be used in conjunction with Case 2, Case 3, and Case 4. Copyright © 1997 by IMD—International Institute for Management Development, Lausanne, Switzerland. All rights reserved. Not to be used or reproduced without written permission directly from IMD.

fourteen autonomous divisions which resulted from a reorganization in the early 1990s. The move toward decentralization showed Ciba-Geigy's commitment to getting closer to the customer, encouraging cost-consciousness in the divisions, and providing a climate to encourage individual initiative.

Ciba-Geigy's financial performance was heavily dependent upon the cyclical chemical industry. In 1994, the chemical industry was in a downturn. Thus, Healthcare contributed only 40 percent of turnover but accounted for over 50 percent of operating profits (refer to Exhibit 2). On an after tax basis, Healthcare contributed upward of 70 percent to profits. The appreciation of the Swiss franc in recent years had considerably depressed Ciba-Geigy's profitability.

Self Medication was created as a segment within Ciba-Geigy's healthcare area in 1983. It gained status as a separate division in 1992 as a result of the consolidation of Zyma SA[1] and Ciba's self-medication activities. Self Medication had two autonomous business units, Ciba US, located in New Jersey and responsible for the U.S. OTC business, and the Zyma, based at Nyon, Switzerland, and responsible for all other geographies (refer to Exhibit 3). In 1994, Ciba Self Medication's (Ciba) sales of U.S.$823 million ranked it tenth in the world with a 2 percent market (refer to Exhibit 4). Geographically, Ciba generated the majority of its OTC sales in Europe (refer to Exhibit 5). Germany was its biggest European market, generating 17 percent of sales, with the United Kingdom second largest at 7 percent of sales, followed closely by Switzerland.

Historically, Ciba had a limited R&D pipeline for its prescription products. To compensate, the company entered into numerous joint ventures with biotechnical companies and other small, research-based pharmaceutical companies. In addition, Ciba

---

1. At the time, Zyma SA was a wholly owned subsidiary of Ciba-Geigy.

Exhibit 1 ● Ciba Corporate Organization 1994

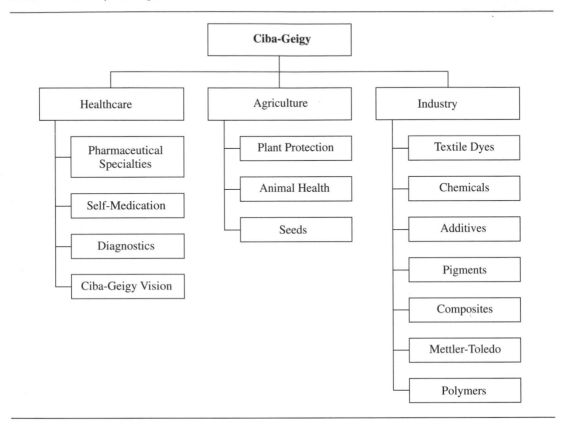

Exhibit 2A ● Financial Overview of Ciba Group ($mn)

	1990	1991	1992	1993	1994
Net sales	$16,254	$17,387	$18,317	$18,683	$18,189
R&D costs	1,692	1,803	1,939	1,817	1,774
Operating profit	852	1,056	1,254	1,949	2,251
Profit after tax	852	1,056	1,254	1,468	1,578
Total assets	21,572	23,460	25,243	26,204	26,270
Shareholders funds	12,749	13,464	14,910	14,090	12,770
Cash	3,061	3,521	4,345	5,950	6,739
Short-term debt	2,851	2,916	2,706	2,843	2,928

Exhibit 2B ● Ciba-Geigy 1994 Sales and Profits by Division

Division	% of Sales	Operating Profits % of
Healthcare	40%	51%
Agriculture	22	21
Industry	38	28

Exhibit 2D ● Financial Results of Healthcare Group ($mn)

Segment	1993	1994
Pharmaceuticals	$5,789	$5,355
Self Medication	826	823
Ciba US		226
Zyma		597
Diagnostics	578	534
Ciba Vision	895	960
R&D	1,936	1,891

Exhibit 2C ● Ciba-Geigy Sales and Operating Profits by Division, 1994

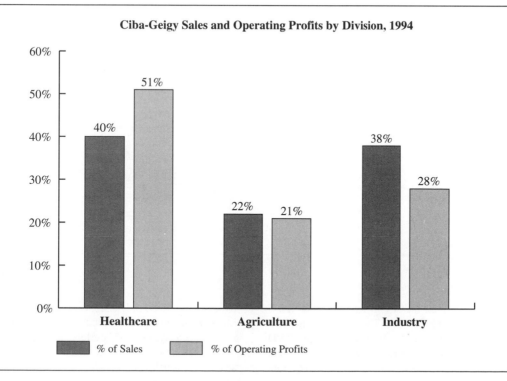

Ciba-Geigy Sales and Operating Profits by Division, 1994

Exhibit 3 ● Ciba Self Medication Division

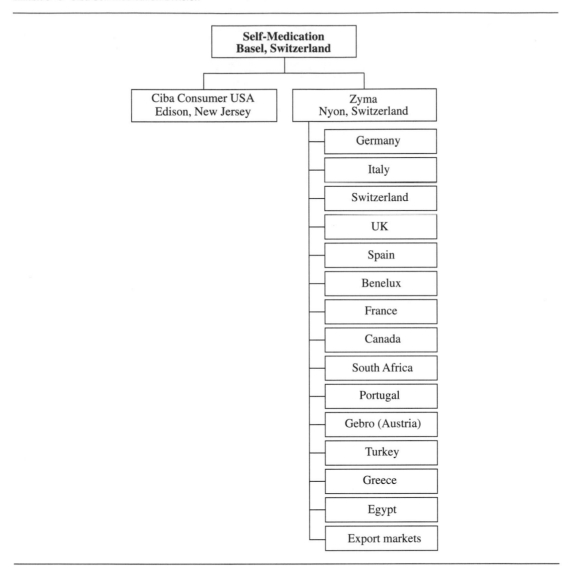

acquired several businesses to strengthen its OTC portfolio (refer to Exhibit 6). The pharmaceutical division as a whole increasingly concentrated on R&D for cardiovascular disease, central nervous system (CNS) disorders, cancer, inflammation, allergy, and bone disease. R&D did not concentrate solely on finding new chemical entities. Ciba also actively explored new delivery systems. This effort yielded such innovations as transdermal patches used for smoking cessation (Nicotinell).

Exhibit 4 ● OTC Company Rank, 1994

Rank	Worldwide	SOM %	United States[a]	SOM %	Europe	SOM %
1	J&J/Merck	5.4%	Johnson & Johnson	11.0	Rhône-Poulenc Rorer	3.6
2	American Home Products	4.9	American Home Products	9.0	Sanofi/Sterling	3.2
3	Warner Wellcome	4.7	Procter & Gamble	7.6	Bayer	3.2
4	Procter & Gamble	4.2	Warner Wellcome	7.5	Warner Wellcome	2.7
5	Bayer	3.1	Bristol-Myers Squibb	4.0	Boehringer Ingelheim	2.4
6	Sanofi/Sterling	2.8	SmithKline Beecham	3.5	Roche	2.2
7	Bristol-Myers Squibb	2.8	Schering-Plough	3.3	SmithKline Beecham	2.2
8	SmithKline Beecham	2.7	Abbott Laboratories	3.2	American Home Products	2.1
9	Rhône-Poulenc Rorer	2.6	Bayer	3.0	Pierre Fabre	2.1
10	Ciba-Geigy	2.0	Sanofi/Sterling	2.3	Servier	2.0
11					Ciba-Geigy	1.9

a. Ciba's purchase of Rhône-Poulenc Rorer's North American OTC business at the end of 1994 placed them in the top ten U.S. OTC companies.

Source: OTC Review 1994.

MARKET SEGMENTS

Ciba's OTC products covered a range of product categories (refer to Exhibit 7). Ciba's strongest categories were cough/cold, gastrointestinal, circulatory, and skin treatments (refer to Exhibit 5). Ciba also had a growing presence in the smoking cessation market. In common with other OTC manufacturers, Ciba's product portfolio in Europe contained semi-ethical products,[2] making the company vulnerable to government cost-reduction measures.

Cough/Cold and Other Respiratory

The global cough/cold segment generated sales of U.S.$7.1 billion in 1994. Ciba's estimated revenues were about U.S.$198 million, or 3 percent share of the market. Products in this segment treated ailments related to cough, cold, sore throat, hayfever, and asthma. Ciba focused mainly on the cold remedies subcategory with several products in the cough and sore throat remedies categories, as well.

Ciba's only pan-European OTC brand[3] was Otrivin,[4] a nasal decongestant. Otrivin's competitive positioning as "The most advanced and effective nasal decongestant you can buy" helped it achieve the top position in that category in Belgium, Germany, Netherlands, and the United Kingdom. It was ranked second in Switzerland. Otrivin was also available in Italy, Spain, the United States, and Canada (refer to Exhibit 7). Otrivin was Ciba's second-largest brand

2. Semi-ethical products are those that are non–prescription-bound but are still prescribed by some doctors (and thus reimbursed).

3. A pan-European brand was one that spanned numerous European countries and to which the same base marketing strategy was applied.

4. Also known as Otrivin and Otriven, depending on the country.

Exhibit 5A ● Ciba's Expected OTC Sales by Region, 1995

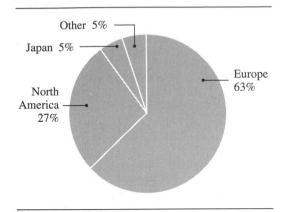

Source: Datamonitor.

Exhibit 5B ● Ciba's Expected OTC Sales by Category, 1995

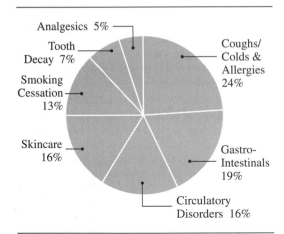

Source: Datamonitor.

with 1994 SFr. 63.8 million[5] (refer to Exhibit 8). Otrivin was Europe's fourth-largest self-medication cold remedy behind Vicks, which held the top three rankings. In the nasal decongestants category, Otrivin ranked second, giving way only to Vicks Sinex.

Ciba marketed Otrivin with slightly different

5. Includes all sales of Otrivin, prescription and nonprescription, except those in the United States.

names in different markets, making it difficult to advertise with a pan-European approach. As such, Ciba used national campaigns to market the product, including different pack designs in each country. Direct promotion accounted for 18 percent of sales in 1993. In Germany and Belgium, Otrivin was the top advertiser in the nasal decongestants category, achieving 24 percent and 60 percent share of voice (SOV) in those markets.[6] The second-biggest advertiser in the German market, Sinex, had 20 percent SOV. In Belgium, Rhinospray achieved an SOV of 20 percent. In all other markets, Otrivin's consumer advertising spends did not rank it among the top three brands. Across Europe, Otrivin's advertising to sales ratio of 18 percent ranked it second to Sinex with an A/S ratio of 50 percent. Ciba's goal was to leverage Otrivin more widely across the cough/cold market with line extensions into, for example, oral decongestants.

Another nasal decongestant, Efidac/24, was launched in the United States at the end of 1993. Its main attraction was its innovative delivery system, which allowed the medicine to be released into the body gradually over a twenty-four-hour period. At launch, Ciba spent over U.S.$30 million to promote this new technology. It achieved first-year sales of U.S.$28.7 million. Ciba believed twenty-four-hour coverage would appeal to consumers, since most other medicines in this category lasted four to six hours only.

The Fisons acquisition in 1992 added two allergy and sinus relief products, Allerest and Sinarest, to Ciba's U.S. portfolio. Prior to the acquisition, Allerest commanded a 7 percent share of the U.S. allergy relief market, placing it third in 1991 behind Benadryl and Chlor-Trimeton. Allerest's nondrowsy formulation made it attractive to consumers who were wary of products causing drowsiness, such as Tavist. Both Allerest and Sinarest lost share as new, more innovative products were introduced to the market.

Digestive and Other Intestinal Remedies

Digestive remedies was an important OTC market for Ciba with 1994 sales of approximately U.S.$156 million translated into a 3 percent share of the global

6. Total advertising spending on nasal decongestants in Germany was SFr. 19.3 million compared to only .9 million in Belgium.

Exhibit 6 ● Historical Development of Ciba and Its OTC Operations

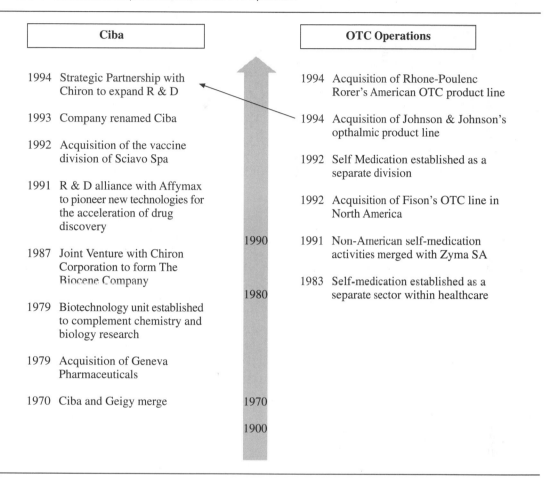

Ciba		OTC Operations
1994 Strategic Partnership with Chiron to expand R & D		1994 Acquisition of Rhone-Poulenc Rorer's American OTC product line
1993 Company renamed Ciba		1994 Acquisition of Johnson & Johnson's opthalmic product line
1992 Acquisition of the vaccine division of Sciavo Spa		1992 Self Medication established as a separate division
1991 R & D alliance with Affymax to pioneer new technologies for the acceleration of drug discovery		1992 Acquisition of Fison's OTC line in North America
	1990	1991 Non-American self-medication activities merged with Zyma SA
1987 Joint Venture with Chiron Corporation to form The Biocene Company		1983 Self-medication established as a separate sector within healthcare
1979 Biotechnology unit established to complement chemistry and biology research	1980	
1979 Acquisition of Geneva Pharmaceuticals		
1970 Ciba and Geigy merge	1970	
	1900	

Source: Datamonitor.

digestive remedies market. Digestive and other gastrointestinal medications treated such ailments as constipation, diarrhea, heartburn, and indigestion. Most of Ciba's sales in this segment were generated from laxatives treating constipation. The acquisition of Maalox from Rhône-Poulenc Rorer in 1994 gave Ciba a stronger entry point into the U.S. antacid market for indigestion.

Importal was perhaps the backbone of Ciba's gastrointestinal segment. Launched as a semi-ethical laxative in France in 1990, the brand quickly moved into several other European countries. Italy, Belgium, and Spain were other high sales markets for Importal, although it was not ranked in the top ten in any of those countries. Importal was ranked among the top five in France only. Importal was one of few products marketed in France that had reached such rank.[7]

Promotion of Importal accounted for 18 percent

7. The French market is much different from other European markets in terms of government regulation and the attitudes of doctors, pharmacists, and consumers.

Exhibit 7 ● Ciba Self Medication Key OTC Brands, 1994

	France	Germany	Italy	Spain	United Kingdom	United States	Japan	Other
ANALGESICS								
Systemic		Eu-Med	Neo-Cibalgina[f]		Librofem	Ascriptin Doan's Q-Vel		
Topical					Proflex[m]	Eucalyptamint Myoflex		Voltaren Emulgel: Belgium Switzerland[z]
COUGH/COLD								
Cold remedies		Otriven[c] Vibrocil	Otrivine	Otrivin[k]	Otrivine[n] Do-Do Mu-Cron	Otrivin Privine Allerest Sinarest Efidac/24		Otrivine: Canada Belgium Netherlands Vibrocil: Belgium
Cough/sore throat remedies			Sinecod Resyl		Bradosol	Delsym		Delsym: Canada Sinecod: Turkey Orofar: Belgium
Allergy remedies						Efidac/24		
DIGESTIVE REMEDIES								
Antacid/indigestion remedies				Bicarbonato Torres Munoz[l] Fructosel		Maalox[r]		
Laxatives	Importal[b]	Neda- Fruchtewurfel[d] Biolax	Importal	Importal		Dulcolax[s] Fiberall Perdiem[t] Maalox A-D		Importal: Belgium Netherlands Switzerland
Antidiarrheal								
DERMATOLOGICALS								
Acne remedies					Tri-Ac Cepton			
Antifungals						Desenex[u] Cruex[v] Ting		
Antihemorrhoidals			Proctidol			Nupercainal Americaine		

Anti-itch products	Eurax	Fenistil[e]	Eurax Fengel[g]	Fenistil	Eurax[o]	Caldecort	Eurax	Fenigel: Belgium
Therapeutic Moisturizers				Halibut				
Wound care			Bialcol[h] Neril[i]		Savlon Very Dry Savlon[p]			
Medicated shampoo						Caldesene		
Lip treatment					Lypsyl			
DIETARY SUPPLEMENTS								
Vitamins						Sunkist		Webber: Canada
Minerals					Slow Fe	Slow Fe[w]		
Fish oil			MaxEPA					
SLIMMING AIDS						Acutrim		
HABIT CONTROL								
Smoking cessation			Nicotinell[j]		Nicotinell[q]			
EYE CARE[a]								
Contact lens solution						Aosept[x] Quick Care		
Artificial tears						HypoTears[y]		
Decongestant						Vasocon A		

a. Sales and profits for eye care are accounted for in the Ciba Vision division's financial statements.
b. Ranked 5th with 3% share of U.S.$105 mn market.
c. Ranked 1st with 22% share of U.S.$54 mn market.
d. Ranked 4th with 5% share of U.S.$98 mn market.
e. Ranked 4th with 7% share of U.S.$26 mn market.
f. Ranked 3rd with 8% share of U.S.$87 mn market.
g. Ranked 3rd with 13% share of U.S.$10 mn market.
h. Ranked 6th with 6% share of U.S.$35 mn market.
i. Ranked 4th with 7% share of U.S.$21 mn market.
j. 15% share of U.S.$4 mn market.
k. Ranked 6th with 9% share of U.S.$11 mn market.
l. Ranked 6th with 4% share of U.S.$33 mn market.
m. Ranked 4th with 7% share of U.S.$19 mn market.
n. Ranked 1st with 55% share of U.S.$8 mn market.

o. Ranked 2nd with 39% share of U.S.$4 mn market.
p. Ranked 1st with 50% share of U.S.$6 mn market.
q. Ranked 1st with 55% share of U.S.$8 mn market.
r. Ranked 4th in U.S. Antacid market.
s. Ranked 4th in U.S. Non-Fiber Laxatives market.
t. Ranked 4th in U.S. Fiber Laxatives market.
u. Ranked 3rd in U.S. Foot Powder market and 4th in U.S. Athlete's Foot Remedy market.
v. Ranked 1st in U.S. Jock Itch Treatment market with 36% share of U.S.$23.9 mn market.
w. Ranked 2nd in U.S. Iron market.
x. Ranked 3rd in U.S. Contact Lens Solution market.
y. Ranked 2nd in U.S. Artificial Tears market.
z. Ranked 1st with 25% share of U.S.$26 mn market.

of 1993 sales. Another 30 percent went to field force allocation for promotion to the medical profession. Importal was available in sachet form. Ciba intended to further build Importal's brand equity through line extensions and new delivery systems (e.g., cubes and liquid). Importal was still highly semi-ethical, and the company hoped to position the brand more as a consumer product in the future.

In 1991, Dulcolax and Fiberall competed in the U.S. laxatives market for Ciba. Dulcolax accounted for over half of the gastrointestinal sales for the company. In 1994, Dulcolax ranked fourth in the U.S. market for nonfiber laxatives. However, the brand's sales represented less than 5 percent of the U.S. laxatives market. Marketing rights for the U.S. sale of Dulcolax were licensed from Boehringer-Ingelheim in 1990. Boehringer-Ingelheim retained marketing rights outside the U.S. market. Fiberall generated less than one-third of the sales of Dulcolax. It was given little advertising support and was repositioned as a value brand[8] by Ciba. Fiberall was available in chewable tablets, wafers, and powder form.

Maalox was the main reason for Ciba's acquisition of Rhône-Poulenc Rorer's North American OTC business in 1994. As an antacid, it faced tough competition from the introduction of H_2 antagonists. Maalox had a strong image, which was used to launch two line extensions in 1993: Maalox Anti-Gas and Maalox Antidiarrheal. Original Maalox ranked fourth in the U.S. antacid market in the twelve months to July 1994 with sales of U.S.$58.7 million (11.4 percent share of market).

Circulatory Remedies

Circulatory remedies achieved a 4 percent share of the global OTC market. Hemorrhoidal treatments were the most well-known products in this segment. Although Ciba's portfolio did not contain any strong products with this indication, Ciba had about 8 percent of the circulatory remedies market due to Venoruton, a medication used to improve circulation in the veins. Venoruton was used mostly by women as a night medication to prevent restless, achy legs. If left untreated, poor circulation could lead to varicose veins.

Venoruton was available worldwide in seventy countries throughout Europe, Latin America, Africa, Australia, and New Zealand. The drug was semi-ethical in all markets. Sales were highest in Germany at SFr. 56 million in 1993. Spain, Italy, Belgium and the United Kingdom rounded out the top five, but sales in those four countries combined were less than the total for Germany. Venoruton's different pricing strategies in many of the countries, causing parallel importing in some instances.[9] Venoruton was available in two forms, systemic and topical. The systemic version tended to have a higher price and thus was less likely to be offered OTC. The topical version, however, was more likely to be taken without prescription by consumers.[10]

The company's intention was to switch the brand to OTC status in as many markets as possible, thus building OTC sales through direct consumer promotion. In 1994, government-imposed classification changes in Italy changed Venoruton to a nonreimbursable, nonprescription drug, but did not automatically grant consumer advertising approval. Ciba did not immediately apply for OTC with advertising status. Venoruton enjoyed a good reputation among pharmacists and was generally considered effective. Ciba hoped to continue support of the product to medical professionals in those countries where the product was still reimbursed, while branching out with new forms in those markets where the product could become completely OTC.

Skin Treatments

Skin treatments were the fourth-largest product segment worldwide, with a 12 percent share of the global OTC market. Products in this segment treated a broad range of ailments, including dry skin, dandruff, athlete's foot, jock itch, cold sores, and cuts and scrapes. Ciba offered several brands for skin treatments. Perhaps the two most important were the Desenex family of foot care products in the United States and the anti-itch remedy, Fenistil, in Europe. Ciba generated approximately 16 percent of its 1994 OTC sales in the skin treatments segment.

Desenex was another US brand acquired in the

---

8. A value brand was generally priced lower than other brands in the same segment.

9. Parallel importing occurred when products were cheaper in one country than another, making it financially attractive for a wholesaler to buy the products in one country and sell them at a much higher price in another.

10. *OTC News Company Monitor,* June 1995, p. 190.

Exhibit 8 ● Ciba Self Medication Sales of Top Zyma Products (SFr. mn)

Product	1992	1993	1994
Venonuton	156.6	115.4	109.8
Otrivin	52.2	50.1	63.8
Fenistil	46.2	44.0	50.5
Importal	31.8	30.2	34.4
Nicotinell	N/A	N/A	29.2
Zymaflour	19.1	21.8	24.7
Vibrocil	18.7	18.9	17.5
Neda	14.3	13.0	13.9
Savlon	12.8	12.6	13.4
Voltaren/Emulgel	10.8	11.4	11.7
Total Zyma	700.8	667.0	681.1

Note: These figures include all sales of the products, both prescription and nonprescription. Top products for U.S. operation were not available.

Source: Ciba Self Medication.

Fison's purchase in 1992. It was considered Ciba's most important skin care brand. Ciba invested heavily in the line. In 1994, Desenex was ranked fourth in the U.S. athlete's foot remedy market and third in the foot powder market.

Zyma's third-largest brand was Fenistil, an anti-itch remedy.[11] It was offered in several dosage forms, such as tablets, drops, syrup, injectable phials, and gel. Only the gel was OTC-approved; all other forms were still prescription–bound.[12] The gel accounted for 38 percent of overall sales in 1993 at SFr. 16.7 million. Germany was by far the most important market for the product, where it commanded a 7 percent share of the anti-itch market. Its sales in Switzerland,

11. Also called Fenigel, in Italy and Belgium.

12. Except in Germany, where the oral forms were available without a prescription.

13. Total sales for Fenistil were SFr. 44 million, of which SFr. 12.7 million came from prescription-bound sales. The direct promotion ratio includes promotion for both the prescription- and non–prescription-bound versions of the product.

Portugal, and Benelux were also important. As an OTC, Fenistil competed mostly as a topical antihistamine in the skin irritation market against Parfenac and Polarmine. Eurax, another Ciba product, competed in markets where Fenistil was not available (e.g., France and the United Kingdom). Fenistil's systemic, prescription-bound version competed with antihistamine products like Clarityn, Hismanal, Teldane, and Zyrtec.

Promotion of Fenistil accounted for 13 percent of sales.[13] Fenistil (Fenigel) was the only advertised anti-itch brand in Belgium, where Ciba spent SFr. .05 million in 1993. The brand had 52% SOV in Germany, making it the biggest advertiser in its category. Fenistil was generally positioned as a cooling gel with antihistamine (effects for the relief of mosquito bites and sunburn. It had previously been marketed more as a hay fever medication, but its drowsy side effects were seen as a disadvantage by consumers. As a skin treatment, on the other hand, its drowsiness was more desirable to consumers because it got them through the night without itching.

Smoking Cessation

Habit control represented a relatively small portion of the global OTC market, but it was expected to grow at a compound annual growth rate of 21 percent from 1993–1998. Ciba entered the rapidly growing smoking cessation market on the ground floor with its transdermal nicotine patch, Nicotinell.

At the end of 1994, Nicotinell was available as OTC in six European markets, generating sales of SFr. 29 million, with SFr. 11 million of direct promotion. Germany and the United Kingdom were Nicotinell's top markets, with sales of SFr. 13.9 and 13.4 million, respectively. It ranked second in Europe to Nicorette, which came in both gum and patch forms.[14] Habitrol, as the product was known in the U.S. market, had not been approved for OTC status as of the end of 1994.

Nicotinell's key feature was its slow-release mechanism which gradually allowed nicotine into the system for a twenty-four-hour period. Nicorette's patch, on the other hand, lasted for sixteen hours. Ciba was also working to develop a gum it expected to introduce in 1995.

Analysts expected Ciba to eventually market Nicotinell with a pan-European approach. Ciba chose to package the OTC version of the product in a completely different fashion from the Rx version. Advertising in 1994 centered on building brand recognition and promoting the benefit of twenty-four-hour effectiveness. It's tag line in the United Kingdom was "It Needn't Be Hell With Nicotinell." In Germany and the United Kingdom, Ciba used extensive TV advertising with good initial success.

Oral Care

Oral care accounted for approximately 4 percent of global OTC sales. It included products for tooth decay, bad breath, dentures, and so on. Ciba was not a big player in oral care but offered a very solid product in this category with Zymaflour.

Zymaflour had been introduced as a prescription-

only more than forty years before. Its indication was as a fluoride supplement tablet for babies and children. Sales in 1993 were SFr. 21.8 million, mostly from France and Germany. It ranked second in the overall European fluoride supplement market.

Zymaflour was the only pan-European brand in its category. It was highly semi-ethical—mostly prescribed by doctors to strengthen children's teeth during development. Because it was semi-ethical, Ciba could not do any consumer advertising for the product. Zymaflour built up strong consumer awareness with its standard pink packaging. Pricing of the product varied by country. In Belgium, Ciba attempted to market a toothpaste version of the product as a pure OTC but was unsuccessful in developing a substantial market presence.

Pain Relief

Pain relief was the largest product segment in the world OTC market, with 1994 sales of U.S.$7.3 billion. This segment was very dynamic, with many new product introductions and line extensions by leading players such as Johnson & Johnson (Tylenol) and American Home Products (Advil). Pain relief was generally divided into four therapeutic segments: general pain, muscular pain, migraine, and mouth pain. Ciba generated only 5 percent of its OTC sales in this category, giving them less than a 1 percent share of the total pain relief market.

Ciba marketed several pain relief products in the United States and Europe. Most notable in the United States were Doan's and Ascriptin, neither of which were ranked in the top ten. In Europe, Ciba achieved top-ten rankings with Proflex cream in the United Kingdom and Neo-Cibalgina in Italy.

Voltaren Emulgel, a topical nonsteroidal anti-inflammatory drug (NSAID) for muscular pain relief, was believed to have much potential as a future Rx-to-OTC switch[15]. It had achieved success as an OTC in Switzerland, the only market where it was available on a nonprescription basis. For 1994, Voltaren Emulgel achieved sales in Switzerland of SFr. 7.5 million, 25 percent of the market for muscular and arthritic pain remedies. The oral prescription version of

---

14. Nicorette had 51 percent of the European market (43 percent gum and 8 percent patch), while Nicotinell had 32 percent (patch). The next closest competitor was Nicopatch, at 10 percent.

15. Emulgel was a trademark of Ciba-Geigy; its galenic presentation was in between a cream and a gel.

Voltaren was the single most important product in Ciba's pharmaceutical portfolio. More switches to OTC status of Voltaren Emulgel were discussed.

Ciba acquired the distribution rights to Doan's in 1987. The product possessed a strong brand name and was positioned specifically as a backache medicine. Sales dropped 5 percent in 1994 to U.S.$21 million. Products such as the Bayer Select line offered by Sterling Health also targeted niche markets such as backaches. Doan's PM, a line extension for relief of pain during sleep, gained slightly in 1994 to reach U.S.$5 million in sales.

The RPR acquisition gave Ciba its top-selling analgesic, Ascriptin. Sales of aspirin products had been relatively flat or declining in recent years, and Ascriptin held an insignificant share of the market.

Vitamins, Minerals, and Nutritional Supplements

The global OTC segment, vitamins, minerals, and nutritional supplements (VMS), was broadly defined, and there were discrepancies between countries as to what products were included. Even so, approximately 10 percent of global OTC sales occurred in VMS.

Ciba had few offerings in this category, its strongest being Sunkist and Slow Fe in the U.S. market. Vitamins accounted for roughly 4 percent of the U.S. operation's total OTC sales in 1994.

Ciba's Sunkist Vitamin C product was the fourth-ranking product in its category in the twelve months to March of 1995. It held a 5 percent share compared to Pharmavite's 19 percent share with its Nature Made Vitamin C tablet. The U.S. market for vitamin C was approximately U.S.$135.5 million at retail selling price. In the U.S. iron category, Slow Fe ranked second behind Geritol. Ciba's product claimed 14 percent of the U.S.$64.9 million dollar market (retail selling price).

MANAGEMENT STRUCTURE & DECISION-MAKING

In 1992, when Ciba Self Medication became a separate division, Ciba US and Zyma were two separate OTC organisations. Both reported to Pierre Douaze, who headed both the Pharmaceutical and Self Medication divisions at Ciba's corporate headquarters in Basel, Switzerland. The relationship between the OTC operations and corporate headquarters was very much at arms length, according to Eric Decosterd, head of Markets & Marketing at Zyma during this period. Even between the Pharmaceutical and Self Medication divisions very little information sharing occured.

At Zyma, located in Nyon, Switzerland, a few miles from Geneva Airport, the *Committee de Direction* (CD) made all key decisions. Its chairman, Remo Denti, also served as president of Zyma. Reporting to Denti were five committee members: Business Development, Production, Markets & Marketing, Research & Development, and Finance. This committee, along with its subcommittees, was the coordinator for all of Ciba's OTC operations outside of the United States.

"Product decisions funneled through the CD and were basically on a country-by-country basis, because it was mainly Europe," said Decosterd, explaining that Ciba's Self Medication business outside of Europe and the United States was almost nonexistent.

As far as business decisions were concerned, planning input meetings (PIM) were held each May or June, which gave countries the chance to explain to CD members what they foresaw happening in their market in the upcoming year. The CD came to the meeting with its own preconceived forecast. The purpose of the meeting was to reconcile the two views and build a business strategy for the next year. Individual meetings were held with each country. Once all of the meetings had taken place, it was up to the head of Markets & Marketing to consolidate the information and see what the global strategy looked like and then go back to the countries with corrective measures. Ciba management described this as a "bottom up, top down" approach to decision making.

Product development decisions were handled differently from the overall business strategy. For those types of decisions, an International Product Committee (IPC) composed of the CD chairman, the heads of Development and Markets & Marketing, and representatives from the five biggest countries, met two or three times a year to discuss product development ideas. Development for major brands was done at the Zyma facility in Nyon, with local brand development done in the countries.

Each country's management team was structured similarly to the CD, with a general manager (GM) at the head and production, marketing, field force, and finance managers reporting to the GM. Financial reporting was done on a country-by-country basis. While each country had control of implementing its own strategy, it was not allowed to introduce new products without the approval of the CD, even if the brand was to be sold only in that market.

INTERNATIONAL CATEGORY MANAGEMENT

Ciba did not have a clear international marketing strategy it applied to all OTC brands. In addition, marketing was performed separately for its U.S. and Zyma operations. At Zyma, each country took control of its own marketing. Until 1992, there was loose coordination of international brands. When Self Medication became a division in 1992, an international category manager (ICM) system was created. Each market segment had its own ICM, who coordinated the strategies of products that were offered in more than one country.

Philip Cross, head of Strategic Marketing Management, and his team began setting up the ICM structure by looking at the portfolio for each segment. With the help of the three lead countries for the particular segment, they developed a category strategy. Cross explained, "This involved identifying Ciba's key brand and geographic strengths by market segment, defining realizable midterm brand share objectives, and focusing marketing and product development resources accordingly." Once the strategy had been put in place, it was up to the countries to implement it. Cross and his team had no direct authority to mandate the individual countries to adopt any given strategy.

Implementing the ICM system was Ciba's first real attempt at a more coordinated approach to international OTC marketing. Six group brands evolved, which were offered across Europe. A proactive approach was taken in marketing these products. Ciba's ten key multilocal brands, which were offered in several countries only, were looked at in a more reactive fashion by the ICM.

OTC PORTFOLIO STRATEGY

Cross described Ciba's European OTC portfolio:

None of Ciba's brands could be considered blockbusters. Like most of today's successful OTCs, they hadn't been launched as consumer brands but, through doctor prescription and pharmacist recommendation, had evolved over the years to become familiar names. Today, however, the pace needed to be accelerated and the brands more actively shaped and managed.

Ciba generally used acquisitions and some licensing agreements to fuel product growth, in addition to switches from the pharma division. According to Raja Rajagopal, head of Business Development, "Part of Ciba's acquisition strategy was a natural response to the consolidation of the fragmented OTC industry."

"We set ourselves on a course to get into new markets or to build to a certain size in markets like the United States. So our strategy then was driven by the need to gain some respectable business volume in that market." The quality of the products purchased was not the main criteria. Rather, emphasis was placed on gaining critical mass in a specific geography. This strategy was used to get a start in the United Kingdom, Germany, Spain, and the United States, for example. There were bigger, higher quality acquisitions available in the early 1990s, but corporate headquarters in Basel chose not to take advantage of them. "They could not be justified financially," said Rajagopal.

A prime example was the sale of Sterling Health in 1994, which Ciba initially took an interest in. There were executives within Ciba, such as newly appointed head of the Self Medication division, Roland Jeannet, who tried to convince Ciba-Geigy executives to place a competitive bid. However, he could not convince them to take such a huge step in their OTC business. "To put it into perspective, Sterling sold for U.S.$3 billion. Several months later, we purchased RPR's North American OTC business for U.S.$400 million," stated Jeannet.

GEOGRAPHIC SETUP

The largest Ciba Self Medication manufacturing facilities were in the United States and at the Zyma

Exhibit 9 ● Ciba Self Medication: Operating Units, 1994

OPERATING UNITS IN:		Marketing/Sales	Production	Development
EUROPE				
Switzerland	Headquarters		X	Complete
Austria	Affiliate	D[1]		MR
Benelux	Affiliate	D P		MR
France	Affiliate	D		MR
Germany	Affiliate	D P	X	MR G
Greece	Division	P		MR
Italy	Affiliate	D P	X	MR
Poland	Division	D P		MR
Portugal	Affiliate	D P		MR
Spain	Affiliate	D P	X	MR G
Switzerland	Affiliate	D P		MR
Turkey	Division	D P		MR
United Kingdom	Division	P S		MR G
NORTH AMERICA				
USA	Division	P S	X	Complete
Canada	Division	P S	X	MR G
AFRICA, ASIA, AND PACIFIC RIM				
Egypt	Division	D P S	X[2]	MR
South Africa	Division	D P S		MR

Field force visiting: Doctors: D   Pharmacists: P   Supermarkets: S

Development: Medical/Regulatory: MR   Galenical: G

1. Joint Venture Zyma/Gebro

2. Joint Venture Ciba/Sandoz

headquarters in Nyon, Switzerland. Production centers were also located in Canada, Egypt, Germany, Hungary, Italy, and Spain (refer to Exhibit 9). Country subsidiaries sourced products in different ways. Basically, they could either produce locally, source them from Nyon, buy from a Ciba operation in a third country, or purchase from a Ciba pharmaceutical manufacturing site in their own country. Products sourced from Nyon were generally those that were considered international brands (e.g., Venoruton). Countries with their own manufacturing sites did not necessarily produce all of their own products, and they sometimes opted to get them from Nyon or from another country. Government regulation in countries such as Egypt and Hungary forced at least some local production to be done. The U.S. operations sourced largely locally.

COST STRUCTURE[16]

Ciba obtained most of its OTC products through switches from its pharma division or by acquiring other company's products. Most of its R&D was spent on reformulating Rx versions of drugs or developing new delivery systems. R&D was generally 5–10 percent of sales (refer to Exhibit 10).

Cost of goods sold for Ciba was comprised of variable and period expenses and usually amounted to 30–35 percent of wholesale price. Period expenses included: direct labor, equipment (depreciation and repairs & maintenance), quality control, and production overhead. Raw materials and packaging costs were the variable part of the manufacturing costs.

Active ingredients, or raw materials, used in Ciba's manufacturing process were less expensive than those for the pharma division. This was mainly due to the fact that ingredients used in OTC products are more commonly available. Together, the active ingredients and the excipients accounted for one-third of the variable materials cost, with packaging accounting for the other two-thirds.[17] Packaging was much more complicated than processing and much more labor-intensive. Each country required different packaging, resulting in small batch sizes and frequent changeovers for packaging equipment. Packaging equipment tended to be much more expensive than processing equipment.

Direct labor ran from 4–7 percent of cost of goods sold, with equipment and quality control at less than 2 percent. Production overhead was another 8–13 percent and included personnel administration, information systems, and other plant infrastructure costs.

Transportation and rebates to wholesalers added another 5–9 percent to the final cost of the product.

Marketing and sales was a major expense for Ciba, averaging 35–45 percent of the wholesale price. Ciba marketed to the trade, to medical professionals, and to consumers. Also included in this percentage were brand management and sales force expenses, which ran at about 5–9 percent and 7–11 percent, re-

16. Actual data disguised. Ciba's cost structure was broadly similar to industry-wide averages. Data cited in case reflects OTC industry averages.

17. Excipients are the components other than the active ingredients that comprise the final form of the drug.

Exhibit 10 ● Ciba Self Medication Cost Structure

Business Operaton	Proportion of Wholesale Price
RESEARCH & DEVELOPMENT	5–10%
COST OF GOODS SOLD	30–35%
Variable Expenses	
Raw Materials (⅓)	4–6%
Packaging (⅔)	8–12%
Period Expenses	
Direct Labor	4–7%
Equipment	1%
Quality Control	1%
Overhead	8–13%
TRANSPORTATION & REBATES	5–9%
MARKETING & SALES	35–45%
Brand Management	5–9%
Sales Force	7–11%
Customer Service	2–5%
General Advertising	10–15%
Trade Promotion	4–8%
Consumer Promotion	2–5%
Medical Promotion	2–5%
GENERAL & ADMINISTRATIVE	5–10%
PROFIT	10–20%

Note: Cost structure shown represents average values for OTC industry.

spectively. In addition, Ciba included its customer service expenses under marketing and sales, which averaged 2–5 percent.

General advertising expenditures accounted for 10–15 percent of sales. Promotion to the trade and to both medical professionals and consumers averaged 4–8 percent respectively. Consumer and medical advertising were at about 2–5 percent, respectively.

General and administrative expenses for Ciba

Self Medication ranged from 5–10 percent, allowing Ciba to earn a profit margin of 10–20 percent.

DEVELOPING A CIBA SELF MEDICATION STRATEGY

With the strategy review in full swing at the end of 1994, Jeannet expected that a complete proposal to the Ciba Group would have to be made by early spring 1995. The review process would take two steps. First, Jeannet and his team would need to get the support of the Ciba Health sector, where the Self Medication Division reported. Secondly, the plan would be presented to the Ciba Group executives for final approval.

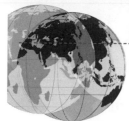

CASE 5

Interactive Computer Systems Corp.

In September 1990, Peter Mark, marketing manager of Interactive Computer Systems Corporation,[1] was faced with a perplexing conflict between his company's USA sales group and the European subsidiaries. The USA sales group had begun to sell a display controller which had been developed in Europe. The product had been selling in Europe for several years, and sales were relatively strong. Now, however, several major European customers had begun to purchase the product through their USA offices and ship it back to Europe. The Europeans were complaining that the U.S. pricing was undercutting theirs and that they were losing sales volume which was rightfully theirs. Both the U.S. and European groups claimed that their pricing practices followed corporate guidelines and met the profit objectives set for them.

INTERACTIVE COMPUTER SYSTEMS CORP.

Interactive Computer Systems Corporation (ICS), headquartered in Stamford. Connecticut, was a large, multinational manufacturer of computer systems and equipment. The company made a range of computer

●

This version of this case was prepared by Professor Jean-Pierre Jeannet based on an earlier version by Mark Uhrich as a basis for class discussion rather than to illustrate either effective or ineffective handling of an administrative situation. Copyright © 1996 by IMD, Lausanne, Switzerland. The International Institute for Management Development (IMD), resulting from the merger between IMEDE, Lausanne, and IMI, Geneva, acquires and retains all rights. All rights reserved. Not to be used or reproduced without written permission from IMD, Lausanne, Switzerland.

1. Names and data are disguised. All prices are stated in U.S. dollars.

systems and was best known for its workstations. ICS was considered one of the industry leaders in that segment of the computer industry, which included such companies as Digital Equipment, Hewlett-Packard, and Sun Microsystems.

The company was primarily a U.S.-based corporation, with the majority of its engineering and manufacturing facilities located in the eastern United States. In addition, ICS had manufacturing facilities in Singapore, Germany, Brazil, and Taiwan, and a joint venture in South Korea.

Sales were conducted throughout most of the world by means of a number of sales subsidiaries with sales offices located in Canada, Mexico, Brazil, Argentina, Chile, Japan, Australia, and most European countries. Elsewhere, sales were conducted through a network of independent agents and distributors.

PRODUCT LINE

The ICS line of products was centered around a family of powerful workstations. *Workstation* was the popular term referring to small to medium-sized computer systems, which were used in a wide variety of engineering applications including industrial control, telecommunications systems, laboratory applications, and small business systems.

In addition to the computer central processing units (CPUs) and memory units, ICS produced a line of peripheral devices required for making complete computer systems. These included devices such as disk storage units, printers, video and hard-copy terminals, display units, and laboratory and industrial instrumentation interface units. These various peripherals were used as appropriate and combined with the final computer systems to meet the specific customer's requirements. ICS produced most of these products in-house, but some, such as printers, were purchased to ICS specifications from companies specializing in those products.

ICS manufactured several central processing units, which were positioned in price and performance to form a product family. They all had similarity of design, accepted (executed) the same computer instructions, and ran on the same operating system (master control programs). The difference was in speed, complexity, and cost. The purchaser was able to select the model which economically met the performance requirements of the intended application.

This family of CPUs, together with the wide range of available peripheral devices, formed a family of computer systems offering a considerable range of price and performance but with compatible characteristics and programming.

MODEL 2000 COMMUNICATIONS INTERFACE

A communication interface was a peripheral device used for transmitting data to or from the computer system. The specific product in question was the model 2000 communications interface, a multiline programmable multiplexer.

The 2000 provided the interface for many separate communications lines, which were connected by means of specially designed connectors on the module. Such multiline interfaces were typically called multiplexers after the manner in which they worked internally. They offered the advantages of more efficient space utilization and lower per-line costs compared with the normal alternative of a separate single-line interface per line. Depending on the computer vendor, multiplexers come in various sizes such as 2, 4, 6, 8, 16, 32, and 64 lines.

ICS already had multiplexers in its line of high volume standard products. The specified advantage of the 2000 was its programmable nature. It could be loaded with software to handle any of several different protocols directly in the interface, using its own microprocessor on the module. Since these functions had previously all been performed by a program running in the computer, the 2000 relieved the computer of this load and freed it up to do other work. The result was a net improvement in system speed and power.

The model 2000 was designed in 1987 at ICS's small European engineering facility assigned to its German subsidiary, Interactive Computers GmbH, in Frankfurt and was manufactured there for shipment worldwide to those ICS subsidiaries who were selling

the 2000. Sales had initially started in Europe and then spread to other areas. Sales volumes are given in Exhibit 1.

INTERSUBSIDIARY TRANSACTIONS

With the exception of the Korean joint venture, all of ICS's subsidiaries were wholly owned, and products moved freely between them. ICS had set up its procedures and accounting systems in line with the fact that it was basically a U.S.-based company manufacturing a uniform line of products for sales worldwide through various sales subsidiaries. For the major product lines, the only differences by countries were line voltages and some minor adaptations to comply with local government regulations.

Although the subsidiaries in the various countries were essentially sales subsidiaries functioning as sales offices to sell products in those countries, they were separately incorporated entities and wholly owned subsidiaries, operating under the laws of that particular country. Careful accounting of all transactions between the parent company and the subsidiaries had to be maintained for the purpose of import duties and local taxes.

When a customer ordered a computer system, the order was processed in the subsidiary and then transmitted back to the parent company (ICS) in the United States to have the system built. The order paperwork listed the specific hardware items (CPU, memory size, disk units, etc.) wanted by the customer,

Exhibit 1 ● Model 431 Sales Volume (Units), Selected Countries

	1987	1988	1989	1990
Germany	30	100	110	100
U.K.	5	40	60	70
France	10	20	50	40
Canada	0	0	5	5
Switzerland	3	20	30	15
Australia	0	0	10	30
United States	0	2	80	200

and each system was built specifically to order. The component pieces were built by ICS in volume to meet the requirements of these specific customer systems orders. Like most companies, ICS expended a great amount of effort attempting to accurately forecast the mix of products it would need to meet customer orders.

When the customer's system, or any product, was shipped to the subsidiary, the subsidiary "bought" it from the parent at an intercompany discounted price, or "transfer price," of list minus 20 percent. The level of subsidiary transfer price discount was established with two factors in mind:

- It was the primary mechanism by which Interactive repatriated profits to the U.S. parent corporation.

- The 20 percent subsidiary margin was designed to give the subsidiaries positive cash flow to meet their local expenses such as salaries, facilities, benefits, travel, and supplies.

Import duties were paid on the discounted (list minus 20 percent) transfer price value according to the customs regulations of the importing country. Some typical import duties for computer equipment are shown in Exhibit 2.

Most countries were quite strict on import/export and customs duties and required consistency in all transactions. Therefore, all shipments were made at the same discounted transfer price, including shipments among subsidiaries and shipments back to the United States.

PRICING

ICS set prices worldwide based on U.S. price lists. which were referred to as "Master Price Lists," or MPLs. Prices in each country were based on the MPL plus an uplift factor to cover the increased cost of doing business in those countries. Some of these extra costs were:

- Freight and duty, in those countries where it was included in the price (in some countries, duties were paid for separately by the customer).

Exhibit 2 ● Import Duties for Computer Equipment for Selected Countries[a]

United States	5.1%
Canada	8.8
Japan	9.8
Australia	2.0
European Union countries	None between EU countries; 6.7% from outside EU countries

a. These are typical amounts only. The topic of customs duties is quite complex. It varies with the type of goods, even within an industry (computer systems may be one rate, while computer terminals may be another, higher rate and parts a third rate), and by country of origin.

- Extended warranty: in some countries, the customary warranty periods were longer than in the United States, for example, one year versus ninety days.

- Cost of subsidiary operations and sales costs, to the extent that they exceed the normal selling costs in the United States.

- Cost of currency hedging: in order to be able to publish a price list in local currency, ICS bought U.S. dollars in the money futures market.

Uplift factors were periodically reviewed and adjusted if needed to reflect changes in the relative cost of doing business in each country. Typical uplift factors for some selected countries are shown in Exhibit 3.

Each subsidiary published its own price list in local currency. The list was generated quarterly by use of a computer program which took a tape of all the MPL entries and applied the uplift and a fixed currency exchange rate which had been set for the fiscal year. This price list was used by all salespeople in the subsidiary as the official listing of products offered and their prices.

SPECIAL PRODUCTS

In addition to its standard line of products which were sold worldwide in volume, ICS had a number of lower

Exhibit 3 ● Typical Country Uplift Factors: Local Price = Master Price List + Uplift %

United Kingdom	8%
Germany	15
France	12
Switzerland	17
Sweden	15
Australia	12
Brazil	20
Canada	5

volume, or specialized, products. The model 2000 communications interface was considered one of these. Specialized products were typically not on the MPL, and prices were set locally by each subsidiary wherever they were sold. They were either quoted especially on request for quote basis or added to a special price list supplement produced by each country. This was a common procedure in the computer industry.

To support the sales of the specialized products, ICS had a separate team of specialists, with one or more specialists in each subsidiary. They were responsible for the pricing of their products and had a high degree of independence in setting prices in each subsidiary. The specialist or team in each subsidiary was responsible for all aspects of the sales of their assigned products and essentially ran a business within a business.

For the purposes of internal reporting to management, the specialists were measured on achieving a profit before tax, or PBT, of 15 percent, which was the ICS goal. The results were shown on a set of internal reports which were separate from the legal books of the subsidiary. The purpose of the internal reports was to give ICS management more information on the profitability of its various product lines. These reports took the form of a series of profit and loss statements of operation by line of product with overhead and indirect costs allocated on a percentage of revenue basis. For these internal P&L reports, the cost of goods was the actual cost of manufacture (in-

ternal cost) plus related direct costs instead of the discounted price paid by subsidiaries and shown on their official statements of operation.

2000 SALES IN EUROPE

The model 2000 communications interface was designed in 1987 by the European engineering group in Frankfurt as a follow-up to some special engineering contracts for European customers. It was introduced in the European market in 1988, where it grew in popularity.

The 2000 was produced in Frankfurt only on a low-volume production line. The manufacturing and other direct costs amounted to U.S. $1,500 per unit. Because there were no tariffs within the EU and shipping costs were covered by allocated fixed costs, there were no other direct costs. The allocated fixed costs in Europe were running at 47 percent of revenue. Thus, a contribution margin of 62 percent was required to achieve a 15 percent PBT. Based on these costs, a list price of U.S. $3,900 had been set within the EU. The resulting P&L is shown in Exhibit 4.

Because of the popularity of this product, it had been listed on the special products price list in most European countries. Within the EU, the price had been set at the same level, with any variation due only to local currency conversions. In European countries outside the EU, the price was increased to cover import duties.

At the above price, the 2000 had gained market acceptance and had grown in popularity, especially in

Exhibit 4 ● Model 2000 European Profit Analysis (in U.S. dollars)

European List Price	U.S. $3,900
Manufacturing and Other Direct Costs	1,500
Contribution Margin	2,400
	62%
Allocated Fixed Costs (47%)	1,833
PBT	U.S. $567
	14.5%

Germany, the United Kingdom. and France. Its customers included several large European based multinational companies of major importance to ICS in Europe. These customers designed specific system configurations and added programming to perform specified applications and shipped the systems to other countries, either to their own subsidiaries for internal use (for example, a factory) or to customers abroad.

2000 SALES IN THE UNITED STATES

The 2000 was brought to the attention of the U.S. sales group in two different ways. In sales contacts with U.S. operations of some European customers, ICS was told of the 2000 and asked to submit price and availability schedules for local purchase in the United States. U.S. customers expressed irritation at being told that the model was not available in the United States.

Secondly, the U.S. sales force also heard of the 2000 from their European counterparts at sales meetings, where the Europeans explained how the 2000 had been important in gaining large accounts.

As a result of this pressure from customers and the sales force, the U.S. special products specialists obtained several units for evaluation and in 1989 made the 2000 available for sale in the United States.

Originally, the U.S. specialists set the price equal to the European price of $3,900. However, it became obvious that the U.S. market was more advanced and more competitive, with customers expecting more performance at that price. As a result the price had to be reexamined.

The 2000 was obtained from Frankfurt at the internal cost of $1,500. Transportation costs were estimated at $200. In the U.S. accounting system, import duties and transportation were not charged directly and were absorbed by general overhead. This came about because ICS was primarily an exporter from the United States, with very little importing taking place. Consequently, it was felt that import costs were negligible. Thus, the only direct cost was the $1,500 internal cost. Overhead and allocated fixed expenses in the United States averaged 35 percent.

The result was, as shown in Exhibit 5, a revised price of $3,000 with a contribution margin of 50 per-

Exhibit 5 ● Model 2000 U.S. Profit Analysis

U.S. list price	$3,000
Manufacturing cost	1,500
Contribution margin	1,500
	50%
Allocated fixed costs (35%)	1,050
PBT	$450
	15%

cent and a PBT of 15 percent—the ICS goal. Following this analysis, the U.S. price was reduced to $3,000. The 2000 was not listed on the main U.S. price list but was quoted only on an RPQ basis. Subsequently, this price was also listed on special products price list supplements which were prepared by the U.S. product specialists and handed out to the sales force in each district.

CURRENT SITUATION

The repricing of the 2000 to $3,000 was instrumental in boosting U.S. sales. The sales volume continued to grow, and some large customers were captured. These customers included existing ICS customers who previously used other, lower-performance communications interfaces or had bought somewhat equivalent devices from other companies who made "plug compatible" products for use with ICS computers. Also, a good volume of sales was being obtained from the U.S. operations of European multinationals who were already familiar with the product. ICS's U.S. group, who had first viewed the European designed product with suspicion, was now more confident about it.

But the Europeans were not entirely happy with the situation. Recently, they had started complaining to ICS management that the U.S. pricing of the 2000 was undercutting the European price. This was causing pressure on the European subsidiaries to reduce the price below the $3,900 they needed to meet their profitability goals. Pressure was coming from customers who knew the U.S. price and from European salespeople who, as a result of travel to the United

States or discussions with U.S. colleagues, knew the U.S. price and what the uplifted European price "was supposed to be."

The price difference had also been noticed by several of ICS's larger European multinational customers. They started buying the 2000 through their U.S. offices and reexporting it, both back to Europe and to other countries.

So far, three customers had done this, two German firms and one French customer. Several additional customers were showing definite signs of "shopping around."

This loss of customers to the United States was particularly painful to the Europeans. They had invested considerable amounts of effort into cultivating these customers.

In addition, the customers still expected to receive technical and presales support from their local ICS office (that is, European) as well as warranty and service support, regardless of where they placed the purchase order. Attempts to discuss this with the customers or persuade them to purchase in Europe had not been successful. Typical reactions had been "That's ICS's problem" (U.K. customer) and "But are you not one company?" (German customer).

In brief, the ICS European subsidiaries were complaining that they were "being denied the prof-itable results of their own work" by the unfair pricing practices of the U.S. parent company.

In the eyes of the U.S. team, however, they were pricing in accordance with corporate guidelines to achieve a 15 percent PBT. They also maintained that the market did not allow them to price the 2000 any higher. Furthermore, they felt that they were simply exercising their right to set their own country prices to maximize profits within their specific country market.

The U.S. group was so pleased with the U.S. market acceptance of the 2000 that they wanted to begin an aggressive promotion. As an important part of this, they were now planning to add the 2000 on the official ICS U.S. price list. This was viewed as a key to higher sales since, especially in the United States, products tended to be sold from the regular price list, and the sales force tended to lose or ignore special price list supplements.

At this point, both the European and U.S. specialists were upset with each other. Both sides maintained that they were following the rules but that the actions of "the other side" were harming their success and profitability.

It had been a long day, and it was time to go home. As he turned his car out into the traffic on High Ridge Road, Mark was still feeling confused about the issues and wondering what should be done.

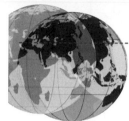

CASE 6

ICI Paints (B): Considering a Global Product Organization

In the spring of 1993, Herman Scopes, chief executive officer (CEO) of ICI Paints, was having a discussion with the members of the company's International Business Team (IBT) about how the paint industry had changed over the past few years:

The passage of time has increasingly impressed upon us the rate at which markets are becoming international and global in nature. Over the past few years, ICI Paints has become an agglomeration of companies; global, but not necessarily globally managed. Moreover, as a result of past practices, we have an organizational structure that is, for the most part, based on geographic regions, not global product lines. As I look at the present business environment, however, I wonder whether that is the best arrangement and how the remainder of the IBT views the situation. Specifically, is our regional management structure, which has served us well in the past, appropriate for the rest of the decade?

In contrast to regional executives, who managed several of the company's products in one or more countries, some felt that ICI Paints should appoint worldwide business leaders with global product line responsibility. Doing so, however, raised all kinds of questions—such as the ability to maintain a local image in, say North America and Asia, with a product

manager based in the United Kingdom. Adopting an organization based on global product lines also raised communication issues; would people feel able to relate to a product line organization that was worldwide in scope? Despite the potential problems, a global product organization offered distinct advantages in terms of allocating resources, deciding priorities, and making investment decisions. For Herman Scopes and his colleagues on the IBT, the question was whether the company should move from a regional to a global product organization and if so, how.

IMPERIAL CHEMICAL INDUSTRIES PLC

The Imperial Chemical Industries (ICI) was formed in 1926 by the merger of Great Britain's four major chemical companies: Nobel Industries Limited, the United Alkali Company, the British Dyestuffs Corporation, and Brunner, Mond, and Company Limited. At that time, the newly formed ICI was divided into nine groups: alkalis, cellulose products, dyestuffs, explosives, fertilizers, general chemicals, rubberized fabrics, lime, and metals. Beginning in the 1930s, ICI's dyemakers used their knowledge of chemistry to diversify into plastics, specialty chemicals, and pharmaceuticals—higher-margin products that later became ICI's core businesses. In 1991, those core businesses were structured along product and geographic lines into four principal areas: Bioscience Products, Specialty Chemicals and Materials, Industrial Chemicals, and Regional Businesses. In the same year, the ICI Group reported a turnover of $22.1 billion, profits of $1.8 billion, and employed 128,600 persons around the world.

Sometime in the early 1990s, executives began considering breaking up ICI into smaller companies. In doing so, it was proposed, new companies would be better prepared to devote the amount of management attention and resources needed in an industry where the return on investment had gradually declined over the preceding twenty years. Had the reorganization occurred in 1992, ICI would have been split into two companies; one was to retain the company name with interests in industrial chemicals, paints, and explosives, while the other company—with the proposed name of Zeneca—was to include drugs, pesticides, seeds, and specialty chemicals. (Exhibit 1 gives financial data on how the two firms would have looked if they had been split in 1992.)

Organization of ICI Paints

In 1991, ICI Paints was the largest paint manufacturer in the world and accounted for $2.9 billion, or 13 percent, of all sales within the ICI Group of companies. In the same year, ICI Paints operated manufacturing plants in twenty-four countries, had licensees in an additional sixteen countries, all of which manufactured and marketed coatings in the company's main application segments: decorative, automotive OEM, automotive refinish, can, powder, and coil. (Refer to Exhibit 2 for a list of ICI Paints manufacturing companies, minority holdings, and licensees.)

Like other multinationals, ICI Paints traditionally structured its operations on the basis of individual

Exhibit 2 ● ICI Paints Territorial Spread

ICI PAINTS MANUFACTURING COMPANIES

Australia	Italy	Spain
Canada	Malaysia	Taiwan
Ireland	Mexico	Thailand
Fiji	New Zealand	United Kingdom
France	Pakistan	United States
India	Papua New Guinea	West Germany
Indonesia	Singapore	

ICI MINORITY HOLDINGS

Botswana	South Africa
Malawi	Zimbabwe

COMPANIES MANUFACTURING UNDER LICENSE

Brazil	Kenya	Sudan
Colombia	Korea	Trinidad
Cyprus	Madagascar	Turkey
Ecuador	Portugal	Venezuela
Japan	Saudi Arabia	Yemen
Jordan		

Exhibit 1 ● ICI-Zeneca Turnover & Operating Profit (Loss), 1992

Turnover ($mn)	Zeneca	Operating profit (loss) ($mn)
$228	Trading & Misc.	(18.2)
1,429	Specialties	39.5
1,961	Agrochemicals & Seeds	129.2
2,447	Pharmaceuticals	741.8
	New ICI	
$2,827	Materials	(38)
5,396	Industrial Chemicals	(25.8)
2,052	Regional Businesses	12.2
836	Explosives	89.7
2,402	Paints	174.8

markets. That is, executives had profit and loss responsibility for the full range of ICI products within a given market. Following the acquisitions of the 1980s, however, the management of ICI Paints felt that its customers could be better served by managers with a multicountry product line responsibility. To this end, ICI brought the management of Mexico, Canada, and the United States together under a regional CEO who reported to Herman Scopes in the United Kingdom. Similarly, regional constructs were devised for Europe and Asia. By 1990, the array of ICI Paints' subsidiaries and licensees was organized along geographic and business lines (as shown in Exhibit 3).

Within their respective regions, each regional CEO had profit and loss responsibility for the entire paint business. Also, within each region and reporting to the regional CEO, ICI Paints had country managers, territorial general managers (TGMs), and busi-

Exhibit 3 ● Previous Organization Chart, 1988–1990

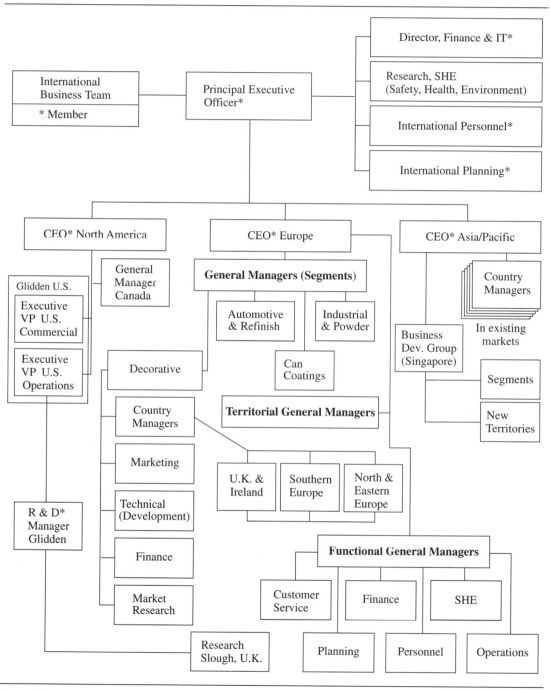

Source: Company records.

* Denotes International Business Team member.

ness area general managers (BAGMs). As the name implied, country and territorial managers supervised more than one of ICI Paints' product lines on a geographic basis, while business area general managers concentrated on the products of only one of ICI Paints' application segments. Because the latter were not required unless an individual segment reached a certain size, territorial general and business area general managers were sometimes one and the same person. In those areas where both existed, profit and loss results were a shared responsibility.

At ICI Paints, major decisions were always discussed and decided upon by an International Business Team (IBT), chaired by Herman Scopes. Additional members included the three regional CEOs, and four other executives with either functional or segment responsibility (as shown in Exhibit 4). Typically, executives were nominated to the IBT because of their ability to contribute to the development of the ICI Paints Group rather than their specialties or specific skills. Once part of the IBT, members were assigned "portfolios" based on their own talents and experience. Occasionally, these responsibilities changed when there was a change in the composition of the IBT.

Yet another important aspect of the way ICI Paints operated was its use of international leaders (ILs), persons drawn from each of the company's core business areas as well as three out of five of the following functional areas: finance, information technology, operations, research & development, and management development. Typically, international leaders drawn from the core businesses acted as facilitators or coordinators. And though they did not have profit and loss responsibility, international leaders were responsible for developing global strategies in their respective application segment. Most recently, the company had appointed a worldwide safety, health, and environment (SHE) executive whose presence as an IL increased management's awareness of environmental issues.

Though the strategy making and coordination processes differed among ICI's application segments, in general, strategies were developed at the business, or operational, level by the international leaders and their teams. In turn, these strategies were proposed to the International Business Team which met six to eight times per year in various locations.

Exhibit 4 ● Members of the International Business Team (IBT)

Herman Scopes	CEO Paints
John Danzeisen	Chief Executive North America
Peter Kirby	Chief Executive Asia Pacific
Denis Wright	Chief Executive Europe International Leader Decorative
Adrian Auer	Chief Financial Officer
Nigel Clark	International Leader, Operations and Personnel
Brian Letchford	International Leader, Automotive and Can Coatings
Alex Ramig	International Leader, R&D
John Thompson	Chief Planner

THE WORLD PAINT INDUSTRY

In 1991, the world paints and coatings industry was valued at $46 billion at suppliers' prices, corresponding to a volume of 13.5 billion liters. Generally speaking, the industry included a range of products such as pigmented coatings, or paints, as well as unpigmented coatings like stain and varnish, used to decorate and/or protect different substrates. Analysts and participants alike divided coatings sales into two main classes: decorative or architectural paints, used in decorating buildings and homes, and industrial coatings, which provided functional properties and added value to manufactured goods. Typically, decorative coatings were high-volume, low-priced goods and commanded low margins. Industrial coatings, on the other hand, were high priced and focused on niche markets. (Refer to Exhibits 5 and 6, respectively, for a breakdown of world paint sales by market sector and region.)

Exhibit 5 ● World Paints by Market Sector

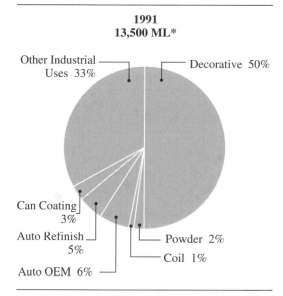

1991
13,500 ML*

Other Industrial Uses 33%

Decorative 50%

Can Coating 3%

Auto Refinish 5%

Auto OEM 6%

Powder 2%

Coil 1%

*ML = million liters.

Note: Excludes central and eastern Europe, the Middle East, and Africa.

Exhibit 6 ● World Paint Markets by Region

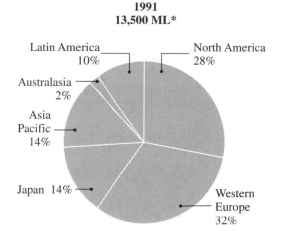

1991
13,500 ML*

Latin America 10%

North America 28%

Australasia 2%

Asia Pacific 14%

Japan 14%

Western Europe 32%

*ML = million liters.

Note: Region definitions are as follows:

1. Western Europe = The United Kingdom, France, Germany (including former East Germany), Italy, Spain, Portugal, Belgium, the Netherlands, Denmark, Finland, Norway, Sweden, Austria, Ireland, Greece, and Turkey.

2. North America = The United States and Canada.

3. Asia Pacific = India, Pakistan, Sri Lanka, Thailand, Malaysia, Singapore, Indonesia, Taiwan, Hong Kong, China, and Korea.

4. Australasia = Australia and New Zealand.

5. Latin America = Brazil, Argentina, Mexico, Ecuador, Uruguay, Colombia, and Chile.

6. Excludes Commonwealth of Independent States, eastern Europe, the Middle East, and Africa.

Decorative Paints

By far, decorative coatings was the largest single segment in the industry. Overall, the potential demand for decorative coatings in any country was influenced by climate, construction methods, and lifestyle, together with the collective successes of the local paint industry in presenting its offering to private and professional consumers in a readily accessible and attractive form. From this baseline, variations in demand were driven primarily by changes in real disposable income and in real interest rates, the latter already being an indicator of the level of construction activity and house moves.

In the decorative segment, paint sales were further classified according to two major user groups, each of which accounted for roughly half the sales in the segment. As the name implied, the professional market consisted of professional painters, further subdivided into restorers, new housing contractors, and

commercial contractors. Sales to the professional market were either through small independent stores or branches of manufacturers. The second segment consisted of individual do-it-yourself (DIY) users who bought paint through a variety of retail stores.

Retailing   Traditionally, decorative paints had been sold in small shops or hardware stores, but recent developments in the DIY segment were substantially changing the retailing process. In recent years, in fact, the DIY segment had increased its share to slightly over half the decorative market. In part, the increased share reflected a change in the way consumers viewed paint. Though once considered a lowly commodity, at the start of the 1990s, domestic paint was beginning to be seen as a household fashion accessory, adding value to the object it coated. In other words, the market for household paint, like that for beans, soap, and fish fingers, had become retail-led and susceptible to all the pressures which afflicted grocery producers. While the supermarket's rise to eminence in food and packaged goods took thirty years, the storming of the trade by DIY superstores happened in only ten years

Worldwide, these developments were most evident the in Anglo-Saxon countries—the United Kingdom, the United States, and Australia, to a lesser degree in northern Europe, and considerably less in southern Europe. To clarify, in the late 1960s and early 1970s specialist store chains like High Street in the United Kingdom and Sherwin-Williams in the United States replaced most small shops. Thereafter, variety department stores and supermarkets such as Woolworth, Sears, JC Penney, and Montgomery Ward in the United States, and Tesco in the United Kingdom took the lead in retailing decorative paints; at one point, it was reported that Sears had reached a 30 percent U.S. market share through its own branding. In concert with the growing popularity of variety department stores and supermarkets, however, DIY superstores—i.e., sheds—soon gained importance. In the United States, for example, the opening of stores like Home Depot cut Sears' market share in half. In the United Kingdom, the number of specialist stores declined from about 20,000 in 1979 to some 11,000 in 1988, and large DIY chains such as B&Q, Texas, and Pay Less accounted for 65 percent of all sector sales.

Throughout this retailing cycle, the marketing task of the paint manufacturer changed at each turn. In the first cycle, independent distributors and wholesalers gave way to manufacturer-owned stores and outlets. When the chains took over, increased buying power led to bargaining over shelf space. Thereafter, the supermarket or departmentalized variety stores brought private labels. Finally, the superstores narrowed the brand choice by typically carrying just one advertised brand and their own private label, and the reduced number of brands led to the disappearance of many retail paint suppliers.

In 1991, the decorative segment accounted for 50 percent of the value of all paint sold in the world, or roughly 6.67 billion liters. Geographically, North America accounted for 30 percent of these sales; western Europe, 32 percent; Japan, 9 percent; and the rest of the world, 29 percent. One analyst pointed out that despite the size of Japan's population and economy, decorative paints accounted for a surprisingly small share of the country's coatings sales. He attributed this to the fact that traditional, domestic architecture in Japan, with its paper partitions, meant that millions of square feet of walls were not painted.

Industrial Paints

In contrast to decorative coatings, demand for industrial coatings depended on a country's manufacturing profile, vehicles versus electronics or furniture versus textiles, for example. That is, industrial coatings tended to have more specialized uses than decorative coatings and included paint for cars, ships, planes, boats, white goods, cans, and thousands of other applications. In this segment, properties such as corrosion, abrasion resistance, and the ability to withstand high temperature or wet weather were important purchase criteria. To monitor the market, participants further classified industrial coatings according to application: automotive OEM (original equipment manufacturers), automotive refinish, can coatings, powder, and coil. Each segment had its own particular customer group and usually required its own technology and application base.

Automotive OEM   The automotive paint segment consisted of paint sales to automobile manufacturers—usually global companies—for use in their assembly plants. In this segment, users applied coatings by immersing an entire car body in a "paint bath" in which the paint carried an electric charge, opposite from that of the car body, resulting in a corrosion resistant finish. Because of the service requirements associated with maintaining electrolytic paint baths, as well as the desire to provide a consistent color wherever cars were assembled, automotive OEM customers preferred paint suppliers that were both local and global in nature. That is, customers favored suppliers able to provide a consistent color around the world yet, at the same time, deliver local service. As a result, paint manufacturers tended to locate their factories close to automotive assembly plants and stationed their personnel permanently at automotive sites. When purchasing coatings, automotive OEM customers usually maintained a major supplier for each top coat and base coat, and a second supplier for smaller volume applications "to keep the big ones honest." In 1991, the volume of paint sold to car manufacturers was roughly 791 million liters, or 6 percent of the industry volume, with sales distributed among North America, 22 percent, western Europe, 27 percent, and Japan, 34 percent.

Automobile Vehicle Refinishing   The refinish segment included paints and coatings for repairing automobiles. Although the volume of paint sold in this market was smaller than the automotive OEM segment, it was a larger segment by value due to its higher sales price and was, in fact, the most profitable segment in the industry. Refinish customers were primarily small paint shops which needed quick and frequent deliveries, usually on a daily basis. Typically, paint manufacturers supplied these customers with mixing schemes through local distributors, who combined basic colors and shades with solvents to obtain a correct color match. Because there were some 10,000 different shades and some 60 different colors to select from, a refinish company had to have access to the color and paint shops of car manufacturers. And because automobile makers wanted to ensure that, if necessary, car owners could get their cars refinished wherever they were purchased, car manufacturers were interested in worldwide coverage. Not surprisingly, refinish paint manufacturers profited when they had access to all locations of a car maker because then they could supply the widest possible color range in any geographic market. Worldwide, the refinish segment accounted for 5 percent of industry sales, which were distributed among North America, 39 percent; western Europe, 23 percent; and Japan, 13 percent.

Can Coatings   As the name implied, can coatings were applied inside tin and aluminum cans to make them corrosion resistant for use as food or beverage containers. In 1991, can coating sales were concentrated among four groups: Continental Can, Pechiney-Triangle (which included former American and National Can), Carnaud-MetalBox, and Crown Cork and Seal, as well as their licensees, all of which operated canning lines around the globe. Because these canning companies were expected to provide a consistent taste for globally marketed products such as Coca-Cola, they in turn expected their suppliers to provide local service at each of their canning sites. In 1991, the can coating segment accounted for only 3 percent of the world paint market, with sales distributed among North America, 41 percent; Europe, 27 percent; and Japan, 16 percent.

Powder Paints   In contrast to other coatings, powder paints were 100 percent solids in the form of pigmented resin powders, usually electrostatically sprayed onto a grounded metal substrate and then cured by heat. Because powder paint could be applied in layers of 50–60 microns—five times as thick as wet paint, it was far more durable, retained its color longer, and resisted abrasions for up to twenty years. As a result, powder paint was ideal for coating domestic appliances such as washing machines or refrigerators, as well as metal surfaces on the outside of buildings which were subject to extreme weather conditions. Despite these advantages, powder paint had two limitations. First, because powder paint left thick layers, it could not be used in applications such as can coating where thin layers of coating were a must. Second, because powder coatings had to be cured by heat, there was an upper limit to the size of an object which could be coated.

In addition to the functional properties they imparted to a given substrate, powder paints had a major advantage over solvent-borne paints in that they released no toxic fumes into the atmosphere. As well as reducing emissions, powder coatings avoided the problem of waste disposal, as any stray powder was collected and reused. By contrast, wet paint always had a residual waste which had to be disposed of.

Worldwide, the market for powder coatings was growing 10–20 percent per year and was seen as a possible substitute for up to 50 percent of paint being applied to metal. In Europe, where the powder process was pioneered, the substitution already amounted to roughly 20 percent compared to about 10 percent in the United States. Although major user groups included automotive component suppliers, the metal furniture industry, and domestic appliance manufacturers, most powder makers were also looking into applying colored coatings to inferior grades of plastic, thus enabling them to compete with the attractive high-quality plastics used for chairs and garden furniture. As one analyst pointed out, the trick was to develop a paint that could be cured at relatively low temperatures, so that it did not melt the plastic. Other potential new applications included car engine blocks, baskets inside automatic washing machines, and the steel reinforcement bars used in concrete. One analyst commented that manufacturers were also experimenting with high-gloss powder finishes that could eventually be used for car body work. Worldwide, powder coatings accounted for only 2 percent of industry sales and were distributed among Europe, 54 percent; North America, 21 percent; and Japan, 10 percent.

Coil Coatings   The coil-coating segment derived its name from coiled steel or aluminum, which was given a decorative or industrial coating before the main manufacturing step or construction process. Typically, steel or aluminum coils were unrolled on automatic lines and the coating was applied by roller or spray. They were dried and hardened, and then the metal was coiled up again for shipment to manufacturers. Upon receipt, manufacturers could bend or stamp the metal into a required shape—such as a refrigerator cabinet or building cladding—without damaging the painted surface. In Europe, coil-coating customers included major metal producers such as British Steel, Sollac of France, Phoenix (part of the Belgian Cockerill group), Hoesch of Germany, Svenska Stal of Sweden, and La Magona of Italy.

In 1991, roughly 60 percent of coil-coated steel and 50 percent of coil-coated aluminum in Europe went to the building sector. Other important outlets were the automotive industry, domestic appliances, and packages. Also in Europe, it was estimated that, although manufacturers produced roughly 2.2 million tons of painted steel per year in the form of car and commercial vehicle bodies, 95 percent of that steel was painted after assembly. In other words, industry used only 110,000 tons of prepainted coil, and coil coaters hoped that more European manufacturers would follow the example of Nissan's Sunderland, United Kingdom, plant which used precoated car body panels. In terms of world paint sales, coil coatings represented less than 1 percent, or roughly 181 million liters, of industry sales. Geographically, these

sales were concentrated in Europe, 34 percent; North America, 33 percent; and Japan, 22 percent.

COMPETITION

Despite the takeover activity of the 1980s, in 1991, roughly 10,000 paint companies remained active around the world. In general, these competitors could be grouped into two categories: large multinational companies and primarily domestic manufacturers. In the first category, the ten largest companies accounted for 35 percent of industry sales, employed hundreds if not thousands of people, and were sometimes part of larger chemical companies. Typically, these players made and marketed coatings products in all, or almost all, of the industry's market segments, having attained their size by acquiring smaller companies. (Refer to Exhibit 7 for information on the top twelve paint companies.)

At the other end of the spectrum, small companies had sales under $10 million and employed fewer than ten persons. Normally, these smaller manufacturers concentrated production on one or only a few segments, usually in their home markets, and they sometimes augmented their sales by OEM relationships with other specialist paint companies.

ICI PAINTS' COMPETITIVE POSITION

Worldwide, ICI Paints' competitive position varied as a function of region and application segment (as shown in Exhibit 8).

Decorative

By far, decorative paints was ICI's strongest product line, accounting for 62 percent of the company's 1991 sales. Despite ICI Paints' worldwide strength in the decorative segment, however, it was not the biggest in some regional markets, and market shares varied considerably by country. In western Europe, for example, ICI had only a 5 percent market share, behind Akzo with 8 percent and Casco-Nobel with 7 percent. In the United Kingdom, on the other hand, ICI's Dulux product line accounted for an estimated 37 percent of all retail paint sales and included Dulux Vinyl Silk Emulsion, Dulux Matte Emulsion, Dulux Vinyl Soft

Exhibit 7 ● ICI's Principal Paint Competitors

	Coatings as % of group sales	1990 sales (million liters)	1990 sales ($ mn)	Average RONA 1987–1990	Key market sectors	Area of significant direct competition with ICI
INTERNATIONAL						
PPG	38%	515	$1,963	26%	Motors, Refinish, Decorative—U.S.	Refinish, Decorative—U.S.
BASF	7	485	c. 1,945	15	Motors, Refinish, Can	Refinish, Can
AKZO	23	485	2,160	15	Decorative—Europe, Refinish, Motors	Decorative—Europe, Refinish
Courtaulds	31	300	1,767	25	Marine, Can, Powders, Decorative	Can, Powders, Decorative—Australia
REGIONAL—AMERICAS						
Sherwin-Williams	100	535	2,338	26	Decorative, Refinish	Decorative
Dupont	3	265	c. 1,160	?	Motors, Refinish	
Valspar	100	230	539	24	Decorative, Can, Wood, Coil	Can
REGIONAL—EUROPE						
Casco Nobel	37	250	892	20	Decorative, Coil, Wood, General Industrial	Decorative—UK
Hoechst	4	220	1,160	c. 10	Motors, Refinish	Refinish
REGIONAL—ASIA						
Nippon	100	350	1,374	20	Motors, Refinish, Marine, Decorative, Coil	Decorative, Refinish, Motors
Kansai	100	275	1,080	19	Motors, Refinish, Decorative, Marine, Can, Coil	Refinish, Motors
ICI	13%	805	$2,927	17%	Decorative, Refinish, Can, Powders	

Sheen, Dulux Satinwood, Dulux Gloss Finish, Dulux Non-Drip Gloss, Dulux Definitions, Dulux Undercoat, Dulux Options, and Dulux Weathershed. Dulux was also known for its Natural Hints product line, consisting of nine or ten shades of off-white colors.

In North America, ICI Paints, through Glidden, its U.S. subsidiary, had an estimated 13 percent share of market, second only to Sherwin-Williams with 20 percent and well ahead of Benjamin Moore with 7 percent. And though ICI Paints had no decorative paint sales in Japan, it had a 5 percent market share in the rest of the Asia Pacific region, second only to Nippon Paint with 6 percent.

Industrial

Automotive Refinish   After the decorative segment, the automotive refinish segment was ICI Paints'

Exhibit 8 ● Breakdown of ICI Paints Sales by Region and Application Segment, 1991

| Segment | % Market Share by Region | | | *Application Segment's Share (%) of Total ICI Paint Revenues* |
	Europe	*N. America*	*Asia Pacific*	
Decorative	5%	13%	5%	62%
Auto OEM	4	0	15	3.4
Auto Refinish	11	1	14	13
Can	32	44	19	9
Coil	2	10	6	1.6
Powder	4	14	2	2

largest segment, representing roughly 13 percent of company turnover. Similar to the decorative segment, sales of paint in the automotive refinish segment varied by region. In western Europe, for example, ICI Paints had an estimated 11 percent market share, behind Hoechst with 19 percent; BASF, 18 percent; and even Akzo at 11 percent. In North America, ICI had only a 1 percent share of the refinish market, well behind Du Pont with 31 percent; PPG and Sherwin-Williams with 22 percent each; BASF, 13 percent; and Akzo, a 6 percent market share. Despite having no sales in this segment in Japan, ICI was in first place in the Asia Pacific region with a 14 percent market share, ahead of Korea Chemical with 13 percent; Kansai, 6 percent; and Kunsul and Nippon, each with 5 percent of the market.

Automotive OEM   With only 3.4 percent of ICI Paints' total sales, the automotive OEM coatings segment was among the smaller of the company's product lines. In western Europe, ICI had only a 4 percent share of this market segment, well behind PPG with 31 percent; Hoechst, 25 percent; BASF, 18 percent; and Akzo, 8 percent. In 1991, ICI sold the Canadian portion of its automotive OEM business to PPG. Thereafter, in North America and Japan, ICI was not present in the automotive OEM segment. In the rest of the Asia Pacific region, though, the company had a 15 percent market share in this segment, second to Korea

Chemical with 23 percent, but well ahead of Dong Ju with 9 percent; Goodlas Nerolac, with 7 percent; and Daihan and Shen Yan, with 5 percent each.

Can   Worldwide, can coatings accounted for roughly 9 percent of ICI Paints' sales. Geographically, ICI was a distant leader in western Europe with a 32 percent market share, well ahead of BASF with 16 percent, Dexter with 15 percent, and Courtaulds with 11 percent. ICI was also a formidable competitor in can coatings in North America with 44 percent of the market, more than twice the share of its closest rival—Valspar with 20 percent, and considerably ahead of BASF and Dexter with 12 percent and 10 percent of the market segment, respectively. Despite a strong presence in western Europe and North America in can coatings, ICI had no sales in this segment in Japan. It was, however, by far the leader in the rest of the Asia Pacific region with 19 percent of that market. In terms of market shares, its closest rivals in that part of the world were Courtaulds and Kunsul, each with a 9 percent share of market.

Coil   In 1991, sales of coil coatings by ICI accounted for a mere 1.6 percent of all sales; in western Europe, several competitors led in this segment. In decreasing order of market share, these competitors were Becker, 18 percent; Sigma 13 percent; Casco-Nobel, 12 percent; PPG, 9 percent; Akzo and Courtaulds, 7 percent each; Kemira, 3 percent; and BASF, Dexter, Grebe, Hoechst, Salchi, and ICI, 2 percent each. In the North American coil-coating segment, ICI was tied for fourth place with Lilly at a 10 percent market share; Valspar was the leader with 21 percent, followed by Morton, 19 percent; and Akzo, 16 percent. As with its other coatings, ICI had no sales in Japan but did have 6 percent of the Asia Pacific market for coil coatings, behind Nippon, 22 percent; Kansai, 17 percent; Korea Chemical, 13 percent; and Daihan, 10 percent.

Powder Powder coatings represented approximately 2 percent of ICI Paints' 1991 sales and, in western Europe, accounted for 4 percent of all sales in that segment. Powder competitors with greater market shares were DSM, 13 percent; Becker, 11 percent; Courtaulds, 9 percent; and Hoechst, 6 percent. In North America, ICI's powder paints had a 14 percent market share, second only to Morton with 17 percent, yet still ahead of Ferro with 13 percent; Valspar, 12 percent; and Fuller O'Brien, 9 percent. In the Asia Pacific region, ICI's powder coatings had only a 2 percent share of market; there, leading competitors and their market shares were Daihan and Korea Chemical, 15 percent each; Jotun, 9 percent; Chokwang, 4 percent; and Kunsul, 3 percent. To bolster its presence in the powder segment, in 1991 ICI began merger discussions with Ferro. Though the deal was never concluded, a merger of Ferro and ICI would have made that company the worldwide leader in powder coatings.

DESIGNING AN ORGANIZATION FOR THE 1990S

At ICI Paints, management sought to have an organization in the 1990s that was both global- and territory-oriented, that supported R&D centers of excellence in certain locations, and maximized resources among the company's different operations and locations. At the same time, the company intended to concentrate on its key application segments on a global basis, and wanted to exploit opportunities in the European Union and Asia Pacific regions.

ICI Paints' organization had already evolved over time and, by 1992, several changes had been made (refer to Exhibit 9). In both the North American and European regions, territorial general managers had been eliminated, moving the entire organization away from a territorial approach to a more brand-oriented structure.

Upon review, some of ICI Paints' executives felt that, in order to succeed in the future, the company needed to focus more directly on and better coordinate the activities of its main application segments. To this end, executives cited four advantages in moving toward a global product organization. First, it was believed that a global product organization would enhance ICI's ability to serve a customer base that was itself becoming increasingly global. For customers with global operations—such as can coating companies and automobile makers—a single product and service package that was applicable worldwide was bound to be appealing.

Second, executives cited the substantial cost benefits of standardizing ICI's products. To emphasize this point, it was mentioned that reducing the number of the company's refinish top coats from twenty-four to ten would save upward of $17 million on a product line with an annual turnover of approximately $300 million.

Third, executives believed that a global product organization would have additional benefits in terms of resource allocation. As an example, one manager mentioned that with increasingly expensive pollution abatement equipment, it did not make sense to have as many manufacturing plants. Rather, he stressed, the company should consider consolidating the number of plants and upgrading the remainder to world-class manufacturing standards. In fact, it was believed that some thirty of the company's sixty-four plants were common sites for a number of paint products.

Last, the executive mentioned that, in a truly global product organization, there would be a much greater chance to transfer experience from one market to another. For example, he described how an application developed for a can coating customer in North America, while not identical, had a number of parallels to the needs faced by can coating customers in Europe.

In contrast to these advantages, another group of executives pointed out that although some of ICI Paints' customer needs had become global, there were still substantial differences among individual markets. In the U.S. decorative segment, for example, Glidden had a 13 percent market share, was priced be-

Exhibit 9 ● Present Organization Chart, 1992

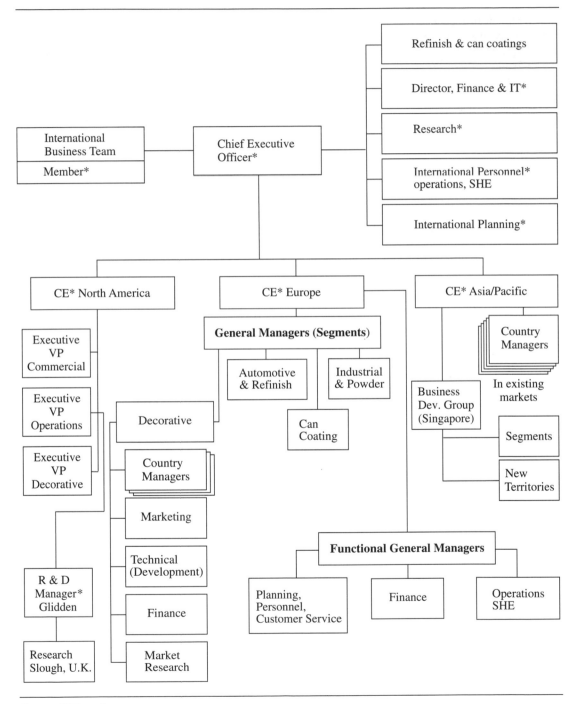

*Denotes IBT member.

low other brands, and distributed to DIY customers through mass merchandising outlets such as Wal-Mart. Because Glidden did not compete in the premium sector, it was seldom purchased by small-scale professional users like interior decorators. In contrast to Glidden in the United States, ICI's premium brand—Dulux—had a 37 percent market share in the United Kingdom. As a result, in 1993 ICI launched the Glidden brand in the United Kingdom, aiming it toward commercial contractors—a segment in which Dulux had been weak. John Thompson commented further:

To establish Dulux as a global brand, the U.S. market might be the next logical step. However, we estimated that a countrywide launch would cost ICI Paints $50 million over four to five years. An important issue would be not only determining the timing of such a large-scale project, but also resolving the positioning of Glidden versus Dulux.

In conjunction with trying to establish a global brand, the group went on to say that reducing the number of paint formulations and standards might well yield savings, but at the risk of jeopardizing ICI's sensitivity to local market conditions. "How would you feel," he asked, "if you worked at Anheuser-Busch and your 'local' can coating salesman was in fact based in the U.K?" Then too, the executives pointed out that, in theory, it was easy to reduce the number of manufacturing plants. In practice, however, local management and governments would hardly be receptive to the unemployment created due to such restructuring. As well, the executives men-

tioned that because many of ICI Paints' production assets were shared, business area general managers were largely responsible for business volume in an application segment, yet did not have full asset responsibility. In fact, no more than 75 percent of the company's assets could be clearly attributed to individual product lines.

SUMMARY

Before meeting with the IBT again, Scopes reviewed in his mind how his industry had changed and, in particular, what those changes implied for the organizational structure of ICI Paints. He recalled the words of one industry analyst, who said that the worldwide merger and acquisition activities of the 1980s were merely part of the ongoing globalization of the paint industry. At the start of the 1990s, the analyst believed that the globalization process was driven by three factors: first, the need to service customers with international manufacturing operations such as can makers, vehicle assembly, and domestic appliances; second, the need to service customers dealing with the aftercare of internationally traded products such as vehicles and ships; and last, the need to amortize the ever-growing costs of research, product development, and marketing over a broad volume base. With these thoughts in mind, Scopes turned to the IBT to renew the discussion on developing a new organizational structure at ICI Paints and the role of the territorial general managers, the business area general managers and, particularly, the international leaders in the 1990s.

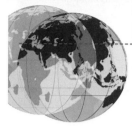

CASE 7

Gillette International's TRAC II

In mid-1972, Gillette International's management was considering the introduction of its new shaving system, the TRAC II, in some of its foreign markets. The blade had been introduced only nine months earlier in the U.S. market with considerable success. However, existing blade production capacity was limited, and the company could not serve all markets at the same time. Consequently, management was carefully evaluating which markets should get top priority for the TRAC II and how to combine this market selection process with an appropriate pricing strategy. In addition, the company was keenly aware of its main competitors, Schick of the United States and Wilkinson of the United Kingdom. The introduction of Gillette's newest product, the Platinum Plus, had been successful in most foreign markets; however, a number of executives believed the Platinum Plus's performance was below potential and wanted to avoid some of these negative experiences with the TRAC II introduction.

COMPANY BACKGROUND

The Gillette Company was a Boston-based consumer goods manufacturer with annual sales in 1971 of $730 million. The company was best known for its shaving

This case was prepared by Robert Howard under the direction of Jean-Pierre Jeannet, Visiting Professor at IMD and Professor of Marketing and International Business at Babson College. This case was prepared for class discussion rather than to illustrate either effective or ineffective handling of an administrative situation. This case was based on earlier work by Robert Roland, M.B.A. candidate at Babson College. Copyright © 1988 by IMD, Lausanne, Switzerland. The International Institute for Management Development (IMD), resulting from the merger between IMEDE, Lausanne, and IMI, Geneva, acquires and retains all rights. All rights reserved. Not to be used or reproduced without written permission from IMD, Lausanne, Switzerland.

product line, which was marketed worldwide and where Gillette continued to be the major company both in the United States and abroad.

The company's main operating units were Gillette North America, Gillette International, and other companies under the Diversified Companies group (see Exhibit 1). Gillette North America included four product divisions: Safety Razor, Paper Mate, Toiletries, and Personal Care.

The Safety Razor Division was responsible for the Gillette shaving business within the United States. The Toiletries Division marketed such products as deodorants, antiperspirants, shaving creams, and hair grooming products for both men and women, including the leading brands Right Guard and Foamy.

The Personal Care Division marketed women's toiletry products such as hair sprays, cream rinses, home permanents, and hair conditioners, as well as a line of portable hair dryers (Max, Super Max, and Max Plus for Men). After only one year in national distribution, Gillette held second place in the competitive market for hand-held dryers.

Gillette's Paper Mate Division was responsible for marketing writing instruments in the United States and was the leader in porous point pens. The Paper Mate Division also sold ballpoint pens and refills, broadtip markers, and glue and had recently entered the lower price segment with a new line of ballpoint and porous point pens.

The Diversified Companies group included a range of recent acquisitions located both in the United States and abroad. Acquired in 1967, Braun AG of West Germany was a leading manufacturer of electric housewares. Its largest lines were electric razors, coffeemakers, digital clocks, and some photographic products. In electric shavers, Braun was the market leader in Germany and its products were distributed in many European markets. Shavers were not sold in the United States due to a licensing agreement signed with an independent company in

Exhibit 1 ● Gillette Organization Chart

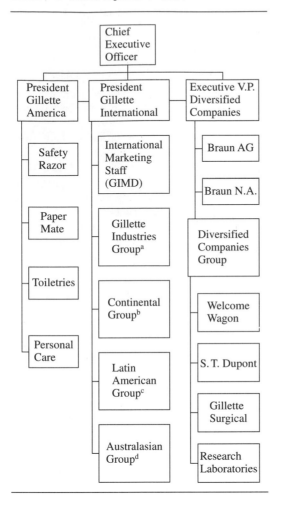

a. United Kingdom, S. Africa, and export departments to Ireland, Iceland, Greece, Eastern Europe, Near and Middle East, and African markets.
b. France, Germany, Italy, Spain, and affiliated sales companies in Scandinavia, Benelux, Alpine, and Portugal.
c. Argentina, Brazil, Colombia, Mexico, and Venezuela plus Latin American sales companies and export to Chile, Peru, Puerto Rico, Guatemala, Honduras, Costa Rica, Salvador, Nicaragua, Ecuador, Bolivia, Paraguay, Dominican Republic, Aruba, Curaçao, Guyana, Surinam, Barbados, and the Bahamas.
d. Australia, New Zealand, Japan, Hong Kong, and Southeast Asia.

Source: Company records.

1954 which was due to expire in 1975. Also part of this group was Welcome Wagon, a community service company acquired in 1971. Welcome Wagon was a service used by local businesses to acquaint new arrivals in the community with local companies and their services.

Safety Razor Division

The Safety Razor Division marketed Gillette's principal product line—shaving equipment and blades—in the U.S. market. Gillette was the world's leading blade manufacturer and the major factor in the U.S. market. The company marketed a full range of blades including double-edged stainless steel blades (Super Stainless Steel and Platinum Plus) as well as an older line of carbon steel blades (Super Blue, Blue, and Thin). Gillette sold its Techmatic Razor Blade and Lady Sure Touch on the band concept. In the United States, the Safety Razor Division also imported a line of disposable lighters under the name Cricket which was produced by Gillette's S. T. Dupont affiliate in France. Starting in the fall of 1971, the division began marketing the TRAC II, Gillette's latest shaving product based on a twin blade shaving system. 1971 had brought record sales and profits for the division, and the outlook for 1972 indicated another top performance.

International Division

Gillette International was responsible for marketing the majority of Gillette's products abroad. The company sold its products in more than 170 countries and territories, with shaving products accounting for most of the volume. International sales had been steadily increasing as a percentage of corporate sales and accounted for more than 40 percent of Gillette's volume. Because of the higher profitability of international operations, Gillette International accounted for half of the company's profits, as seen in Exhibit 2.

The president of Gillette International was also the executive vice president for international operations at corporate headquarters in Boston. The president was supported by a staff of international marketing experts located at Gillette's International Marketing Department (GIMD) in Boston. The staff was responsible for interacting with regional and

Exhibit 2 ● The Gillette Company Development of Sales and Profits, 1967–1971 (in millions of dollars)

Year	Total company		Blades and razors		Foreign operations	
	SALES	NET PROFITS	SALES	NET PROFITS	SALES	NET PROFITS
1967	$428	$57	$193	$38	$167	$20
1968	553	62	238	40	221	23
1969	610	65	250	44	256	29
1970	673	66	262	46	289	33
1971	730	62	270	41	327	33

country level managers on marketing, planning, and strategic issues and would set priorities for introduction when a supply of products was limited.

Reporting to Gillette International's president were four regional managers, each responsible for a group of markets. The Gillette Industries Group in London controlled Gillette operations in the United Kingdom and South Africa and export operations to Ireland, Iceland, Greece, eastern Europe, the Middle East, and Africa. The group's only manufacturing facility was located in the United Kingdom.

Also located in London was the Continental Group, with responsibility for subsidiaries in France, Germany, Spain, and Italy. The Continental Group also controlled the marketing operations of affiliated sales companies in Scandinavia, the Benelux countries, Portugal, Switzerland, and Austria. This group's plant facilities were located in Germany, France, and Spain.

Gillette International's other two regional operations were based in Boston. The Latin America Group headed subsidiary operations in Argentina, Brazil, Colombia, Mexico, and Venezuela and was responsible for export and sales in Chile, Peru, Puerto Rico, and all of the countries in Central America and the Caribbean area. The group's manufacturing plants were located in Brazil, Argentina, Colombia, and Mexico.

Gillette International's fourth regional group was the Australasian Group with responsibility for Australia, New Zealand, Japan, Hong Kong, and Southeast Asia. Its major plant facility was located in Australia.

THE DEVELOPMENT OF SHAVING TECHNOLOGY

Carbon Steel Blades

King C. Gillette, the company founder, introduced the first safety razor in 1895. The company was granted an exclusive patent in 1904 on an improved version of its blade, which was followed by the development of the double-edged blade. In the 1930s, Gillette introduced carbon steel blades under the brand name Gillette Blue. These blades were thinner than earlier blades, had lacquer applied to the surface, and offered an improvement in shaving comfort and blade life.

The introduction of the Super Blue blade in 1960 represented a quantum step in technology. The Super Blue came with a silicon coated treatment which was baked on to give it extra hardness. This new process significantly improved the quality of shaving, although the shave quality tended to decline more rapidly than with previous blades after reaching a certain point. The blade was priced at 6.9 cents per unit and quickly became the standard in the industry. Customers once accustomed to the more comfortable shave of the Super Blue found it very difficult to return to the older carbon blades. For about eighteen months, Gillette was able to exploit this product advantage before competitors could introduce similar products.

Stainless Steel Blades

In August 1961, another quantum leap in shaving technology occurred when Wilkinson Sword, a U.K. company, introduced a Teflon-coated stainless steel blade. The coating process was actually developed earlier by Gillette, and Wilkinson paid a royalty to Gillette for its use. Stainless steel was much harder than carbon steel and could absorb the high temperature generated in the Teflon coating process. However, because of this hardness, a stainless steel blade could not be sharpened as easily as a carbon blade. Stainless steel blades offered a high quality shave consistent over a relatively long time and were a considerable improvement for the user over carbon steel blades. Wilkinson introduced its new blade first in the United Kingdom and then launched it in the United States but did not have sufficient supply to satisfy the entire U.S. market. In response, both Gillette and Schick, the principal U.S. competitors, countered with crash development programs before Wilkinson could become fully established in major markets.

In 1963, Gillette introduced a Teflon-coated stainless steel blade under the brand name Stainless (Silver Gillette in Europe). The major hurdle to overcome was the manufacturing process, as the new blades required specially designed equipment. The Stainless blades were improved by a factor of 2 to 3 in blade life over the carbon, double-edged blades. Gillette was able to maintain market leadership in the United States because Wilkinson moved too cautiously with its product rollout and did not have a fully developed marketing function.

In 1965, Gillette introduced its first modern shaving system consisting of the Techmatic razor band technology. Rather than using single blades one after another, the Techmatic came equipped with a cartridge that contained a band of blades. The user would never have to touch a single blade; thus the Techmatic offered added convenience although blade quality was equal to the stainless steel blades. Techmatic's introduction was well timed and had a lead of six months over all competitors, resulting in a 2 percent gain in market share. The Techmatic was Gillette's first entry into shaving systems other than the double-edged blade.

Platinum Treated Blades

In 1969, Gillette made another improvement in its blades by adding a platinum chromium alloy. This new blade, marketed in the United States under the brand name Platinum Plus, further increased blade life and shaving comfort but was not considered a technological breakthrough. The blade was also introduced in European markets under various names which included the word *platinum.*

In 1970 it was once more Wilkinson of the United Kingdom reaching the market with an innovation. Wilkinson launched its Wilkinson "Bonded" blade, consisting of a single blade enclosed in a plastic casing. The term *bonded* meant that the blade remained permanently fixed in a cartridge. Although Gillette had been working on a twin blade cartridge, it was not ready for product launch at the time of the Wilkinson introduction. Fortunately for Gillette, Wilkinson did not have sufficient resources to make a major impact on the market.

In 1971, after combining Techmatic plastics knowledge with an innovative twin blade design, Gillette introduced the TRAC II. This was a major evolution from the single blade, double-edged razor and provided an entirely new concept in blade making. Although Wilkinson's Bonded razor gave the public its first experience with a cartridge product, the TRAC II represented the next step forward in cartridge design. Combined with Gillette's previous blade expertise, this shaving product was the most advanced in the industry in terms of quality and blade life (see Exhibit 3).

COMPETITION

Gillette Experience Prior to 1960

During the early development of the shaving industry, Gillette had almost no significant competition. The company got its first major break during World War I when U.S. soldiers were required to be clean shaven. By the end of the war, Gillette had sold some 3.5 million razors and about 52 million blades to the military forces, giving Gillette a substantial advantage over other razor companies. Another big step occurred in 1939 when Gillette spent 50 percent of its entire advertising budget to sponsor the U.S. baseball World Series. By World War II, Gillette had the dominant share of the blade market. Market shares reached an all-time high in the early 1940s with 55–60 percent in the double-edged segment and about 40 percent of the entire market. The advent of television gave Gillette another boost.

Exhibit 3 ● Blade Quality versus Blade Life

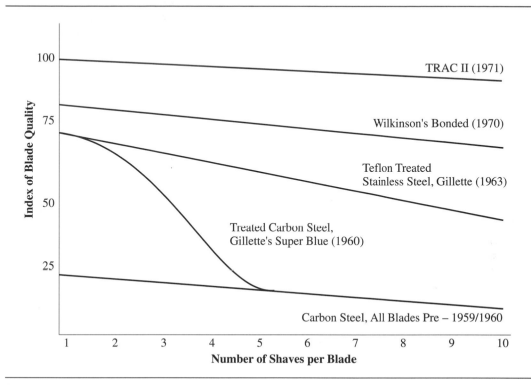

Source: Company records.

Gillette did not face real double-edged blade competition in the United States or abroad until the early 1960s. Before that time, Wilkinson of the United Kingdom was not a major factor and Schick was only of minor concern in the United States. Gillette was much more concerned with electric razors, particularly abroad, where the pricing of electric shavers tended to be lower than in the United States. With a smaller price gap between electric and wet shaving and with many customers preferring electric over wet shaving, Gillette was gaining market share in a stagnant or even declining segment.

Recent Developments: The Platinum Plus Experience

Gillette International's latest worldwide product introduction was the launch of Platinum Plus blades in early 1970. The Platinum Plus represented a product improvement and had been well received in the United States in the fall of 1969. In 1970, a number of key foreign markets were offered access to the Platinum Plus technology. However, because production machinery was only available in limited volume, Gillette had to introduce the product selectively. By 1972, all markets had been introduced to the Platinum Plus blade albeit with varied success.

From the outset, Gillette International gave its local managers considerable freedom in selecting the positioning strategy for the new blade. As a result, different countries chose different strategies. Some market introductions were unsuccessful by Gillette standards, and the company wanted to learn from these mistakes before introducing the TRAC II.

After reviewing the introduction of Platinum Plus in Europe, management came to a consensus on what had gone wrong. To gain further insight on the European scene, management looked closely at the U.K., German, and Brazilian experiences.

The U.K. subsidiary, faced with intensive competition in the U.K. market and a scarcity of retail shelf space, had decided to introduce Platinum Plus as its new top-of-the-line blade in place of Super Silver. Super Silver and Wilkinson's top blade had been similarly priced and selling at about the same volume. When Gillette withdrew Super Silver and introduced the higher priced Platinum Plus (with platinum coating), the company lost some of its share to Wilkinson because some users were unwilling to upgrade to the new product. As a result, Gillette lost overall market share and had not been able to regain it.

In West Germany, the Gillette subsidiary also faced intensive competition from Wilkinson. With a surplus of blade products in the retail trade, the German subsidiary opted to provide an improved product by adding a platinum coating to its top-of-the-line brand Super Silver and introduce the new product as Super Silver Platine. However, this variation brought only mixed success for Gillette.

By contrast, the Brazilian operation went ahead with the largely U.S. type strategy, by adding the new Platinum Plus to its existing product line, which included the Super Silver. This strategy proved successful. As a result of the Platinum Plus experience, management at Gillette International felt that local management should not decide on the introductory program. Rather than local companies proposing their own strategies, Gillette International's management preferred to give the local subsidiaries detailed instructions. If the decision did not suit the local market, then local management could argue its case. At the start, however, there would be a more standardized marketing and positioning strategy largely based on the U.S. experience.

Schick in the United States and Abroad

Schick, a fully owned subsidiary of Warner-Lambert, was Gillette's major competitor. Schick Safety Razor Co. manufactured injector and double-edged blades in the United States, Canada, Sweden, and the Netherlands as well as in Japan, where Schick was the dominant company in the wet shaving segment. Sales of Schick in 1972 were estimated at $47 million. In the

United States and most other markets, Schick's market share was about one-third of Gillette's or less.

Schick's marketing strategy tended to emphasize print advertising or promotions such as free samples, in-store displays, or write-in offers. Schick was capable of introducing new blade types quickly and could be expected to react to Gillette within twelve to eighteen months after a new product introduction. But, like Gillette, Schick was constrained by the scarcity of machinery needed to introduce new products. In January 1972, Schick had entered Schick Super II, a product similar to TRAC II, into the shaving system market on the West Coast of the United States. By mid-1972, however, Schick Super II had still not reached full national distribution. Full-scale national television support had also not yet taken place. Most television exposure in the U.S. market was through partial sponsorship of the 1972 summer Olympics which were going on at the time.

Wilkinson on All Continents

Wilkinson, a British company, was not a serious competitor to Gillette until it introduced a treated stainless steel blade in 1961. Wilkinson had been marketing an untreated stainless blade since the mid-1950s with little success. Total sales for 1971 amounted to about £24 million ($60 million), of which the shaving portion accounted for about £18 million ($40 million). Wilkinson had experienced growth rates of 20 percent in recent years and had approximately 75 percent of its sales overseas.

Wilkinson operated its main manufacturing facilities in the United Kingdom, where it employed more than 1,300 people. The company's only other full manufacturing facility was in West Germany. Partial manufacturing and packaging were done in the United States, Australia, South Africa, and Spain.

When the treated stainless steel blade was first introduced, Wilkinson did not have sufficient capacity to satisfy demand, and the result was only a 20 percent erosion of Gillette's U.K. market share. After its introduction in the United Kingdom, Wilkinson moved into the West German market in 1962 and, on a limited basis, into the United States at the end of 1962. In addition to capacity constraints, Wilkinson did not have a fully developed marketing operation outside its key markets and, thus, could never capitalize on the Teflon-coated stainless steel blade. The only exception was the U.K. market, where Wilkinson's market share was larger than Gillette's.

Wilkinson's market share and market position differed considerably from market to market. As the major domestic producer, Wilkinson enjoyed a large share of the U.K. market. Its introduction of the "Bonded" razor ahead of Gillette had helped consolidate its market share further. It was estimated that Wilkinson's share was moving close to 50 percent for all blades sold in the United Kingdom. In Germany, Wilkinson continued to defend its share of about 30 percent. The same local subsidiary was also responsible for selling in Austria and Switzerland, where the company's market share had been increasing.

In Italy, Wilkinson had been able to increase its market share to about 20 percent as a result of introducing the Wilkinson Bonded system. Although Wilkinson maintained its own subsidiary in Italy, sales and distribution were handled by Colgate-Palmolive. In France, distribution and marketing were in the hands of Reckitt & Colman. In Spain, the company had started construction of full-scale manufacturing facilities which were expected to come on stream in 1974.

In other European countries, Wilkinson also relied on the distribution arrangements with established consumer products companies. In Denmark, Norway, Sweden, and Holland, Wilkinson products were marketed by Colgate-Palmolive. Wilkinson blades were marketed in Greece by Unilever, one of the world's largest consumer products companies, and in Ireland by Beecham, a U.K.-based personal products company. Distribution was also handled by Reckitt & Colman in South Africa, where Wilkinson's share had increased beyond 10 percent with the introduction of the Bonded blade. Wilkinson blades were also distributed in many Middle Eastern countries out of a Beirut office.

In Asia, Wilkinson blades were marketed in Japan, Australia, and New Zealand. The Australian market position improved considerably with the introduction of the Bonded blade. In Japan, Wilkinson was marketed through Lion, a major Japanese personal products company.

In the United States, where Wilkinson's share was about 10 percent, marketing had been handled exclusively since 1970 by Colgate-Palmolive, the large, U.S.-based multinational consumer products company. In Canada, where Wilkinson had a market share of about 20 percent, its blades were distributed by John A. Houston Ltd. Throughout Latin America, Wilkinson used independent distributors to market in Brazil, Colombia, the Dominican Republic, Haiti, Paraguay, Uruguay, and Venezuela.

THE TRAC II OPPORTUNITY

Manufacturing Overview

The manufacturing process of the TRAC II system consisted of three distinct phases: the manufacturing of the blade, the manufacturing of cartridge parts, and the assembly of these blades and cartridge parts into the TRAC II system. Each one of these stages offered particular challenges to Gillette. The key problem, however, had turned from making the system work to adding sufficient capacity. Although it was difficult to forecast exactly how much blade capacity would be available for Gillette International, it was felt that each gain in annual volume of 150 million units would take twelve to eighteen months.

Blade Manufacture

The blade manufacturing process alone consisted of six stages. In the first stage a continuous strip of soft steel, purchased in coils the width of one blade, was mounted on a wheel for perforation. Perforations in the steel served as guides for additional blade cartridge components and also enabled soap and water to pass through. Oil used in cutting these perforations was removed before the steel passed into a hardening furnace with three temperature zones. The hardening gave the blades an extended life of eleven to fourteen shaves. After leaving the furnace, the steel was cooled in an annealing process before being rewound onto a wheel for sharpening.

In the sharpening process, the perforated and hardened steel strip was ground to remove rough steel from the blade's cutting edge, followed by rough sharpening and honing (refined sharpening process). Once the honing process had put a cutting edge on the blade, the steel strip was cut into individual blade lengths and the individual blades airblown onto blade holders. Blade holders transferred stacks of razor blades to blade magazines, which passed through a washing cycle before vacuum phase sputtering.

The contents of each magazine were automatically unloaded onto a sputtering knife. Twelve sputtering knives were positioned around a sputtering post of chromium and platinum with the cutting edge of the razor blades facing the sputtering post. Using a technique known as ion deposition, chromium and platinum were transferred from the sputtering post to the blades' cutting edge.

In the final step, the blade edges were coated with Teflon and passed through a sintering furnace which baked the Teflon onto the blade and enhanced the bonding of chromium and platinum to the razor's cutting surface.

Cartridge Assembly

Each TRAC II cartridge contained two individual razor blades, as well as several plastic and metal parts. Cartridge assembly began with black plastic guard caps that were fed from a bowl of caps into a chute, with each cap positioned so that its plastic alignment studs were face up.

The first razor blade in the cartridge assembly was set on a guard cap, with the plastic alignment studs passing through the blade perforations. A spacer was set on top of the first blade, followed by a second blade and, lastly, the top plastic guard cap. This was a very delicate operation since the relationship of the two blades to the cartridge was critical to providing shaving comfort. A slight pressure was applied to seal the assembled cartridge before it was moved to an automated inspection stage.

If the automated scanning device verified that all parts were included and properly aligned in the cartridge assembly, the cartridge was relayed to a dispenser tray. A plastic cartridge dispenser was positioned over the dispenser tray and five TRAC II cartridges pressed into place. Once assembled, these dispensers were transported to another area for final packaging. (For an overview of the manufacturing process, see Exhibit 4.)

Equipment as Bottleneck

Manufacturing equipment for the production of razor blades had specific requirements and was not purchased on the open market. Instead, Gillette produced its own equipment in company-owned tool shops in Boston, the United Kingdom, and France. For TRAC II production, new equipment was needed for blade perforation, hardening, and sharpening. New equipment was also needed for the production of plastic elements such as guard caps and dispensers as well as for assembly and loading operations. The longest lead times (twelve to eighteen months) were for the procurement of sharpening equipment. For plastic parts production, molds had to be produced which also required high-precision tools.

For years, Gillette tool shops had been operating at full capacity. In recent years, Gillette had suffered from undercapacity in production, with output often a step or two behind actual demand for Gillette blades. As a result, Gillette's top management decided to add to existing capacity so that manufacturing capacity would always exceed demand by 10 percent. Consequently, just when the tool shops were busy providing this additional equipment, TRAC II increased the burden even more. It was estimated that Gillette was able to add about 150 million units of TRAC II (dispensers containing five cartridges) every twelve months, or about 12.5 million units per month. The Boston plant was using all its output to satisfy demand in the United States, and the North American division wanted still more products out of the newly planned capacity expansion. Given the nature of tool production, there was no short-term solution for expanding total output beyond the rate of 12.5 million units per month.[1]

PRICING ISSUES

Pricing was a main consideration in the launch of TRAC II abroad. Gillette International viewed pricing as the key to increasing market share and to maintaining or improving margins in each market. Pricing was dependent on a number of factors, any one of which could be used as a basis for selecting a final price policy. These factors were production costs, marketing costs, and competitor pricing.

---

1. The 150 million dispensers refer to annualized capacity increase; for example, after twelve months, the annualized output for the next twelve months would be increased by 150 million units (or 750 million blades).

Exhibit 4 ● Gillette TRAC II Manufacturing Overview

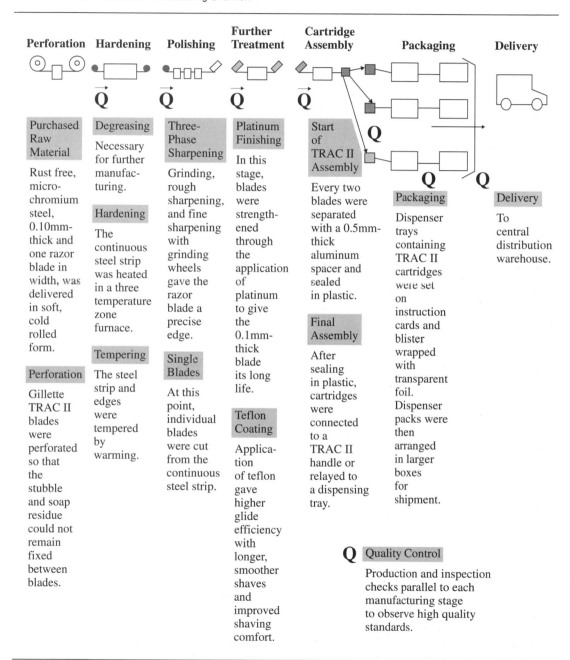

Perforation	Hardening	Polishing	Further Treatment	Cartridge Assembly	Packaging	Delivery

Purchased Raw Material

Rust free, micro-chromium steel, 0.10mm-thick and one razor blade in width, was delivered in soft, cold rolled form.

Perforation

Gillette TRAC II blades were perforated so that the stubble and soap residue could not remain fixed between blades.

Degreasing

Necessary for further manufacturing.

Hardening

The continuous steel strip was heated in a three temperature zone furnace.

Tempering

The steel strip and edges were tempered by warming.

Three-Phase Sharpening

Grinding, rough sharpening, and fine sharpening with grinding wheels gave the razor blade a precise edge.

Single Blades

At this point, individual blades were cut from the continuous steel strip.

Platinum Finishing

In this stage, blades were strengthened through the application of platinum to give the 0.1mm-thick blade its long life.

Teflon Coating

Application of teflon gave higher glide efficiency with longer, smoother shaves and improved shaving comfort.

Start of TRAC II Assembly

Every two blades were separated with a 0.5mm-thick aluminum spacer and sealed in plastic.

Final Assembly

After sealing in plastic, cartridges were connected to a TRAC II handle or relayed to a dispensing tray.

Packaging

Dispenser trays containing TRAC II cartridges were set on instruction cards and blister wrapped with transparent foil. Dispenser packs were then arranged in larger boxes for shipment.

Delivery

To central distribution warehouse.

Q Quality Control

Production and inspection checks parallel to each manufacturing stage to observe high quality standards.

Pricing Based on Production Costs

Production costs at Gillette were classified into two parts: manufacturing costs and initial investments costs. Manufacturing costs were defined as the sum of direct material, direct labor, and variable manufacturing overhead. The manufacturing costs of the new TRAC II were about twice the cost of the Platinum Plus blade, which averaged $.03 per unit. Initial investment costs for new processes at Gillette were normally 20 percent higher than prior blade processes. Added capital investment for the TRAC II, however, was substantially higher than for previous blade manufacturing processes because of the technology level and amounted to $10 million per 100 million units (dispensers at five blades each). As with the older line of blades, these investment costs would be reduced over time as volume increased and added equipment depreciated. A typical depreciation period was about six years. If the TRAC II were priced on the basis of total production costs, Gillette's typical ex-factory price for blades would give the company a gross margin of 70 percent. Out of this gross margin, the company would have to cover all direct marketing and general administrative expenses.

Pricing Based on Marketing Costs

Gillette's marketing costs tended to be higher for a new brand since the bulk of advertising expenditures would shift to the latest product. At the time of the TRAC II introduction, advertising expenditures for overseas markets were concentrated on Techmatic and Platinum Plus. If these expenditures were to be shifted to the TRAC II, management needed to decide on the changeover rate. Under ideal circumstances, these expenditures could be shifted at the same rate as customers upgraded brands. In the United States, the Marketing Research Group had charted trade-up patterns since 1960. When the Super Blue was introduced, it cannibalized Blue Blade sales, enabling Super Blue to achieve predominant market share after only eighteen months. Similarly, when Platinum Plus was added to Gillette's product line, customers traded up from the stainless steel blade at roughly the same rate. This type of data was not available for countries other than the United States, but management felt it could use these data as an estimate for trends in the European marketplace.

Initial interest in and purchase of the TRAC II was particularly dependent on two things. One was the newness of the product. Management in Boston felt that once the TRAC II was launched, there would be a certain period of vulnerability because of its level of sophistication. Whether trading up from a previous Gillette product or switching brands, a consumer would have to spend an initial $1.50 for a TRAC II handle to accommodate TRAC II cartridges. Secondly, therefore, the potential for cartridge sales was dependent on the number of TRAC II handles. The only experience Gillette had had with such a sophisticated trade-up was the Techmatic. Excluding the Techmatic, all of Gillette's other successor blades were compatible with the same razor handle. Hence, the level of advertising had to be sufficient to generate early sales of the sophisticated TRAC II while at the same time balancing demand with a limited supply in each key market.

Pricing to Gain Market Share

The pricing policy chosen to cover production costs and advertising expenses would certainly influence market share. In the past, a new product would be priced at a certain premium over its predecessor. The size of this price premium would have varying effects on resulting market share. Given Gillette's pricing strategy with country by country differences, adding a 10–20 percent premium for a sophisticated new product such as TRAC II could result in success in some markets and low performance in others.

Past new product introductions served as an example. On average, Gillette's Super Blue sold at a 38 percent premium over Gillette's Blue. The first stainless steel blade, marketed as Super Silver in most European markets, was sold at about twice the retail price of the Super Blue.

The Gillette Techmatic was marketed at a substantial premium over the Platinum Plus. The amount of this price premium depended on the various competitive factors and differed from market to market. In 1971, the premium was about 50 percent over the Stainless Steel in both Germany and the United Kingdom. However, the price base was not identical, and actual retail prices for the two markets differed.

Given the key market data in Exhibits 5 and 6, Gillette management was concerned with creating a

Exhibit 5 ● Size of Key Markets

Market	Estimated blade sales (1972) (in millions of blades)
United States	1,772
United Kingdom	361
West Germany	296
France	429
Italy	266
Spain	160
Canada	170
Argentina	250
Brazil	500
Mexico	310
Sweden	35
Holland	50
Japan	1,300

Source: Company records.

pricing policy that would lead to intracompany trade-up as well as intercompany brand switching.

Options for Gillette International

Having reviewed the manufacturing costs and anticipated demand patterns. Gillette management considered three pricing strategies: (1) in accordance with production cost differences, (2) at a constant premium over the now top Platinum Plus, or (3) at a uniform world price for all countries.

Pricing in relation to production costs would allow Gillette its existing margin structure and would take into consideration the new equipment investment. On the other hand, there were some markets where margins were lower than desired, and a constant margin would not increase margins in these countries.

If management chose to price at a constant premium, there would be a real potential for price dif-ferences between markets. Such price differences between markets would not be easy to equilibrate once a product had been established at a certain price level. Furthermore, the differences could lead to product arbitrage (parallel imports).

The threat of parallel imports had always been a problem for Gillette and encouraged some managers to support the world pricing policy. Although this policy would alleviate parallel imports, it could put the TRAC II price out of reach in some markets, which would affect market share. And, although this policy would reduce product arbitrage, a uniform price would open up doors to competitors with various lower cost products and with identical products priced at a lower level.

Whichever policy was chosen, Gillette's management constantly had to keep the competition in mind. Gillette had to continue and increase its TRAC II supply with one-third of all new output going to the U.S. market. The decision to go international had been made, but only the remaining two-thirds of new output could be spread among those key markets.

Gillette had to move rapidly to reach its overseas markets before Schick introduced its Super II and before Wilkinson had a replacement for its own Bonded blade. The importance of getting to a market first was reinforced by the Marketing Research Group's findings on timing and market share. That meant, all things being equal regarding pricing, quality of product, and distribution, that the market share potentials to the second, third, and fourth entrants would be no more than 30 percent, 18 percent, and 12 percent, respectively, of the market leader.

Based on previous experience, the window of opportunity for the TRAC II would last twelve to eighteen months. Given that this time lead represented the number of months Schick and Wilkinson needed to invest several million dollars to achieve production capability, management had to make its decisions soon. Furthermore, the precise combination of pricing policy and selected target markets had to match and preserve Gillette's image as world leader in the shaving industry.

Exhibit 6 ● Key Market Shaving Data

	MALE POPULATION (IN MILLIONS)	% OF WET SHAVERS	Share of market			Manufacturing		
			G	S	W	G	S	W
United States	67.6	73%	58	23	10	X	X	
United Kingdom	19.7	72	40	3	42	X		X
W. Germany	21.7	40	59	6	31	X		X
France	17.4	50	65	23	5	X		
Italy	17.2	74	65	3	19			
Spain	11.7	48	70	17	4	X		X
Canada	7.4	58	55	23	19	X	X	
Argentina	8.1	75	95	1	0	X		
Brazil	21.5	97	85	3	4	X		
Mexico	10.0	95	80	5	0	X		
Sweden	3.1	39	54	45	1		X	
Holland	4.6	32	60	30	3		X	
Japan	40.0 (approx.)	n/a	14	64	n/a			

Source: Company records.

*Share of male wet shavers.

Note: n/a = not available; G = Gillette; S = Schick; W = Wilkinson.

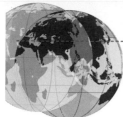

CASE 8

Toyota: Repositioning the Brand in Europe (A)

February 1999: As Toyota Motor Europe—Marketing and Engineering (TMME) entered the new millennium, the mood in the company was upbeat and realistic. In 1998 Toyota had achieved record sales in 10 European countries, and TMME had topped Nissan's sales in Europe for the first time ever. Further growth was expected; import restrictions that had hindered the progress of all Japanese brands were due to be lifted entirely on December 31, 1999. At last, Toyota could really make progress in Europe.

The appointment of Mr. Fujio Cho as President of Toyota Motor Company in early 1999 provided additional impetus. Mr. Cho took over from Mr. Hiroshi Okuda. Mr. Okuda led Toyota's globalization efforts and later became Chairman of the Board. Mr. Okuda had made a firm commitment to European operations by setting up a new factory in France and putting Toyota Europe on a growth strategy. In addition, he installed a new President at TMME and hired a senior marketing executive from the Volkswagen Group. Mr. Cho fully endorsed the objective of increasing Toyota's European market share from 3% to 5% by 2005. For TMME's Corporate Identity & Brand Management Team, this was a challenge to relish:

We will develop Toyota into an important European player. This will neither be easy, nor will it happen overnight. If we reach world standards with regards to customer satisfaction and product experience, then we can be successful.

Research Associates George Rädler and Madoka Hokamura prepared this case under the direction of Professors Sean Meehan and Dominique Turpin as a basis for class discussion rather than to illustrate either effective or ineffective handling of a business situation. Selected data in the case have been disguised and are not intended for research purposes. Copyright © 2000 by IMD—International Institute for Management Development, Lausanne, Switzerland. All rights reserved. Not to be used or reproduced without written permission directly from IMD, Lausanne, Switzerland.

Among the challenges the Corporate Identity & Brand Management Team needed to address urgently was brand image. There was a strong feeling within TMME that the brand was poorly positioned relative to its potential and revitalization was in order. A team led by TMME's Marketing Director had been looking at this issue and needed to recommend a way forward.

JAPANESE CAR MANUFACTURERS—FACING NEW REALITIES

For many of Japan's car manufacturers, the ongoing recession in Japan had been a "nightmare." Domestic car sales had plummeted because of economic uncertainty and a weak replacement market for cars. Within one decade, the domestic replacement cycle for cars had been prolonged from 7 to more than 11 years.

Contrary to industry expectations, the Japanese market had declined by 12% to only 5.9 million vehicles (passenger cars and trucks) in 1998. In the case of Nissan, sales had dropped by 13.4%, and capacity utilization had hit levels below 60%. Having lost money in six out of seven years, it had been forced to sell a 36.8% equity stake to Renault in 1999. This followed Ford's taking of a 33% stake in Mazda.

Never before had foreign markets been so important for the Japanese manufacturers. However, they faced fresh obstacles, in particular the strengthening of the yen. Selling purely on price was no longer an easy option.

TOYOTA MOTOR COMPANY

The Toyota Motor Company (TMC) was established in 1937. It evolved from being a major domestic into one of a handful of global players (*refer to Exhibit 1 for an overview of Toyota's global activities*). Toyota's corporate culture was a very successful mix of traditional values like quality and cutting-edge technological innovations. Its lean manufacturing system had turned it into one of the most profitable auto manufacturers in the world.

In 1997, largely to help insulate it from adverse domestic economic conditions, Toyota announced the "New International Business Plan," a spending package that totaled $16.2 billion over three years. The expansion would also help Toyota reap economies of scale, mainly in R&D and marketing functions. The plan included capacity expansion to 1.2 million units in North America and 400,000 units in Europe. The expansion was led by a set of criteria that Toyota employees referred to internally as guiding principles (*refer to* **Figure 1**).

As for all Japanese carmakers, 1998 was a tough year for Toyota at home and in the rest of Asia. In Japan, sales fell 12.3% to 1.67 million units; in Asia,

Figure 1: Toyota's 7 Guiding Principles

1. Honor the language and spirit of the law of every nation and undertake open and fair corporate activities to be a good corporate citizen of the world.

2. Respect the culture and customs of every nation and contribute to economic and social development through corporate activities in the communities.

3. Dedicate ourselves to providing clean and safe products and to enhancing the quality of life everywhere through all our activities.

4. Create and develop advanced technologies and provide outstanding products and services fulfilling the needs of customers worldwide.

5. Foster a corporate culture that enhances individual creativity and teamwork value, while honoring mutual trust and respect between labor and management.

6. Pursue growth in harmony with the global community through innovative management.

7. Work with business partners in research and creation to achieve stable, long-term growth and mutual benefits, while keeping ourselves open to new partnerships.

sales fell 48% to 131,000 units. In contrast, Toyota's sales in North America grew by 14.8% to 1.49 million units. Europe was also up, growing 15% to 541,000 units. Other parts of the world accounted for sales of 700,000 units.

By 1998 Toyota and its affiliated brands (Lexus and Daihatsu cars, as well as truck maker Hino Motors) was the third largest car company in the world, producing some 5.2 million vehicles (*refer to* **Exhibit 2** *for market shares worldwide*).

Mr. Cho, the President of TMC, was fully committed to making Toyota a success in Europe. In the mid-1980s Mr. Cho was a team member for Toyota's first plant in the US. He later became President of the Toyota's American manufacturing arm. Upon his return to Japan, he was in charge of corporate planning—one of his major assignments included the European strategy. One of Mr. Cho's close allies was Mr. Akira Imai. After spending 10 years with Toyota in the US and Canada, Mr. Imai returned to Japan in 1996. There he was instrumental in developing Toyota's business expansion strategy for Europe. In January 1999 he became President and CEO of TMME.

THE EUROPEAN MARKET FOR AUTOMOBILES

With 1998 sales of 14.3 million vehicles (up from 11.9 million in 1994), the European market was one of the world's largest (*refer to* **Exhibit 3** *for the historical data on market size*). Germany, Italy, the UK, France and Spain were particularly critical as they accounted for over 80% of all Western European sales. Most of the growth resulted from niche markets, such as sport utility vehicles (SUVs) and multi-purpose vehicles (MPVs). MPVs had grown from 1.5% of the total market in 1994 to 5.7% by 1998. However, between 1994 and 1998, traditional mass-market segments such as "small high" had fallen from 28.1% to 24.4%. Ford was the only non-European brand to make an impact on the market. Its mainstream models, aimed at the so-called "medium," "small high" and "small low/economy" segments, were in particular demand (*refer to* **Exhibit 4** *for the top 10 selling brands and the market size/growth by segment*). In addition, Ford had extensive production capability in Europe and was embraced as quasi-domestic by many mainstream drivers.

Several manufacturers were struggling with the changes in the market. Between 1995 and 1998, Ford

Exhibit 1 ● Toyota's Global Operations

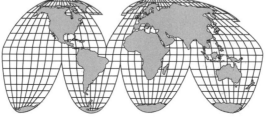

North America:
- 4 regional offices
- nearly 1,600 dealers
- 8 manufacturing bases
- nearly 18,000 employees

Europe:
- 24 distributors
- 3,700 dealers
- 2 manufacturing bases

Japan:
- >300 dealers
- Nearly 5,700 outlets
- 15 manufacturing bases
- >45,000 employees

Asia (excl. Japan):
- 10 importers
- 150 dealers
- 17 manufacturing bases
- >22,000 employees

Latin America/ Caribbean:
- 44 importers
- nearly 400 dealers
- 5 manufacturing bases
- nearly 4,000 employees

Africa:
- 50 importers
- 400 dealers
- 2 manufacturing bases
- >7,000 employees

Middle East & Southwest Asia:
- 18 importers
- >200 dealers
- 4 manufacturing bases
- >1,000 employees

Oceania:
- 18 importers
- more than 300 dealers
- 1 manufacturing base
- >4,000 employees

Source: Toyota

and GM's Adam Opel division had seen its Western European market share decline from 13.7% to 11.8% and from 13.4% to 11.3% respectively. Both companies were lacking popular niche models such as roadsters and convertibles. Moreover, the success of diesel engines had taken many car companies by surprise— their penetration rate had risen to around 30% of the market. These changes in the market had required carmakers to be responsive to the market. The winners included Volkswagen, which had been able to increase its share of the Western European market from 16.7% in 1995 to 18.0% in 1998.

OPENING OF THE EUROPEAN MARKET TO THE JAPANESE

The European market was heavily protected. Governments favored their domestic "national champions" manufacturers; import restrictions had been launched in selected markets as early as 1975. Strict regulations made it almost impossible for dealers to add a Japanese brand as a second brand in their showrooms. Officials from the European Union (EU) negotiated

with the Ministry of International Trade and Industry (MITI) in Tokyo to limit Japanese vehicle exports to 1.23 million units starting in 1993. In 1996 this was lowered to 1.066 million. The agreed limit for 1999 was 1.1 million. The UK, France, Italy, Spain and Portugal had additional import restrictions. Although these restrictions were going to be lifted at the end of 1999, car manufacturers still had to pay an EU-imposed duty of 10% on all imported vehicles. Adverse exchange-rate movements put Japanese importers at an even greater disadvantage. UK-based production did not help overcome the exchange-rate problem because the sterling had not joined the common European currency. Some analysts argued that these factors were of little material impact.

Import restrictions that took effect in 1993 to keep the Japanese in check proved largely irrelevant . . . although the strong yen didn't help, the Japanese fell flat in Europe in large part by failing to adapt to local tastes. Europe was crowded with companies just making the kind of small, economical cars the Japanese had introduced to the US. Not enough attention was

Exhibit 2 ● Market Shares in Western Europe, USA and Japan

Western Europe
New registration

		1998 Volume	%
Volkswagen Group		2,588,197	18.0%
	Volkswagen	1,574,836	11.0%
	Audi	494,649	3.4%
	SEAT	361,254	2.5%
	Skoda	157,458	1.1%
GM Group		1,644,801	11.5%
PSA Group		1,634,103	11.4%
	Peugeot	958,078	6.7%
	Citroen	676,025	4.7%
Fiat Group		1,561,984	10.9%
Renault		1,539,974	10.7%
Ford Group		1,456,152	10.2%
BMW Group		818,947	5.7%
	BMW	451,015	3.1%
	Rover	349,932	2.4%
Mercedes-Benz		631,471	4.4%
Volvo		240,502	1.7%
Japanese		1,695,309	11.8%
	Toyota	429,071	3.0%
	Nissan	424,782	3.0%
	Honda	213,290	1.5%
	Mazda	209,996	1.5%
	Mitsubishi	181,028	1.3%
South Korean		382,914	2.7%
Total (incl others)		14,341,246	100.0%

USA
Sales

	1998 Volume	%
GM/Saab	2,458,689	30.0%
Ford/Jaguar	1,559,190	19.0%
Toyota	867,814	10.6%
Daimler Chrysler	866,328	10.6%
Honda	860,471	10.5%
Nissan	411,375	5.0%
Volkswagen Group	265,874	3.2%
Mazda	186,501	2.3%
Mitsubishi	147,956	1.8%
Subaru	147,833	1.8%
BMW/Land Rover	131,599	1.6%
Volvo	101,171	1.2%
Others	181,288	2.2%
Total	8,186,089	100.0%

Japan
New registration

	1998 Volume	%
Toyota	1,139,585	27.8%
Nissan	687,321	16.8%
Honda	588,949	14.4%
Suzuki	359,869	8.8%
Mitsubishi	323,810	7.9%
Daihatsu	292,336	7.1%
Mazda	239,902	5.9%
Fuji-Subaru	192,921	4.7%
Isuzu	2,607	0.1%
Imports	265,848	6.5%
Total	4,093,148	100.0%

Note: The sales for the American market do not include light commercial vehicles. These vehicles (pick-up trucks, SUVs) account for 50% of the American market.

Sources:

"Western Europe: Leading Shares of the New Car Market." The Economist Intelligence Unit: *Motor Business Europe,* Feb. 1999: 184

"Sales by Manufacturer." The Economist Intelligence Unit: *Motor Business International,* Jan. 1999: 151

"Japan's Domestic Passenger Car Market by Manufacturer." The Economist Intelligence Unit: *Motor Business Japan,* March 1999: 15

Exhibit 3 ● The European Car Market

New registration

	1993	1994	1995	1996	1997	1998	1998 (%)	CAGR (1993–1998)	Toyota's Market Share	All Japanese Market Share
Germany	3,194	3,209	3,314	3,496	3,528	3,740	26.1%	3.2%	2.5%	12.30%
Italy	1,890	1,672	1,731	1,732	2,412	2,364	16.5%	4.6%	1.4%	5.30%
UK	1,778	1,911	1,945	2,026	2,171	2,247	15.7%	4.8%	3.5%	14.90%
France	1,721	1,973	1,931	2,132	1,713	1,944	13.6%	2.5%	1.5%	4.60%
Spain	745	910	834	911	1,014	1,192	8.3%	9.9%	1.1%	6.70%
Netherlands	392	434	446	474	478	543	3.8%	6.7%	4.6%	20.80%
Belgium	376	387	359	397	396	452	3.2%	3.8%	5.3%	15.30%
Austria	285	274	280	308	275	296	2.1%	0.7%	4.0%	20%
Switzerland	257	266	268	282	271	300	2.1%	3.2%	6.0%	22.30%
Sweden	124	156	170	180	225	253	1.8%	15.3%	5.5%	15.90%
Portugal	250	233	201	218	213	248	1.7%	-0.2%	2.0%	10.70%
Greece	148	113	125	140	162	179	1.2%	3.9%	9.9%	28.20%
Denmark	84	140	136	142	153	158	1.1%	13.5%	9.0%	26.30%
Ireland	64	80	87	115	137	146	1.0%	17.9%	11.5%	29.70%
Norway	61	85	91	125	128	118	0.8%	14.2%	10.2%	31.10%
Finland	56	67	80	96	105	126	0.9%	17.7%	12.7%	27.20%
Luxembourg	26	25	23	27	28	32	0.2%	4.5%	3.9%	11.90%
Total	11,451	11,934	12,021	12,790	13,408	14,341	100.0%	4.6%	3.0%	na

Sources: The Economist Intelligence Unit, IMD Research

paid to tailoring cars for Europe and carving out niches in the market.

Source: Miller, Scott.
"Tune Up: Japanese Car Makers Vow to Stop Treating Europe Like the U.S."
The Wall Street Journal Europe, *December 20, 1999*

Regardless of whether it was macro economic forces such as duties or currency conditions or the voice of the market or both, at 11.5%, the collective market share of the Japanese in Europe (as low as 4.6% in France) suggested lots of room for improvement.

POSITIONING OF JAPANESE MANUFACTURERS IN EUROPE

Both traditional and modern mainstream segments were the largest segments, accounting for around 31% of the market (*refer to **Exhibit 5** for an overview of European customer segments*). Japanese cars were popular in lower income segments. The cars were perceived as offering value for money, but they lacked distinctive brand images. Moreover, many Japanese manufacturers were experiencing difficulties in Europe. In the case of Mazda, 1998 sales in France were only 44% of their 1991 level. Other manufacturers experienced similar

fluctuations in demand (*refer to **Exhibit 6** for the sales development of different Japanese brands in Europe*).

Korean manufacturers had been attacking the traditional segment of Japanese brands. Attractive designs and the strong devaluation of the Korean currency had led to considerable increases in volume. Hyundai, for example, had been able to increase its European sales by 61% to 198,000 units between 1996 and 1998; over the same period, Daewoo had increased its sales by 71% to 168,000 units. Although the Koreans were no longer the fearful threat they had once been, they still recorded sales of around 400,000 units in Europe. A Toyota manager commented:

Traditionally, we served the value seekers. They wanted a car for a good price and with a wide selection of standard equipment. The strong yen and the Korean success have eroded this success somewhat.

Besides the Koreans some of the well-established European companies had become a force in Toyota's traditional segment. Fiat had started importing low-cost models from Latin America while VW had positioned Skoda as its entry brand. Skoda benefited from the technology transfer and saw its sales rising from 225,000 units in 1995 to 363,000 units in 1998.

Exhibit 4 ● 1998 Market Overview—Western Europe

Top 10 Selling Brands

	Unit Sales
Volkswagen	1,574,836
Opel/Vauxhall	1,644,801
Fiat	1,561,984
Renault	1,539,974
Ford	1,456,152
Peugeot	958,078
Citroen	675,025
Mercedes	631,471
Audi	494,649
BMW	451,015

Market Segments

Segment	Units Sold 1994	As a %	Units Sold 1998	As a %	Change 1994/98 in %	Toyota Models
Premium	1,412,021	10.7	1,792,069	11.2	+26.9	Lexus
Large	288,464	2.2	173,180	1.1	-40.0	Camry
Medium	2,095,843	15.9	2,357,738	14.7	+12.5	Avensis
Small High	3,701,164	28.1	3,899,179	24.4	+5.4	Corolla
Small Low/ Economy	4,004,038	30.5	4,581,141	28.7	+14.4	Starlet
MPV	175,272	1.3	893,068	5.7	+409.5	Previa, Picnic
SUV	292,117	2.2	460,442	3.0	+57.6	RAV4
Sports	172,131	1.4	333,812	2.1	+93.9	Supra, Celica
Other	72,674	0.5	48,056	0.3	-33.9	
Light Commercial Vehicles	944,040	7.2	1,473,933	9.4	+56.1	
Total	**13,157,764**	**100**	**16,012,618**	**100**	**+21.7**	

Source: TMME

Exhibit 5 ● Brand Perceptions in the European Market

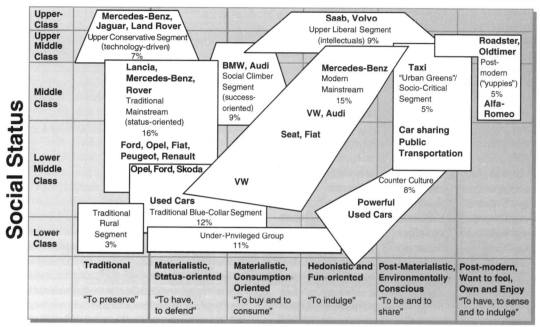

Source: Marketing Systems Essen, Eurosensor by Impulse/Sigma

Traditional Segments

Upper Conservative Segment:

• Traditional European elite, conservative, religious, increasingly technocratic values

Traditional Mainstream:

• Seek status, performance and enjoyment in moderation

Traditional Blue-Collar Segment:

• Skilled, blue-collar workers from innovative industries

form an attractive target segment, flexible in their brand selection and willing to spend a lot of money on cars.

Traditional Rural Segment:

• Predominantly in Italy and Spain

Underprivileged Segment:

• Not very competitive in the job market anymore, poor, cannot afford their desired "products," frustrated

Mainstream Segments

Social Climber Segment:

• Consumption-oriented, average education, sporty

• Aim for the lifestyle of the "elite" and are afraid of their social decline

Modern/Progressive Mainstream:

• Young and middle generation, mostly well-educated, good income

• Willing to spend more than others on cars, open for new/other brands

Counter Culture:

• Trying to escape routine, leading to "teenager lifestyle protest," nevertheless stable value orientation, value community feeling

Exhibit 5 ● Brand Perceptions in the European Market, *cont.*

Segments striving for a variety of lifestyles, high tolerance towards different lifestyles and cultural "openness"

Upper Liberal Segment:

• Elite, combines postmaterial values of emancipation and individuality striving for financial success and epicurean philosophy of life, search for a equilibrium between work and spare time

"Urban Green"/ Socio-Critical Segment:

• 1968 generation or believers in this idea, post materialistic convictions and philosophies, trying to fit their beliefs into the post-modern microcosmos

Postmodern:

• Live in European metropolis, "avant gardistic" self-confidence

• Firm belief that they control their own destiny—see the environment (fellow creatures, products, art, philosophy, religions) as a construction kit

• Multiple identities, and changes/reversibility of trends in their construction kit are well possible

---

Some Japanese models were very popular in higher segments, e.g., Japanese brands accounted for 9% of the European SUV market.

TOYOTA IN EUROPE

Toyota started exporting to Europe a few years after its 1957 entry into the US market. Toyota first established operations in "marginal markets," which had neither domestic car manufacturers nor high levels of competition. After gaining some experience in these markets, Toyota started to attack Europe's high volume markets like the UK and France (*refer to* **Figure 2**).

By the late 1960s Toyota had a presence in a considerable number of markets. Nevertheless, only five countries absorbed more than 3,000 units per year. They were Finland, Belgium, Denmark, Switzerland and the Netherlands (in order of volume). The main selling points of the cars were their novelty and their simplicity. The success in these countries was based on strong importers. In Switzerland, for example, Emil Frey had a national presence and was able to introduce the brand very quickly. However, in many other countries finding distributors and dealers had proved difficult. Some existing dealers were only allowed by law to carry one brand; others were afraid of the risk of starting a new brand. Where allowed, Toyota tried to encourage "dual brand dealers." In several markets, Toyota took over dealers from discontinued brands (e.g., Talbot and Simca of France). In Germany, Toyota initially relied on a sales network that comprised agricultural machinery dealers, gasoline stations and car repair shops.

In the mid-1970s, Toyota also started to acquire the first leasing companies for its vehicles. In 1976 Toyota exported more than 200,000 units annually to Europe for the first time, and by 1980, the company hit the 300,000 mark. By 1997 Toyota had the highest market shares in Finland, Norway and Ireland (*refer to* **Exhibit 3**), but Germany and the UK still accounted for 40% of total sales (*refer to* **Figure 3**). Across Europe, consumers recognized Toyota for its outstanding quality and responsiveness.

The Role of TMME

Toyota Motor Company Brussels (TMC Brussels), the European operation of Toyota, was set up in Belgium in 1970. The company established a technical center in 1987 and a market research center in 1989. By 1989, TMC was trying to coordinate its diverse European operations via an office: TMC Brussels was renamed TMME, and its objective was to "oversee and coordinate Toyota's sales and parts distribution as well as product planning activities" (*refer to* **Exhibit 7** *for an overview of TMME's operations*). Some distributors reported to TMME; a few of the larger ones reported directly to TMC.

With the success of the European market entry, TMC started to acquire stakes in distributors and wholesalers (*refer to* **Figure 4**).

Regardless of these streamlining efforts, TMME was still dealing with 24 distributors in 1998. The distributors could select their own advertising agencies or rely on material from TMME. The most widely used agency was Saatchi&Saatchi, but it was only

Figure 2: Entry Dates for Toyota in the European Market

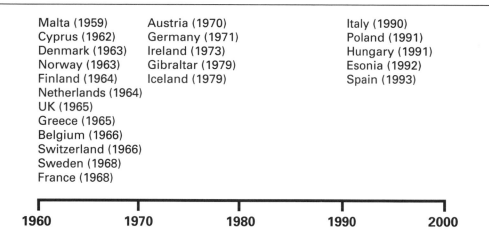

Malta (1959)	Austria (1970)	Italy (1990)
Cyprus (1962)	Germany (1971)	Poland (1991)
Denmark (1963)	Ireland (1973)	Hungary (1991)
Norway (1963)	Gibraltar (1979)	Esonia (1992)
Finland (1964)	Iceland (1979)	Spain (1993)
Netherlands (1964)		
UK (1965)		
Greece (1965)		
Belgium (1966)		
Switzerland (1966)		
Sweden (1968)		
France (1968)		

1960   1970   1980   1990   2000

Figure 3: Toyota in Europe

	Toyota's New Vehicle Registrations (1997)	% of Toyota's West European Sales	1997 New Registrations of Japanese-badged Passenger Cars
Austria	13,400	3.1	55,388
Belgium	24,100	5.7	60,866
Denmark	20,100	4.7	40,130
Finland	16,000	3.8	28,389
France	23,500	5.5	81,794
Germany	94,100	22.1	406,679
Greece	19,500	4.6	43,229
Ireland	17,100	4.0	42,823
Italy	23,600	5.5	137,495
Netherlands	26,800	6.3	102,524
Norway	18,700	4.4	38,618
Portugal	15,700	3.7	33,745
Spain	12,500	2.9	102,817
Sweden	n/a	n/a	35,824
Switzerland	21,100	5.0	60,412
UK	79,200	18.6	340,752
Total	**425,400**	**100%**	**1,611,485**

Note: Actual sales only reached 391,300 units in 1997. New registrations included registered demo cars, etc.

Sources: "Japanese Manufacturers in Western Europe: yet further expansion," Economist Intelligence Unit (EIU): *Motor Business Japan,* 2nd quarter 1999: 24ff; "A strategic profile of Toyota—the heavyweight remains strong," Economist Intelligence Unit (EIU): *Motor Business Japan,* 4th quarter 1998: 55.

Figure 4: Ownership Structure

TMC Owned Distributors:	Significant Stakes in Distributors:	Independent Importers:
Czech Republic	Hungary	Austria
Denmark	Norway	Belgium
Finland	Poland	Cyprus
France	Portugal	Greece
Germany	Spain	Ireland
Italy		Netherlands
Sweden		Switzerland
UK		

Source: Toyota.

used in five markets including the UK, France and Poland. Distributors were free to choose whether they wanted to use material produced by TMME or produce their own material. Competing car manufacturers were moving toward single agencies for many markets with VW using one agency for twelve markets.

By 1998, Toyota had 3,700 dealers in Europe. The main requirement for its dealers was profitability; "sales targets" were secondary. Because of Toyota's past, a large proportion of dealers in selected countries were relatively small, with average sales of 224 cars per outlet. The European average stood at 283 cars per outlet. In contrast, the mass of manufacturers such as Fiat, Opel and VW had achieved sales of 671 units, 550 units and 456 units respectively (*refer to Exhibit 8 for an overview of Toyota's sales network in Europe*). Mr. Tatsuo Takahashi, former president of TMME, remembered:[1]

We had to gain sales in the markets where we were weak, and that meant in the southern half of Europe where export restrictions had limited our penetration. We were not merely increasing the number of dealers, we were also concentrating on getting quality dealers who were strong and efficient.

Toyota had started to run a European-wide warranty program as of mid-1995, but other than that, the co-operation among the different distributors was lim-

1. See "Face to face: with the president of Toyota Motor Europe," EIU *Motor Business Europe,* 3rd quarter 1998, page 4.

ited. Several managers in TMME were rallying for a more centralized approach in order to reduce duplication among the distributors. But TMME was facing regulatory changes. The EU directive known as the "Block Exemption," which allowed manufacturers to operate exclusive dealer networks, was going to expire in 2002. This put additional pressure on Toyota, and a Toyota manager recalled the US experience:

We remember the deregulation of dealers in the US. Toyota continued to have exclusive dealers dedicated to Toyota that are very profitable and motivated.

BECOMING A EUROPEAN PLAYER

Sales forecasts for 1999 were strong. Sales of the newly launched Avensis model were expected to reach 180,000 units. Toyota was building a new factory in France for its Yaris model, a small car developed at the European design center in Brussels by European designers for the European market. Finally, European managers had obtained the commitment they felt necessary for becoming a "European player." The Yaris was to have a local content of 60%. Besides the Yaris, Toyota had an outstanding product range. This was the time to press for changes (*refer to Exhibit 9 for the new products in the pipeline*).

Challenge 2000

As part of its drive to achieve its targeted 5% market share in Europe—profitably—TMME embraced Chal-

Exhibit 6 ● Sales of Japanese Brands in Western Europe in 1998

	Toyota			Nissan			Honda		
	Units	Sales as a % of Total	1998 Sales as a % of 1991 Sales	Units	Sales as a % of Total	1998 Sales as a % of 1991 Sales	Units	Sales as a % of Total	1998 Sales as a % of 1991 Sales
Austria	11,643	2.6	61.1	8,098	1.8	44.8	5,761	2.7	85.1
Belgium	24,064	5.5	83.4	14,137	3.2	49.7	6,397	3.0	100.5
France	28,084	6.4	168.9	27,878	6.3	86.6	14,095	6.5	96.1
Germany	94,965	21.5	83.8	92,924	21.1	61.5	48,247	22.3	76.8
Italy	32,524	7.4	694.5	52,071	11.8	299.3	24,005	11.1	291.1
Netherlands	25,466	5.8	101.1	18,693	4.2	59.2	7,881	3.6	94.6
Spain	20,706	4.7	198.2	53,290	12.1	188.6	16,033	7.4	618.1
Switzerland	14,535	3.3	51.8	4,079	0.9	25.0	4,941	2.3	73.3
UK	82,567	18.7	200.2	101,430	23.1	158.0	61,048	28.2	216.1
Others	106,824	24.2	n/a	67,270	15.3	n/a	28,043	13.0	n/a
Western Europe Total	**441,378**	**100.0**	**n/a**	**439,870**	**100.0**	**n/a**	**216,451**	**100.0**	**n/a**

	Mazda			Mitsubishi			Suzuki		
	Units	Sales as a % of Total	1998 Sales as a % of 1991 Sales	Units	Sales as a % of Total	1998 Sales as a % of 1991 Sales	Units	Sales as a % of Total	1998 Sales as a % of 1991 Sales
Austria	13,424	6.2	51.8	8,111	4.2	69.4	6,316	4.0	105.0
Belgium	7,692	3.6	43.2	11,079	5.8	122.7	5,710	3.6	118.6
France	7,572	3.5	43.9	5,043	2.6	134.1	11,240	7.2	460.1
Germany	87,053	40.5	80.3	62,473	32.7	70.9	35,432	22.6	99.7
Italy	-	-	-	13,544	7.1	133.9	17,875	11.4	151.3
Netherlands	16,238	7.5	56.0	14,799	7.7	141.9	16,348	10.4	103.2
Spain	4,636	2.2	170.3	12,264	6.4	327.5	14,784	9.4	142.0
Switzerland	7,730	3.6	59.4	8,901	4.7	77.7	2,458	1.6	55.4
UK	29,962	13.9	151.2	20,938	11.0	169.1	19,309	12.3	346.0
Others	40,775	19.0	n/a	34,020	17.8	n/a	27,356	17.4	n/a
Western Europe Total	**215,082**	**100.0**	**n/a**	**191,172**	**100.0**	**n/a**	**156,828**	**100.0**	**n/a**

Source: "Japanese Manufacturers in Western Europe: Yet Further Expansion." Economist Intelligence Unit (EIU): *Motor Business Japan,* 2nd quarter 1999: 199ff.

lenge 2000. Challenge 2000 was kicked off during a three-day event for 200 top managers from the different distributors in Europe. During this event, the participants raised a number of issues:

- *Cost of Ownership:* How to further reduce the cost of owning a Toyota, thus optimizing the cost-benefit relationship.

- *Customer Delight:* How to further improve customer satisfaction.

- *Network Development:* How to improve operational efficiency and profit margins of dealers.

- *Brand Management:* This involved two steps. The first part dealt with the goals of turning Toyota into a more desirable brand in Europe. This included developing a vision and value

proposition for the "New Toyota" brand. The second part involved developing communication strategies for this repositioning.

On each of these dimensions, studies had taken place, and improvement programs were being implemented across Europe. TMME's Marketing Director actively participated in the study on brand management. Several issues had emerged:

- Characteristics for Toyota's tangible brand identity included low pride, weak design appeal, strong for value for money and equipment, weak for safety and environment.

- Toyota's intangible brand personality was seen as a cold, secretive Japanese brand, cautiously introverted. Customer focus was low.

Exhibit 7 ● Overview of TMME

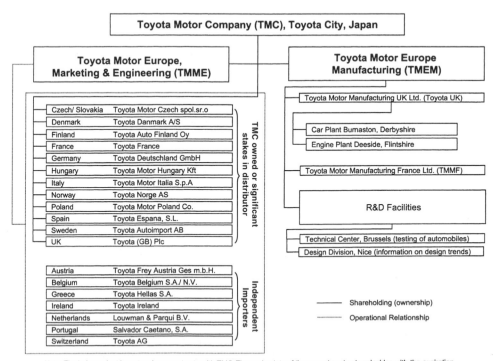

Note: The independent importers have contracts with TMC. The expiry date of the current contracts coincides with the expiration of the current EC Block Exemption Regulation at the end of 2002. Exception: Switzerland expires December 2009.

Source: TMME

- The existing customer base was skewed towards the older generation with a conservative lifestyle and mindset.

- Toyota and other Japanese manufacturers lagged behind the majors in awareness, consideration and preference by a large margin. There were important differences on these dimensions from market to market. Lexus appeared particularly weak (*refer to Exhibit 10*).

- In the volume market, some manufacturers had staked out distinct positions. VW was clearly associated with "robustness," Ford as "classic," Renault as more "friendly." Toyota was considered "intelligent" and "modern" (*refer to Exhibit 11 for a perceptual map of the main manufacturers*).

- Some manufacturers, through the use of broad model ranges, had achieved broad appeal across many of the value segments. Ford, for example, appealed to traditionalists who were predominantly lower/middle class drivers; it also appealed to upper class traditionalists through its Jaguar brand and to post-modernists with liberal lifestyles through Volvo.

- Analyses of perceptions of car owners country by country confirmed the belief that Toyota's brand image varied a lot country by country (*refer to Exhibits 12 to 16 for selected country profiles*). The variation resulted from varying levels of competition, historic import restrictions, independent pricing mechanisms, distinct consumer preferences and the independent marketing communications strategies implemented by fairly autonomous distributors.

For TMME, Challenge 2000 was of great importance and many executives were actively preparing for the Pan European Dealer Meeting in Barcelona in March

Exhibit 8 ● Toyota's Sales Network in Europe (1998)

	Ger	Fr	UK	It	Spain	Bel	Por	Den	Greece	Ire	Swe	Aus	Fin	Switz
Number of Official Dealers														
-99 units	301	33	29	32	22	66	2	21	10	0	30	74	5	43
100-199 units	202	76	50	34	29	60	112	36	23	3	38	38	27	34
200-299 units	51	49	66	42	41	29	0	22	15	7	15	6	16	9
300-499 units	31	48	53	46	29	11	0	18	17	30	4	3	8	5
500-599 units	14	22	37	27	19	2	0	2	14	14	1	3	8	2
600-1,000 units	2	0	3	5	5	0	0	0	4	2	0	0	2	0
Total	**601**	**228**	**238**	**186**	**145**	**168**	**114**	**99**	**83**	**56**	**88**	**124**	**66**	**93**
Number of Official Sub-Dealers														
-99 units	169	75	0	23	14	72	0	1	9	0	18	47	0	289
100-199 units	5	0	0	0	0	0	35	1	1	0	0	1	0	2
200-299 units	1	0	0	0	0	0	0	0	0	0	0	0	0	0
300-499 units	2	0	0	0	0	0	0	0	1	0	0	0	0	0
500-599 units	0	0	0	0	0	0	0	0	0	0	0	0	0	0
600-1,000 units	0	0	0	0	0	0	0	0	0	0	0	0	0	0
Total	**177**	**75**	**0**	**23**	**14**	**72**	**35**	**2**	**11**	**0**	**18**	**48**	**0**	**291**

Source: TMME

1999. At this meeting, top managers from TMC and TMME wanted to communicate their vision about Challenge 2000 to the dealer network in Europe. For this meeting, over 7,000 European dealers and their spouses were expected.

WHAT NEXT?

TMME's Marketing Director assessed that there was an urgent need to enhance the appeal of the Toyota brand, make it more desirable, connect with customers' emotions. He also believed it essential that Toyota be true to itself. After all, it had recently stated its core values: quality and responsiveness. But this wouldn't set Toyota apart from its competition; the company also needed to identify and agree on which values would do this.

As the managers were evaluating their options, they considered three options for repositioning their brand:

• Japanese Brand: This approach would involve positioning the Japanese side of Toyota more interestingly. However, market research revealed that, in general, Europeans were not very aware of Japan and Japanese culture.

• European Brand: This approach would be similar to Toyota's approach in Canada and the US. In Canada, the Toyota symbol often appeared with a maple leaf. In the US, the company had several image campaigns that stressed Toyota's contribution to American society. However, market researchers were uncertain how to position Toyota as a European brand. After all, the consumers kept their regional attitudes, and national tastes were very strong.

• Global/International Brand: Toyota positioned as a global player.

As part of Challenge 2000, it had become clear that something had to be done to reposition the brand. Mr. Imai and Mr. Cho were looking forward to receiving recommendations on how to proceed.

Exhibit 9 ● Planned Product Portfolio

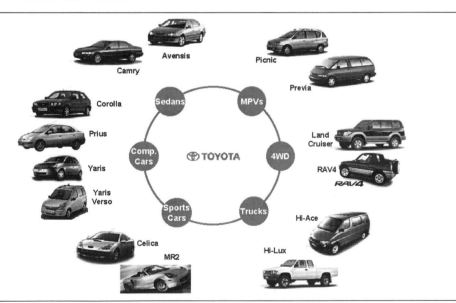

Source: TMME

Exhibit 10 ● Brand Perceptions in the European Market

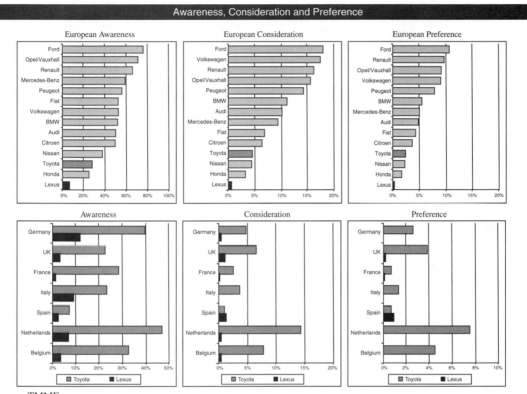

Source: TMME

Exhibit 11 ● Brand Positioning Map

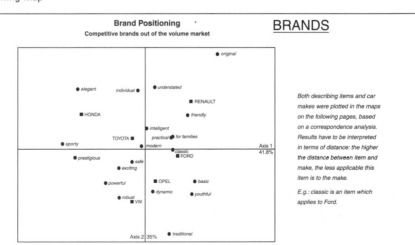

Source: TMME

Exhibit 12 ● Market Overview—Belgium (1998)

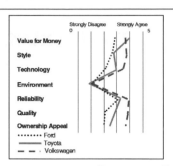

Top 10 Brands:	
	Units Sold
Volkswagen	56,281
Renault	48,132
Opel	43,270
Ford	38,654
Peugeot	37,919
Citroen	32,562
Toyota	24,064
Audi	18,579
Mercedes	16,368
BMW	15,290

Market Segments	1998 Units	Share (%)	Toyota/ Lexus Seg. Share
Luxury High	2,616	0.6	1.91
Luxury Low	21,884	4.8	1.14
Medium High	8,052	1.8	
Medium Low	111,311	24.6	6.04
Small High	134,467	29.7	6.86
Small Low	97,915	21.7	4.72
Economy	12,479	2.8	
Sport/ Special	7,549	1.7	
Sport Utility	9,555	2.1	7.73
MPV	45,841	10.1	
Van	369	0.01	
Others	91	0	
Total Year	452,129		
Growth (%)	12.4		

Belgian Market in General:

• 1998 sales were the highest in six years. Market is strongly recovering from a low of 360,000 units in 1995 (10-year low).

• Taxation has for a long time favored used cars, as consumers have to pay fewer taxes.

• Personal taxation is high, and the law caps salary increases—companies tend to offer cars as a form of remuneration (35% of market).

• Share of Japanese fell from 22% in 1991 to 16.5% in 1998.

Comments on Toyota in Belgium:

• Market Share increased from 4.8% in 1996 to 5.3% in 1998.

• Toyota remains the leader of the Japanese carmakers with sales increase of 30% in the past.

• Toyota is also facing the effects of a general slump for Japanese cars.

Source: TMME

Exhibit 13 ● Market Overview—Denmark (1998)

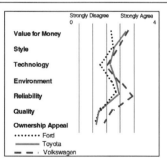

Top 10 Brands:	
	Units Sold
Volkswagen	18,886
Opel	15,486
Ford	15,258
Toyota	14,529
Peugeot	14,000
Citroen	11,386
Mazda	9,349
Fiat	8,869
Skoda	6,507
Renault	5,952

Market Segments	1998 Units	Share (%)	Toyota/ Lexus Seg. Share
Luxury High	243	0.1	4.94
Luxury Low	3,995	2.5	
Medium High	1,902	1.2	8.1
Medium Low	52,449	32.3	15.47
Small High	51,525	31.8	8.08
Small Low	37,208	22.9	
Economy	3,929	2.4	
Sport/ Special	587	0.4	2.73
Sport Utility	498	0.3	10.65
MPV	7,922	4.9	2.74
Van	1,114	0.7	
Others	760	0.5	
Total Year	162,132		
Growth (%)	5.7		

Danish Market in General:

• Very high taxes (up to 240%), normally taxes double the retail price of cars.

• Long replacement cycles, in 1997, still 1 million cars were not equipped with a catalytic converter.

• Volatile market, sales fell from 169,000 in 1986 to only 81,000 in 1990 and rose since then.

• Diesel engines only account for 3% of the market.

• Share of Japanese fell from 42% in 1991 to 25% in 1998.

Comments on Toyota in Denmark:

• Toyota fell from 3rd position to 4th position in 1998.

• Toyota is still suffering from a negative press campaign from 1997. Journalists discovered that the Corolla was potentially dangerous when changing lanes.

Source: TMME

Exhibit 14 ● Market Overview—Germany (1998)

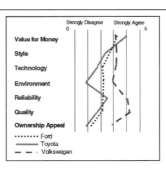

Top 10 Brands:	
	Units Sold
Volkswagen	708,172
Opel	531,975
Mercedes	371,505
Ford	354,712
Audi	243,380
Renault	234,399
BMW	232,012
Fiat	133,611
Nissan	92,923
Toyota	92,851

Market Segments	1998 Units	Share (%)	Toyota/Lexus Seg. Share
Luxury High	34,467	0.9	1.46
Luxury Low	271,356	7.3	0.59
Medium High	73,695	2	1.6
Medium Low	924,052	24.7	2.36
Small High	1,154,389	30.9	3.31
Small Low	602,667	16.1	
Economy	167,222	4.5	
Sport/Special	120,079	3.2	
Sport Utility	88,007	2.4	6.27
MPV	225,059	6	2.19
Van	68,231	1.8	
Others	6,763	0.2	
Total Year	3,735,987		
Growth (%)	5.6		

German Market in General:

- Total sales are still far below the all time record of 4.3 million units in 1992.
- Sales of Japanese cars have fallen from 550,000 units in 1992 to 455,000 units in 1997.
- Korean cars are very popular in former Eastern Germany.
- Total Diesel Market accounts for 15% of the market.

Comments on Toyota in Germany:

- Registrations have fallen from 101,000 units in 1992 to 92,500 units in 1998, but still 16 different products.
- Goal: 2005: 120,000 units.
- High percentage of diesel sales (estimated to reach 38% in 1999).
- Toyota Germany was unprofitable.

Source: TMME

Exhibit 15 ● Market Overview—Greece (1998)

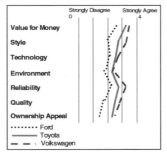

Top 10 Brands:	
	Units Sold
Toyota	18,880
Hyundai	16,673
Fiat	16,060
Citroen	15,739
Opel	11,780
Nissan	11,097
Volkswagen	9,957
Suzuki	9,482
Peugeot	9,015
Seat	7,899

Market Segments	1998 Units	Share (%)	Toyota/Lexus Seg. Share
Luxury High	83	0	1.2
Luxury Low	2,075	1.1	
Medium High	355	0.2	
Medium Low	26,803	14.8	15.36
Small High	56,115	31.1	15.38
Small Low	69,433	38.5	7.35
Economy	11,168	6.2	
Sport/Special	2,742	1.5	
Sport Utility	7,664	4.2	5.25
MPV	3,518	1.9	
Van	153	0.1	
Others	432	0.2	
Total Year	180,541		
Growth (%)	10		

Greek Market in General:

- Sales fell from 199,000 units in 1992 to 156,000 units in 1997 and back up to 180,000 units in 1998.
- The EU has ruled the Greek taxation measures for imported used cars illegal; car park is the oldest in Europe.
- Car penetration is among the lowest in Europe. In 1998: 25 vehicles per 100 inhabitants (EU average: 39).
- A,B,C segment account for almost 80% of the market.
- Japanese share of the market fell from 37% in 1990 to 28% in 1998.
- Koreans are gaining quickly.

Comments on Toyota in Greece:

- Toyota entered the market in 1965, Inchape plc took over in 1987.
- Entry level Corolla accounted for half of Toyota's sales.
- "Incentive driven and unstable due to external factors."
- 85 Toyota dealers (each selling on average 400 cars), tops customer satisfaction ratings.
- Since 1993: market share larger than 10% (from 121,000 in 1993 units to 197,000 in 1998); reduction of import tax from 225% in 1987 to 44.% in 1998.

Source: TMME

Exhibit 16 ● Market Overview—United Kingdom (1998)

Top 10 Brands:	
	Units Sold
Ford	400,280
Opel/ Vauxhall	282,560
Peugeot	181,564
Renault	180,319
Rover	160,323
Volkswagen	128,421
Nissan	101,430
Fiat	92,256
Toyota	79,298
Citroen	76,652

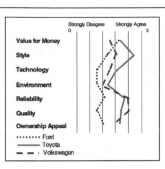

Market Segments	1998 Units	Share (%)	Toyota/ Lexus Seg. Share
Luxury High	19,801	0.9	4.92
Luxury Low	64,495	2.9	3.56
Medium High	50,574	2.3	2.25
Medium Low	600,818	26.7	4.21
Small High	620,351	27.6	3.64
Small Low	575,479	25.6	
Economy	56,508	2.5	
Sport/ Special	66,934	3	4.51
Sport Utility	98,200	4.4	7.63
MPV	89,877	4	2.75
Van	1,137	0.1	
Others	3,228	0.1	
Total Year	2,247,402		
Growth (%)	3.4		

British Market in General:

- Among the highest price levels in Europe.

- Intense competition has led to the incidence of pre-registering of new cars by dealers up to 20% of annual sales volume.

- Percentage of diesels is decreasing from 22.6% in 1994 to 15.3% in 1998.

- Small cars (A/B/C segments) account for 60% of the market.

Comments on Toyota in the UK:

- Toyota: 51% since 01/ 1998. Inchape, the world's largest independent distributor, 49% (it took Toyota 10 years to acquire a controlling stake), Inchape entered 1978, also owns Toyota distribution rights in Belgium, Greece and Luxembourg.

- Inchape distributes Mazda, Toyota, Ford, Rover, VW.

- Fleet buyers get price discounts in between 17% and 35%.

- Toyota's sales have increased from 49,000 units in 1994 to 82,000 units in 1998.

Source: TMME

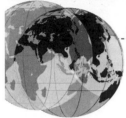

CASE 9

Delissa in Japan (Revised)

We can maintain our presence in Japan or we can pull out . . .

In the fall of 2001 Bjorn Robertson, who had recently been named managing director of Agria, Sweden's leading dairy products cooperative, met with his team to review the international side of the business. The four men sat around a table piled high with thick reports, Nielsen audits, film storyboards, yogurt cups and a mass of promotional material in Japanese. Agria's "Delissa" line of fresh dairy products was sold all over the world through franchise agreements. Several of these agreements were up for review, but the most urgent one was the agreement with Nikko of Japan.

Robertson looked across the conference table at Peter Borg, Stefan Gustafsson and Lars Karlsson, each of whom had been involved with Agria's Japanese business over the past few years, and spoke:

In the light of these results, there are several things we can do in Japan. We can maintain our presence and stay with our present franchisee, we can change our franchisee, or we can pull out. But, let's look first at how badly we are really doing in Japan.

Robertson read out loud to the others a list of Agria's major foreign ventures featuring the Delissa yogurt brand:

USA launch date 1981, market share = 12.5%; Germany launch 1984, market share = 14%; UK launch 1986, market share = 13.8%; France launch 1987, *market share = 9.5%; Japan launch 1991, market share today = 2% to 3%.*

Robertson circled the figure with his marker and turned to look around at his team.

Under 3% after 10 years in the market! What happened?

HISTORY

Agria was founded in 1973 when a group of Swedish dairy cooperatives decided to create a united organization that would develop and sell a line of fresh dairy products. The principal engineers of the organization were Rolf Andersen and Bo Ekman, who had established the group's headquarters in Uppsala, near Stockholm. In 1980, after the individual cooperatives had been persuaded to drop their own trademarks, the Delissa line was launched. This was one of the few "national" lines of dairy products in Sweden. It included yogurts, desserts, fresh cheese and fresh cream. In the two decades that followed, Agria's share rose from 3% to 25% of the Swedish fresh milk products market. Andersen's vision and the concerted efforts of 20,000 dairy farmer members of the cooperative had helped build Agria into a powerful national and international organization.

By 2001 more than 1.1 billion Delissa yogurts and desserts were being consumed per year worldwide. In fiscal year 2000 Delissa had sales of $2.9 billion and employed 4,400 people in and outside Sweden.

Industrial franchising was not very widespread in the 1980s, and few Swedish dairy products firms had invested money abroad. However, Ekman's idea of know-how transfer ventures, whereby a local licensee would manufacture yogurt using Swedish technology and then market and distribute the product using its own distribution network, had enabled Delissa to penetrate over 13 foreign markets with considerable success and with a minimal capital outlay. In contrast, Delissa's biggest competitor worldwide, Danone—a French food conglomerate marketing a yogurt line under the "Danone" brand name—had gone into foreign markets mainly by buying into or creating local companies, or by forming regular joint ventures.

By the time Robertson took over as European marketing director in 1995, the Delissa trademark—with the white cow symbol so familiar in Sweden—was known in different countries worldwide. Delissa was very active in sponsoring sports events, and Robertson—himself a keen cross-country skier and sailor—offered his personal support to Delissa's teams around the world.

When he reviewed the international business, Robertson had been surprised by the results of Agria's Japanese joint venture, which did not compare favorably with those achieved in most foreign markets. Before calling together the international marketing team for a discussion, Robertson requested the files on Japan and spent some time studying the history of the alliance. He read:

Proposal for entry into the Japanese market
In early 1989, the decision was made to enter the Japanese market. Market feasibility research and a search for a suitable franchisee are underway, with an Agria team currently in Japan.

Objectives
The total yogurt market in Japan for 1990 is estimated at approximately 600 million cups (100mn ml). The market for yogurt is expected to grow at an average of at least 8% p.a. in volume for the next 5 years. Our launch strategy would be based on an expected growth rate of 10% or 15% for the total market. We have set ourselves the goal of developing a high quality range of yogurts in Japan, of becoming well known with the Japanese consumer. We aim to reach a 5% market share in the first year and 10% share of market within three years of launch. We plan to cover the three main metropolitan areas, Tokyo, Osaka and Nagoya, within a two-year period, and the rest of the country within the next three years.

Robertson circled the 10% with a red pen. He understood that management would have hesitated to set too high a goal for market share compared with other countries since some executives felt that Japan

was a difficult market to enter. But in 1997 the Japanese operation had not reached its target. In 2001 Delissa's share of the total yogurt market had fallen to 2%, without ever reaching 3%. Robertson had written a note to the Uppsala-based manager responsible for Asian business, stating that he felt Agria's record in Japan in no way reflected the type of success it had had elsewhere with Delissa. He began to wonder why Japan was so different.

The report continued with a brief overview of the Japanese yogurt market:

Consumption
Per capita consumption of yogurt in Japan is low compared with Scandinavian countries. It is estimated at around 5.3 cups per person per year in Japan, versus 110 in Sweden and 120 in Finland. Sales of yogurt in Japan are seasonal, with a peak period from March to July. The highest sales have been recorded in June, so the most ideal launch date would be at the end of February.

Types of yogurt available in Japan—1990
In Japan, yogurt sales may be loosely broken down into three major categories:

- Plain (39% of the market in volume): Called "plain" in Japan because the color is white, but it is really flavored with vanilla. Generally sold in 500 ml pure pack cups. Sugared or sometimes with a sugar bag attached.

- Flavored (45% of the market in volume): Differentiated from the above category by the presence of coloring and jelling agents. Not a wide range of varieties, mainly vanilla, strawberry, almond and citrus.

- Fruit (16% of the market in volume): Similar to the typical Swedish fruit yogurt but with more pulp than real fruit. Contains some coloring and flavoring.

Western-type yogurts also compete directly in the same price bracket with local desserts—like puddings and jellies—produced by Japanese competitors.

Competition
Three major Japanese manufacturers account for about half of the total real yogurt market:

- Snow Brand Milk Products is the largest manufacturer of dairy products in Japan and produces drinking milk, cheeses, frozen foods, biochemicals and pharmaceuticals. Turnover in 1989 was ¥643.322 million (yen).[1]

- Meiji Milk Products is Japan's second largest producer of dairy foods, particularly dried milk for babies, ice cream and cheese. Its alliance with the Bulgarian government helped start the yogurt boom in Japan. Turnover in 1989 was ¥610,674 million.

- Morinaga Milk Industry, Japan's third largest milk products producer, processes drinking milk, ice cream and instant coffee. It has a joint venture with Kraft US for cheeses. Turnover in 1989 was ¥561,783 million.

The share of these three producers has remained stable for years and is approximately: Yukijirushi (Snow Brand) 25%; Meiji 19%; Morinaga 10%.

The Japanese also consume a yogurt drink called "Yakult Honsha" which is often included in statistics on total yogurt consumption as it competes with normal yogurt. On a total market base for yogurts and yogurt drinks, Yakult has 31%. Yakult drink is based on milk reconstituted from powder or fresh milk acidified with lactic acid and glucose. Yakult is not sold in shops, but through door-to-door sales and by groups of women who visit offices during the afternoon and sell the product directly to employees.

Along with some notes written in 1989 by Ole Bobek, Agria's director of international operations, Robertson found a report on meetings held in Uppsala at which two members of Agria's negotiating team presented their findings to management.

Selecting a franchisee
We have just returned from our third visit to Japan where we once again held discussions with the agricultural cooperative Nikko. Nikko is the country's second largest association of agricultural cooperatives; it is the Japanese equivalent of Agria. Nikko is a significant political force in Japan but not as strong

as Zennoh, the National Federation of Agricultural Cooperatives, which is negotiating with Yoplait, one of our French competitors. Nikko is price leader for various food products in Japan (milk, fruit juice, rice) and is active in lobbying on behalf of agricultural producers. Nikko is divided into two parts: manufacturing and distribution. It processes and distributes milk and dairy products, and it also distributes raw rice and vegetables.

We have seen several other candidates, but Nikko is the first one that seems prepared to join us. We believe that Nikko is the most appropriate distributor for Agria in Japan. Nikko is big and its credentials seem perfect for Agria, particularly since its strong supermarket distribution system for milk in the three main metropolitan areas is also ideally suited to yogurt. In Japan, 80% of yogurt is sold through supermarkets. We are, however, frustrated that, after prolonged discussions and several trips to Japan, Nikko has not yet signed an agreement with Agria. We sense that the management does want to go ahead but that they want to be absolutely sure before signing.

The same report also contained some general information on the Japanese consumer, which Robertson found of interest:

Some background information on the Japanese consumer
Traditionally, the Japanese are not dairy products consumers, although locally produced brands of yogurt are sold along with other milk-based items such as puddings and coffee cream.

Many aspects of life in Japan are miniaturized due to lack of space: 60% of the total population of about 124 million is concentrated on 3% of the surface of the islands. The rest of the land mass is mountainous. In Japan, 85% of the population lives in towns of which over one-third have more than half a million people. This urban density naturally affects lifestyle, tastes and habits. Restricted living space and lack of storage areas mean that most Japanese housewives must shop daily and consequently expect fresh milk products in the stores every day as they rarely purchase long-life foods or drinks. The country is fairly homogeneous as far as culture and the distribution of wealth is concerned. Disposable income is high. The

1. $1 = ¥138 in 1989

Japanese spend over 30% of their total household budget on food, making it by far the greatest single item, with clothing in second place (10%).

The market is not comparable to Scandinavia or to the US as far as the consumption of dairy products is concerned. There are young housewives purchasing yogurt today whose mothers barely knew of its existence and whose grandmothers would not even have kept milk in the house. At one time it was believed that the Japanese do not have the enzymes to digest milk and that, only a generation ago, when children were given milk, it was more likely to be goat's milk than cow's milk. However, with the market evolving rapidly towards "Westernization," there is a general interest in American and European products, including yogurt.

Although consumption of yogurt per capita is still low in Japan at the moment, research shows that there is a high potential for growth. When we launch, correct positioning will be the key to Delissa's success as a new foreign brand. We will need to differentiate it from existing Japanese brands and go beyond the rather standardized "freshness" advertising theme.

Distribution

Traditionally, Japanese distribution methods have been complex; the chain tends to be many layered, making distribution costs high. Distribution of refrigerated products is slightly simpler than the distribution of dry goods because it is more direct.

The Japanese daily-purchase habit means that the delivery system adopted for Delissa must be fast and efficient. Our basic distribution goal would be to secure mass sales retailer distribution. Initially, items would be sold through existing sales outlets that sell Nikko's drinking milk, "Nikkodo." The milk-related products and dessert foods would be sold based on distribution to mass sales retailers. The objective would be to make efficient use of existing channels of distribution with daily delivery schedules and enjoy lower distribution costs for new products.

The Japanese retail market

The retail market is extremely fragmented, with independent outlets accounting for 57% of sales (vs. 3% in the US). With 1,350 shops for every 100,000 people, Japan has twice as many outlets per capita as most European countries. Tradition, economics, government regulations and service demands affect the retail system in Japan. Housewives shop once a day on average and most select the smaller local stores, which keep longer hours, deliver orders, offer credit and provide a meeting place for shoppers. Opening a Western-style supermarket is expensive and complicated, so most retailing remains in the hands of the small, independent or family business.

Japan has three major metropolitan areas: Tokyo, Osaka and Nogaya, with populations of 11 million, 3 million and 2 million, respectively. Nikko's Nikkodo, with a 15% share of total, is market leader ahead of the many other suppliers. Nikko feels the distribution chain used for Nikkodo milk would be ideal for yogurt. Each metropolitan area has a separate distribution system, each one with several depots and branches. For instance, Kanto (Great Tokyo)—the largest area with over 40 million people—has five Nikko depots and five Nikko branches.

Most of the physical distribution (drivers and delivery vans) is carried out by a subsidiary of Nikko with support from the wholesalers. The refrigerated milk vans have to be fairly small (less than 2 tons) so that they can drive down the narrow streets. The same routes are used for milk delivery, puddings and juices. Our initial strategy would be to accept Nikko's current milk distribution system as the basic system and, at the same time, adopt shifting distribution routes. Japan's complicated street identification system, whereby only numbers and no names are shown, makes great demands on the distribution system and the drivers.

The Franchise Contract

Robertson opened another report written by Bobek, who had headed up the Japan project right from the start and been responsible for the early years of the joint venture and who had left the company in 1994. This report contained all the details about the contract between Agria and Nikko. In late 1989 Nikko and Agria had signed an industrial franchise agreement permitting Nikko to manufacture and distribute Delissa products under license from Agria. The contract was Agria's standard Delissa franchisee agreement covering technology transfer associated with trademark exploitation. Agria was to provide manufacturing and product know-how, as well as marketing, technical, commercial and sales support. Agria would receive a royalty for every pot of yogurt sold. The Nikko cooperative would form a separate company for the distribution, marketing and promotion of Delissa products. During the pre-launch phase, Per Bergman, senior area brand manager, would train the sales and marketing team, and Agria's technicians would supply know-how to the Japanese.

By 1990 a factory to produce Delissa yogurt, milk and dairy products had been constructed in Mijima, 60 miles northwest of Tokyo. Agria provided Nikko with advice on technology, machinery, tanks, fermentation processes, etc. Equipment from the US, Sweden, Germany and Japan was selected. A European-style Erka filling machine was installed which could fill two, four or six cups at a time, and was considered economical and fast.

Robertson opened another of Bobek's reports, entitled "Delissa Japan—Pre-Launch Data." The report covered the market, positioning, advertising and media plan, minutes of the meetings with Nikko executives and the SRT International Advertising Agency that would handle the launch, analysis of market research findings and competitive analysis. Robertson closed the file and thought about the Japanese market. During the planning phase before the launch, everything had looked so promising. In its usual methodical fashion, Agria had prepared its traditional launch campaign to ensure that the new Agria/Nikko venture would mean a successful entry into Japan for Delissa . . . "Why then," Robertson wondered, "were sales so low after nine years of business?" He picked up the telephone and called Andersen, one of Agria's founders and former chairman of the company. Although retired, Andersen still took an active interest in the business he had created. The next day, Robertson and Andersen had lunch together.

The older man listened to the new managing director talking about his responsibilities, the Swedish headquarters, foreign licensees, new products in the pipeline, etc. Over coffee, Robertson broached the subject of the Japanese joint venture, expressing some surprise that Delissa was so slow in taking off. Andersen nodded his understanding and lit his pipe:

Yes, it has been disappointing. I remember those early meetings before we signed up with Nikko. Our team

was very frustrated with the negotiations. Bobek made several trips and had endless meetings with the Japanese, but things still dragged on. We had so much good foreign business by the time we decided to enter Japan, I guess we thought we could just walk in wherever we wanted. Our Taiwanese franchise business had really taken off, and I think we assumed that Japan would do likewise. Then, despite the fact that we knew the Japanese were different, Wisenborn—our international marketing manager— and Bobek still believed that they were doing something wrong. They had done a very conscientious job, yet they blamed themselves for the delays. I told them to be patient . . . to remember that Asians have different customs and are likely to need some time before making up their minds. Our guys went to enormous pains to collect data. I remember when they returned from a second or third trip to Japan with a mass of information, media costs, distribution data, socio-economic breakdowns, a detailed assessment of the competitive situation, positioning statements, etc. . . . but no signed contract. [Andersen chuckled as he spoke.] Of course, Nikko finally signed, but we never were sure what they really thought about us . . . or what they really expected from the deal.

Robertson was listening intently, so Andersen continued:

The whole story was interesting. When you enter a market like Japan, you are on your own. If you don't speak the language, you can't find your way around. So you become totally dependent on the locals and your partner. I must say that, in this respect, the Japanese are extremely helpful. But, let's face it, the cultural gap is wide. Another fascinating aspect was the rite of passage. In Japan, as in most Asian countries, you feel you are observing a kind of ritual, their ritual. This can destabilize the solid Viking manager. Of course, they were probably thinking that we have our rituals, too. On top of that, the Nikko people were particularly reserved and, of course, few of them spoke anything but Japanese.

There was a lot of tension during those first months, partly because France's two major brands of yogurt, "Yoplait" and "Danone," were getting more aggressive in the Japanese market.

Andersen tapped his pipe on the ashtray and smiled at Robertson:

If it's any consolation to you, Bjorn, the other two international brands are not doing any better than we are in Japan today.

What About These Other European Competitors?

The discussion with Andersen had been stimulating, and Robertson, anxious to get to the bottom of the story, decided to speak to Peter Borg, a young Danish manager who had replaced Bergman and had been supervising Agria's business in Japan for several years. Robertson asked Borg for his opinion on why Danone and Yoplait were apparently not doing any better than Delissa in Japan. Borg said:

I can explain how these two brands were handled in Japan, but I don't know whether this will throw any light on the matter as far as their performance is concerned. First, Sodima, the French dairy firm, whose Yoplait line is sold through franchise agreements all over the world, took a similar approach to ours. Yoplait is tied up with Zennoh, the National Federation of Agricultural Cooperative Association, the Japanese equivalent of Sodima. Zennoh is huge and politically very powerful. Its total sales are double those of Nikko. Yoplait probably has about 3% of the total Japanese yogurt market, which is of course a lot less than their usual 15% to 20% share in foreign markets. However, Zennoh had no previous experience in marketing yogurt.

Danone took a different approach. The company signed an agreement with a Japanese partner, Ajinomoto. Their joint venture, Ajinomoto-Danone Co. Ltd, is run by a French expatriate together with several Japanese directors. A prominent French banker based in Tokyo is also on the board. As you know, Ajinomoto is the largest integrated food processor in Japan, with sales of about $3 billion. About 45% of the company's business is in amino acids, 20% in fats and 15% in oil. Ajinomoto has a very successful joint venture with General Foods for "Maxwell House," the instant coffee. However, Ajinomoto had had no experience at all in dealing with fresh dairy products before entering this joint venture with Danone. So, for

both of the Japanese partners—Ajinomoto and Zennoh—this business was completely new and was probably part of a diversification move. I heard that the Danone joint venture had a tough time at the beginning. They had to build their dairy products distribution network from scratch. By the way, I also heard from several sources that it was distribution problems that discouraged Nestlé from pursuing a plan to reintroduce its yogurt line in Japan. Japanese distribution costs are very high compared with those in Western countries. I suspect that the Danone-Ajinomoto joint venture probably only just managed to break even last year.

"Thanks Peter," Robertson said. "It's a fascinating story. By the way, I hear that you just got married . . . to a Japanese girl. Congratulations, lucky chap!"

After his discussion with Borg, Robertson returned to his Delissa-Nikko files. Delissa's early Japanese history intrigued him.

Entry Strategy

The SRT International Advertising Agency helped develop Delissa's entry into what was called the "new milk-related products" market. Agria and Nikko had approved a substantial advertising and sales promotion budget. The agency confirmed that, as Nikko was already big in the "drinking milk" market, it was a good idea to move into the processed milk or "eating milk" field, a rapidly growing segment where added value was high.

Robertson studied the advertising agency's prelaunch rationale, which emphasized the strategy proposed for Delissa. The campaign, which had been translated from Japanese into English, proposed:

> Agria will saturate the market with the Delissa brand and establish it as distinct from competitive products. The concept "natural dairy food is good to taste" is proposed as the basic message for product planning, distribution and advertising. Nikko needs to distinguish its products from those of early-entry dairy producers and other competitors by stressing that its yogurt is "new and natural and quite different from any other yogurts."

The core target group has been defined as families with babies. Housewives have been identified as the principal purchasers. However, the product will be consumed by a wider age bracket from young children to high school students.

The advertising and point-of-sale message will address housewives, particularly younger ones. In Japan, the tendency is for younger housewives to shop in convenience stores (small supermarkets), while the older women prefer traditional supermarkets. Housewives are becoming more and more insistent that all types of food be absolutely fresh, which means that Delissa should be perceived as coming directly from the manufacturer that very day. We feel that the "freshness" concept, which has been the main selling point of the whole Nikko line, will capture the consumers' interest as well as clearly differentiate Delissa from other brands. It is essential that the ads be attractive and stand out strikingly from the others, because Nikko is a newcomer in this competitive market. Delissa should be positioned as a luxurious mass communication product.

SRT also proposed that, as Japanese housewives were becoming more diet conscious, it might be advisable to mention the dietary value of Delissa in the launch rationale. Agria preferred to stress the idea that Delissa was a Swedish product being made in Japan under license from Agria Co., Uppsala. It felt that this idea would appeal to Japanese housewives, who associated Sweden with healthy food and "sophisticated" taste. The primary messages to be conveyed would, therefore, be: "healthy products direct from the farm" and "sophisticated taste from Sweden." Although it was agreed that being good for health and beauty could be another argument in Delissa's favor, this approach would not help differentiate Delissa from other brands, all of which projected a similar image.

In order to reinforce the product's image and increase brand awareness, SRT proposed that specific visual and verbal messages be used throughout the promotional campaign. A Swedish girl in typical folk costume would be shown with a dairy farm in the background. In the words of the agency, "We feel that using this scene as an eye catcher will successfully create a warm-hearted image of naturalness, simplic-ity, friendliness and fanciful taste for the product coming from Sweden." This image would be accompanied by the text: *"Refreshing nature of Delissa Swedish yogurt; it's so fresh when it's made at the farm."*

Also included in the SRT proposal:

Advertising

To maximize the advertising effort with the budget available, the campaign should be run intensively over a short period of time rather than successively throughout the year. TV ads will be used as they have an immediate impact and make a strong impression through frequent repetition. The TV message will then be reinforced in the press. The budget will be comparable to the one used to launch Delissa in the US.

Pricing

Pricing should follow the top brands (Yukijirushi, Meiji and Morinaga) so as to reflect a high-class image, yet the price should be affordable for the housewife. The price sensitivity analysis conducted last month showed that Delissa could be priced at 15% above competitive products.

Launch

In January 1991 Delissa's product line was presented to distributors prior to launch in Tokyo, Osaka and Nagoya. Three different types of yogurt were selected for simultaneous launch:

- Plain (packs of two and four)
- Plain with sugar (packs of two and four)
- Flavored with vanilla, strawberry and pineapple (packs of two). (Fruit yogurt, Delissa's most successful offering at home and in other foreign markets, would be launched a year or two later.)

All three types were to be sold in 120 ml cups. A major pre-launch promotional campaign was scheduled for the month before launch with strong TV, newspaper and magazine support, as well as street shows, instore promotions, and test trials in and outside retail stores. On March 1, 1991 Delissa was launched in Tokyo, and on May 1, in Osaka and Nagoya.

1994: DELISSA AFTER THREE YEARS IN JAPAN

Three years after its launch, Delissa—with 2% of the Japanese yogurt market—was at a fraction of target. Concerned by the product's slow progress in Japan, Agria formed a special task force to investigate Delissa's situation and to continue monitoring the Japanese market on a regular basis. The results of the team's research now lay on Robertson's desk. The task force from Uppsala included Gustafsson (responsible for marketing questions), Bergman (sales and distribution) and Borg (who was studying the whole operation as well as training the Nikko sales force). The team spent long periods in Tokyo carrying out regular audits of the Delissa-Nikko operations, analyzing and monitoring the Japanese market and generating lengthy reports, most of which Robertson was in the process of studying.

Borg, eager to excel on his new assignment, sent back his first report to headquarters:

Distribution/Ordering system

I feel that the distribution of Delissa is not satisfactory and should be improved. The ordering system seems overcomplicated and slow, and may very well be the cause of serious delivery bottlenecks. Whereas stores order milk and juice by telephone, Delissa products are ordered on forms using the following procedure:

Day 1 A.M.: Each salesman sent an order to his depot.

Day 1 P.M.: Each depot's orders went to the Yokohama depot.

Day 2 A.M.: The Yokohama depot transmits the order to the factory.

Day 2 P.M.: Yogurt was produced at Nikko Milk Processing.

Day 3: Delivery to each depot.

Day 4: Delivery to stores.

Gustafsson agrees with me that the delivery procedure is too long for fresh food products, particularly as the date on the yogurt cup is so important to the Japanese customer. The way we operate now, the yogurt arrives in the sales outlet two or three days after production. Ideally, the time should be shortened to only one day. We realize that, traditionally, Japanese distribution is much more complex and multi-layered than in the West. In addition, Tokyo and Osaka, which are among the largest cities in the world, have no street names. So, a whole system of primary, secondary and sometimes tertiary wholesalers is used to serve supermarkets and retailers. And, since the smaller outlets have very little storage space, wholesalers often have to visit them more than once a day.

I wonder if Nikko is seriously behind Delissa. At present, there are 80 Nikko salesmen selling Delissa, but they only seem to devote about 5% of their time to the brand, preferring to push other products. Although this is apparently not an uncommon situation in many countries, in Japan it is typical—as the high costs there prohibit having a separate sales force for each line.

Borg's report continued:

Advertising

Since we launched Delissa in 1991, the advertising has not been successful. I'm wondering how well we pre-tested our launch campaign and follow-up. The agency seems very keen on Delissa as a product, but I wonder if our advertising messages are not too cluttered. Results of recent consumer research surveys showed only 4% unaided awareness and only 16% of interviewees had any recall at all; 55% of respondents did not know what our TV commercials were trying to say.

A survey by the Oka Market Research Bureau on advertising effectiveness indicated that we should stress the fact that Delissa tastes good . . . delicious. Agria's position maintains that according to the Oka survey, the consumer believes that all brands taste good, which means the message will not differentiate Delissa. Research findings pointed out that Delissa has a strong "fashionable" image. Perhaps this advantage could be stressed to differentiate Delissa from other yogurts in the next TV commercial.

DELISSA IN JAPAN: SITUATION IN AND LEADING UP TO 2001

In spite of all the careful pre-launch preparation, ten years after its launch in Japan, Delissa had less than

3% of the total yogurt market in 2001. Although Agria executives knew the importance of taking a long-term view of their business in Japan, Agria's management in Sweden agreed that these results had been far below expectations.

A serious setback for Agria had been the discovery of Nikko's limited distribution network outside the major metropolitan areas. When Agria proposed to start selling Delissa in small cities, towns and rural areas, as had been agreed in the launch plan, it turned out that Nikko's coverage was very thin in many of these regions. In the heat of the planning for the regional launch, had there been a misunderstanding of Nikko's range?

Robertson continued to leaf through Agria's survey of Japanese business, reading extracts as he turned the pages. A despondent Borg had written:

1998: The Japanese market is very tough and competition very strong. Consumers' brand loyalty seems low. But the market is large, with high potential—particularly among the younger population—if only we could reach it. Nikko has the size and manpower to meet the challenge and to increase its penetration substantially by 2000. However, Nikko's Delissa organization needs strengthening quickly. Lack of a real marketing function in Nikko is a great handicap in a market as competitive as Japan.

Distribution is one of our most serious problems. Distribution costs are extremely high in Japan, and Delissa's are excessive (27% of sales in 1998 vs. 19% for the competition). Comparing distribution costs to production costs and to the average unit selling price to distributors, it is obvious that we cannot make money on the whole Delissa range in Japan. Clearly, these costs in Japan must be reduced while improving coverage of existing stores.

Distribution levels of about 40% are still too low, which is certainly one of the major contributing factors for Delissa's poor performance. Nikko's weak distribution network outside the metropolitan areas is causing us serious problems.

1999: Delissa's strategy in Japan is being redefined (once more). The Swedish image will be dropped from the advertising, since a consumer survey has shown that some consumers believed that "fresh from the farm" meant that the yogurt was directly imported from Sweden—which certainly put its fresh-

ness into question! Ads will now show happy blond children eating yogurt . . .

Over time, the product line has grown significantly and a line of puddings has recently been added. Nikko asks us for new products every three months and blames their unsatisfactory results on our limited line.

By 2001 plain yogurt should represent almost half of Delissa's Japanese sales and account for about 43% of the total Japanese market. The plain segment has grown by almost 50% in the past three years. However, we feel that our real strength should be in the fruit yogurt segment, which has increased by about 25% since 1998 and should have about 23% of the market by next year. So far, Delissa's results in fruit yogurt have been disappointing. On the other hand, a new segment—yogurt with jelly—has been selling well: 1.2 million cups three months after introduction. Custard and chocolate pudding sales have been disappointing, while plain yogurt drink sales have been very good.

Robertson came across a more recent memo written by Gustafsson:

Mid-year Results

Sales as of mid-year 2001 are below forecast, and we are unlikely to meet our objective of 55 million 120 ml cups for 2002. At the present rate of sales, we should reach just over 42 million cups by year-end.

Stores covered

In 2001 Delissa yogurt was sold mainly in what Nielsen defined as large and super large stores. Delissa products were sold in about 71% of the total stores selling Nikko dairy products. We think that about 7,000 stores are covered in the Greater Tokyo area, but we have found that Nikko has been somewhat unreliable on retailer information.

Product returns

The number of Delissa products returned to us is very high compared with returns in other countries. The average return rate from April 2000 to March 2001 was 5.06% vs. almost 0% in Scandinavia and the international standard of 2% to 3%. The average shelf life of yogurt in Japan is 14 days. Does the high level of returns stem from the Japanese consumer's perception of when a product is too old to buy (i.e. 5 to 6 days)? The level of return varies greatly with the type of product: "healthy mix" and fruit yogurt have the highest rate, while plain and yogurt with jelly have the lowest return rate.

Media planning

Oka's latest results suggest that Delissa's primary target should be young people between 13 and 24 and its secondary target: children. Budget limitations require that money be spent on advertising addressed to actual consumers (children), rather than in trying to reach the purchasers (mothers) as well.

However, during our recent visit to Japan, we found that Nikko and the agency were running TV spots—intended for young people and children—*from 11:15 to 12:15 at night.* We pointed out that far more consumers would be reached by showing the spots earlier in the evening. With our limited budget, careful media planning is essential. Nikko probably was trying to reach both the consumer and distributor with these late night spots. Why else would it run spots at midnight when the real target group is children? Another question is whether TV spots are really what we need.

Looking at some figures on TV advertising rates in Japan, Robertson found that the price of a 15-second spot in the Tokyo area was between ¥1.25 million and ¥2.3 million in 2000 depending on the time it was run, which seemed expensive compared with European rates.[2]

Robertson continued to peruse Gustafsson's report:

Positioning

I'm seriously wondering who we are trying to reach in Japan and with what product. The Nielsen and Oka research findings show that plain yogurt makes up the largest segment in Japan, with flavored and fruit in second and third positions. It is therefore recommended that regular advertising should concentrate on plain yogurt, with periodic spots for the second two categories. However, according to Nikko, the company makes only a marginal profit on

2. $1 = ¥124 in 2001

plain yogurt, thus they feel it would be preferable to advertise fruit yogurt.

In light of this particular situation and the results of the Oka studies, we suggest that plain yogurt be advertised using the existing "brand image" commercial (building up the cow on the screen) and that a new commercial for fruit yogurt be developed based on the "fashion concept." We also believe that, if plain yogurt is clearly differentiated through its advertising, sales will improve, production costs will drop and Nikko will start making money on the product.

Last year, to help us understand where we may have gone wrong with our positioning and promotional activities, which have certainly changed rather often, we asked the Oka agency to conduct a survey using in-home personal interviews with a structured questionnaire; 394 respondents in the Keihin (Tokyo-Yokohama) metropolitan area were interviewed in April 2000. Some of the key findings are as follows:

Brand awareness

In terms of unaided brand awareness, Meiji Bulgaria yogurt had the highest level, with 27% of all respondents recalling Bulgaria first and 47% mentioning the brand without any aid. Morinaga Bifidus was in second place. These two leading brands were followed by Yoplait and Danone with 4% unaided awareness and 14% and 16% recall at any time. For Delissa, the unaided awareness was 3% and 16% for recall. In a photo aided test, Delissa plain yogurt was recognized by 71% of all respondents with a score closer to Bulgaria. In the case of fruit yogurt, 78% recognized Delissa, which had the same level as Bulgaria. Awareness of Delissa was higher than Bifidus and Danone but lower than Yoplait. In the case of yogurt drink, 99% of all respondents were aware of Yakult Joy and 44% recognized Delissa (close to Bulgaria).

Interestingly, the brand image of Meiji Bulgaria was the highest of the plain yogurt brands in terms of all attributes except for "fashionability." At the lower end of the scale (after Bulgaria, Bifidus and Natulait), Delissa was close to Danone and Yoplait in brand image. Delissa was considered less desirable than the top three, especially as far as the following characteristics were concerned: taste, availability in stores for daily shoppers, frequency of price discounting, reliability of manufacturer, good for health. Delissa's image was "fashionable." [*"Is this good or bad?" Gustafsson had scribbled on the report. "Should this be our new platform??? We've tried everything else!"*]

Advertising awareness

In the advertising awareness test, half of all respondents reported that they had not noticed advertising for any brand of yogurt during the past six months. Of those who had, top ranking went to Bifidus with 43%, Bulgaria 41% and Delissa in third place with 36%. Danone was fifth with 28% and Yoplait sixth with 26%. Respondents noticed ads for Delissa mainly on TV (94%), followed by in-store promotion (6%), newspapers (4%) and magazines (4%); 65% of the people who noticed Delissa ads could recall something about the contents of the current ads, and 9% recalled previous ads. However, when asked to describe the message of the Delissa ads, 55% of the respondents replied that they did not know what the company was trying to say.

Consumption

77% of all respondents had consumed plain yogurt within the past month: 28% Bulgaria, 15% Bifidus, 5% Yoplait, 4% Danone and 3% Delissa. The number of respondents who had at least tried Delissa was low—22% vs. 66% for Bulgaria, the best scoring brand. In the plain category, Delissa was third of the brands mainly consumed by respondents. Bulgaria was number 1 and Bifidus number 2. In the fruit segment (under yogurt consumed within the past month), Delissa was in third place (5%) after Yoplait (10%) and Bulgaria (8%). Danone was in fourth place with 3%. [*"So where do we go from here?" Gustafsson had scrawled across the bottom of the page.*]

Robertson closed the file on Gustafsson's question.

WHERE DO WE GO FROM HERE?

Robertson looked around the table at the other members of his team and asked, "What happened? We still haven't reached 3% after ten years in Japan!" Robertson knew that Borg, Gustafsson and Karlsson all had different opinions as to why Delissa had performed

badly, and each manager had his own ideas on what kind of action should be taken.

Gustafsson had spent months at Nikko, visiting retailers with members of the sales force, instigating new market research surveys and supervising the whole Nikko-Delissa team. Language problems had made this experience a frustrating one for Gustafsson, who had felt cut off from the rest of the Nikko staff in the office. He had been given a small desk in a huge room along with over 100 people with whom he could barely communicate. The Japanese politeness grated on him after a while and, as no one spoke more than a few words of anything but Japanese, Gustafsson had felt lonely and isolated. He had come to believe that Nikko was not committed to the development of the Delissa brand in Japan. He also felt that the joint venture's market share expectations had been absurd and was convinced the franchisee misrepresented the situation to Agria. He felt that Nikko was using the Delissa brand name as a public relations gimmick to build itself an international image. When he spoke, Gustafsson's tone was almost aggressive:

I don't know what to think, Bjorn. I know I don't understand our Japanese friends and I was never quite sure that I trusted them, either. They had a disconcerting way of taking control right from the start. It's that extreme politeness . . . You can't argue with them, and then suddenly they're in command. I remember when the Nikko managers visited us here in Sweden . . . a busload of them smiling and bowing their way around the plant, and we were bowing and smiling back. This is how they get their way and this is why we had such mediocre results in Japan. Agria never controlled the business. Our distribution set-up is a perfect example. We could never really know what was going on out there because language problems forced us to count on them. The same with our positioning and our advertising . . . "We're selling taste; no, we're selling health; no, we're selling fashion . . . to babies, to grandmas, to mothers." We thought we were in control but we weren't, and half the time we were doing the opposite of what we really wanted.

Bjorn, the Japanese will kill Delissa once they've mastered the Swedish technology. Then, they'll develop their own brand. Get out of the joint venture agreement with Nikko, Bjorn. I'd say, get out of Japan altogether.

Robertson next turned his attention to Borg, who had a different view of the problem. He felt that the Nikko people, trained to sell the drinking milk line, lacked specific knowledge about the eating milk or yogurt business. Borg—who had also taken over sales training in Japan after replacing Bergman—had made several trips a year to train the Nikko people both in marketing the Delissa brand and in improving distribution and sales. He had also trained a marketing manager. Borg had worked closely with the Japanese at the Tokyo headquarters.

Borg said, "I understand how Stefan feels . . . frustrated and let down, but have we given these people enough time?"

"Enough time!" said Gustafsson, laughing. "We've been there for over ten years and, if you look at our target, we have failed miserably. My question is, 'Have they given *us* enough support?'" Turning to Gustafsson, Borg continued:

I know how you feel, Stefan, but is ten years that *long? When the Japanese go into business abroad, they stay there until they get a hold on the market, however long it takes. They persevere. They seem to do things at their own speed and so much more calmly than we do. I agree on the question of autonomy. It's their very lack of Western aggressiveness that enables them to get the upper hand. Their apparent humility is disarming. But, Bjorn, should we really leave the joint venture now? When I first went to Japan and found fault with everything we were doing, I blamed the whole thing on Nikko. After nearly six years of visits, I think I have learned something. We cannot approach these people on our terms or judge them as we would judge ourselves. We cannot understand them . . . any more than they can understand us. To me, the whole point is not to even* try *and understand them. We have to accept them and then to trust. If we can't, then perhaps we should leave. But, Bjorn, I don't think we should give up the Japanese market so easily. As Stefan says, they can be excruciatingly polite. In fact, I wonder—beneath that politeness—what they think of us.*

Karlsson, the product manager, had been looking after the Japanese market for only a short time, having been recruited by Agria from Procter & Gamble 18 months earlier.

Bjorn, for me, perhaps the most serious defect in our Japanese operation has been the poor communication between the partners and a mass of conflicting data. I came into the project late and was amazed at the quantity of research and reporting that had taken place over the last ten years by everyone concerned. Many of the reports I saw were contradictory and confusing. In addition, the frequent turnover of managers responsible for Japan has interrupted the continuity of the project. And, after all the research we did, has anyone really used the findings constructively? How much is our fault? And another thing, have we been putting enough resources into Japan?

There are so many paradoxes. The Japanese seem to be so keen on the idea of having things Western, yet the successful yogurts in Japan have been the ones with that distinctive Japanese flavor. Have we disregarded what this means? Agria people believe that we have a superior product and that the type of yogurt made by our Japanese competitors does not really taste so good. How can this be true when we look at the market shares of the top Japanese producers? It obviously tastes good to the Japanese. Can we really change their preferences? Or should we perhaps look at our flavor?

It's interesting. Yoplait-Zennoh and Ajinomoto-Danone's joint ventures could be encountering similar problems to ours. Neither has more than 3% of the Japanese yogurt market and they have the same flavors as we do.

Robertson listened to the views and arguments of his team with interest. Soon, he would have to make a decision. Almost ten years after launching Delissa with Nikko, should Agria cancel its contract and find another distributor? Or should the company renew the arrangement with Nikko and continue to try to gain market share? Or should Agria admit defeat and withdraw from Japan completely? Or . . . was it, in fact, defeat at all? Robertson was glad that he had gathered his team together to discuss Delissa's future . . . their thoughts had given him new insights into the Japanese venture.

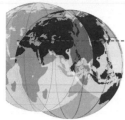

CASE 10

Marriott International: Global Account Management

Marriott International (MI), established in 1927, was a Washington D.C.-based hospitality company with over 2,200 operating units worldwide. In 2000, MI employed 153,000 people in 60 countries and generated $19.8 billion in sales.

Overview

MI had 20 products divided into six segments: Full Service Lodging, Selected Service Lodging, Extended Stay and Corporate Living, Ownership Resorts, Senior Living, and Other Operations. Full Service Lodging consisted of Marriott hotels, resorts, and suites; Renaissance hotels, resorts, and suites; The Ritz Carlton Hotel Company; LLC; and Marriott Conference Center. Selected Service Lodging consisted of Courtyard, Fairfield Inn, Spring Hill Suites, and Armada International. Extended Stay and Corporate Living consisted of Residence Inn TownePlace Suites, Marriott Executive Apartments, and ExecuStay. Ownership Resorts consisted of Marriott Vacation Club International, The Ritz-Carlton Club, and Horizons by Marriott Vacation Club. Senior Living consisted of Brighton Gardens, Marriott MapleRidge, and Village Oaks. Other Operations included Marriott Distribution Services and The Market Place by Marriott. In 1999, 1% of the hotels in the MI system were company owned; the rest were franchised, being owned and financed by third parties. Franchise fees made up 17% of MI's 1999 earnings, base management fees 27%, profit participations 38%, timeshare resorts 15%, and land rentals 3%.

This case was prepared by W. Caleb McCann, MBA, Babson College, under the direction of H. David Hennessey, Associate Professor of Marketing and International Business. The case was drawn entirely from public information sources and written as a basis for class discussion rather than to illustrate either effective or ineffective handling of a business situation. Copyright © 2002 by Babson College, William F. Glavin Center for Global Entrepreneurial Leadership. Not to be used or reproduced without written permission.

International Expansion

In October of 1966, MI expanded internationally by acquiring an airline catering company in Caracas, Venezuela. Between 1967 and 1989, MI acquired restaurant chains, fast-food restaurant chains, airport terminal food services, beverage and merchandise facilities, a vacation timesharing business, two diversified food service companies, a contract food service company, an all-suite hotel chain, a housekeeping maintenance and laundry service, and a rental retirement community. In addition, between 1967 and 1989, MI continued to build its existing hotel and restaurant system, primarily in the United States. In April of 1987, MI completed the largest single-site reservations operation in the United States. Between 1989 and 1995, MI grew from 18 to 60 international (non-U.S.) hotels. In March of 1997, MI acquired Renaissance Hotel Group for roughly $1 billion and increased its international presence to 235 hotels.

Organizational Transformation

In June 1996, a CEO-sponsored task force set up to analyze the effectiveness of the sales force led to the development of a Customer Relationship Management (CRM) program. The CRM program in turn led to a Sales Transformation program in 1997. This transformation program consolidated the sales division, marketing division, and customer services function into one reporting structure and business unit, except for the international sales force. International sales continued to report to international operations. The organizational transformation included the creation of a Strategic Accounts division within the Sales and Marketing division. It was responsible for MI's global and U.S. headquartered national accounts. Global and U.S. headquartered national accounts consisted of approximately 1,500 commercial customers and annual sales of roughly $3 billion. The Strategic Accounts division sits above the hotels' sales forces and builds account teams around qualified commercial customers. In the course of the transformation, MI also consolidated Marriott.com, worldwide reservations, agency sales, and field sales under the Sales and Marketing division.

Before MI had instituted the transformation process and new account management strategy, individual hotels acting alone to create demand handled their own sales and marketing. There was a system-wide sales force of 225,000 that sold for individual properties.

Strategic Selling Through Account Management

The Strategic Accounts division created the MI Alliance Program. The MI Alliance Program was initiated when senior managers realized that major customers, primarily corporations, were demanding more than just hotel rooms; they wanted accommodation solutions. A decision to reorganize the entire sales force within the company was based on three goals: using technology to support connectivity, refocusing the sales force on markets rather than on individual hotels, and developing a global account management program.

In 1998, MI created a Global Account Management (GAM) group. MI hired a GAM team of 12 global account managers. These managers were chosen after review of candidates' detailed résumés, psychological profile testing, and interviews by two vice presidents. GAM directors were approved by a committee of five vice presidents from brand teams, corporate headquarters, and sales and marketing.

There were four levels of account management. Tier IV accounts consisted of several thousand local accounts and new prospects. Tier III consisted of several hundred regional accounts. Tier II consisted of a few hundred national accounts. Tier I, Alliance Accounts, consisted of global business customers. Out of 3,500 total accounts, the GAM group identified 25–50 potential Alliance Accounts, MI's label for high-valued global customers. In 1998, MI's 30 Alliance Accounts accounted for $600 million in revenues and were managed by 12 global account managers.

By 1999, MI's sales force was completely overhauled and organized around customers instead of around properties. In 1999, MI employed over 10,000 sales and reservation associates, all of whom carried out booking requests for any MI property worldwide.

Internal Selling

For the Alliance Program to begin properly, MI had to sell the idea internally. MI faced the challenge of moving the sales force from a traditional transactional structure to an organization focused on account solutions. Since each hotel in the MI system was franchised and managed locally and each had a separate P&L statement, consolidation of account management initially was seen as a loss of control by individual hotel management. To address this issue, MI conducted an internal campaign focused on selling the account strategy program. Communication of the vision, mission and plan was continuous. For every presentation that was given to an external customer selling the account management strategy, three presentations were given to those involved internally. The GAM program was mainly concerned with meeting the needs of strategic accounts and not with filling rooms at individual hotels. During the account management formation and early stages of execution, MI continually communicated urgency for change and every success was celebrated and communicated to all involved. This was achieved through e-mail by relaying real success stories praising work that encouraged and advanced strategic selling. MI brought in customers and conducted one-to-one presentations to help transform the sales team. Quarterly updates were conducted during business reviews. During the first year alone, the vice president of alliance sales conducted over 80 internal meetings addressing alliance accounts. Sales training classes for over 500 people were held every year specifically to demonstrate how strategic account management would change each job in the company.

MI's Alliance Program identified audiences throughout the company who were critical to the success of the alliance program. These groups were targeted with constant communications for the purpose of providing information that helped them understand the program's strategy and gain their support. Alliance program directors and vice presidents were on the agenda of every corporate meeting throughout the organization. Sales newsletters, in-market presentations, monthly conference calls with each account team, and annual business review meetings with executives were some of the other internal communication mediums used to get the message across. Many of these initiatives continued even after the program had advanced beyond its startup period.

Compensation packages for sales teams also changed, moving from calculating sales on "definite roomnights" to "total account revenue". The weighting of revenue component decreased from 80% to 50%, annual account revenue goals were zero based and account team members had a portion of their compensation plans tied to supporting strategic accounts.

Global Account Management

MI Tier I Alliance Account was MI's category for GAM. The GAM strategy was business-to-business focused; that is, the program concentrated on providing a greater level of service to companies that used MI on a regular basis. This was done by profiling and segmenting potential accounts to ensure alignment with the program. Then a GAM team would identify key customers and its influencers, determine its requirements and needs, and develop a customized value proposal for the customer.

MI's goal was to get customers who could be potential alliance accounts to think beyond price and a single point of contact. At first, many customers saw the MI GAM program as only a central point of contact and global pricing agreement. This was important for MI's strategy, but it was only the beginning step. MI's long-term vision was to combine its strengths with that of an alliance account and leverage this relationship to generate solutions and create value for both companies. Building a relationship of trust and satisfying a customer's base expectations was MI's first step in this process. MI's approach was to flawlessly execute an alliance account's initial expectations regarding one point of contact and pricing. Through delivering small successes, MI believed that a relationship of trust would grow and open up the customer to a complete acceptance of the alliance account strategy.

MI's long-term GAM strategy success is illustrated by its relationship with International Business Machine (IBM). MI appointed a strategic account manager to manage the IBM account and to direct a sales team of about 70 to manage the local relationships. A year after MI designated IBM as an alliance account, IBM agreed to use MI as its only supplier when piloting new accommodations, conferences, and other related event programs. In 1998, IBM paid MI over $2 million in cancellation fees for meeting rooms. In that same year, IBM paid MI $15 million dollars for meeting rooms actually used. Thus, IBM was paying over 10 percent of its budget for meetings on cancellation fees.

Through the Alliance Account partnership IBM and MI had built, the two companies worked together to solve this problem. The solution involved connecting MI and IBM internal systems with an electronic bulletin board on which IBM would post canceled meeting rooms to sell to other internal IBM customers. If another IBM customer filled the meeting room, then the cancellation fee would no longer apply. This way IBM dramatically reduced money spent on cancellation fees and MI did not have to assume the costs of filling a previously scheduled meeting room.

Technology

MI aligned its IT organization to reflect the transformation of its sales and marketing functions. This included providing every business and functional division in MI a representative from the IT division, consolidating databases, enhancing data warehousing capabilities, and developing customer profiling capabilities. The IT representatives reported directly to their appointed business or functional division. The Strategic Accounts division had its own IT representative.

MI invested approximately $25 million in a Siebel front office system. MI had about 2,500 employees using the system in 2000 and planned to have between 4,000 and 5,000 employees implemented by the end of 2001. During the Siebel front office system rollout, MI planned to consolidate many of its various customer information databases to improve its storage and use of customer information.

MI kept customer profiles by collecting and storing transaction history, demographics, product and service usage, customer value level, and service history. MI systematically recorded data at each interaction with customers. MI was able to view a complete customer profile across all product and service areas by downloading data from multiple databases. Data warehousing was completely functioning in the consumer business, which enabled MI's loyalty program and reservations for the individual traveler. This was not the case with business customers because the inventory management (meeting rooms and conference sites) was controlled at the property site level. Business customer information and bookings needed to be uploaded to be directly accessed company-wide. The database consolidation and the Siebel system allowed for business customer and individual customer information to be accessible company-wide. In 2001, MI began to develop a total hotel yield management and consolidated inventory system for meeting and conference rooms and meeting space.

Through its website, MI provided customers the ability to browse for hotel rooms, make reservations, link to other travel sites, and create customer profiles. In 2001, MI expected to book $1 billion in business through its website. The Strategic Accounts division planned and conducted pilot programs to develop MI's web presence for business customers. These programs included links to unique sites of interest to business travelers and provided online booking capability for meeting planners by linking into companies' intranets.

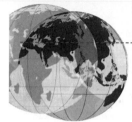

CASE 11

Hewlett-Packard: Global Account Management

Hewlett-Packard Company (HP), established in 1939, was a Palo Alto, California-based technology company with more than 540 sales and support offices worldwide. In 2000, HP employed 88,500 people in 120 countries and generated $48 billion in revenues.

HP's first product was an electronic instrument used to test sound equipment in 1939. In 1957, HP's written objectives along with HP's management style formed the "HP way." Dave Packard delivered the corporate objectives as a way of guiding management decision-making. In 1958, divisions structured with separate profit-and-loss accountability were established. Each product group was a self-sustaining organization responsible for developing, manufacturing, and marketing its own products. Any group that grew to 1,500 people was divided in two and moved to two separate P&L. This autonomy fostered individual motivation, initiative, and creativity, and it gave employees the opportunity to work with broad freedom to achieve common goals and objectives.

In 1959, HP became global and opened a large manufacturing facility in Boeblingen, Germany, and a European headquarters in Geneva, Switzerland. Flexible work hours were introduced at the Boeblingen plant in 1967 and throughout U.S. facilities in 1973. In 1968, decentralization moved decision-making from corporate vice presidents to group general managers who run divisions with related product lines. This allowed compatible units to work together. HP's first step in adopting group structure was combining

●

This case was prepared by W. Caleb McCann, MBA, Babson College, under the direction of H. David Hennessey, Associate Professor of Marketing and International Business. The case was drawn entirely from public information sources and written as a basis for class discussion rather than to illustrate either effective or ineffective handling of a business situation. Copyright © 2002 by Babson College, William F. Glavin Center for Global Entrepreneurial Leadership. Not to be used or reproduced without written permission.

independent operating divisions to form related product groups. HP was again reorganized in 1984 into a four-sector organization that was formed to oversee the growing number of groups. In 1986–1987, all of HP's technical computing activities were put into the same sector. In 1994, Telecommuting polices were formalized, making HP one of the first companies to encourage telecommuting around the world. Employees could work at home or at remote HP offices. HP benefited from reduced office-space requirements and improved employee retention. HP's Intranet, the world's largest at the time, linked its global operations and ensured communication with employees wherever located.

Extended Enterprise

In response to continuous rising expectations and competition, HP introduced technology initiatives to increase speed, reduce costs, and improve quality. These initiatives worked through the Internet both internally and externally, with customers and with suppliers. In 1989, HP implemented its global wide-area network, which has resulted in cost savings of five times the previous system. In 1999, 1.5 million e-mail messages were transmitted daily and the number of megabytes of traffic continued to grow, with the increasing number of attachments.

HP has used its Intranet to increase sales productivity with the aid of its new tool called Electronic Sales Partner (ESP). This tool anticipates the informational needs of HP's sales representatives. It had increased sales productivity and saved HP $125 million per year. It has given sales people access to any information they need to do their job, including field training, product literature, press releases, data sheets, and conference guides all in one place whenever they need it. ESP's primary users were 5,000 sales representatives. In 1999, ESP contained over 40,000 documents and was continuing to grow.

One of the first functions where HP began to

extend information to its trading partners was in order fulfillment and logistics. Its web-based product data management had links with material resource planning (MRP) and corporate parts databases. Its workflow engine controls changes, approvals, versions, notification, and summary statistics. The channel logistics and fulfillment organization distributes HP products to about 250 resellers in the U.S. and Canada, and it pushes $20 billion of product through the reseller channel annually.

Global Account Management

The marketing within the computer systems industry evolved toward a customer-focused approach in the late 1980s and early 1990s for several reasons. First, customers demanded consistent worldwide service and support and increased standardization. Second, technologies changed from a centralized mainframe mode to decentralized networked computers that were linked globally. Multinational customers demanded that vendors be strategic partners who could demonstrate an understanding of specific international business needs and deploy relevant solutions on a global basis. Third, continuous innovation and decreasing time-to-market forced firms to reevaluate their relationships and strategic alliances with customers and suppliers. Fourth, alternative channels of distribution were prevalent and continued to grow throughout the industry.

In 1991, HP implemented a pilot global account management program between its largest division, The Computer Systems Organization, and six of its global accounts. This program originated from the philosophy of customer-based management. HP's global account management program consisted of several elements:

1. *Global client business managers* were assigned executives and account program managers. This level of global account management, offering one interface to account executives, greatly facilitated communications for global account customers.

2. *Experts and specialists on product solutions.*

3. The process of *worldwide contracts* consisted of delivery and implementation primarily through the use of HP's Intranet.

In response to customers' expectations for all parts of HP to behave as one company, HP consolidated its sales model by creating the "Client Business Manager" in 1998. This position was responsible for complete business relationships of customers in HP's Computer Organization. This created some challenges because organization structures below the "Client Business Manager" were not changed or aligned.

Global Account Managers

Global account managers were directed to address customers' demands for consistent worldwide service. Global account managers were located near customers' headquarters, were responsible for directly managing HP's relationship with the global customer, and served as the direct channel of the global account's relationship to HP's distribution channels. The global account manager's responsibilities included coordination of global customer sales, providing customer support and satisfaction, ensuring that HP was seen as one company at all customer locations, working with HP's senior management to ensure that company actions were organized and availability of adequate resources were provided to properly service global account opportunities, and establishing close relationships with senior corporate HP executives assigned to the global accounts.

Global account managers operated under a dual reporting system. They reported to the country/region and industry manager as well as to the global account sales manager accountable for global accounts business in a particular field office. The global accounts sales manager reported to both the field operations manager and to the head of the global account program. Global account headquarters staff reported directly to the global account manager for their field. District sales managers and sales representatives reported both to a global account manager and to a local area sales manager. Dual reporting structures strengthened geographical responsibilities of the sales force and enabled the global account manager to meet a global customer's needs directly, thereby making decisions independent of geography.

Global account managers were evaluated on worldwide performance of their assigned global accounts. Country managers were evaluated on worldwide performance of global accounts headquartered in their country as well as on overall country performance.

HP's global account management program used a measurement system to assess the costs of implementing the program and provide global account performance tracking. Two metrics were involved in the measurement systems: selling cost envelope (SCE) and the account specific field selling cost model (FSC). SCE measured the selling costs associated with obtaining an order and FSC measured all costs associated with the implementation of a global account sales team and supporting costs.

Global account managers were responsible for motivating the local sales teams and country level business managers. In some cases, the business generated by global accounts were 30–40% of a global account manager's business. The global account manager's responsibility to iron out the differences between local needs and global business needs was achieved through meeting, in person, with local sales people and management.

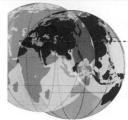

CASE 12

Xerox Corporation: Global Account Management

Global Account Management Overview

Xerox has had a global account management program for 15 years. In 1986, Xerox started with a global account management test program for six major accounts. In 1988, the program was expanded to 12 accounts and then again in 1989 to 24 accounts. Throughout the 1990s, Xerox's global account management program continued to grow and as of September 2001, the company had 150 global accounts.

Global account managers reside in the home country of their assigned account. That country unit incurs a global account manager's salary and expenses, but they take direction from the industry VPs. In Germany, for example, the General Manager has eight global account managers reporting to him, including the global account managers for BMW, Volkswagen, and Allianz Insurance. These global account managers also report to Xerox's VP of Industrial, in the case of BMW and Volkswagen, or Xerox's VP of Financial Services, in the case of Allianz Insurance. Joint reporting in Europe occurs because global account managers are on the books of Xerox's individual country units. In the U.S., global account managers report to the various Industry Vice Presidents who are part of the U.S. management team.

Xerox has over 100 global account managers, each of whom handles one or two accounts. "Tier 1" accounts have a dedicated global account manager in

●

This case was prepared by W. Caleb McCann, MBA, Babson College, and H. David Hennessey, Associate Professor of Marketing and International Business. The case was drawn from a conversation with David Potter, Director Global Account Field Operations at Xerox Corporation, and from public information sources and written as a basis for class discussion rather than to illustrate either effective or ineffective handling of a business situation. Copyright © 2002 by Babson College, William F. Glavin Center for Global Entrepreneurial Leadership. Not to be used or reproduced without written permission.

almost all cases. A few global account managers have other responsibilities, although this is contrary to the design model. For example, the global account manager for a global banking group is also the channel manager for Financial Services in Holland. The reason for this variance from the design is that 80% of Xerox's business with this global banking group is outside of Holland, so Xerox's Holland unit wants to spread the cost of a relatively high-powered sales person over other functions.

Selecting Global Accounts

Xerox has three initial criteria that companies need to meet to become a global account:

- The first criterion is that a potential global account spends at least $10 million a year with Xerox. Tier 1 accounts have global purchases of $15 million and Tier 2 $10 million.

- The second global account criterion is that a potential global account be global in both business practices and organizational structure. Xerox requires global accounts to do business globally but does not require global purchasing. Some Xerox customers conduct business globally but are locally organized and managed. In this situation, even if the customer spends over $10 million a year with Xerox, there is no strategic benefit to Xerox for dedicating a global account manager to the customer.

- Third, a global account must be willing to collaborate with Xerox. Xerox's global account management program goes beyond just selling products and works with global accounts to help develop value added solutions. In order to do this successfully, a global account needs to share their business issues, key success factors, and strategy with Xerox.

Most large customers have multiple brand divisions as well as administration, marketing, and other functions. Part of the challenge for global account managers is being able to get their arms around all of the divisions while managing their time efficiently. That is why Xerox wants to ensure that the customer is willing to make an equal investment in the relationship.

Global accounts have global, regional, and/or local contracts. This gives Xerox flexibility to build relationships and strategically align with customers who do not meet all the global account criteria but are in the process of building a global strategy. For example, in 1999 Motorola was a Xerox global account but was not able to commit to a global contract. At the time, Motorola's only extensive contract with Xerox covered the United States, and this contract was not considered truly comprehensive. However, Motorola had a proactive manager running its Asia operation who wanted to leverage its global account relationship with Xerox and not "wait for those people at headquarters to get their act together." This resulted in Xerox doing a comprehensive Asia deal with Motorola.

Global Account Information Systems

Xerox has a product called Docushare, which is a document sharing group-ware. Docushare allows global account managers to set up web pages without having to use HTTP programming. Xerox's global account managers all have web pages with their own setup, including contract information, price lists, Who's Who, presentations, success stories, and a chat room. Team members on existing accounts can continuously update their Global Account Strategic Plan using Docushare.

There is also a Global Account Management Information System that tracks revenue and machine population in 45 countries around the world. Xerox is in the process of upgrading that system and turning it into the Global Account Reporting System. The upgraded Global Account Reporting System will not only report billed revenue but also will track current booked business and an account's gross profit.

Xerox global account operations also has an internal "best practice" sharing system called Xplane Information Transfer (Xplane i.t.). The idea was developed in Europe and used to share success stories with other global account managers. The "Xplane i.t." memos do three things. One, they highlight applications and solutions so other employees involved in global accounts are aware of them. Two, they give recognition to the people who are responsible for success stories. Three, they provide a constructive piece of news for everybody in the company to say, "Hey, we've had success here, business is good with this account."

Global Account Planning and Coordination

Xerox uses its global account planning process to balance both global and local issues. If Xerox is adding a new global account, key members who will be handling and interacting with the account come together to develop a coordinated plan during the account planning process. In the account planning process, Xerox involves many of the people who will be handling the account, including key members from Xerox's local, corporate, and industry groups, as well as representatives from partners who will be involved and sometimes representatives from the account. The account representative is an executive and comes to the account planning meeting to bring the account's perspective into the planning process. If an executive from the account is not able to attend the account planning meeting, the Xerox global account manager will visit the relevant account executive to collect customer information to be taken in to consideration during the account planning process. Xerox employees involved in the planning process meeting are the ones who will handle major aspects of the account and related initiatives. A global account plan can be updated throughout the year, if needed, on Docushare.

Independent of the account planning meetings, Xerox schedules an annual Global Account meeting that combines a kick-off meeting for the up-coming year, recognition of success, and training.

Xerox controls the account plan from a global perspective through influence and corporate backing. However, friction sometimes does occur between the needs and objectives of global account management and the needs and objectives of product and local management. For example, there may be cases of maverick managers trying to sell out products at the end of June because they want to make their half-year bonus or a country manager may sell to the local division of a global account for 10% less than the global contract stipulates just to get the business. This kind of behavior is technically out of the control of the global account manager because he/she does not have direct control at the local level. However, this is not a major problem for Xerox because, in general, most managers understand and follow the global account management concepts. A manager is hard pressed to argue a conflicting direction if there is a plan that has been put together by the global account team and the customer has sanctioned it. Issues do not escalate very often at Xerox because the global account management program has been working for almost 15 years and managers know that "you shouldn't mess with the global account manager" because people recognize that they have ownership of the account.

Selecting and Developing Global Account Managers

Approximately 50% of Xerox global account managers have been national account managers. These global account managers were usually elevated to the position when an account was elevated from national account status to global account status, but this scenario is not guaranteed. For example, in 2000, Xerox elevated a large server company from a national account in the United States to a global account because of their global expansion. In this case, the person who was the national account manager did not get the job because Xerox industry management did not feel that that person was sufficiently capable of taking on that additional responsibility. National account managers and global account managers have similar jobs at Xerox except for the degree of complexity, difficulty, and cultural acumen required. A national account manager with less refined human management skills might perform well in the U.S. because he/she is dealing with other Americans in English and does not have to master other languages or cultural difficulties.

Global account managers often deal with remote people who do not report to them. In these situations, they must manage through influence. They must understand how to communicate with people from another culture. Xerox understands that a key to success is managing customer perceptions of its people and how they deal with all kinds of issues.

Xerox is in the process of working on professional development and focusing on what is required for the global account manager to be successful on a worldwide basis. Working with Rutgers University and the Strategic Account Management Association,

Xerox has carried out elaborate skill assessment internally with sales people, middle management, senior management, and customers to determine skills and competencies required to be a successful global account manager. Qualified global account managers are difficult to find, and Xerox is constrained by its inability to identify and attract a sufficient number of candidates. Given this situation, approximately one-third of Xerox's global account managers are stretched too thin. Xerox has developed some cultural awareness half-day modules for employees involved in global accounts. These modules create awareness and train participants to use a mental checklist that asks, "What's going on here? Are we having a conflict because we do not treat time the same? Or we do not reason the same way? Or we do not treat status the same way?"

Xerox conducted workshop sessions at the headquarters of Fuji-Xerox Asia Pacific, in Singapore, which brought together country based marketing people and their global account counterparts from the Asia Pacific region and global account managers from around the world. Account managers presented their account plans, made calls on their customers, and listened to what other account managers had to say about business in their respective countries. Xerox found that the participants who were experienced and aware of cultural difference provided greatest value.

Xerox is organized by industry. Five Industry Business Groups develop industry-specific solutions and each industry group is responsible for gathering data and analyzing its respective industry. The five industry business groups are Graphic Arts, Public Sector, Healthcare, Financial Services, and Industrial. Each industry business group is organized into subunits that focus on specific niches. For example, the Industrial Business Group is organized into these sub-units: Aerospace, Automotive and Other Discrete Manufacturing, Petroleum and Chemical, Communications, Consumer Products, Pharmaceutical, Technology, Transportation, and Utilities. Each industry sub-unit has marketing managers who track specific industries. Industry group team members are knowledgeable in their specific industries; about 40% were hired out of those industries. For example, the public sector group hired a person who was an executive with the state of Florida to become the university and education marketing manager. He knew the language and culture of the public sector and the education industry. Each industry group marketing manager puts together training sessions and seminars specific to their industry. It is the responsibility of the industry groups to develop solutions for their particular industries. For example, in the pharmaceutical industry, the new drug approval process is very complicated and it is the responsibility of the pharmaceutical sub-unit to know the procedure, required paper work, and software solutions for the drug approval process.

When it comes to individual global accounts, it is the responsibility of the account manager and the people on the global account team to meet the specific informational requirements of the account. Most of this work is done when the Annual Account Plan is drawn up. As previously mentioned, the annual account planning process at Xerox sometimes includes participation from the global account customer. This provides an account team with valuable first-hand information about their account's business problems and critical success factors. In some circumstances where Xerox has had a strong relationship with a global account or an adept global account manager on the account, customers have volunteered information by saying, "by the way, here are a few areas where I think you can help us."

Xerox global account managers receive training on industries from the industry managers. The global account management program office is focused on what is required to be a successful strategic account manager on a global basis. This includes developing a manager's skills in cultural awareness, reading financial reports, executive communication, managing cross-cultural teams without direct authority, major international economic trends, and understanding the influences of currency fluctuations on business. Xerox is trying to make global account managers trusted advisors to the customer. Xerox can easily lose credibility if a global account manager and a customer are having a conversation and the customer says, "We're going to have to postpone that order in Singapore because of what's been happening with the value of the currency." and the global account manager looks at the customer and asks, "So what difference does that make?" The global account manager should be aware enough to say, "How about if we did an offshore deal and you pay for it in the UK?"

Global Account Measurement Systems

To determine success of its global account management program, Xerox uses both qualitative and quantitative measures. The principle measurement used is year-over-year revenue growth of each global account. Since 2000, Xerox has been measuring gross profit of its global accounts. This has been difficult because of multiple P&L allocations versus actual costs. Xerox also measures customer satisfaction. Some of the softer measures employed are the degree to which Xerox has been able to introduce new technologies into its global accounts, the conversion rate from analog to digital, and the adopt rate of color products.

Xerox's global account managers are compensated based on year-over-year revenue growth and profit growth. A global account manager may also be measured on how well he/she is able to get the global account team to use Docushare and work together as a team.

Creating Value for Global Accounts

A major part of the global account manager's role is to identify unique ways to create value for the account. Xerox has developed most of these solutions with industry orientations, with most of the advancements coming from global accounts. For example, BMW wanted to make vehicle owner manuals personalized and less expensive to produce. Most vehicle owner's manuals included at least four languages of material and instructions for all the possible options. The traditional owner's manual was about an inch-and-a-half thick. This practice wasted paper, was becoming more expensive to print, and had high associated storage costs. Xerox worked with BMW, for almost a year, to create a personalized print-on-demand owner's manual solution. With this solution, BMW was able to provide an owner's manual that was personalized, with the buyer's name printed on the front, in the buyer's preferred language, and with instructions that addressed only the specific options purchased. The new owner's manuals are 80% thinner than the ones previously used and are printed on demand, thus eliminating storage and shipping costs. The personalized print-on-demand owner's manual solution has become almost a generic solution now; Xerox is using this format for mobile-phone companies, like Nokia and Motorola, and television manufacturing companies.

Xerox has also worked closely with global account pharmaceutical companies. Xerox has software that helps pharmaceutical companies manage their proposals involved in the drug approval process. The drug development and testing process needs to be meticulously documented with version control and sign-off for all the different tests for drug approval. If all the documents required for a drug approval process were printed, they would fill a trailer truck. Xerox has worked with their pharmaceutical global account companies to do this electronically.

Another area where Xerox has been successful is in the banking industry. Xerox has been able to help many banks, with the Hong Kong Shanghai Bank as a prime example. Xerox worked with Hong Kong Shanghai Bank to have print-on-demand personalized bank statements. The bank can now actually ask customers, "What language do you want your statement printed in?" and immediately print a personalized version.

Global Account Management Challenges

One of the biggest issues that Xerox faces is the lack of a truly shared value among all senior management as to the importance of the global account management program and the level of support it requires. Nobody wants to give up control. For example, Germany does not want to give up control of BMW, and so they resist having to go into a corporate function. They also do not want their salesperson from Germany to spend all of his time doing business in France, the UK, or Italy. This is because Xerox Germany does not receive credit for revenue developed in other countries while incur-

ring the cost of paying their salesperson's salary and traveling expenses. Germany has eight global account managers on its payroll, and they are only spending about a third of their time in Germany. That is an unfair burden for the current general manager of Germany. There is also the issue of Xerox Germany losing the services, within Germany, of the individual account manager while he is doing business elsewhere.

One challenge for Xerox global account management is to determine how to handle customers who want a global price. Although the customer might want the same prices everywhere, Xerox does not have the same costs everywhere. Many customers do not recognize this, even though they may talk to someone like McDonalds who does not charge the same price for a "Big Mac" everywhere or to automobile companies who do not sell comparable automobiles for the same prices everywhere.

Xerox GAM has not lost too many deals because they could not provide a global price. Xerox has had situations where business has been postponed or lost temporarily when another company was awarded a contract because they claimed they could provide a global price. However, usually these companies cannot actually provide a global price when it comes to delivery. The global pricing problem tends to be with uninitiated customers; their purchasing people want to try to do this because they want a feather in their cap and to be able to say, "We've got the same price everywhere." Xerox could give customers the same price everywhere, if the pricing is smoothed out, but that means some countries would be paying a price higher than what they could get locally.

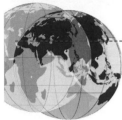

CASE 13

tonernow.com: A Dotcom Goes Global

INTRODUCTION

It was the second week in April 2000. Dotcom euphoria gripped the U.S. economy and venture capital was flowing everywhere. Henry Kasindorf and Rich Katz, young founders of a New Jersey-based brick-and-mortar company recently turned dotcom, had received communications from all over the world soliciting their participation in licensing agreements, partnerships, and other similar relationships. Serious offers had come from Australia, Brazil, South Africa, Central America, and Europe. Their company, tonernow. com, was hot.

Kasindorf and Katz were facing a big question: should operations remain focused on the U.S. or should the company go global? The business was expanding and many issues required immediate attention. Globalization would inject even greater urgency into the situation.

tonernow.com was the e-commerce arm of IQ Computer Products, a company Kasindorf and Katz had founded in 1993. The brick-and-mortar segment of the business, not counting the website, was now selling approximately $5 million. Some two-thirds of this volume went to individual retail clients and one-third to wholesalers and distributors.

The tonernow.com website launched in beta format on September 15, 1999, now carried over 3,000 products at discounts of 30% to 70% off manufacturer list prices. The site also offered a proprietary line of compatible toner products.

●

This case was written by Martha Lanning, Research Associate, William F. Glavin Center for Global Entrepreneurial Leadership, under the direction of JeanPierre Jeannet, F.W. Olin Distinguished Professor of Global Business. This case was written as a basis for class discussion rather than to illustrate either effective or ineffective handling of a business situation. Copyright © 2000 by Babson College, William F. Glavin Center for Global Entrepreneurial Leadership. Not to be used or reproduced without written permission.

Toner was a black, powdered, plastic substance contained in cartridges used in printers, copiers, and fax machines. Toner powder adhered to parts of a drum that had been properly charged for toner coverage. A fuser assembly within the printer or copier machine melted the toner to fuse it to the page, resulting in a sharp text that could not be smudged. When toner ran out, the machines could not function. Toner was critical for office productivity.

COMPANY HISTORY

Kasindorf and Katz had met as freshmen undergraduates at Babson College in 1987, the year Kasindorf achieved recognition for his successful launch of a condom vending machine business. Kasindorf described his rocky beginning as an entrepreneur:

> "I used all my professors. One in law helped me with the contracts, marketing helped me with the brochures. I was fascinated by all the resources that were available, some of the best in the world! I attended a student government meeting and brought the project up for approval, but the Assistant Dean shot me down. I stormed into the Dean's office and got it OK'd. That business was fun, it got my feet wet. There were a lot of legal issues, such as liability if one of the condoms broke. Also, I was a freshman and in the middle of finals I got 12 voice mails from reporters!"

William F. Glavin Center for Global Entrepreneurial Leadership Distributed by The European Case Clearing House, England and USA.
North America, phone: +1 781 239 5884, fax: +1 781 239 5885, e-mail: ECCHBabson@aol.com.
Rest of the World, phone: +44 (0)1234 750903, fax: +44 (0)1234 751125, e-mail: ECCH@cranfield.ac.uk.
All rights reserved. Printed in UK and USA. Web Site: http://www.ecch.cranfield.ac.uk.

Within months, Kasindorf had set up condom dispensers in college bathrooms throughout the Boston area. Two years later he sold the business for $25,000 and used the proceeds to start another venture. The partners laughed as they recalled their early collaboration:

> Kasindorf: "We didn't take much of a liking to each other."
>
> Katz: "We didn't hit it off."
>
> Kasindorf: "I needed a ride, I told him it would take five minutes, it took 40, and he liked me even less! Then we had a Human Communications class together. My only memory is that Rich got a 37 on the midterm and I got a 16.[1] We sort of bonded after that."

The T-Shirt Business

Kasindorf and Katz soon founded a screen-printed T-shirt company operating on campus. The shirts featured creative graphics using well-known consumer goods logos and sold like hotcakes. Kasindorf explained:

> "The copyright hounds had their bounty hunters looking for us. You *do* have to change 20% of the design so you're not infringing on someone else's mark. We had friends at other schools who started selling the T-shirts for us. Then *U.S. News & World Report* came out with the Babson ranking, and we launched a new T-shirt highlighting the No. 1 ranking during homecoming weekend.[2] In 1988–1989, our picture ran in the Babson College publication with the *U.S. News & World Report* ranking."

IQ Computer Products

After graduating from Babson College, Kasindorf and Katz briefly went their separate ways, each working elsewhere. However, in May 1993, they teamed up again, this time purchasing two small manufacturing companies with combined revenues under $300,000. According to Katz, "One was a sole proprietorship, a guy was making toner products out of his garage."

Based on this purchase, Kasindorf and Katz opened business activity in Spring Valley, NY, some 45 miles from New York City. The new enterprise produced toner and employed four people in addition to Kasindorf and Katz: one in customer service, one to perform accounting and clerical tasks, and two in manufacturing. Operations included manufacturing, customer service, accounting, warehousing, and sales.

Recycling toner cartridges was encouraged on an industry-wide basis. The two partners saw this as an advantage, an aspect of the business that would aid in cost control and make the product "recession-proof."

Funding came entirely from cash flow, profits, and a small bank loan. In 1993, the partners held notes to the two original owners. Within two years the notes were paid off.

By 1994, business was exploding out of the 900 square feet facility in Spring Valley. The young entrepreneurs consolidated the two original firms, named the new entity IQ Computer Products (IQCP), and moved the company to its present site in Englewood, NJ. Kasindorf discussed the decision to locate in Englewood:

> "We wanted to stay in New York, and so did the employees. We took it to the State to inquire regarding subsidies and incentives, but they laughed at us because we were under one million dollars in sales. The next week I went to Trenton[3] to talk to the same department, but in New Jersey. They had a team of people assembled in a conference room. They offered training and incentives, and each one made a proposal to us on why we should locate in New Jersey. They welcomed us with open arms."

Growing the Business

During the period 1994–1998, the company added products and diversified as Kasindorf and Katz grew the business. They brought the repair division, previously subcontracted, in-house and hired their own technicians.

In 1994, IQCP sold in three states: New York, New Jersey, and Connecticut. IQCP also serviced a small number of other states by UPS.[4] In 1997 the

---

1. Out of a possible score of 100 on the midterm exam.

2. *U.S. News & World Report* ranked Babson College the No. 1 business school in the U.S. for entrepreneurial studies.

3. Capital of the state of New Jersey.

4. United Parcel Service, a delivery service.

company began using Federal Express to offer three-day delivery to California with standard ground rates. That same year, business expanded into Canada. By 1998, IQCP was selling in 14 states, mainly in the Northeast but also in California and Colorado.

The partners elaborated on the importance of building customer relationships.

Katz: "We felt we could sell products other than those we manufactured. Our customers told us they wanted other products. Our customers asked us because the level of service we offered was so far above what other companies offered."

Kasindorf: "We hand-delivered the product, no matter how large or small the order. Our rep showed up with a nice shirt and our IQCP logo, offered to clean the printer and install the customer's cartridge so it would achieve optimal performance. People started to see the attention we gave."

Katz: "When we started, quality was a major issue in the industry."

Kasindorf: "People are leery of this industry. Therefore, it's important for us to appear as legitimate as possible. We advertise in the *New York Times,* we bring large customers here to tour our facility."

Katz: "We encourage people to call our reference list. We've had long-standing relationships with our customers, and they rave about us. We are very, very careful here. It's a 'razor blade' product, people come back and buy it again and again. We want people to have an experience second to none. If there's a problem, we replace it with no charge and we handle it quickly."

Kasindorf: "We sell to some of the largest law firms in New York City. We are right there when their laser printers need repair. They rely on us."

Website Launch

In 1998, Kasindorf and Katz made the decision to go dotcom. They looked at what was necessary for their company to remain successful and determined that it would be essential to develop an e-commerce strategy and get online. As Kasindorf put it, "We knew we had to now or we'd be left behind."

Kasindorf and Katz knew what was successful *offline,* and they wanted to translate that to *online.*

They also wanted to avoid cannibalizing their existing business. The primary options were either to create online ordering for existing clients or to create an entirely new entity as the e-commerce solution.

Kasindorf and Katz decided to create a new entity. They would develop it as an e-commerce arm of the IQCP business. They needed to launch a website, and they would require it to be:

- Serious and straight forward
- User-friendly
- Easy to navigate
- Fun with a couple of unique twists

The partners hired a full-service PR firm. In addition, they hired a freelance media consultant to do media planning.

Kasindorf: "We knew we did not want to do this in-house. We met with a lot of big communications companies and realized the budget we had to develop the site was low. We also realized we'd probably get lost in some of these companies. So we decided to look for more of a boutique-type web developer. We found a great little company in Silicon Alley."

Katz: "Henry really oversaw the process. We trust our vendors, but we really wanted to have a heavy hand in terms of how the site was developed. We knew how our customers wanted the experience to feel."

Kasindorf: "For eight months, it was all I did. It was tremendously stressful! Even as good as the developers were."

Katz: "We had to develop all the relational links. It was 3,000 products!"

The staff in-house set about developing a large relational database that would allow prospective customers to shop four ways: by key word, brand, product type, or product number. The project took six months and thousands of "man-hours" with five people dedicated full-time. The complete project cost approximately $200,000, half of which went to development alone.

The team designed the database to cross-sell and up-sell each product so that when a prospective customer input a product specification, the website would automatically offer helpful suggestions. The up-sell offered suggestions such as, "this printer also takes product so-and-so, we have these products at different prices, do you want to buy it/these also?" The cross-sell offered tonernow.com's own branded products once the customer had input a selection, for example a compatible or related product version, some manufactured on a private label basis and others by tonernow.com.[5] The cross-sell also offered incentives such as double points for a rewards program.

Kasindorf described the complexity of the project:

> "We had fantastic developers, but they did not know anything about product. It was up to us to develop the back-end issues. We learned through focus groups that most people really don't know what they need. Also, product numbers are long, and there's no apparent connection between the number and the product. We wanted to make the site user-friendly, for people to get what they wanted in two clicks or less. Most competitor sites require five clicks or more. There is nothing out there like our proprietary database, it's unique to the industry. We have people who want to license use of the database because of how powerful it is."

The Ambush Campaign

The next task was to develop a budget for the first three months after launch. An important part of this step was to look at the different vehicles for advertising. The budget would allocate money for various types of advertising such as banner ads, email marketing, radio, TV, and billboard.

The partners examined many names for the new entity and finally found one they liked. It was owned by a cyber-squatter, so they bought it. The new name would be *tonernow.com*.

The original plan was to launch the website in June, but it quickly became apparent that June would be impossible.

> Kasindorf: "There was no way for June to work. September 15 was Internet World at the Javits Center.[6]

5. As an input example, product EPS-SO2-0089.

6. The Jacob K. Javits Convention Center, New York's premier trade show and convention venue with more than 814,400 square feet of exhibit space.

We decided on an ambush campaign. No display at the expo. We had men dressed in white jumpsuits with the tonernow.com logo, in front of a giant tonernow.com billboard, handing out shopping bags with T-shirts to each person."

Katz (laughing): "We really used our T-shirt expertise!"

Dotcom Results

Once the website was launched, resulting activity was entirely new business. No activity migrated from the brick-and-mortar operation to the website. Kasindorf and Katz had decided to maintain two separate profit centers and market to two separate databases. They would possibly migrate individual customers, two-thirds of the brick-and-mortar segment of the business, to the website at a later time. They had not publicized the website to their traditional customers in order to avoid cannibalization. Moreover, the website sold at lower margins, and significant customer migration would have reduced margins overall.

Gross sales rocketed upward. From initial sales volume of a few thousand dollars in December 1999, by January 2000 business had jumped 115%, by February 209%, and by March 118%.

Going for Venture Capital

The partners soon turned their attention to crafting a business plan.

> Katz: "Toward the end of the year was when we started to focus on VC. It had always been understood that at some point, we'd get venture capital and take the company public."

> Kasindorf: "We had first-mover advantage, we were more a 'click-and-mortar' rather than e-commerce. Very appealing to the VC people. We'd shown we could grow in a brick-and-mortar way. It was more a question of how much equity we'd have to give up and who we'd go with, not <u>if</u> we'd go."

The partners expected to get exactly what they sought in the first round, but they were in for a few surprises. The first surprise was that profitability was not required.

> Kasindorf: "In our projections we were showing profitability after two years. Investment bankers,

consultants, and VC people told us we were *not showing a loss!"*

Katz: "It just made sense to us, that we were in business to make a profit."

Kasindorf: "Another thing! We'd walk into a VC meeting wearing business suits, not ripped jeans, wearing tattoos and carrying our skateboards. The first meeting we ever had, we walked out of there with a $37 million valuation."

Katz: "We began to get offers on the table. Then in spring the NASDAQ got hit hard."

THE TONER SUPPLIES INDUSTRY

The toner supplies industry was a highly fragmented segment within the larger office supplies industry. In 1999 the market for toner supplies was estimated at $30 billion. Players in the market included OEMs, office superstores, dealers of equipment such as copiers, printers and fax machines, catalog distributors, and re-manufacturers.

Customers were extremely sensitive to price and convenience. When toner ran out, the productivity of an office machine was placed on hold until new toner could be supplied. Thus, same day delivery was a key to success.

Laser copying and printing had dramatically changed the industry in recent years. Developments such as color printing had placed new demands on paper quality. Paper needed to be able to handle black and white toner printing as well as printing that used the newer four-color toner technology. Color toner particles had recently been made smaller in order to improve print quality.

Competition

Toner cartridges and inkjet cartridges formed a highly specialized niche segment of the office supplies industry. Toner and other supplies carried a much higher margin than hardware. Within this segment there was no single dominant player. Several large companies held a major share of the toner supplies market: Hewlett-Packard (H-P), Lexmark, Xerox, IBM, Canon, and Ricoh, among other OEMs.

In early 2000, Konica Corp. and Minolta Co. both of Japan announced an agreement in the areas of information technology equipment and printer toner production. The agreement involved a joint venture to manufacture toner.

In 1999, H-P had launched a new line of toner supplies, eliptica, to compete with Xerox. Two years earlier Xerox had begun to offer H-P-compatible laser printer cartridges, and the eliptica line was H-P's counterstrike response. After only eight months of operation, H-P surprised the industry in spring 2000 by announcing the end of the eliptica venture in order to re-focus on other strategic growth opportunities.

H-P was the world's largest maker of printers, and China was the world's fastest growing market. Printer sales in China totaled some $900 million in 1999. H-P had been selling printers in China since the mid-1980's and now controlled almost one quarter of the market.

Cartridge Recycling

The resale of toner and related products was highly profitable, with gross margins ranging from 20% to 70%. Empty toner cartridges that had been used could be returned to be recycled. The process ideally involved cleaning and refitting the cartridge as well as filling it with new toner. However, many re-manufacturers used shortcuts and provided recycled cartridges of poor quality.

Industry Fraud

Fraud was a serious problem for the industry. Customers using counterfeit supplies risked poor equipment performance, low supply yields, inferior print quality, toner leakage, high cartridge failure rates, and increased equipment downtime.

Illegal operations typically contacted potential victims by telephone, misrepresenting themselves as having taken over the previous toner supplier's operation, or as a firm that worked in tandem with the legitimate supplier. These "telemarketers" sold low quality goods to unsuspecting customers. Advances in communications technology had increased the opportunity for this type of fraud.

Xerox had been working with federal authorities to crack down on counterfeit toner distributors. In 1999 federal agents raided a warehouse in Milwaukee seizing 47,000 counterfeit supplies boxes estimated at a market value of $8 million.

BUILDING A STRATEGY FOR THE FUTURE

In spring 2000, Kasindorf and Katz had been shopping their company to venture capital people with the expectation of increasingly lucrative offers. However, the valuation of tonernow.com had tanked when the NASDAQ plummeted.

The deals now on the table were lower than the partners had previously considered desirable. Moreover, taking one of the deals would force them to relinquish at least some measure of control to their funding source.

Overview of the Current Business

Since 1994, tonernow.com had grown significantly. The firm employed 30 people and sold in all 50 states. Over 3,000 different products were offered with approximately 40 manufactured in-house. Some 10% of the products covered 80% to 90% of the market. tonernow.com sourced OEM products from vendors and also provided 300 compatible products that were not OEM-branded. Compatibles were manufactured either by tonernow.com or by another firm and sold under the tonernow.com name.

The mission of tonernow.com was to become the best known brand in the imaging supplies industry. The objective was to deliver high-end value through e-commerce while offering the following service elements:

- The Web's largest selection of toner products
- A superior website with built-in guidance tools and support designed for cross-selling and up-selling to products with superior margins
- Discounts from 30% to 70% lower than manufacturer's prices
- Service and maintenance programs for business equipment
- A rewards program with incentives for return customers
- Free next-day shipping with Federal Express
- Email reminders and an auto-ship program
- Online and offline ordering options
- National advertising

Customer Service: A Key to Success

The company had retained many of its original customers as a result of superior customer service.

Kasindorf: "When we were just 23 and starting out, people saw the commitment we had to serving them. Among our customers we have very low attrition rates. Companies we were doing business with in 1993 are still our customers."

Katz: "We definitely benchmark other companies. We look at them to see if they're doing something right. And we learn from our customers."

Kasindorf: "As we've grown, there have been a lot of internal pressures. The ability to have two partners running the business is unique in that we're able to feed off each other in certain ways. We're able to do that in a way that has really contributed to our growth. Our roles are not completely pigeonholed, we have insight into each other's areas, and that's beneficial."

Katz: "When we first started, we were both into selling, selling, selling. We had no idea how things would develop. As you grow, there's always the issue of costs getting out of control. As a result, I am now more involved with the operations. Henry is more the outside guy who handles sales and marketing. He instituted the procedures of how we deal with customer relations. I've kinda stayed inside and developed cost-cutting measures. We run a manufacturing operation, and neither of us had any manufacturing or engineering background. Also, we have some very big competitors. They've put obstacles in our way, and we've had to figure out how to get around them."

Changing Realities

By spring 2000, tonernow.com had attracted attention from outside the U.S. Katz remarked that the attention had been entirely unsolicited:

"We got noticed through trade shows. But as soon as we became a dotcom, it added instant credibility. When people saw the functionality of the site, they were just wowed by it. International contacts were also wowed by it. Once they got into our site, they saw we had a great deal to offer."

A number of deals had been proposed, and the partners were now considering options for international expansion. They would need to examine every aspect of the business: from legal to operational, from inquiry handling to delivery process, including customer relationships and confirmation of shipping dates. The move from small domestic player to globalization posed many challenges, among which might be any or all of the following:

- Licensing the technology
- Setting up licensing agreements
- Dealing with royalties
- Collecting payment via credit card
- Translating foreign currency into U.S. dollars
- Access to tonernow.com's proprietary database
- Restrictions to impose on website use run through other countries
- How to maintain control of the technology
- Cross-cultural revisions of website to make it readily understandable
- Legal requirements of setting up business activity
- Sameday delivery

Options on the Table

tonernow.com had received communications from Europe, Australia, Brazil, Central America, and South Africa. (**Exhibits 1–3**) In some cases, a concrete business proposal had been offered. Suggestions included the following:

Gateway page: This element would enable a customer in a foreign country to log on to the tonernow.com website and then be directed to the specific site for his/her geographic region.

Localization: Making cultural and linguistic changes in the website or gateway page in order to give the look and feel of the local country.

Licensing: Making the website structure and content available in a non-U.S. setting, including templates,

shipping, database, product information, and costing data, among other elements. Specifically, licensing would provide website content, brand relationships, and alternative revenue though co-op funds available with the brands. In addition, a licensing agreement would include:

- International contacts for global contracts
- Comprehensive collateral materials
- Outbound marketing material (bulk email copy, promotions, online coupons)
- Launch support
- Development of local media affiliations
- Proprietary strategic information

The structure that would be required to handle business differed for each geography, and the partners did not want to undertake a different strategy for each region. Kasindorf saw this as a "monumental chore." He was also concerned about the level of service:

"Who would send the second confirmation that confirms the ship date? C.O.D. orders and credit card orders online are an issue, because some people don't want to input their credit cards online. Who will handle customer service inquiries? Certainly you want someone local to do this."

Brazil: The contact company had connections with all the major players, including the government. They had come to CEBIT, the major industry trade show in Hanover, Germany, looking for opportunities. For tonernow.com to go into Brazil as an aftermarket supplier might make sense because entry barriers were high. Katz stated:

"We found there was only one licensee there for each manufacturer. To bring us in on a gray market basis would kill our margins. We would have to come in selling our own branded product because the distribution channels are so tight."

Australia: tonernow.com had exhibited at a large print industry show in California where they met an Australian distributor of toner supplies. The partners recalled his offer:

"He told us, 'we want to use your site in Australia, how can we do this?' Licensing the technology would result in people getting access to our proprietary database. The alternative would be to set them up as licensees of the technology to use the site in their restricted geographic territory. We did the analysis, to look into running the site for them, and also collecting payment with credit cards in Australian dollars."

CONCLUSION

Conducting business internationally would require playing the game with more than one set of rules. (**Exhibit 4**) Whether to globalize or remain domestic was the big question. tonernow.com was a small, new company. It shared little in common with firms running large global operations. The partners considered the ramifications of setting up business on an international scale:

Katz: "In the U.S. when you shake on it, it's a done deal, but in other countries you're not sure. Also in some countries, to get a domain name is very expensive. Fraud overseas is a lot harder to combat than fraud in the U.S."

Kasindorf: "We've started to question everything. Sales are very strong, site revenues are growing, but we're bleeding because of the costs associated with doing business in this manner: advertising, overhead, promotions 'buy one, get one free' to gain market share. We are about eight months late with what we were trying to do because the landscape has changed so much. We've gotten into a difficult financial situation thinking we did not <u>need</u> to be as profitable as we had planned."

Katz: "A lot of dotcom casualties have already happened. We want to be very careful."

Exhibit 1 ● Europe

EMAIL FROM HENRY TO EUROPE

I enjoyed meeting you and discussing our mutual e-commerce interests. At this point we are in discussions with firms in various regions who are interested in forming alliances to build the tonernow.com brand on a global level.

    It would be helpful if you could provide me with an understanding of your interest in working with tonernow.com and whether you are interested in pursuing further discussions. Many synergies exist between our firms, and a well thought out strategy of how we could work together would be mutually beneficial.

EMAIL FROM EUROPE TO HENRY

Further to our recent telephone conversations and meetings, I have thought long and hard about how we could take this opportunity forward. The opportunities I see are as follows:

    1. We could fulfill tonernow.com orders to customers within their countries and also fulfill a manufacturing role for tonernow.com.

    2. We could bring on other companies in Europe who can also fulfill customer requirements in both.

3. We could introduce various OEMs to the tonernow.com distribution model.

I will call you tomorrow to discuss the above in more detail. I would like to work with you on these options but need to know whether they fit in with your plans. Other considerations are: languages for Europe, software compatibility (i.e. order processing and stock system reconciliation), and dealer blind shipping timescales.

Exhibit 2 ● Brazil

EMAIL FROM BRAZIL TO HENRY

As we talked about in Germany, one of the product lines we have interest to work with, and have been talking about, is the ink jet cartridges. So far it looks to us like it would not be good in Brazil to work with remanufactured cartridges, and we are evaluating the possibilities for importing compatible ones. We have received several proposals for that, mainly from European and Asian companies. One has a strong capability to give huge discounts on their lines, and we are about to receive some samples from them in order to test quality matters.

EMAIL FROM HENRY TO BRAZIL

In terms of your market analysis for Brazil, I believe that a strategy with compatible products would be very effective for you. Please understand that there are many companies in the market producing and distributing "compatible" toner cartridges that are "remanufactured." Our firm produces and distributes both types of products.

I realize this may be a bit confusing, but packaging requirements enable us to use the term "compatible" if a certain amount of internal components are replaced during our production process. I realize that there are many companies throughout the world that would like to earn your business for the Brazil market, and I recommend that you proceed slowly and cautiously as this can be very complex.

We can develop a comprehensive user-friendly website for you specifically for your market. The website can be a useful marketing tool for your sales reps, and your customers will appreciate the fact that they can access the information online, order product or simply get product reference information. We can negotiate with the various suppliers on your behalf to produce products for your market under the brand name on a private label basis, therefore you will not be tied to any one manufacturer's brand except your own.

Exhibit 3 ● Central America

EMAIL FROM HENRY TO CENTRAL AMERICA

We are currently undergoing our first round of venture capital financing. I have recruited some senior members for our senior management team and one of the first steps we are taking is to partner with a major distributor in the European market. I am currently analyzing the possibilities for Latin America and the Caribbean in this market.

Currently the U.S. and European markets are highly fragmented and lack a dominant player. Our focus is to become the world leader in these markets via the Internet. We have relationships with many of the OEMs in each of the markets that we are targeting, and they will be working closely with us to achieve our objectives.

Please let me know if you have an interest in working with us, in what territories you can provide distribution, with which manufacturers you currently have relationships, and whether you have or are planning to implement an e-commerce strategy.

EMAIL FROM CENTRAL AMERICA TO HENRY

Thanks for your continued interest. The opportunity to distribute the recycled toners is not as clear-cut for us as it would be for other companies. Let me explain. We have been approved to distribute (product xyz) in several countries of Central America. We will be investing a lot to open operations in each of these countries.

I know that some non-original supplies are being imported into these countries, and we certainly do not have 100% share of the original toner market, so there is room for growth. My main concern is that we may only substitute the (product xyz) toners for yours, thereby lowering our sales volumes and possibly the margin. The margin is the clincher.

I have no idea what your toners sell for and how much I can earn on each one. I'm sure you will have good news for me in this department. Please send me your price list and the credit terms we could work on. I'm sure we will be able to do something together.

Exhibit 4 ● Legal Advice

(Excerpt from an entity in Europe)

As you are aware, in many jurisdictions it is necessary to have some sort of local presence before a local domain name can be obtained. We can assist in helping you satisfy these local presence requirements, whether it be by setting up a branch office or a limited company, registering a trademark or in some cases just providing a local address. We hope to be able to provide a seamless service.

As you will appreciate, setting up said alliance will involve a lot of work on our part and although we are some way down the line, it will inevitably take some time, possibly another couple of months, to put in place all the necessary arrangements and set up the technology. However, in the meantime, we have been approached by a number of clients of (company name) who wish to proceed more quickly.

We have already gathered a substantial amount of information and made contacts in most jurisdictions. In many we are in a position to begin offering our services. If you provide us with a list of the jurisdictions in which you are interested, we will forward to you further information regarding whether there is a local presence requirement in those jurisdictions, and if there is, the easiest option for satisfying this requirement.

In setting up this project, one of the most difficult issues to date has been ascertaining the costs of setting up local entities in each jurisdiction. Where it is possible to determine the actual costs, it is apparent that there are significant differences in costs. Therefore to simplify matters to date we have been suggesting a fixed fee per country. This gives you as the client a greater degree of certainty and makes it easier for us to manage the process and achieve consistency in the services we are offering.

However, if there is a relatively small number of countries, you may prefer to work individual fees for each country. We can discuss this with you in more detail when your exact requirements are known.

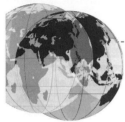

CASE 14
EURO RSCG Worldwide: Global Brand Management in Advertising

INTRODUCTION

It was the first week of April 2000. Bob Schmetterer, chairman and CEO of Euro RSCG Worldwide (Euro RSCG), was conferring with his chief of staff and two members of the Network Development team at the headquarters office in New York. Formed in 1991, the new company had blazed ahead of competitors and by 1998 had reached the No. 5 global position among the world's top 20 advertising firms. Euro RSCG had set aggressive goals for the new millennium, and Schmetterer explained what this would mean:

> We've set a vision for ourselves to be the leading network of the new century. We need to find new ways, better ways than our competition. We don't want just a level playing field. We want the playing field to be *uneven*.

The team was examining global brand management, a topic that had been the focus of a recent meeting in February. Agency leaders from the Euro RSCG network had convened in Florida to explore divergent models for handling global clients, with particular emphasis on the increasing demand for a broad array of integrated services.

The issue had become pressing for an important global client. In only the last six months, the client

●

This case was written by Martha Lanning, Research Associate, William F. Glavin Center for Global Entrepreneurial Leadership at Babson College, under the direction of Jean-Pierre Jeannet, F.W. Olin Distinguished Professor of Global Business at Babson College and Professor of Strategy and Marketing at IMD. The case was written as a basis for discussion rather than to illustrate either effective or ineffective handling of a business situation. Copyright © 2001 by IMD—International Institute for Management Development, Lausanne, Switzerland. All rights reserved. Not to be used or reproduced without written permission directly from IMD, Lausanne, Switzerland.

had approached Euro RSCG for a new solution. As Schmetterer put it:

> They turned to us and said you've done some great creative advertising for us, but that's not what we need. We need something more.

It was critical for Euro RSCG to develop a comprehensive strategy for handling global clients. Several successful models existed or were beginning to emerge as the firm responded to client needs. The central question was how to balance customization and localization with high quality global service. Schmetterer summed it up:

> More and more companies are looking for one partner, or maybe two or three, that can work with them globally. How to handle these clients is really crucial. Probably only a dozen agencies all over the world can deal with multinational assignments. In the advertising and communications business, there are no models to follow. What has become clear to us is that it is not *where* on the map you have the dots, it's *the lines between the dots* that count. The key is our ability to deliver to clients a strategically coordinated set of activities that meet their needs.

COMPANY HISTORY AND BACKGROUND

In 1991, two French advertising agency groups, Eurocom and RSCG, merged to form Euro RSCG Worldwide. In April 1997, Bob Schmetterer was appointed CEO. One of his first strategic decisions, primarily to broaden geographic presence and exposure, was to move company headquarters from Paris to New York.

By 2000, Euro RSCG had become a leading global player in the advertising industry, operating 202 agencies with more than 8,500 employees in 75 countries. (*Refer to Exhibit 1.*) In over half of these countries, Euro RSCG was among the top ten advertising agencies. The corporate headquarters office used the name

Exhibit 1 ● Euro RSCG Worldwide (as of January 18, 2000)

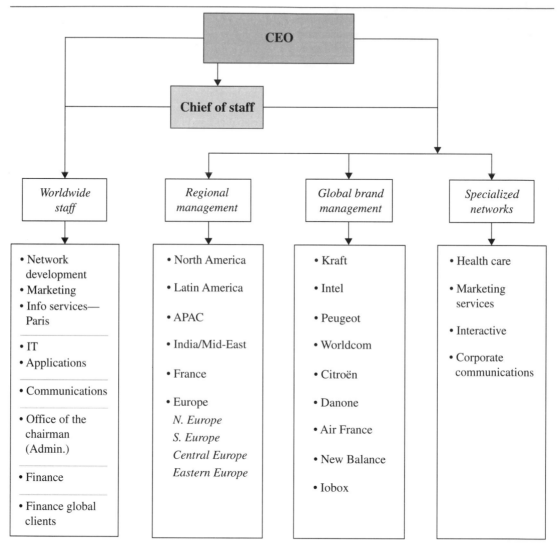

Source: Company information.

Euro RSCG Worldwide. Individual operating agencies used the name Euro RSCG plus the agency name, such as Euro RSCG BETC in Paris, and Messner Vetere Berger McNamee Schmetterer Euro RSCG in New York.

Euro RSCG Worldwide was a division of Paris-based Havas Advertising. Havas Advertising was 20% owned by Havas SA, also based in Paris. Havas SA was the oldest and largest publishing concern in France and ranked among the world's largest media companies. Havas SA was a subsidiary of French utility conglomerate Vivendi[1]. (*Refer to Exhibit 2.*)

Business Activity

Euro RSCG was a full-service advertising network. Business was divided into four geographic regions: Europe, North America, Latin America, and Asia/Pacific, which included India and the Middle East. Activity for 1999 is shown in the table below.

Region	Rank	Gross Income	Billings
Europe	1	$781.3 million	$5.178 billion
North America	6	$378.4 million	$3.578 billion
Latin America	8	$74.9 million	$587.5 billion
Asia/Pacific	17	$65.0 million	$439.9 billion

The four core business areas were advertising, marketing services, healthcare, and corporate communications. Euro RSCG used a matrix structure which incorporated a fifth core business area, interactive, throughout each of the other four. The service array included the following:

1. In early 2000, Vivendi was negotiating the acquisition of Seagram, the Canadian entertainment and liquor conglomerate. The deal was expected to go for $34 billion in mid-year and would transform Vivendi from a diversified conglomerate into one focused on environmental services and communications. The proposed company, Vivendi Universal, would become the world's second largest media group behind the pending union of America Online and Time Warner Inc. The new company would combine media, publishing, and entertainment content with fixed-line and mobile telephone and Internet access. Vivendi's strategy was to control the subscriber base in order to maximize revenue from services offered. The Bronfman family of Canada owned 24% of Seagram shares outstanding and had signed a binding commitment to vote in favor of the deal.

Also in early 2000, Havas Advertising Group was negotiating the purchase of Snyder Communications, a US-based advertising and marketing services firm with operations closely tied to the Internet. The pure stock deal was valued at $2.1 billion.

- *Advertising:* Integrated communications solutions utilizing television, print, radio, outdoor, and other media venues.

- *The Sales Machine:* A branded marketing services network. Ranked No. 2 worldwide and comprised of 76 agencies in 40 countries. Consulting, direct marketing, sales promotion, event marketing, sales force motivation, database marketing, and interactive.

- *Euro RSCG Worldwide Healthcare:* A network of 43 agencies in 38 countries, providing a full range of marketing and communications solutions to clients such as pharmaceutical companies in the healthcare industry. Ranked No. 3 worldwide.

- *Euro RSCG Corporate Communications:* A worldwide public relations network comprised of more than 80 agencies in 40 countries, providing corporate communications, reputation management, internal communications, marketing communications, public affairs, investor relations, employee communications, media relations, and institutional communications.

- *Euro RSCG Interaction:* A network of 40 interactive agencies in 11 countries, providing consulting, interactive advertising and websites, e-commerce, interactive TV, and other activities. Euro RSCG Interaction was ranked No. 8 among all interactive networks and No. 1 among advertising company interactive networks.

Through 1999, Euro RSCG had grown and gained market share. (*Refer to Exhibit 3.*) Billings and income in all four geographic regions and all core business areas had increased. Margins and profitability had risen, making a favorable impression on Havas Advertising Group investors. Gross income had advanced 22% and operating profit 38%. By early 2000, marketing services, healthcare, and corporate communications offered potential for higher profit margins than traditional advertising, and Euro RSCG had begun to weight advertising less heavily as demand grew for an expanded range of services.

Client Service Structure

Euro RSCG offered service through a "client-focused network," an integrated multi-disciplinary matrix

Exhibit 2 ● Havas

Havas Advertising, based in Paris, operated both Euro RSCG and Campus, an ad agency network targeting smaller markets in Germany, Italy, and the UK. Havas Advertising owned 45% of Media Planning, a media buying firm which provided service in 14 countries. Havas Advertising was pursuing a strategy of acquisition in the multimedia segment and had divested outdoor advertising operations.

Havas SA, which owned 20% of Havas Advertising, had begun in Paris as a publishing company. The oldest and largest media company in France, Havas SA maintained holdings throughout Europe including periodicals, advertising, book publishing, and multimedia.

Havas SA was a subsidiary of Vivendi, a utility conglomerate formerly known as Générale des Eaux. Vivendi was a diversified global company based in Paris with operations in some 90 countries. In Asia, Europe, and the US, Vivendi produced electricity through two subsidiaries and operated waste management, rail, and road transportation companies. Vivendi also held full or partial ownership of several television and telephone networks in Europe.

Havas Advertising, Havas SA, and Vivendi

	1999 Sales Revenues (€ million)*	No. of Employees
HAVAS ADVERTISING	1,208	8,451
HAVAS SA	3,300	18,600
VIVENDI	41,623	234,800

* €1 = US$1.06.

The Four Divisions of Havas Advertising

Division	Territory	Operations
Euro RSCG Worldwide -A global advertising agency network	Europe, North America, Asia/Pacific, India/Middle East, Latin America	Global agency network
Media Planning -A worldwide integrated media resource	Europe, North America, Asia/Pacific, Latin America	Media specialist
Campus -A group of independent agencies	France, Germany, Italy, Spain, UK, Brazil	Independent agency group
Diversified Agencies -A group of specialized communication companies	Europe, North America	Specialized communication services

Source: Public information.

Exhibit 3 ● Euro RSCG Worldwide Business Activity by Client Industry Segment 1999

Rank by Growth Rate	Client Industry Segment	Growth % 1998–1999	Rank by % of Business Activity
1	Tourism/Travel	248.3	11
2	Financial services	87.7	7
3	Fashion/Clothing	76.0	12
4	Healthcare	67.2	1
5	Telecommunications	20.4	3
6	Food/Beverage	19.9	5
7	Retail	19.4	8
8	Industry/Energy	19.1	14
9	Hygiene/Beauty	16.9	9
10	Automotive	13.3	2
11	Media	11.5	10
12	Technology	4.2	4
13	Leisure/Household Equipment	(19.4)	6
14	Household	(19.6)	13

Source: Company information.

capable of providing both global and regional brand management. (*Refer to **Exhibit 4**.*) The leadership, array, and level of services were based on actual client needs in all regions. A Euro RSCG executive commented:

> The company is very decentralized to enable such a customizable service package. The upside is that there's a lot of flexibility for innovation and entrepreneurial action. The downside is that it's complicated to mobilize network level behavior. To resolve this, we rely on collaborative technology tools that bring us together to meet the needs of the client. Our client-focused approach to global services is also a part of this. We're starting to build these systems more and more, but we want to keep the organizational model open enough so we can still remain innovative. We are shaping a new kind of international structure, one that dynamically leverages the best of our local talent and worldwide resources.

Global Business Enablers

Schmetterer's strategy was to grow a network composed of entrepreneurial companies able to implement solutions in their own local markets. Much recent growth had come from acquisitions in all geographies and all core businesses. As a result, the network was composed of entrepreneurial agencies with local market strength. Euro RSCG was addressing the challenge of coordinating these agencies into a global network for client solutions through two major technology initiatives:

- *Euro RSCG StarLink:* StarLink was a secure, proprietary, Internet-based collaboration tool. Access was restricted to the client and the network agencies working on a given project. Multiple agencies could engage with the

Exhibit 4 ● Client-Focused Network

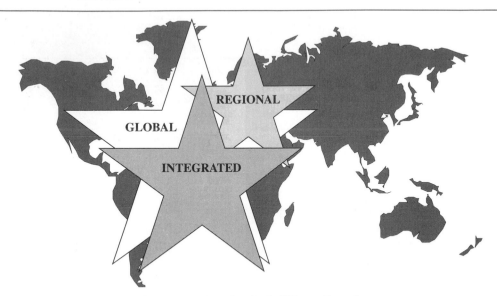

A Model for Global Client Service

Global Service

- **Brand Management**
  New York
- **Interactive** Lead Agency Salt Lake City
  Paris – Hong Kong – Tokyo – São Paulo –
  Sydney – London – Amsterdam
- **Consumer & Business**
  Lead Agency New York
    Advertising
    Paris – Hong Kong – Tokyo – São Paulo
    Database & Direct Marketing
    London – Hong Kong – Sydney

Regional Service

- **Brand Management**
  Paris – Hong Kong – Toyko – São Paulo
- **Advertising**
  Paris – Hong Kong – Toyko – São Paulo
- **Interactive** Lead Agency Salt Lake City
  Paris – Hong Kong – Tokyo – São Paulo –
  Sydney – London – Amsterdam
- **Database & Direct Marketing**
  London – Hong Kong – Sydney
- **Consumer & Business**
  Lead Agency New York
    Advertising
    Paris – Hong Kong – Tokyo – São Paulo
    Database & Direct Marketing
    London – Hong Kong – Sydney

Integrated Service

- **Marketing Communications**
  Markets Worldwide

Source: Company information.

client. The tool allowed upload and download of workflow and corresponding approval via PC, thus facilitating jobs containing creative work and media planning. StarLink provided an open link to all worldwide resources and a global approach to teamwork.

- *Euro RSCG StarNet:* StarNet was a company-wide, web-based intranet. Euro RSCG used StarNet internally. It contained a news area, a database of contact information for all employees, community areas to bring together interest groups, and a resource center for sharing and storing materials. Employees could upload and download reports and other resources based on topic.

Euro RSCG expressed its vision for client service as "a commitment to applying new organizational concepts and information technology in ways that make us the leading network of the new century." (*Refer to Exhibit 5.*)

Corporate Culture

Euro RSCG was by far the youngest company among the top global players. In 1998, the firm was seven years old, whereas the average age of the top ten competitors was 81 years old. Schmetterer viewed this as a key success factor:

> Competing on the same playing field with brands that have been around for decades has challenged us to be different, to position ourselves as the most attractive global agency network for clients of the new century.

Euro RSCG as a global company had become a networked, multi-cultural family of agencies. Euro RSCG staff represented many cultural and linguistic backgrounds. The firm emphasized creativity and considered it a strength to be able to provide bold and innovative solutions for clients. (*Refer to Exhibit 6.*)

In autumn 1998, Schmetterer had summarized his thoughts about the organization as he introduced the first issue of *Star Magazine*, the company publication:

> Euro RSCG is filled with dynamic people who are embracing innovation and creativity. It is one of our most important differences and it really sets us apart from other groups. I hope this new magazine captures some of the energy that I have felt in my visits with thousands of you over the past year. To-

Exhibit 5 ● Euro RSCG Worldwide: Our Vision

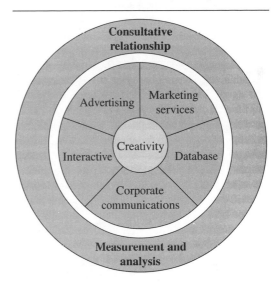

Source: Company information.

gether we made great strides. Together we have begun to create a clarity of culture, to see ourselves as a multi-cultural network based on a clear, precise vision, clear leadership, clear organization, shared values, and shared trust. Our leadership isn't one person; it's groups of people having distinct responsibilities. You should be extremely proud of all that we have accomplished together.

THE ADVERTISING INDUSTRY

The advertising industry was characterized by extremely rapid change across every market, driven by global evolution of the consumer economy. (*Refer to Exhibits 7 and 8.*) Major worldwide trends in early 2000 overlapped one another and included the following:

- Advances in technology
- Consolidation of industry players
- Globalization of industry players and also of their clients
- Changes in the nature of client relationship
- Media and communications advances, which affected all dimensions of the industry
- Expansion in the menu of services offered, in response to client demand.

Exhibit 6 ● Creative Work by Euro RSCG—Evian Ads

Exhibit 6 ● (continued) Iobox Ads

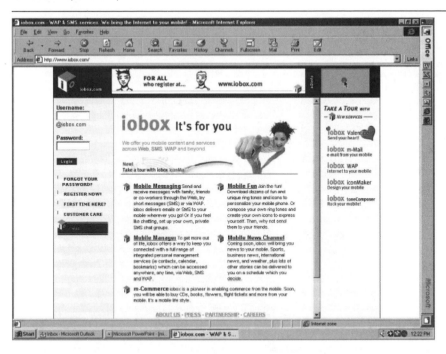

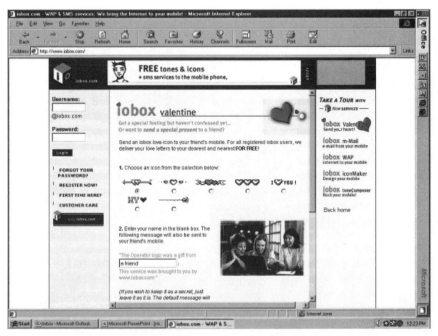

Exhibit 6 ● (continued) Intel Ads

Exhibit 6 ● (continued) Intel Ads

Exhibit 6 ● (continued) Novartis Ads

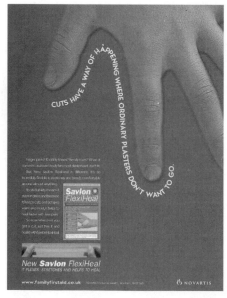

Source: Company information.

Competition

During the 1960s, firms had begun to consolidate into holding companies. As service offerings expanded through the 1990s, it became expedient to merge or acquire. Geographic expansion in response to market growth and customer demand led to both globalization and consolidation, which were intertwined and often gave rise to one another. Many traditional agencies had grouped together into powerhouses with a global reach, and activity could no longer be viewed as limited by geography or service.

By the late 1990s, the worldwide advertising industry was dominated by large holding company groups operating numerous agencies. (*Refer to **Exhibits 9 and 10**.*) Of the top 100 ad agencies worldwide, 90 ran international operations. Most were wholly or partially owned by a holding company and operated as subsidiaries or affiliates. The holding company structure allowed subsidiary firms to benefit from parent company support and resources (financing) while conducting business with product competitors.

The closeness of the traditional relationship between ad agencies and their clients, based on loyalty and confidentiality, had begun to constrain business growth for two reasons. Agencies declined to handle more than a single client in a given industry, and clients preferred not to share the same agency with a direct competitor. The holding company structure alleviated these issues.

The Regulatory Environment

In the US, the advertising industry had long been subject to regulation by several entities: the Food and Drug Administration (FDA), the Federal Trade Commission (FTC), trade organizations such as the National Advertising Division of the Council of Better Business Bureaus, and numerous "grass-roots" and civic groups. Recently, controls on the advertising of pharmaceutical products had been relaxed, and drug firms such as Pfizer (Viagra) had moved forward with new ad campaigns.

In Europe, differing national regulations added a greater level of complexity. According to the Treaty of

Exhibit 7 ● Ad Industry Spending

Quick Facts:

- US dominated ad industry with 62% of worldwide expenditures. Within US, ad agencies concentrated mainly in New York. Japan held No. 2 worldwide position with 15% of ad expenditures. Markets in Germany, Brazil, and the UK experiencing rapid growth.

- 1999 spending: US revenues $200.8 billion with 7.6% yearly growth. Worldwide revenues $417 billion of which public relations and direct marketing composed $200 billion. Non-US annual spending estimated over $112 billion. The top ten ad firms accounted for one-third of total sales.

- Largest customers: automobile industry $9.5 billion, retail $7.6 billion. Companies that spent the most: General Motors No. 1 ($2.173 billion in 1998), Procter & Gamble No. 2, and Philip Morris No. 3.

- Technology and Internet firms quickly gaining position as big spenders. This segment nearly tripled ad expenditures in five-year period 1995–2000. Estimated 1999 ad expenditures $2 billion, with firms such as Apple Computer, America Online, Intel, and Microsoft increasing ad budgets as sales rose.

- Media segments: No. 1 medium for advertising in US was television. Other media included newspapers, radio, magazines, outdoor, telephone directories, direct mail, and the Internet. Online and interactive advertising had most rapid growth.

- Industry predictions: Online ad spending to hit $32 billion and compose 8% of total US ad market by 2005. Internet ad spending to reach $2 billion in 1999 and subsequently experience extraordinary growth.

- Surveys in late 1999 indicated significant dissatisfaction with online advertising. Approximately 24% of executives contacted reported discontent with online ad campaigns.

- Japan: 1999 spending declined for traditional media but jumped 111% to $220 million for Internet advertising.

- China: 1994 to 1999 ad industry growth 45%. Over 3,500 ad agents in Beijing. Top ten firms were foreign ad companies targeting foreign customers. Increasing competition viewed as positive influence likely to raise professional standards and service quality of Chinese firms. Expenditures: No. 1 food, No. 2 cosmetics, No. 3 household electrical goods.

Source: Public information.

Rome, once a company had satisfied the laws of its own country, another state could not impose further restrictions unless specific conditions were met, such as overriding issues relating to the public interest. However, the regulatory impact on advertising was far from resolved, in light of conventions still in place such as those listed below:

- Greece banned TV toy advertising between 7:00 a.m. and 10:00 p.m.

- Some countries required candy advertising to feature a toothbrush symbol

- Differing national rules on: how much of the human body may be revealed; discounting,

special offers, free gifts, and promotions; promotion of alcohol, tobacco, financial services, and pharmaceuticals.

Service Array

The traditional service array of advertising, direct marketing, sales promotion, event promotion, and interactive had broadened to include PR, corporate communications, consulting, analysis, measurement, database services, and media buying and planning. The dividing line between advertising and PR had begun to disappear as agencies expanded from creating an ad to creating and maintaining a brand. Most of the top agencies now ran PR divisions or subsidiaries.

Exhibit 8 ● Ad Growth by World Markets 1999

Rank by Growth Rate	Country Market Area	Annual Growth Rate (%)	GDP 1999 ($US billion)	Ad Spending as % of GDP	Estimated Total Ad Spending ($US billion)
1	China	18.2	1,031.1	0.48	4.943
2	Portugal	16.0	107.4	1.49	1.601
3	Taiwan	10.7	296.3	1.56	4.637
4	Belgium	8.4	255.5	0.69	1.768
5	Philippines	7.2	85.2	0.89	0.760
6	South Africa	7.0	128.2	1.27	1.628
7	Greece	5.6	128.2	1.18	1.510
8	Czech Republic	5.5	50.5	1.01	0.511
9	Austria	5.2	217.9	0.80	1.741
10	India	5.0	435.6	0.39	1.702
11	Canada	4.7	648.8	0.81	5.286
12	Puerto Rico	4.6	33.5	4.06	1.360
13	Netherlands	4.1	384.7	0.93	3.587
14	Australia	4.0	420.0	1.27	5.331
15	Finland	3.9	129.5	0.88	1.139

Source: Public information.

Growth of the marketing services segment was fueling development and expansion of agencies dedicated to this niche alone. Clients were directing more money to promotions that produced visible ROI for their marketing expenditures, for example sampling programs ("try it, you'll like it") both in stores and via direct mail. Also, new client categories were moving into promotional activity, in many cases clients whose industries had only recently been granted legal permission to advertise. Examples were utilities and healthcare, as well as computers, software, electronics, automobiles, and retailers.

The broadening service array led to an increase in the number of niche service providers, with e-commerce players competing for advertising dollars, thus giving clients greater choice and negotiating leverage. Some insiders predicted that large advertising and marketing service firms would evolve into even larger professional service firms offering management consulting, software development, and venture capital. Others predicted the advent of agency boutiques with niche operations providing highly specialized services.

The media specialist had become a key player. Large global clients typically sought a single specialist to design a global media strategy. In some cases, the media specialist took precedence over the creative agency and dealt directly with large advertisers. Media specialists contributed profit margins averaging over 20%, whereas creative agencies generally contributed profit margins of approximately 15%. Many ad groups ran a media specialist subsidiary (StarCom of Leo Burnett and MediaVest of Mac-Manus).

Exhibit 9 ● The Top Agency Networks Worldwide

Group	1995–1999 CAGR (%)	1999 Gross Income (US$ million)	1998 Gross Income (US$ million)	1997 Gross Income (US$ million)	1996 Gross Income (US$ million)	1995 Gross Income (US$ million)
Dentsu	2.2	2,109	1,786	1,927	1,930	1,930
McCann-Erickson Worldwide	12.8	1,865	1,640	1,451	1,299	1,154
BBDO Worldwide	13.3	1,415	1,304	990	925	858
J. Walter Thompson	6.0	1,270	1,177	1,121	1,073	1,007
EURO RSCG Worldwide	**18.5**	**1,269**	**1,019**	**883**	**824**	**643**
Grey Advertising	11.3	1,193	943	918	842	777
DDB Needham Worldwide	8.2	1,078	1,007	920	848	786
Publicis Communication	13.6	1,009	765	625	677	606
Leo Burnett Co.	4.5	958	933	878	866	804
Ogilvy & Mather Worldwide	7.1	938	861	838	793	714
Young & Rubicam	13.0	905	879	781	707	556
FCB Worldwide	n/a	897				
Lowe Lintas & Partners Worldwide	11.8	888	656	621	606	568
Hakuhodo Inc.	–3.6	828	735	848	898	959
TBWA Worldwide	25.8	796	782	476	366	318
D'Arcy Masius Benton & Bowles	7.5	664	617	607	525	497

Source: Public information.

Exhibit 10 ● Agency Network Rankings Across Geographic Regions (Figures as of March 2000)

		United States	*Europe*	*Latin America*	*Asia/Pacific*
7 truly global agencies*					
McCann-Erickson	IPG	3	2	1	4
J. Walter Thompson	WPP	2	10	2	5
Young & Rubicam	YNR	7	5	4	8
BBDO Worldwide	OMC	8	4	5	6
DDB Worldwide	OMC	9	7	9	12
Ogilvy & Mather	WPP	10	6	7	7
Grey Advertising	GREY	1	8	15	13
4 geographically lopsided agencies, within reach of truly global					
Euro RSCG	**Havas**	**6**	**1**	**8**	**19**
Lowe Lintas & Partners	IPG	13	9	10	15
Leo Burnett	BDM	5	13	6	11
Foote, Cone & Belding	TNO	4	16	3	18
5 quasi-global agencies					
Publicis	Publicis	25	3	14	16
DMB&B	BDM	11	12	11	20
TBWA Worldwide	OMC	12	11	17	17
Bates Worldwide	CDA	16	14	18	9
Saatchi & Saatchi	SSA	14	15	16	14

*This category represents the top 10 firms in the US and in Europe, and the top 15 firms in Latin America and Asia/Pacific.

Source: Public information.

Service Delivery

Traditional delivery of service encompassed multiple stages of activity typically coordinated by an account executive: planning, design, media purchasing, and production. The agency and client first worked together to develop an advertising and marketing strategy. Next, a brief was produced for the creative team addressing specifics such as the message to be conveyed, definition of the target audience, and the medium for communication. Advertising text and images were then developed by art directors and copywriters. The following stage, production, could require physical production of signage as well as photographic shoots for TV commercials. Photographic shoots could be costly and time-consuming. Media planning and buying staff chose outlets for the media mix, and traffic staff coordinated logistics. The final agency task was to ensure that the media did indeed publish or broadcast the advertisement as contracted.

Service delivery was changing rapidly, and the creation of an ad campaign could not be assumed to follow the traditional pattern. Increasingly, the goals of an agency were to redefine and redesign client and customer relationships. Expanding use of Internet advertising had begun to erase distinctions among marketing, sales, branding, promotions, and fulfillment. Dividing lines for budgetary allocation of expenditures had also become blurred, with funding drawn not only from advertising but also from sales, operations, and information technology budgets.

Branding

The concept of branding was evolving to meet changing global realities. No longer a single message for a single consumer, a brand spoke to multiple constituencies: manufacturer, distributor, consumer, corporate alliances, joint ventures, employees, investors, and analysts. The brand message needed to be easily understood by all constituencies including across geographic and cultural boundaries.

Models for branding had typically been driven by advertisers providing solutions to client problems through idea delivery. Branding was now reaching into personal belief systems to offer choices about personal identity. Concepts such as social responsibility and environmental sustainability were starting to play a role. According to one industry specialist, "the great brands will be driven by simple ideas bigger than advertising."

The quest for brand loyalty had generated new types of advertising and promotion. The ultimate goal was to capture market share. Database marketing allowed highly focused targeting of a specific customer segment. Loyalty marketing (direct mail, special values, and targeted communications) had become popular in consumer industries such as pharmaceuticals, hospitality, and toys.

EURO RSCG GLOBAL ACCOUNT MANAGEMENT

Euro RSCG served a broad range of clients in multiple industries. (*Refer to **Exhibit 11**.*) Although many clients operated globally, Euro RSCG did not necessarily serve a given client worldwide, often working in one or more regional or country market areas. Each client was handled differently, and service delivery was based on response to individual client needs. Clients operated at varying levels of internal profitability and globalization, and they ran differing strategies for expansion or retrenchment. Thus, service needs were by no means uniform, even among

the larger multi-national or global firms. (*Refer to **Appendix 1**.*)

Schmetterer and his team were addressing the issue of how the company should manage global clients. The key themes Euro RSCG emphasized were entrepreneurialism, innovation, technology, flexibility, and multi-culturalism. Schmetterer believed Euro RSCG held an advantage over competitors: "Most of our competitors grew from a large central office with a 50 or 60 year heritage of working in a more homogeneous culture. We are a much more multi-cultural company." He saw the need to forge a new approach based on relationship management:

> We have to take a global point of view about interactive advertising and marketing. We need to be part of our clients' future thinking. Part of showing them how to be heroes in their own industries. Part of many other things that in the traditional advertising world we're not so much a part of. We need to find a unique way of managing our global client *relationships,* not just *account management.*

However, for a variety of reasons, managing the relationship was not always easy. With one client, it seemed that by the time Euro RSCG established a good working relationship, the contact had either changed position or left the company. A Euro RSCG manager commented on staff turnover within this firm:

> Every time they let the dust settle, there's a change. You work for somebody, then the person is gone. For an agency, this is difficult. It's not easy to build a relationship in a situation like this. You have to work constantly on building trust.

The Service Menu

Euro RSCG delivery of global client service was changing rapidly, influenced by growth and expansion of Euro RSCG itself, and also by growth and expansion of clients. Schmetterer viewed the company as a full service, integrated organization. (*Refer to **Exhibit 5**.*) He recognized that as the industry moved toward an expanded range of services, the service array would be a key to success:

Exhibit 11 ● Euro RSCG Global Client Relationships

Company	Years*	Advertising	Media Services	Interactive	Corporate Communications
Air France	2	X	X	X	X
Airbus	4	X	X		X
Alberto Culver	1	X			
American Home Products	11	X			X
Auchan	3	X	X		X
Aventis	3	X	X		X
Bayer	31	X	X		X
BNP Paribas	3	X	X		X
Canal+	16	X	X	X	
UTC	1	X	X		X
Cartier	2	X			
Citroën	24	X	X	X	X
CNN	<1	X		X	
Dell	8	X	X		
Diageo	3	X	X		X
Elf	8	X	X		X
Eurofighter	3	X	X		X
Freemarkets	<1	X			
Ford (Volvo)	9	X	X	X	
GlaxoSmithkline	26	X		X	
Groupe Danone	29	X	X	X	X
Immarsat	1	X			X
Intel	10	X	X	X	X
JP Morgan	2	X			
Kraft Foods	22	X	X		
L'Oréal	25	X	X	X	X
LVMH / Louis Vuitton	10	X	X		X
Microsoft	6	X	X	X	
Nestlé	23	X	X		X
Novartis	8	X	X		X
P&G	20	X	X	X	X
Peugeot	19	X	X	X	X
Pfizer-Warner-Lambert	5	X	X		
Pharmacia	3	X			X
Sara Lee	5	X	X		
Schering Plough	16	X	X	X	
Skyteam	<1	X	X	X	
Union Chimique Belge (UCB)	2	X			
Vivendi	3	X	X		X
Worldcom	10	X	X	X	

* Years as Euro RSCG global client.
Source: Company information.

A much larger array of activities—that puts a whole different picture on how we organize ourselves in terms of global clients. There are so many activities we now deploy for the client. It requires much more of a team-based client approach.

Schmetterer noted that with some clients the question was how to deliver a full array of global services in each of the client's regions, whereas for others, Euro RSCG had already worked this out with some degree of success. A Euro RSCG executive addressed the complex issue of integrated service:

Portfolio management and integration are the centerpieces of our strategy today. They are at the heart of our acquisition and globalization efforts. The progression of our business from a stack of services, none of which work together, to an integrated set of services that provide seamless, media-neutral solutions to our clients—of course it's very easy to say this is what we do, but it takes a lot of attention to actually implement.

Euro RSCG's Model for Global Service

Considering which models had proved effective, Schmetterer noted:

We have 30-some clients we are dealing with on a relatively global basis, but we have no one way of dealing with this. Over the last 18 months, a new way of working has developed with Intel. We have appointed someone to work with that relationship who has a very strong way of handling it, and we have a twice-yearly face-to-face report card. There are also other models worth looking at but being managed in a different way. There seems to be a lot of positive feeling about how New Balance, a client much smaller than Intel, is being managed out of our New York agency, and there are probably about a dozen others. There's a new client, literally only a few weeks old. They contacted our agency in London to ask for help setting up in Europe, then our Hong Kong office to set up there.

The global service model Euro RSCG used for Intel was considered effective. Intel was seen as an exciting

account and attracted the best people. George Gallate, Global Brand Manager for the Intel account, remarked that "among people who work on it there's pretty high enthusiasm."

Intel global headquarters were located in Santa Clara, California. (*Refer to* **Appendix I.**) The company organized marketing on a global basis and split activity into two segments: business and consumer. Santa Clara led most programs, and strong regional operations matrixed to Santa Clara ensured locally relevant activity consistent with global direction.

Euro RSCG had won Intel's global business in 1996.[2] The service objective was to reflect client structure and style, and Euro RSCG had therefore created five geographic service regions: North America, Europe/Middle East/Africa, Asia/Pacific, Japan, and Latin America. The North American region took the global lead. Within this region there was a lead Euro RSCG agency for each part of the business they worked on: advertising, business interactive advertising, Internet content development, database marketing, and point of purchase (POP). This structure was replicated in each region.

The global lead agencies were: MVBMS Euro RSCG[3] for advertising; FUEL NA, an integrated marketing services company attached to MVBMS, with a focus on interactive advertising, database marketing, and POP; and Euro RSCG DSW Partners (Salt Lake City) for interactive content.

Euro RSCG had established a brand management team to assure global integrated activity across each discipline. The team included a global brand manager (Gallate) based in New York and a brand manager for each region. The regional brand managers, based in Paris, Hong Kong, Tokyo, and São Paulo, held responsibility for the relationship with Intel in their geography. The global brand manager was responsible for the overall relationship and worked with lead agencies and regional brand managers in a client-focused partnership. Gallate elaborated:

The client does global integrated marketing. We have set up our network to do this. We provide

2. Prior to winning the global account, Euro RSCG had managed the Intel account in Asia/Pacific and had also purchased the agency in the US that serviced Intel.

3. Messner Vetere Berger McNamee Schmetterer Euro RSCG located in New York.

client-focused networks to create a total brand experience. Each network reflects the unique structure and requirements of the client. Our mission is to improve the value of the network to Intel and the value of Intel to the network. Given our integrated structure, if we focus on this, we have a very successful relationship. We are their marketing communications partner. We act as an extension of the client. They operate in a highly competitive marketplace, and because of the prestige of the account, so do we. There are many agencies in many disciplines that covet the Intel account.

More than 350 people worked on the Intel account including a total of 58 Euro RSCG agencies. Brand management facilitated a matrix structure wherein regional offices observed "dotted line" reporting to New York and local offices "dotted line" reporting to regional centers. Building and managing a network in this manner relied on three factors:

- A sense of partnership, shared responsibility, and shared success across the network, facilitated by regular face-to-face meetings and weekly teleconferences.
- Having the right people. Gallate phrased it "people networking as opposed to just a network of people." The prestige of the account attracted good people.
- Technology enablers. Euro RSCG had partnered with Intel to develop StarLink which in addition to a range of other tools served to enhance speed, quality, and relevance of the work flow.

Gallate believed the requirements for success on the Intel account were:

- Strength in understanding the client's brand, with a vision for their direction
- Strength in understanding the client's customers
- Ability to help position the client's products
- Speed facilitated through networking and technology
- Partnership within the network and with the client
- A global focus.

Whereas the Intel service model was global in both aspects of the term (the client operated globally, and Euro RSCG served the client globally), the service structures Euro RSCG had adopted for other clients operating in multiple markets differed considerably. Among multi-market service models, some exhibited varying stages of globalization while others remained international. Euro RSCG had found more than one model successful, and direct competitors offered examples of other service formats as well. (*Refer to Appendix II.*) Drivers that had typically shaped service models were:

- Geographic locations in which the client operated
- Geographic market areas and/or service activities for which the client turned to Euro RSCG as opposed to competitors
- Client propensity for expansion
- Service array required
- Client budget.

DEFINING THE RELATIONSHIP

Danone

Danone products fell into three categories: biscuits, dairy, and water. (*Refer to Exhibit 6 and Appendix I.*) Euro RSCG worked with Danone in biscuits and water, handling the two differently as a result of how Danone had managed its own development. In water, Danone had internationalized its key brand, Evian. In biscuits, Danone had purchased leading brands in several countries.

Danone sold biscuits in many countries under different brands, having acquired the local market leader and retained its name, and in many cases its original recipes, in most geographic markets. Danone sold water internationally under mainly one brand name, Evian, and under a second brand name also positioned internationally, Volvic.

The challenge for Euro RSCG with Danone was to become more international. In order to gain influence at an international level, Euro RSCG had moved into a consulting relationship in addition to advertising. Euro RSCG had created an international brand platform for both water and biscuits, advised on portfolio organization in both segments, and worked on best practices in each country market.

Key issues had recently included the following:

- **Branding:** developing a single worldwide brand platform for Evian.
- **New product launch:** recommending the launch of a "slim water" to expand the Danone portfolio and to match a competitor.
- **Synergy:** facilitating international synergies in the biscuit segment.
- **Organization:** adapting to a group in a different stage of internationalization.
- **Impartiality:** separating the international team from the French team.

Marianne Hurstel, an executive with International Brand Consulting and Coordination at Euro RSCG BETC, discussed the Danone account:

> Danone is looking for a partner able to help them both define their future strategy and participate in its implementation. Danone is looking for a network that will complement their own international needs, one with strong authority over local agencies.

Iobox

Iobox was a small new company based in Helsinki, Finland. It specialized in mobile Internet services, Wireless Application Protocol (WAP), and other emerging communications technologies.[4] The firm had launched its first products in April 1999 and now operated with a pan-European strategy in Finland,

Germany, Sweden, and the UK. Iobox maintained offices in London, Helsinki, Munich, and Stockholm and employed 40 people.

Although Iobox was not yet a global player, the firm had established a strong base with stable financing and operations. A syndicate of international investors (UK, Finland, US, Italy) led by Morgan Stanley Dean Witter Capital Partners contributed financing. The executive team combined experience in engineering, finance, and management.

Iobox had initiated the relationship with Euro RSCG in February 2000. (*Refer to* **Exhibit 6**.) While considering expansion into Germany and the UK, the firm had approached MHI/Euro RSCG, the agency office near Munich, which had in turn contacted Euro RSCG Worldwide in London. Euro RSCG had put together a comprehensive presentation outlining the industry, entry costs, competitor activity, and options for approaching the target market (a "guerrilla-type" approach *vs* traditional advertising).

Iain Ferguson, CEO of Marketing Services in Europe at the Euro RSCG Worldwide office in London, and Ben Robinson, project director for the Iobox assignment, discussed the relationship. Ferguson described the early rapport:

> The client was taken aback by the level of insight we presented. Decisions were made there and then, and they appointed us on the spot. There was strong synergy, and we were able to provide real insight into the marketplace. Iobox had no international structure, no people, no practices. Effectively they were building up from scratch. The relationship was developed largely by Ben. He moved around a lot, flying to the various markets. We've deployed a fast-track team. Ben

---

4. Iobox led the market for wireless Internet services in Europe with over 400,000 customers. Revenues came from user service fees, revenue sharing with content providers, vendors, and other partners (Yahoo!). Products included messaging services, personal management, information services, and other wireless applications. Iobox specialized in easy-to-use services from an Internet platform to mobile users (e-mail to mobile phone).

The wireless communications industry was expanding with unprecedented speed, and Iobox was well positioned to succeed. Currently Europe had 82 million mobile phone users, and this number was expected to reach 195 million within two years. Among world markets, Europe had the most rapid growth in the mobile phone segment. In addition,

it was estimated that the number of Internet users in Europe would expand from 41 million to 136 million in the two-year period 2000–2002.

WAP was available globally and was expected to catch on quickly in Asia where mobile phones had far higher market penetration than PCs. In spring 2000, the number of Internet users in Asia/Pacific excluding Japan was growing at an annual rate of 40%. E-commerce was growing at an annual rate of 109%. Cell phone penetration in Hong Kong was 60% of the total population. Telecommunications firms expected WAP services to become a major source of revenue as the technology caught on. Key attractions for customers were expected to be retailing, mobile banking, stock trading, and airline ticketing.

directs it totally, he is running the Euro RSCG end of the relationship and the Iobox business.

Robinson continued:

> We have not handled this as a traditional account. A team was assembled for this project based on insight the team members have, on their intuitive level of understanding of the company, its target consumers, and the product.

Iobox required far more than the traditional array of advertising services. The fast-moving client looked to Euro RSCG for event creation, investor communications, database management, strategy advisement and formulation, and managing the corporate website. Euro RSCG had been able to use internal resources for most of the skill sets required, including direct consulting expertise.

Euro RSCG had taken the lead in strategy with the business model and timing, and also with internal and external communications. Decisions were approached jointly, and Iobox had the final word. Approximately four people in each of the four market areas, Finland, Sweden, Germany, and the UK, worked on the assignment.

Communication played a key role in the success of the relationship. StarLink, the Euro RSCG proprietary communication tool, had been central to rapid decision-making, an element absolutely critical for the client. StarLink provided nearly real time communication capability, and approval of advertising could be given via this system. Ferguson explained:

> StarLink was one of the benefits we talked about at the very first meeting. The tool is sophisticated and takes some time to deploy, so we decided to create a mini-StarLink out of London. Concept development, notes on meetings—if a meeting was taking place in London, the guys in Germany would see it almost in real time.

Branding was pan-European. Globalization was not yet imminent, in spite of the fact that by spring 2000, market penetration had already reached the level anticipated for summer 2000. Ferguson and Robinson agreed that branding would be uniform and that prominent themes would be used as the client expanded, but that messaging would need to vary according to individual markets. Since Iobox targeted both industry and consumer customers, language, especially "street" language, would require a customized approach.

The full importance of this client relationship would remain unknown at least for the near future. In financial terms, the relationship had been profitable from the outset, although the client did not yet represent a major portion of worldwide activity. Ferguson and Robinson considered the relationship and learning important especially because of the dynamic new sector. Ferguson addressed the element of unpredictability:

> Where will this thing go? We don't really know. It's a narrow base on which to build a fast-growing relationship. We think we've done a good job. But it's bound to be a roller coaster.

In a comparatively short time, Euro RSCG had won a high level of trust based on performance and speed. The account had been conducted with transparency on both sides, and this fact had greatly facilitated problem resolution without conflict or misunderstanding. Ferguson commented on the shared trust:

> Because of the core team Ben has put together, they turned to us to assume a broader role. Iobox tells us "this is what we *could* do, what *should* we do?" We give them recommendations. If we had made these claims on day one, we would not have been credible.

Robinson believed the defining moment was "the very first piece of work we did for them, the briefing in Helsinki." He recalled the event:

> Getting approval from the client and also from the investor, and delivery of the material to San Francisco in less than 72 hours, that set the pace for the relationship. They come to us now and say, "these are the issues we're facing, how do you think we should handle them?" That whole process really did set the tone of trust.

New Balance

Euro RSCG had begun work with New Balance as a small US client in 1989.[5] Euro RSCG began to serve the client in Europe in 1998. In 2000, full service was provided in the US, France, Germany, and the UK. Additional service was handled on request in the Netherlands, Italy, and Sweden with full service planned for these markets in the coming year. MVBMS Euro RSCG was the lead agency worldwide, and Euro RSCG in Paris oversaw activity in Europe.

Management of the New Balance account had progressed toward globalization in a unique way. Due to a limited budget, service had expanded through a "piggy-back" relationship with a New York-based account that had established representation throughout Europe. A total of 25 people in the US and Europe worked on New Balance. Two were dedicated full-time, an account supervisor and an account executive.

Pamela Moffat, account director for New Balance at MVBMS Euro RSCG, described how the account was handled:

> When the chance to partner with New Balance in Europe came up, we jumped on it. We had helped them grow from a small niche brand to a significant player in the US and hoped to be able to do the same in Europe. What we didn't anticipate was that their small budget would demand finding a more creative, less traditional way of servicing them. We were lucky to find a structure already established which allowed us to hit the ground running.

In Europe, local agencies had previously developed their own advertising for New Balance. Lack of a consistent position had caused New Balance to be seen more as a fashion brand than a performance brand, a

departure from its core identity. Euro RSCG had stepped in with a single message based on performance. According to Moffat, "We now have a coordinated message in Europe. Performance is all we talk about." The requirements for success on the New Balance account were:

- Changing the brand image successfully in Europe
- Providing tactical support as the client expanded
- Maintaining the relationship as a partnership
- Serving the client effectively within a limited budget
- Communication, mainly by e-mail so that all shared the same expectations.

Moffat discussed Euro RSCG strategy:

> Our strategy was to take what we've learned from our success in the US and translate that around the world. We needed to have one voice and one consistent position worldwide. To achieve that, we focused on the brand's heritage, *running,* to re-establish their performance credentials. We use the same tag line, "Achieve New Balance," around the world. Initially this proved difficult because of the play on words in English. However, the European team managed to find an effective translation. The tag line appears in both English and the local language in all countries. It was important for us to keep this tag line because it communicates both the physical and spiritual benefits of using the product.

Novartis

Swiss-based Novartis held the No. 4 position in the worldwide pharmaceutical industry. Novartis was a global company with worldwide business in three segments: healthcare (mainly prescription), consumer health (mainly known in the US as over-the-counter, or *OTC,* also known in Europe as self-medication or *SM*), and agribusiness. (*Refer to Appendix I.*) Euro RSCG worked with Novartis in prescription health care and OTC.

Novartis operations in each geographic market enjoyed a certain measure of autonomy in decision-making.

---

5. New Balance Athletic Shoe, Inc., based in Boston (US), manufactured performance-oriented athletic footwear. The company operated five production sites in the US as well as facilities in other countries. Worldwide business activity in 63 countries was divided into the following geographic markets: Africa, Asia/Pacific, Europe, Middle East, Central America/Caribbean, North America, and South America. New Balance was one of the fastest growing athletic footwear brands in the US and by early 2000 had risen to the No. 4 position. The brand was expanding rapidly in the US, partly as a result of its orientation toward the serious runner.

Thus, Euro RSCG provided global service for Novartis in the UK but did not currently work with Novartis in the US. Euro RSCG had handled the Novartis-UK assignment, in the consumer health segment with Voltaren 12.5 *mg,* as a European account only since February 2000. Service was centralized and covered advertising and marketing. Euro RSCG had previously worked with Novartis as a regional or local client in several countries. The client relationship had begun with Canada in 1992, the UK in 1996, France in 1997, and Switzerland in 1998. Although client headquarters were in Switzerland, the US operations of Novartis wielded a strong influence everywhere.

Peter Koerfgen, European coordinator for the Novartis account, discussed the service structure:

> The philosophy of Euro RSCG is to offer the best talent for the client, regardless of which country. A project champion is selected based on expertise. The project champion then selects the team members, choosing people from whichever agency and whichever country he wishes, based on expertise. It's very international and depends on who knows the therapeutic area, the competition, and the product.

Several issues had generated concern on both sides of the relationship. In one case, as a result of a particular incident, a US agency in the Euro RSCG network had been excluded from working with certain areas of Novartis. Novartis in the US had therefore declined to work with Euro RSCG, creating international repercussions. Koerfgen weighed the implications:

> This is a very interesting point for global account management. You have to be a clean global network to work with these big global companies. One little mosaic in the network can destroy the entire relationship.

Novartis, the product of a 1996 merger between pharmaceutical firms Sandoz and Ciba-Geigy, had continued significant internal change including a December 1999 merger of its agribusiness with another company. Staff turnover after the merger had impacted the client relationship. According to Koerfgen, "We get assignments for projects, but the project sometimes gets abandoned according to the focus of the new managers."

Global branding would require future attention, and Koerfgen addressed this issue:

> Novartis management identified global branding as a weakness, and significant efforts are now underway to make global branding stronger. In some countries, the product name and strategy are different. With some tactics, Novartis is very local, very decentralized. There is a debate going on about which is better in pharmaceutical marketing. Personally, I believe you have to have a global brand and present it globally, with minor adjustments for the local market. Novartis now has global brand teams, separate from their therapeutic areas. This is new at Novartis. We mirrored their organization when we put together our global teams.

CONCLUSION

Schmetterer and his team were now considering models for global brand management. The questions revolved around whether to adopt one service model as an overlay. Should the Intel model, or parts of it, be used with other clients? Should a matrix structure lead the organization? Should service be structured by brand rather than by geography or discipline? At recent meetings, a number of issues had been raised:

1. **Compensation was changing:** In some cases, commissions were being linked to performance. For example, some firms paid a fee for services plus an incentive tied to sales. Across Asian markets in general, commissions were simply being cut back, some as low as zero to five percent. Margins had been severely impacted by the recent economic downturn.

2. **Representation:** In early 2000, Euro RSCG internal analysis suggested that the company was

   • Under-represented in PR

   • Under-represented in the overall markets of Germany, Asia (specifically Japan), and the US

- Over-represented in advertising
- Over-represented in France.

3. **Targets for improvement:**
   - Pitching and attracting new global brands
   - Keeping and improving management of existing global brands
   - Financial accountability and control, improving results from global clients
   - More transparency in reporting
   - Centralization of some processes.

Euro RSCG was now facing important strategy decisions. A key question was whether to copy other services or create something entirely new. Schmetterer believed the pace of change within the industry imposed a sense of urgency. He addressed the issues of change management and leadership for the new century:

Obviously we're not alone in understanding that the world is changing and that our place in it is changing. This is still an evolving medium and our issue needs to be how do we take a position as a leader that allows us to be the most attractive agency for clients in the new century. Most of the people who work in our organization have worked at one or more of our competitors and bring with them a heritage of understanding how others do it. There's a part of me that wants to say "OK, let's look at who does it best and adopt their system." But on the other hand, systems have changed, communications and technology have changed. The speed of change is not fully appreciated. I know that what I say today is already six months *behind* the speed of change. We need to find a way to build in much more anticipation of client needs and a way to use speed to execute our response to client needs.

APPENDIX I
Euro RSCG Global Clients

A sample listing of multi-national and global companies that either had been or were currently clients of Euro RSCG. Represented by Euro RSCG in multiple but not necessarily all markets of the client's operation. Equivalent information about activity with each client was not available. Companies listed in alphabetical order.

Citroën and Peugeot

Head Office	Sales 1998 (US$ billion)	No. of Employees	Products	Markets
France	39.425	156,500	Autos, parts, motorbikes, scooters, industrial machinery, light armored vehicles	France 35%, UK 14%, Spain 12%, Germany 10%, Italy 7%, other EU 13%, other 10%

In early 1997, Citroën contracted Euro RSCG agencies in six European countries to spearhead the launch of a new automobile series in 31 countries of Europe, South America, and Asia. The Euro RSCG Paris agency coordinated activity with partners in Germany, Italy, Spain, the Netherlands, and the UK. Numerous advertising commercials featured supermodel Claudia Schiffer, one a crash test from which Claudia emerged without a scratch, another with Claudia kissing a frog who turned into a handsome driver of a Citroën.

APPENDIX I (continued)

Danone

Head Office	Sales 1998 (US$ billion)	No. of Employees	Products	Markets
France	15.106	78,900	Bottled water, dairy (yogurts, cheese, dairy desserts), biscuits (cookies, crackers, snacks)	France 37%, other Europe 39%, other worldwide 24%

Evian, produced by Groupe Danone, was a natural spring water bottled exclusively at its source in the French town of Evian-les-Bains, scenically located on the shore of Lac Leman (Lake Geneva) in the Alps. Since the Middle Ages, the site had been renowned for the curative, rejuvenating effects of the natural waters. As a modern consumer product, the water was not treated or processed in any way. Bottles were filled, sealed, and shipped to over 120 countries.[6]

A key point for advertising, bottled water was known as low margin and difficult to transport. Moreover, any product was virtually indistinguishable from another once out of the bottle. Therefore, marketing expertise and the ability to reach the consumer with an impact were of great importance.

In 1999, a Euro RSCG advertising campaign for Evian created a sensation in France with 20 babies performing an aquatic ballet. The shoot required 70 babies, six nannies, as well as many parents, and was professionally choreographed. Because Evian, the market leader in bottled waters, had become known as a specialty water for babies, the company devised a strategy to motivate consumers to drink Evian at any age. The ad campaign chose the babies as a symbol of youth, demonstrating the mythical regenerative powers of Evian and communicating "a true sense of happiness, optimism, and rapturous well-being."

Intel

Head Office	Sales 1999 (US$ billions)	No. of Employees	Products	Markets
US	29.389	70,200	Microprocessors, chips, networking, wireless, and branded products	North America 45%, Europe 28%, Japan 7%, Asia/Pacific 20%

6. In early 2000, the so-called "water wars" for the Asian market were just heating up. Market volume was estimated at $3 billion with a yearly growth rate of 10%. Over the next five years, bottled water sales were expected to grow 150% in China alone. Danone was estimated to hold a 25% market share in China and Indonesia as No. 2 in Asia overall behind Nestlé. The highly fragmented market had already attracted a large number of international and regional competitors. Since 1998, Danone had spent over $500 million to acquire controlling shares of the largest brand of bottled water in Indonesia and of a major brand of mineral water in China.

APPENDIX I (continued)

Louis Vuitton

Head Office	Sales 1998 (US$ billion)	No. of Employees	Products	Markets
France	8.126	33,000	Wines, champagnes, cognacs, cosmetics, perfumes, fashion apparel, luxury goods	France 18%, other Europe 19%, Japan 15%, other Asia 18%, US 21%, elsewhere 9%

WorldCom

Head Office	Sales 1999 (US$ billion)	No. of Employees	Products	Markets
US	37.1	77,000	Leading edge Internet protocol services; a full range of advanced services such as local, long distance international, data, wireless, conferencing, and more	US 84%, Brazil 6%, other countries 10%

WorldCom had enjoyed a long-standing client relationship with Euro RSCG. Upon the 1998 merger of MCI and WorldCom, the new company chose Euro RSCG to develop a message assuring business customers that WorldCom was now positioned to revolutionize communications and offer even better products, service, and value than either partner had been able to offer before the merger. Due in part to Euro RSCG's successful television commercial and 12-page advertising insert to the Wall Street Journal on the merger closing date, WorldCom lost no customers and the stock price rose dramatically.

Novartis

Head Office	Sales 1999 (US$ billion)	No. of Employees	Products	Markets
Switzerland	19.979	81,854	Healthcare (prescription), consumer health (OTC & nutrition), agribusiness	Americas 48%, Europe 37%, Asia/Africa/Australia 15%

Source: Public information.

APPENDIX II
Competitor Models for Global Service

Young & Rubicam: (New York) The Key Corporate Account (KCA) program, developed to coordinate service delivered globally and to integrate solutions, used client teams from separate disciplines and offered incentives based on service quality. The strategy was to increase penetration of KCAs by winning new assignments and by increasing the service array. Y&R guided brand development through a highly quantified process using measurement tools. Y&R had committed to serving global branding needs by electronic linkage of agency offices and by creative idea and resource sharing.

DDB Needham Worldwide: (New York) One position, the worldwide director, managed the global account relationship providing centralized leadership and added value. Specific responsibilities were to develop the worldwide business plan, to grow revenue and increase market penetration, and to manage profit and loss of the global account. Within each region, a secondary role, the regional account director, was designated to identify opportunities or problems, defend local and regional profit and loss, and lead regional account directors in preparing the business plan.

J. Walter Thompson: (New York) Corporate executives managed the global accounts. They oversaw worldwide profit and loss, client/agency relationships, and the quality of creative work. Corporate executive responsibility took precedence over that of local and regional managers. The structure allowed limited local initiative. A comprehensive service, Thompson Total Branding, aimed at local, regional, and global clients to provide tools and methodologies for enhancing creativity. Service consistency was a strength.

D'Arcy: (New York) D'Arcy Masius Benton & Bowles operated under the shortened name D'Arcy. A Worldwide Management Team known as the "Loop Team" ran global accounts. The objective was to manage each global brand with the fully integrated synergy of all disciplines. A senior worldwide management supervisor reporting to the CEO led the team, which included senior people from marketing services, strategic planning, and corporate PR, plus a senior creative director and a senior media director.

Leo Burnett: (Chicago) Global service was delivered by a team that provided fully integrated service structured according to management of a given brand. The brand team was centralized. Special strengths lay in integration and media planning.

McCann-Erickson: (New York) The firm delivered global brand management through a subsidiary. Service included both management and building of global brands. Operational objectives covered service to local and regional clients. A company within the McCann network, FutureBrand, was dedicated to brand consulting. It was believed that the top five clients made up 30% of the firm's income and 50% of profit. Integration was considered a weakness.

Ogilvy & Mather Worldwide: (New York) The firm provided fully integrated services. Traditional and new services, as well as media marketing, were offered to all clients. The integrated service package was offered regardless of whether the client played globally. Ogilvy placed strong emphasis on branding in all markets.

Source: Public information.

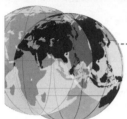

CASE 15

Manchester United PLC

Manchester United was not only one of the most successful clubs in the history of British football but also Europe's highest valued publicly traded soccer franchise. (*Refer to Exhibits 1 and 2.*) Manchester United PLC was listed on the London Stock Exchange in 1991. In June 2003 its market capitalization was £390 million.[1]

On the pitch it had won the 2002/03 Premier League thus securing itself a spot in the lucrative European Champions League the following season. However, the team would be playing without their star David Beckham, England's captain, who had agreed to a £25 million transfer to Real Madrid on 17 June 2003.

Through decades of success and failure, the hundred-year-old club had continued to attract strong support. Over the years it had built an estimated fan base of 50 million all over the world.

Whereas the group's principal activity was the operation of a professional football club, other related and ancillary activities focused on building and commercially exploiting its global brand.

Manchester United has this emotional base, a sort of legendary quality that easily sees it through bad times on the pitch. I'd guess that they can handle five or so bad years and not really hurt the brand.

In the sporting franchise category, Manchester United is way out in front of anyone else in brand terms. It almost rivals the great consumer brands for recognition.[2]

Research Associate Lisa (Mwezi) Schupbach prepared this case under the supervision of Professors Robert S. Collins and Jean-Pierre Jeannet as a basis for class discussion rather than to illustrate either effective or ineffective handling of a business situation. We should like to acknowledge the support of Gerry Boon, Partner in Charge, Deloitte & Touche Sport, in the preparation of this material. Copyright © 2003 by IMD—International Institute for Management Development, Lausanne, Switzerland. All rights reserved. Not to be used or reproduced without written permission directly from IMD, Lausanne, Switzerland.

CLUB HISTORY: ON THE PITCH[3]

Manchester United Football Club was founded in 1878 as Newton Heath LYR (Lancashire and Yorkshire Railway) and joined England's Football League (founded in 1888) in 1892. In 1902 J.H. Davis, a wealthy local brewer, saved the club from impending bankruptcy and changed its name to Manchester United.

Davis had ambitions to create a major footballing power and invested heavily, particularly in the development of the ground at Old Trafford. The club won the First Division Championship in 1908 and the Football Association (FA) Cup a year later. (*Refer to Exhibit 3 for Manchester United honors.*)

The Busby Era: Building a National Powerhouse

In the 1920s and 1930s the club sank into relative obscurity, and during World War II the Old Trafford stadium was severely damaged. In 1945 the directors appointed Matt Busby to rebuild Manchester United. Busby, who would become a legend in international football, managed the club for the next 25 years.

Busby and Jimmy Murphy, as coach, first built a team that was capable of challenging for domestic honors. Manchester United finished second to Liverpool in the 1946/47 Football League campaign, its best showing in 36 years. There was further cause for optimism when the Reserves won the Central League championship the same season. The club went on to win the FA Cup in 1948.

1. Exchange rate June 2003 £1.00 = US$1.64 = €1.4

2. Richard Buchanan, Interbrand, The Celebrity, Forbes Global, July 2002

3. Extracts from *Winners & Losers: The Business Strategy of Football,* Szymanski Stefan & Tim Kuypers. London: Viking, 1999 and company sources: Manchester United website: www.manutd.com

Exhibit 1 ● Top Ten Largest Operating Profits in the UK: 2000/01

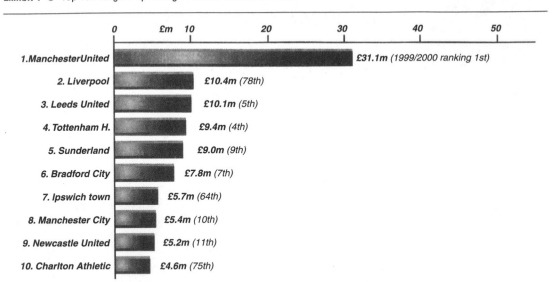

Note: *The figure in brackets against each club denotes its overall ranking in terms of reported profits/(loss) for the 1999/2000 season. Rankings for 1999/2000 (79 clubs) and 2000/2001 (74 clubs) relate to those clubs for which the information was available to us in each year.*

Comment:

The chart of the top ten clubs in terms of largest operating profit consists entirely of clubs that were in the Premiership in that season. Manchester United again tops the table, with operating profits three times greater than its closest rival.

Manchester United's operating profits have been at least three times greater than its closest rival's for the last three seasons—Liverpool (2000/01), Arsenal (1999/2000) and Aston Villa (1998/99): A significant competitive advantage given that, in general terms, operating profit represents the money available for investment in infrastructure and playing squads.

Source: Deloitte & Touche Sports analysis, June 2002

Success on the pitch brought fans flooding back—more than 1 million in the 1947/48 season. The club was out of debt and the rebuilding of Old Trafford was completed by 1947.

Busby had placed his stamp on Manchester United and made it "his" club. From the beginning, he insisted on management control and consulting the players, and emphasized that it was management, not the directors, who were best placed to make football decisions. This was revolutionary at a time when managers were generally more like trainers.

The Busby Era: Going European

Manchester United's league wins in 1956 and 1957 qualified the team for the newly established European Championship. This meant taking the game away from home. Scheduled passenger airline services and floodlighting made regular competition among European clubs feasible, and television promised to make it profitable.

In 1958 disaster struck. Eight of the team were killed and many others injured in a plane crash on the return flight from a semi-final game against Red Star Belgrade. The tragedy was felt not only at home by British football fans but also abroad. It changed the attitude of many towards the club and made it a household name.

Busby went back to rebuilding the team, which reached the final of the FA Cup later in the year.

Busby acquired Denis Law for a record £115,000 in 1963. Together with the maturing Bobby

Charlton and George Best from the Youth Development Team, Manchester United was able to field one of the most potent and admired groups of players in football. In 1968, after winning numerous national honors, Manchester United became the first English team to win the European Cup. The club had become a strong revenue generator with an extraordinarily talented team, exciting football and a growing fan base.

It was at this time that the dominance of the "big five" of English football (Manchester United, Liverpool, Everton, Arsenal and Tottenham Hotspur) was recognized. The transfer market served to create significant wage differentials between players, and by the late 1960s clubs needed to have a significant income in order to afford star players.

The Doldrums

After Busby retired in 1971, Manchester United enjoyed relatively little success over the next 20 years. Indeed the club was ignominiously relegated to the second division in 1974. This lasted only a season and three FA Cup victories in the following ten years provided some consolation. Yet Manchester United was still able to finance one of the more expensive teams in the country due to its ability to generate income.

Exhibit 2 ● The Market's Top Ten

Highest valued for Europe's top-tier publicly traded
soccer franchises

Company/Country	Market Cap ($ mil)
Manchester United/*England*	466
Juventus/*Italy*	241
Rangers/*Scotland*	139
Arsenal/*England*	135
Lazio/*Italy*	111
Roma/*Italy*	96
Ajax/*Netherlands*	73
Borussia Dortmund/*Germany*	58
Newcastle United/*England*	50
Parken/*Denmark*	49

Source: Soccer Investor, July 2002

The Alex Ferguson Era

The arrival of Alex Ferguson as manager in 1986 was the beginning of a slow turnaround and the building of yet another champion team. Winning the FA Cup in 1990 allowed the club to return to European competition after an absence of five years.

With the French player Eric Cantona in the squad, Manchester United won the inaugural Premier League Championship in 1993. This was its first title in 25 years, and this success spurred the team on to win a further 6 championships over the next 8 years.

At home, the club was a leading member of the Premier League. In Europe, it was a founding member of the G-14, the group of leading European clubs, and it had a seat on the board of UEFA's Club Forum. At the global level, Manchester United had helped shape international transfer policy through representation on a key policy-making committee at FIFA, the sports' world governing body.

CLUB HISTORY: IN THE BOARDROOM[4,5]

From Club to Business

When the club won the FA Cup in May 1977, it was on the verge of bankruptcy and was bought by Harry Edwards, a wealthy businessman, who ran a meat factory with revenues ten times those of Manchester United. In 1980 his son, Martin Edwards, was brought in as Chairman of the club. Edwards introduced management techniques to cut through the "romance" of football and to run Manchester United as a professional business. Success on the field was no longer sufficient to keep a club alive.

Going Public

As the lean years became leaner, Martin Edwards resorted to the stock market, the second club to do so. In 1991, eight years after Tottenham, Manchester United raised £7 million in a stock market flotation. In doing so it transferred its fixed assets and non-footballing

---

4. Extracts from *Winners & Losers: The Business Strategy of Football,* Szymanski Stefan & Tim Kuypers. Harmondsworth: Penguin, 1999

5. *Source:* UBS Warburg, May 2002

Exhibit 3 ● Manchester United Honors

European Champions Clubs Cup:
1968, 1999
European Cup Winners Cup:
1991
FA Premier League:
1993, 1994, 1996, 1997, 1999, 2000, 2001, 2003
Football League Division One:
1908, 1911, 1952, 1956, 1957, 1965, 1967
FA Challenge Cup:
1909, 1948, 1963, 1977, 1983, 1985, 1990, 1994, 1996,
1999
Football League Cup:
1992
Intercontinental Cup:
1999
UEFA Super Cup:
1991
FA Charity Shield:
1908, 1911, 1952, 1956, 1957, 1965*, 1967*, 1977*,
1983, 1990*, 1993, 1994, 1996, 1997 (*as joint holders)

Source: Manutd.com

Exhibit 4 ● Market Capitalization May 2002

Market capitalization	£0.32 bn/USso 47 bn
Shares in issue	260 m
Free float	88%
Average volume ('000)	877
5 years earnings growth rate	+8%
Management share incentive	Y
www.manutd.com	

---

business to a public limited company (PLC), so that the company, not the club, would receive a substantial part of future advertising, sponsorship and promotional income as well as the rental income from the use of the grounds. Furthermore, whereas the Football Association had to approve the appointment of directors of member clubs, these rules would not apply to the new company. Most importantly, the company was not affiliated to the FA and was therefore not bound by the FA's restrictions on the payment of dividends. The PLC owned the club, Manchester United, which was affiliated to the FA and did not pay a dividend. (*Refer to **Exhibits 4** and **5** for market capitalization and share price performance since flotation.*)

In 2002 Manchester United PLC generated over £145 million in income with an operating cash flow of £42.9 million. The redevelopment of Old Trafford had been funded internally, and a further share issue

raised £16.6 million for a new 100-acre training ground. (*Refer to **Exhibit 6** for financial highlights.*)

BUILDING THE BUSINESS

By 2002 Manchester United PLC had grown into a holding company that owned Manchester United Football Club, Manchester United Merchandising (Agency Company), Manchester United Catering (Agency Company) and Manchester United Interactive. The club's official channel, MUTV, was a joint venture between Manchester United PLC, Granada and British Sky Broadcasting (BSkyB). Each partner owned 33.3% of MUTV. The ultimate authority in Manchester United belonged to the shareholders, who appointed directors to the PLC board. The largest shareholders were BSkyB, with 9.9%, and Cubic Expression Company, with 8.65%.

Manchester United described its business strategy as follows:

Manchester United's ambition to be the most successful team in football will be achieved by developing a successful and sustainable business. To this end, the football and commercial operations of Manchester United work hand-in-hand. There really is "only one United."

With 50m fans worldwide, our twin-track business strategy is to grow existing and new domestic revenues while also unlocking the substantial commercial potential represented by the Club's global fan base.

The business of Manchester United is built on the three strong foundations of football, fans, and media. Football is our core activity, the fans are our

Exhibit 5 ● Share Price Performance since IPO

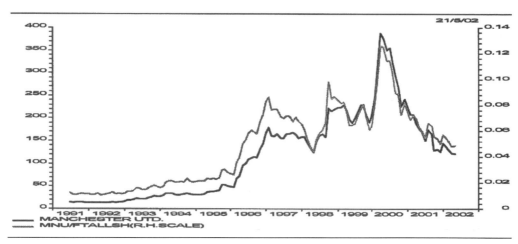

Source: Datastream

greatest asset and the media the most effective means of bringing the two together.[6]

Football: Developing the Team's Assets

Stadium

Old Trafford, with a seating capacity of 67,700 (up from 42,000 in 1991) was the largest football stadium in England and internationally recognized as one of the finest in the world. It hosted the Champions League final in 2003, the first time that the UEFA event was held at an English club ground. Its facilities included corporate booths, hospitality suites, conference rooms and a museum.

The Squad

The first team squad comprised 22 players, all but one of whom had represented their countries. Of the 12 players from the United Kingdom, 9 had come up through the Youth Academy.

Manchester United ensures an evolutionary development of the first team squad by acquiring and selling

experienced players and developing the younger players through our Academy and overseas alliances. For example the acquisition of Rio Ferdinand is complemented by the internal progress of Wes Brown and John O'Shea.[7]

A player was considered an asset to be capitalized and amortized over time. As of January 2002 Manchester United carried £65.2 million of unamortized player contracts on its balance sheet. (*Refer to **Exhibit 7** for details of amortization of players' contracts.*)

Talent

Manchester United had always emphasized the development of its own talent rather than an over-reliance on the transfer market. As Busby said:

If my club decides to buy a player, we do so only because every other method of filling a place in the United team has failed.

The tradition continued under Ferguson with the £8 million investment in the club's Youth Academy, testament to the club's commitment to developing

6. Peter Kenyon, Chief Executive, Manchester United PLC, Annual Report, 2002

7. Manchester United PLC, Annual Report, 2002

Exhibit 6 ● Financial Highlights

Financials (£m)

Yr to Jul	2001	2002	2003F	2004F
Income statement				
Turnover	129.6	146.1	148.0	152.0
EBITDA	39.3	41.6	47.0	47.0
Net financial charges	0.7	0.0	0.5	1.5
Operating exceptionals	0.0	(0.2)	0.0	0.0
Adj pre-tax profit	21.7	15.8	18.0	18.5
Corporate exceptionals	0.1	16.5	0.0	0.0
Profit/Loss on sale of tangible fixed assets	0.0	0.0	0.0	0.0
Amortization of goodwill	0.0	0.0	0.0	0.0
Pre-tax profit	21.8	32.3	18.0	18.5
Taxes	(6.8)	(5.8)	(5.8)	(5.9)
Extra-ordinary items (net)	0.0	0.0	0.0	0.0
Minorities	0.0	0.0	0.0	0.0
Preference dividend	0.0	0.0	0.0	0.0
Net profit	15.0	26.5	12.2	12.6
Balance sheet				
Total fixed assets and L/T investments	195.6	212.3	217.2	215.3
Working capital	(64.6)	(67.2)	(75.1)	(82.3)
L/T Non-interest bearing liabilities	5.1	8.6	8.0	8.0
Enterprise net assets	125.9	136.5	134.1	125.0
Group equity	124.7	137.4	147.7	154.0
Net debit	1.2	(0.9)	(13.6)	(29.0)
Capital employed	125.9	136.5	134.1	125.0
Cash flow				
Operating cash flow	50.9	42.9	47.0	47.0
Cash taxes	(7.4)	(9.4)	(5.8)	(5.9)
Net financial charges (CF)	0.5	0.1	0.5	1.5
Gross cash flow (after tax)	44.0	33.6	41.7	42.6
Capital Exp. (net of disposals)	(7.8)	(0.9)	(6.0)	(6.0)
Free cash flow	36.2	32.7	35.7	36.6

All Sources: Company data, ING estimates

Note:

• Manchester United's final FY02 results were above our expectations, and further reasonable progress should be achieved in the current year.

• Significant long-term potential remains for television and overseas merchandising revenue, with shorter-term concerns over media rights values.

Comments:

Good FY02 outcome. Stated profits before tax showed an increase from £21.8m to £32.3m with the benefit of £17.4m of player disposal profits. Adjusted profits before tax, exceptional items and player trading declined from £21.7m to £15.8m after a rise in the player amortization charge from £10.1m to £17.6m. On this basis, adjusted earnings per share emerged

Exhibit 6 ● Financial Highlights, *cont.*

---

at 4.7p (vs. 5.8p) with a one-off reduction in the tax charge from 31% to 23%. A total dividend of 3.1p (vs. 2.0p) was declared, including a special 1.0 payment to reflect the benefit of high player disposal profits and low tax charge.

Mixed operating performance. Match-day revenue (UK and Europe) was up 8.7%, from £51.8m to £56.3m, representing c.39% of group turnover, and reflected average attendance at Old Trafford of 67,160 and reaching the semi-final stage of the European Champions League (ECL). Media income was up 66.3%, from £31.2m to £51.9m (c. 36% of total turnover), due to the first year of the new UK television deal and success in the ECL. Commercial turnover was down slightly, at £26.5m (vs. £27.4m), with the early termination of the Umbro contract off-setting an increase from Vodafone. Merchandising revenue declined from £19.2m to £11.4m, reflecting a planned reduction ahead of the transfer of the business to Nike. On the cost front, operating expenses increased from £75.8m to £96.5m including a 40% rise in staff costs to £70m.

Progress expected in current year. In FY03 there will be a significant uplift in commercial income, mainly as a result of the new Nike sponsorship contract, but merchandising revenue will effectively disappear. We anticipate modest growth in match-day turnover, and roughly unchanged media income, assuming the club reaches stage two of the ECL. With most of the playing squad now on long-term contracts, increases in operating expenses should be less dramatic. We forecast profits before tax and player trading of £18.0m for FY03, giving earnings per share of 4.7p on an expected 32% tax charge.

---

young players. First team players Beckham, Biggs, Brown, Butt, O'Shea, Scholes, Stewart and the Neville brothers were all graduates of the Academy.

Fans: Developing the Fan Base[8]

To be a supporter of Manchester United meant different things to different people. But for most supporters, watching a game at Old Trafford was the ultimate experience.

I was born into the United family. Both my father and my grandfather supported United and my kids do now. My grandfather took me to my first game when I was 10 years old. I could not get over the noise, it was all a blur but at the same time it was magic.[9]

With an estimated fan base of 50 million, Manchester United had become one of the best-supported teams on the planet. While home games were played in front of 67,000 fans, millions of others followed the action on television, radio or the web. Such loyalty was priceless and the envy of the club's rivals.

The geographic spread of the fan base was unmatched in sports. In the UK and Ireland, Manchester

United had 11.1 million fans, in Scandinavia another 3.4 million, with the rest of Western Europe totaling 9.6 million. There were approximately 4.2 million fans in North America, and just under 4 million in Australasia and Africa. The largest base for Manchester United, however, was Asia, with almost 17 million fans.

There were more than 200 registered branches of the Manchester United Supporters' Club (MUSC) in 24 countries throughout the world. By becoming a member of either an adult or junior section, fans could enjoy a raft of benefits including priority booking of tickets for home matches.

Over the years the fans had become more demanding. They wanted a continuously winning team, a professional game in a comfortable stadium, the provision of meals, snacks and refreshments as well as memorabilia and closer contact with the players they supported.

Media: Bringing the Fans and Football Together

The Manchester United website—manutd.com—available in English and Chinese, documented the various components of the club's communication portfolio. Its *United* monthly magazine was available on a subscription basis. Fans could also subscribe to MUTV, which carried six hours of programming each day. This was available through a number of content providers both in the UK and internationally. Club news and match highlights from any league game

8. *Source:* UBS Warburg, May 2002

9. Quote from a Manchester United supporter, www.manutd.com

Exhibit 7 ● Amortization of Players' Contracts

Joined squad in	Total no. players	Number of trainees	Acquisition cost	Unamortised cost 3/11/02
94/95 or before	7	4	£5.7m	Nil
95/96	2	2	-	Nil
96/97	3	-	£3.1m	Nil
97/98	-	-	-	Nil
98/99	2	1	£12.7m	£3.8m
99/00	2	-	£5.9m	£2.2m
00/01	1	-	£7.8m	£5.9m
01-02	8	3	£58.2m	£52.8m
Others			£1.3m	£0.5m
	25	10	£94.7m	£65.2m

Source: Manchester United

since 1992 could be accessed through MU.tv, its online video channel. The club even offered free Internet access through ManUFree.net and an Internet newsletter.

BUSINESS MODEL: REVENUES

Participation in national and international cup and league competitions allowed qualifying clubs access to greater sponsorship and television revenues. However, as transfer fees and salaries for star players increased, alternative sources of income needed to be developed.

By 2002 Manchester United had diversified its revenue sources considerably. (*Refer to Exhibit 8 for an overview of how Manchester United made its money.*)

Gate Receipts

(*Refer to Exhibits 9a to 9c and Exhibit 10 for details of gate receipts and profits by competition.*)

Manchester United played in front of sell-out crowds. Gate receipts, including program sales and membership fees, were the club's largest source of income. The gross margin was 90% and over 70% of the total was received in advance.

The 5,500 executive box seats sold at a premium over the standard season ticket price of £475, which entitled the holder to attend all 27 home games. Manchester United's 126,000 members could enter a ballot for 14,500 match day tickets.

Competition Revenues

Manchester United earned additional revenues from domestic cup and European competitions. These were mostly derived from gate receipts, television, qualifying and victory bonuses. These revenues were of course dependent upon success in each competition. In 2002 Manchester United's run in the Champions League accounted for 76% of group operating profits before amortization and exceptional costs.

Additional revenues were derived from the hiring out of the stadium and attendance at pre-season games.

Conference and Catering

(*Refer to Exhibit 11 for details of conference and catering revenues.*)

By 2002 the conference and catering division was generating almost £8 million in revenue. Two-thirds of catering revenue was generated on match days. Four thousand meals were served in the Manchester Suite, a 1,000-seat banqueting hall, and nine executive suites. Additionally snacks and refreshments were served at 45 kiosks around the ground. The suites were a potential source of significant non-match day revenues.

The club also operated the Red Café, a 200-seat theme restaurant, located in the stadium. Manchester United expected to capitalize on the Red Café brand by offering franchises throughout the world while retaining an 8% stake of the share capital. The first

Exhibit 8 ● How Manchester United Made Its Money

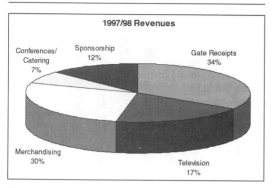

Source: Deloitte & Touche FourFourTwo Rich List, 1998

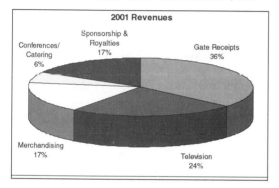

Source: Manchester United PLC, Annual Report, 2001

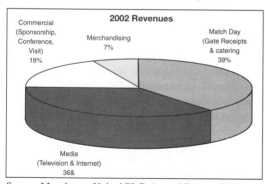

Source: Manchester United PLC, Annual Report, 2002

opened in Singapore and was the home of the local MUSC.

Television and New Media Income

*(Refer to **Exhibits 12** and **13** for details of television receipts and revenue forecasts.)*

A significant proportion of television revenue was dependent upon Manchester United finishing in the top four of the Premier League each year and thereby qualifying for the lucrative European Champions League (ECL). In 2002 media income was £51.9 million, or 36% of total revenue, and reflected the club's successful run in the ECL.

Most of Manchester United's Premier League games were televised either live on BSkyB or other pay-per-view channels, or in ITV highlight packages. All games were shown on a delayed basis on MUTV and incorporated additional analysis from players.

Manutd.com was designed to build on match-day excitement with previews, match tracker and post-match analysis. The objective was to increase the number of unique users and time online. The website was to be enhanced to more effectively communicate and build relationships with the club's global fan base. It was also an important tool for data capture.

Through initiatives such as MUTV (with BSkyB and Granada), the relaunched website (now being extended by Terra Lycos with foreign language versions), and the launch of MU NOW!, the mobile phone service (with Vodafone), we are enhancing our ability to deliver branded services to customers anywhere in the world.[10]

Sponsorship and Royalties

*(Refer to **Exhibits 14a** and **14b** for details of sponsorship revenues and forecasts.)*

The stereotype of the football club–sponsor relationship was one involving a company contributing money to the club every season in return for a hospitality box, free tickets and a chance to hobnob with the chairman and players after every home game. Over the years this had changed as top clubs created "Best of Breed" partnerships with influential companies designed to promote, market and sell their

10. Manchester United PLC, Annual Report, 2002

Exhibit 9a ● Gate Receipts: 1998-2004E (£m)

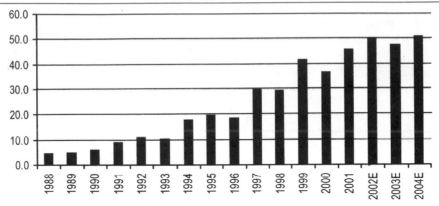

Exhibit 9b ● Gate Receipts Estimates: 2001A-2004E

£m	H1A	H2A	2001A	H1A	H2E	2002E	2003E	2004E
Executive boxes	6.6	5.2	11.8	7.4	5.1	12.5	13.4	14.3
Season tickets	9.2	3.7	12.9	11.6	3.7	15.3	16.1	16.9
Membership fees	0.5	0.0	1.0	0.8	0.9	1.7	1.8	1.9
Other	5.0	4.0	9.0	5.5	4.1	9.6	10.1	10.6
Total premier league	21.3	13.5	34.8	25.3	13.8	39.1	41.3	43.6
European Cup	4.0	3.7	7.7	4.7	4.4	9.1	3.5	4.0
FA Cup	1.0	0.0	1.0	0.5	0.0	0.5	0.5	0.5
League Cup	0.0	0.0	0.0	0.0	0.0	0.0	0.0	0.0
Programme sales	0.7	0.5	1.2	0.8	0.5	1.3	1.3	1.4
Other	1.4	0.1	1.5	0.6	0.4	1.0	1.8	2.3
Total gate recipts	28.4	17.8	46.2	31.9	19.1	51.0	48.4	51.8

Sources: 9a: Man Utd report & accounts / UBS Warburg estimates; 9b: UBS Warburg estimates

products and services to both the club's fans and a wider public.

Given Manchester United's global appeal and recent football achievements—last season they won an unprecedented treble of league championship, FA Cup and European Cup—they were never short of partners. It was a question of making the right choice.[11]

Manchester United had recently replaced its two major sponsors: Sharp with Vodafone and Umbro with

11. Patrick Haverson, *Financial Times,* 14 February 2000

Nike. Sharp's 18-year deal at £2.3 million per year expired in 2000, while Umbro's 6-year £42 million contract terminated in 2002. Umbro supplied kit for the England team as well as other leading clubs.

In August 2002 Nike became Manchester United's exclusive kit and merchandise sponsor. In addition Nike would become the official kit supplier—the manufacturer, marketer and seller of licensed apparel and merchandise bearing Manchester United's trademarks and the operator of the club's global retail operations. The 13-year deal was for £133.4 million over the first six years, rising to £303 million over the entire period.

Exhibit 9c ● Tickets Sold by Type: 2002/03E

	Number of seats	*Price range (inc VAT)*
Season tickets		
Standard	41,000	£437-513
Executive-box*	5,500	£1,088-4,098
Match day tickets		
Visiting club	3,000	£21
Hospitality packages	1,700	£55-150
Sponsor/complimentaries	1,000	NA
Other (members)	14,500	£18-27
Total	66,700	

Source: USB Warburg
*includes all home games but excludes 1000 tickets for promotional purposes

It also included performance incentives—for example, payments would be reduced if Manchester United did not compete in European competitions or finish in the top half of the Premier League. Net profits from the licensing, merchandising and retail operations were to be shared equally between the two parties.

The deal with Vodafone was for £30 million over four years, with the company and the club sharing revenues from wireless Internet services sold to Manchester United fans.

Vodafone, the world's largest mobile telecommunication company, was ideally positioned to exploit the convergence of media technologies that delivered interactive programming and content to consumers via personal computers, laptops, television and mobile phones.

We decided early on we wanted our next partner to be in the media environment because we think in the long term that is the area that will gain us the most benefit and give us the most value to our supporters.[12]

As a global provider of WAP communications, Vodafone launched MU NOW! to deliver a range of information and entertainment services via fans' mobile phones.

Other sponsors included Budweiser, Pepsi, Ladbrokes (sports betting within the stadium and interactive gaming worldwide), Dimension Data (business services, website development and CRM

12. Peter Kenyon, Chief Executive, Manchester United PLC, *Financial Times,* 14 February 2000

Exhibit 10 ● Profit by Competition

£m	2001A	2002E	2003E	2004E
Premier League	11.5	7.0	16.0	20.0
European Champions League	19.1	22.9	15.7	17.0
FA Cup	0.5	0.5	0.5	0.5
Worthington Cup	0.5	0.5	0.5	0.5
EBIT	31.6	31.2	32.7	38.0

Source: UBS Warburg estimates

Exhibit 11 ● Conference and Catering Revenues: 1988-2004E (£m)

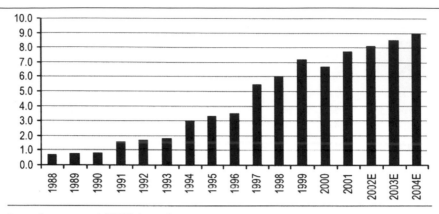

Source: Company accounts/UBS Warburg estimates

Exhibit 12 ● Television Receipts: 1998-2004E (£m)

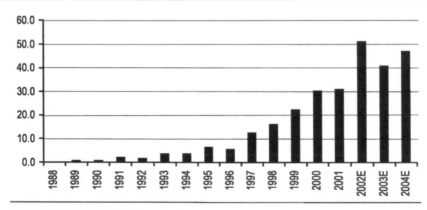

Source: Manchester United/UBS Warburg estimates

programs), Terra Lycos (Chinese website, sales agent for English language site), Fuji, Century Radio and Wilkinson Sword.

In addition Manchester United generated £1.2 million through MU Finance, which had been established in 2001 to build on the success of the club's credit card and savings account affinity products. MU Finance, a partnership with MBNA Europe Bank, Britannia Building Society, Zurich Financial Services and the Bank of Scotland, offered a range of financial services including personal loans, general insurance, mortgages and investment products to Manchester United supporters.

Merchandising and Other Revenues

(*Refer to* **Exhibit 15** *for details of merchandising and other revenues.*)

Since the early 1990s Manchester United had transformed an essentially mail order business for the sale of replica kits and memorabilia into a lucrative merchandising operation. The deal with Nike was the next step in the evolution of the club's merchandising strategy, namely to offer fans a complete lifestyle package in the form of high quality leisurewear.

Nike was to assume responsibility for the distribution and sale of all Manchester United's branded merchandise. It was forecasting sales of £1 billion

Exhibit 13 ● Television Revenue Forecast: 2001A-2004E (£m)

£m	H1A	II2A	2001A	H1A	H2E	2002E	2003E	2004E
Premier League—BSkyB	4.8	7.5	12.3	9.6	15.0	24.6	24.3	27.8
Premier League—other	0.6	1.5	2.1	2.0	5.1	7.1	8.5	9.0
Pay-per-view	0.0	0.0	0.0	0.4	0.2	0.6	1.2	2.4
FA Cup	0.3	0.0	0.3	0.3	0.3	0.6	0.0	0.0
League Cup	0.0	0.0	0.0	0.0	0.0	0.0	0.0	0.0
European Cup	9.3	7.2	16.5	11.9	6.5	18.4	9.0	10.0
Television revenues	15.0	16.3	31.2	24.2	27.1	51.3	43.0	49.2

Source: UBS Warburg estimates

Exhibit 14a ● Sponsorship and Royalty Revenues: 1988-2004E (£m)

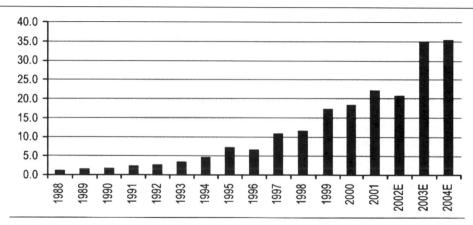

Source: Company data/UBS Warburg estimates

Exhibit 14b ● Sponsorship Revenue Estimates: 2000-2004E (£m)

£m	2000	2001	2002E	2003E	2004E
Umbro	11	11	9	-	-
Sharp	5	-	-	-	-
Vodafone	-	6	7	8	9
Nike	-	-	-	20.8	20.8
Other	3.5	5	5	6.2	6.2
Total	18.5	22.4	21.0	35	36.0

Source: UBS Warburg estimates

Exhibit 15 ● Merchandise and Other Revenue Forecasts

£m	H1A	H2A	2001A	H1A	H2E	2002E	2003E	2004E
Other	14.3	9.3	21.9	9.2	3.8	13.0	4.0	5.0

Source: UBS Warburg estimates

through the "Niketown" shops that would comple-ment Manchester United's own megastores.

It's a clear intent by Nike to plough its huge resources into making the United deal a huge financial success. Nike's marketing will be on a scale never before seen in Europe. No shirt sells like theirs worldwide—it ab-solutely hammers the rest and that's why Nike was willing to pay such a huge amount. But it's not just the shirt. Having United as your football flagship raises the whole company.[13]

Nike's ability to deliver an integrated global market-ing campaign for the simultaneous launch, in 58 countries, of the new team kit was illustrative of the potential of the partnership.

Other sources of income were small though var-ied. The museum attracted some 200,000 visitors each year. The United Trading Estates, land acquired for the North Stand extension, included properties rented to third parties. The Manchester United Devel-opment Association ran its own lottery as a tax effi-cient way of raising funds.

13. People Sport, 2001

BUSINESS MODEL: COSTS[14]

Increases in players' wages and transfer fees as well as the amortization of players' contracts were of con-cern to the Group. (*Refer to **Exhibit 16** for details of the cost structure.*)

Wages

(*Refer to **Exhibit 17** for details of players' wages.*)

The players' wage bill had begun to escalate in the mid-1990s. Contributing factors were the lifting of restrictions on the number of foreign players in the squad, the Bosman ruling of 1995, and the club's own ambitions. With success in the European Champions League a perennial goal, Manchester United had to compete for the best players.

Manchester United continues to invest in strengthen-ing the squad to improve playing performances, while recognising the need to manage our wage costs and transfer spending prudently.[15]

14. *Source:* UBS Warburg, May 2002

15. Peter Kenyon, Chief Executive, Manchester United PLC, Annual Report, 2002

Exhibit 16 ● Cost Structure: 2001A-2003E

£m	2001A	% revenue	2002E	% revenue	2003E	% revenue
Sales	129.5	100.0	142.6	100.0	136.4	100.0
Cost of sales	22.1	17.1	16.0	11.2	7.3	5.4
Wages & salaries	50.0	38.6	69.0	48.4	72.0	52.8
Depreciation	7.5	5.8	6.0	4.2	6.0	4.4
Admin	18.3	14.1	22.2	15.6	21.0	15.4
Total costs	97.9	75.6	113.2	79.4	106.3	77.9

Source: UBS Warburg estimates

Exhibit 17 ● Players' Wages: 1988-2004E (£m)

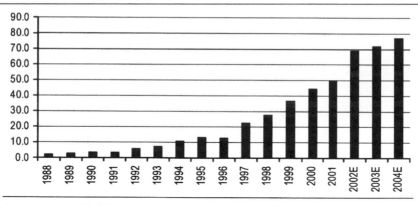

Source: Company data/UBS Warburg estimates

Apart from their salary, players received bonuses related to performance in domestic and European Cup competitions. This was estimated at 6% to 9% of payroll. Manchester United had signed most of its players on long-term contracts. Coaching staff were as important as the players and Manchester United continued to strengthen its resources here. In 2002 the group hired the internationally respected Carlos Queros as first team coach, and brought in two new youth team coaches.

Manchester United PLC had 495 permanent staff and 1,300 or so match-day staff.

Player Transfer Costs

(*Refer to Exhibits 18, 19 and 20 for details of players' contracts and net transfers.*)

Until the late 1990s Manchester United had essentially offset the acquisition costs of players with the proceeds from the sale of not only first team players but also players nurtured in the Youth Academy. The picture changed in 1998 when the club began to enter the transfer market more frequently. In 2001 Manchester United acquired Juan Sebastian Veron and Ruud van Nistelrooy for a total of £47.1 million. A year later Rio Ferdinand, an England defender, was transferred from Leeds for £29.3 million.

MATCHING MANCHESTER UNITED

As a business, Manchester United occupied a very special position in the world of football. This had been achieved over decades by focusing on (1) the

Exhibit 18 ● Net Transfers: 1988-2004E (£m)

Players contract expiry

	Number	Average age at 30/6/02	contracts expire				
			30/6/03	30/6/04	30/6/05	30/6/06	30/6/07
Goalkeepers	2	28	-	-	1	1	-
Defenders	6	26	2	-	1	1	2
Midfielders	10	26	2	-	2	5	1
Forwards	4	27	1	-	-	3	-
Total	22	26	5	-	4	10	3

Source: Manchester United

Exhibit 19 ● Net Transfers: 1988-2004E (£m)

H1 player trading account

£m	Original cost	Gross transfer cost	Net profits
Greening	0.9	2.0	1.7
Wilson	-	1.5	1.4
Stam	10.8	16.0	8.3
Cole	6.3	5.7	4.8
Others	-	-	0.1
Total	18.0	25.2	16.3
Less amortization			-8.4
Player trading			7.9

Source: Manchester United

power of the brand it had created, (2) the football team at the center of the business and (3) its customers, who lay at the center of its thinking. The club aimed to connect the team with its customers by delivering the Manchester United experience to them wherever they were in the world, and by generating profits and creating shareholder value in the process.

Manchester United was the envy of its rivals and the benchmark in a world that was often governed more by passion and emotion than by systematic boardroom business decisions.

Exhibit 20 ● Net Transfers: 1988-2004E (£m)

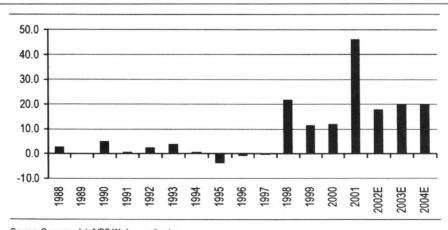

Source: Company data/UBS Warburg estimates

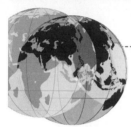

CASE 16

Real Madrid Club de Fútbol

In June 2003 Real Madrid paid €35 million to Manchester United for David Beckham, England's captain. Indeed, Beckham and his advisers had nixed a more lucrative offer of €43 million that Barcelona had made to United.

It is not that we make efforts, but there are some footballers who wish to join Real because it is a very attractive team right now. Last year Ronaldo happened to be ready to leave his side and this year Manchester and Beckham agreed to go separate ways, but, only and exclusively to play in Real, you can be sure of that. It has been a bit of a coincidence.[1]

In its hundred-year history, Real Madrid had brought home 29 League titles, 9 European Cups, 17 Spanish Cups, 2 UEFA Cups and 2 World Cup Championship titles. In 2000 FIFA recognized Real as the "Best Club of the 20th century." Its new president, Florentino Pérez, had not only wiped out the club's high level of debt through a property deal exploiting the enviable location of Real's training grounds but had also bought a string of players with the proceeds. These players included international stars such as Figo, Ronaldo and Zidane, acquired for a total of €182 million.

●

Research Associate Lisa (Mwezi) Schüpbach prepared this case under the supervision of Professors Robert S. Collins and Jean-Pierre Jeannet as a basis for class discussion rather than to illustrate either effective or ineffective handling of a business situation. We should like to acknowledge the support of Gerry Boon, Partner in Charge, Deloitte & Touche Sport, in the preparation of this material. We should also like to acknowledge Ernesto Mancosu for his contribution. Copyright © 2003 by IMD—International Institute for Management Development, Lausanne, Switzerland. All rights reserved. Not to be used or reproduced without written permission directly from IMD, Lausanne, Switzerland.

Under Pérez the club was

. . . trying to invent itself as a global brand to challenge Manchester United of England, the richest club in the world and a household name from the Shetland Islands to Singapore. [. . .]

[Its mission was] the creation and exploitation of a global brand, using high profile—and very expensive players—as standard-bearers to break into new markets[2]

CLUB HISTORY[3]

Forming the Club

Madrid Foot Ball Club was officially founded by a group of fans on 6 March 1902. The first board of directors decided on the team's gear, imitating the famous London Corinthians: white shorts and T-shirt, blue socks and cap, and the coat of arms embroidered in color over a purple band.

The club's premises were in the backroom of the Al Capricho store, owned by founding member Juan Padrós and his brother Carlos. The changing rooms were in the La Taurina Tavern.

Between 1902 and the outbreak of the Civil War in 1936, the club was served by seven presidents, many of whom were ex-players. Under their leadership, the focus was on results. (*Refer to **Exhibit 1** for the club's list of honors.*)

1. Florentino Pérez, Real's President, quoted on *www. realmadrid.com:* "Beckham agrees £25m move to Madrid," 18 June 2003

2. Keith Johnson. "Madrid's Valdano Pursues Validation." *Wall Street Journal* [Brussels], 23 April 2002

3. *www.realmadrid.com*—Real Madrid C.F. Official Web Site

Exhibit 1 ● Real Madrid List of Honors

LIST OF MAJOR TROPHIES WON:
League titles (29)

1932, 1933, 1954, 1955, 1957, 1958, 1961, 1962, 1963, 1964, 1965, 1967, 1968, 1969, 1972, 1975, 1976, 1978, 1979, 1980, 1986, 1987, 1988, 1989, 1990, 1995, 1997, 2001, 2003
European Cups (9)

1956, 1957, 1958, 1959, 1960, 1966, 1998, 2000, 2002
King's and Generalissimo's Cups (17)

1905, 1906, 1907, 1908, 1917, 1934, 1936, 1946, 1947, 1962, 1970, 1974, 1975, 1980, 1982, 1989, 1993
Spanish "Supercups" (6)

1988, 1989, 1990, 1993, 1997, 2001
Intercontinental Cups (2)

1960, 1998
UEFA Cups (2)

1985, 1986
League Cup (1)

1985

LOSING FINALISTS IN:
European Cups (3)

1962, 1964, 1981
King's and Generalissimo's Cups (14)

1929, 1930, 1933, 1940, 1943, 1958, 1960, 1961, 1968, 1979, 1983, 1990, 1992, 2002

- First player to score a goal in official competition for Real Madrid: Arthur Johnson, 13 May 1902 versus Barcelona
- First game between Real Madrid and Barcelona: Real Madrid 1 Barcelona 3, 13 May 1902
- Number of players who have turned out in official competition for Real Madrid between March 1902 and March 2002: Total 1,217
- Spanish region with most supporters' clubs (*peñas*): Andalucía (352)
- Spanish region with least supporters' clubs: The Basque Country (12)
- Oldest living *socio* (club member): Paula Carrillo (born 12.1.1900)
- Worst league finish: 11th (out of 14) 1947-1948
- Club's most capped player for Spain: Fernando Hierro (90)
- Teams most played against in European competitions: Internazionale (15), Bayern Munich (12), Anderlecht (10)

Source: Phil Ball. *White Storm: 100 Years of Real Madrid.* Edinburgh: Mainstream Publishing Company, 2002

Arthur Johnson, a former player, was hired as the club's first coach in 1910. The same year, the club built its first ground, the O'Donell, an unfenced earth pitch which it rented for 1,000 pesetas a month. Two years later, financed by the 450 club members, the pitch was fenced with wood and the first stands were built, with a capacity of 216.

In 1920 King Alphonso XIII granted the club the title "Real," meaning "royal." Shortly afterward the Real Madrid Football Club ventured on its first tours abroad, to Portugal and Italy. Subsequent tours were organized to England, Denmark and France (1926) and the US (1927).

By the 1920s Madrid had become the soccer capital of Spain with two major teams—Real and Atlético. In 1924 Real Madrid inaugurated its new Chamartín Stadium—the first to be wholly owned by the club. Its capacity was eventually expanded to 22,500.

Under Luis de Urquijo (1929–1933), a financier, some of the top players of that time were signed. For example, Ricardo Zamora transferred to Real for the then incredible sum of 150,000 pesetas (equivalent to €900 today!). As runners up in the very first season of Spain's League Championship in 1929, Real fielded a team in which only four players were from Madrid. Real took the trophy for the first time, in an unbeaten season, in 1931/32.

After the Civil War, during which the Charmartín Stadium was used as a prisoner-of-war camp, reconstruction of the club fell to two ex-presidents: Adolfo Meléndez (1939–1940) and Pedro Parages (1941–1943).

The Santiago Bernabéu Era: 1943–1978

Santiago Bernabéu, who had joined Real as a player in 1912, became president on 15 September 1943 and led the club for 35 years until his death in 1978. During his reign Bernabéu created teams which not only dominated the Spanish League but also played in the European Cup Final nine times, winning six matches. His vision was to turn Real Madrid into the best soccer club in the world and he paved the way for his successors.

Bernabéu's first major project was to buy land to build a new stadium, La Castellana, which was completed in 1947. Six years later, the original capac-

ity of over 75,000 was increased to 120,000, and soon afterwards the stadium was renamed Santiago Bernabéu Stadium.

By the 1950s, new player signings were paying off, and Real's star players such as Alfredo Di Stéfano (Argentinean) and Ferenc Puskas (Hungarian) would go on to become legends of the international game. (In 1967 Real hailed the former as the greatest player in football and, three years' later, appointed him emeritus and honorary president.)

The early 1950s saw changes in the way the club operated. Senior management became involved in marketing and in negotiations with the governing bodies of soccer. In 1955/56 Real played in—and won—the first European Cup. Back on home territory, in 1961 the club won 24 out of 30 games, in effect obtaining the title five weeks in advance. No Spanish team had achieved so many records in the League.

In 1963 the Ciudad Deportiva sports complex, situated on 11 hectares of land a mile from the stadium, was opened. It housed football and baseball fields, an athletics stadium and a basketball stadium—the latter for 5,200 spectators—swimming pools, a gym and a skating rink. There were also administrative offices, a cafeteria and changing rooms.

In the later years of his reign, Bernabéu celebrated the stadium's 25th anniversary (1972) and the club's 75th anniversary (1977) in style.

The Era of Transition: 1978–2000

After Bernabéu's death, Real Madrid entered a period of transition. President Luis de Carlos (1978–1985) was succeeded by Ramón Mendoza (1985–1995), marking the beginning of a productive, yet financially challenging, phase for the club. On the pitch, Real Madrid had produced one of its best teams, which won the UEFA title in 1985, after five years with no success in the League. By the end of the 1990 season, it had obtained its fifth domestic title in a row and scored a record 107 goals in 38 games. However, due mainly to lavish spending on the transfer market, the club's debt had risen to unacceptable levels and Mendoza was forced to resign.

Under his successor, Lorenzo Sanz (1995–2000), a commemorative exhibition was organized to celebrate the Santiago Bernabéu Stadium's 50th anniversary in 1997. During Sanz's presidency Real Madrid won its seventh and eighth European Cup titles, in 1998 and 2000, as well as one intercontinental cup and one League Cup. However, Sanz was unable to get rid of the inherited debt, which was said to have accumulated to €260 million. Rumors of his implication in some questionable dealings outside football contributed to his not being reelected in 2000.

The Pérez Era: 2000–to date

Pérez took up the presidency promising to increase the club's income and to have honest and transparent management. He defined a new organizational structure in three areas, with an overall general director. (*Refer to* **Exhibit 2** *for the organizational chart.*)

Pérez quickly set about eliminating Real Madrid's debt. He negotiated the rezoning of Ciudad Deportiva, north of Madrid's financial district. About 20% of the land was sold to private developers for office buildings; the remainder was ceded to local and regional governments to build a public car park and a 20,000-seat sports pavilion. He sold the club's training ground for more than €300 million. (*Refer to* **Exhibits 3** *and* **4** *for details of revenues and expenses, and the balance sheet.*)

In 2002 he secured a new site, Parque de Valdebebas, for the club to develop and build a new, state-of-the-art Sports City, including training facilities for the first football and basketball teams, and facilities for the junior teams and club members. Pérez had wiped the slate clean:

"Not only do we not have debt, but we have cash," he said in an interview. "As of now we have been paid 378m Euros and we still have 120m Euros to come. [We have more than enough] to construct a new 120m Euros, 120-hectare training ground [and] we want to build something spectacular."[4]

Pérez remained fiercely loyal to the club's desire to be private and not seek a listing on the stock exchange. He publicly defended the members' position:

The members don't want the club to be a public limited company. The club plays with feelings and the feelings of madridistas (Real fans) are deeply rooted in our hearts.[5]

Real Madrid was owned by its 70,000 club members, who were ordinary fans. By comparison, Manchester United was a quoted PLC owned by its shareholders, most of whom were financial institutions.

While this means that the Spanish Club cannot go to the capital markets for finance, at least the Real Chairman does not have to devote time and energy to keeping shareholders happy in the way that the United top brass most certainly do. United also has shareholder dividends to think about. United builds its football team in order to make its money; Real makes money in order to build its team.[6]

FOOTBALL: DEVELOPING THE TEAM'S ASSETS

The Stadium

In the early 1980s the Bernabéu Stadium was once again renovated—this time in order to comply with FIFA, UEFA and Spanish League standards and regulations concerning crowd safety and comfort. Capacity was reduced from 120,000 standing to 75,000 seated. In November 2000 Pérez unveiled a refurbishment project to add between 5,000 and 10,000 seats to the stadium, and an adjoining events hall and club museum. Work was expected to be completed around 2005.

Other Facilities

As a Sports Club, Real maintained other facilities for the benefit of its members, including two artificial grass pitches, plus terraces with room for 1,000 spectators to encourage the younger football and baseball teams. There was also a 600-member tennis club, with covered and open-air courts.

---

4. David Owen and Thilo Schafer. "A weight off Real shoulders: Football Real Madrid: A $180m property deal promises to relieve the club of its burdensome debt." *Financial Times* [London], 29 December 2001

5. ibid.

6. ibid.

Exhibit 2 ● Organizational Structure

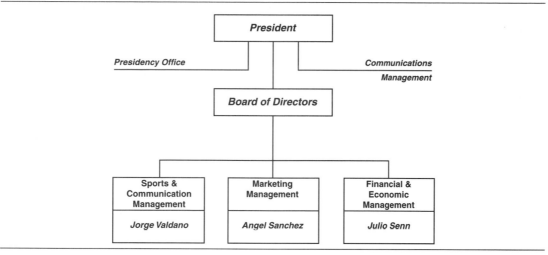

Source: www.realmadrid.com

The Squad

The first team had 25 players, of whom 16 were Spanish. Five had moved up through Real's youth scheme. In addition to the competitions, the team played in 16 friendly matches during the 2002 season.

Real Madrid was the first club to start hiring players from outside its immediate area, i.e. Madrid, for comparatively high sums of money. In keeping with the club's tradition, Pérez continued the policy of buying the best players to perpetuate the team's winning style of play.

A number of the club's star players came back as managers or coaches and took on important executive positions. The club's policy—continuing Bernabéu's dream of creating the best club in the world—was that the best people to build on were those who had been and would continue to be committed to the "Real Madrid cause." They knew the culture of the club and its values.

By 2003 Real Madrid had signed Figo for €60 million (2000); Ronaldo for €45 million (2001); Zidane, the former French national team captain, for a record-breaking €77 million (2002); and Beckham, the England captain and former Manchester United player, for €35 million (2003).

Beckham's €6 million salary was the same as that of Real Madrid's leading players and comparable with what he had earned with Manchester United.

[Beckham] is a very good player, he has such a powerful image that people sometimes forget about his skills on the field. It is not only that he plays good football, he is also a good professional and is in perfect physical condition. Regarding the club's signing policy, Valdano admitted "it is about signing top world footballers as they already come with a great publicity potential. The reputation of the club increases with them, they reinforce our brand."[7]

Talent

Real Madrid also had first, second and third divisions, as well as "lower category" teams for younger age groups.

When Di Stéfano became manager in 1982, he placed a lot of emphasis on Real's Youth Scheme, referred to as *la cantera* (the quarry). Fans also supported the youth development program feeding the first team. With the arrival of Pérez, Real planned to invest heavily in the program and also open football and basketball schools around the world to scout for teenage talent with the potential to be first team players.

---

7. www.realmadrid.com: Beckham: "I could not let this opportunity pass me," 18 June 2003

Exhibit 3 ● Revenue and Expenses Breakdown (in € thousands)

	2001/2002	2000/2001
INCOME		
Membership fees	7,705	7,034
Season ticket sales	17,730	15,752
Rent of boxes and VIP zones	6,888	3,170
Ticket sales and competitions	14,528	14,105
Income from U.E.F.A. and F.I.F.A.	10,479	9,759
Picture rights	438	
Rebroadcast rights	47,072	45,049
Income from rights to concessions	1,031	1,032
Income from advertising	22,511	23,115
Income from merchandising	15,943	11,580
Other income	7,351	5,176
Lending of players	516	30,946
Financial income	4,075	
Extraordinary income	376,240	121,684
Total	**532,507**	**288,400**
EXPENSES		
Personnel expenses (salaries & wages)	137,246	117,636
Travel, room and board expenses	4,402	4,096
Advertising, publicity and public relations	2,600	3,180
Cost of purchases	8,002	5,235
Amortization / depreciation	285,854	62,884
Provisions	1,071	4,828
Expenses of participation in competitions	1,084	422
Remaining expenses	30,794	26,166
Financial expenses	9,713	16,544
Extraordinary expenses	40,281	4,891
Total	**521,047**	**245,887**
Results	**11,460**	**42,520**

Source: Real Madrid Annual Reports 2001/02 & 2000/01

Fans: Developing the Fan Base

Real Madrid had over 70,000 fans who were members of the club. Fans had to apply for membership, and there was a waiting list. The selection criteria were strict, and members' behavior was monitored and evaluated before membership was renewed each year.

In the late 1990s the club developed a number of initiatives for members, including establishing a Member Care Office; upgrading the Supporters Clubs department; and introducing a fan card which, among other things, entitled members to discounts on merchandise and preferential booking of tickets.

Exhibit 4 ● Balance Sheet (in € thousands)

ASSETS	June 30, 2002	June 30, 2001
Fixed Assets	190,422	358,920
Intangible sports assets	-	186,209
Player acquisition rights	333,738	275,625
Amortization	(333,738)	(89,416)
Other intangible fixed assets	31,195	47,833
Cost	81,740	81,168
Amortization	(50,545)	(33,335)
Tangible fixed assets	96,243	98,580
Cost	134,956	123,233
Depreciation	(23,540)	(24,653)
Provisions	(15,173)	-
Long-term financial investments	62,984	26,298
Deferred income	143	478
Current assets	284,943	152,940
Inventory	1,980	658
Debtors	129,577	132,833
Group and associated accounts receivable	1,227	-
Official organizations and television	11,113	12,746
Sports entities	8,085	20,143
Sundry debtors	85,595	79,226
Personnel	1,515	1,504
Government bodies	30,528	26,633
Provision for doubtful debts	(8,491)	(7,419)
Short term financial investments	150,680	6,010
Cash	2,706	13,439
TOTAL ASSETS	**475,508**	**512,338**

LIABILITIES	June 30, 2002	June 30, 2001
Partnership equity	67,951	61,863
Capital fund	53,315	21,719
Revaluation reserve	8,548	8,548
Yearly profit	6,088	31,596
Deferred income	60,147	76,377
Provisions for liabilities and expenses	23,853	19,487
Long-term liabilities	141,055	103,478
Loans with financial institutions	-	45,210
Sundry creditors	39,655	17,423
Interclub funds	39	78
Other debts	101,361	40,767
Short-term liabilities	182,502	251,133
Loans with financial institutions	5,764	110,736
Salaries payable to team personnel	57,203	43,431
Debts for acquisitions and services received	16,106	8,950
Sundry creditors	69,373	63,943
Government bodies	7,244	5,545
Accrued expenses	26,812	18,528
TOTAL LIABILITIES	**475,508**	**512,338**

Source: Real Madrid Annual Report 2001/02

By signing foreign players such as Zidane, Figo and Ronaldo, the club won fans in France and North Africa, Portugal, and Brazil. The club also signed a promising young Japanese midfielder as much for his footwork as for the football-crazy home market he would open up. And it took this a step further by securing Manchester United's Beckham to play for Real.

Much of the reasoning behind signing the England captain . . . is Beckham's ability to break open markets in the Far East. His first public appearance in Japan, a country where nine out of 10 people know his name, will be in the white of Madrid.[8]

The Real Madrid Foundation aimed to reach out to the club's existing fans and to create new ones. Alongside its sporting and training activities for children and young adults, it fulfilled a humanitarian and sociocultural function, working with handicapped children and juvenile offenders; running drug abuse prevention programs and helping to integrate immigrants.

Media: Bringing Fans and Football Together

As early as the 1950s, Bernabéu had introduced an information bulletin for fans, which was later replaced by a club magazine. In 2002 Real Madrid launched *las Peñas del Real Madrid* (*Real Madrid Circles*), a monthly publication to keep all Circle (a separate Members Club supporting Real Madrid) members informed. Throughout the season, an official program was distributed free of charge at all games played in the stadium.

The club had an official website (www. realmadrid.com)—available in Spanish, English and Japanese—to communicate with its fans by providing easy access and information for members. Real Madrid games were televised on five continents, and it also had its own television channel, which was jointly managed with Sogecable SA (one of whose brands was Canal+).

8. Tim Rich and Alan Nixon: "Beckham agrees £25 million on move to Madrid: Real look to capitalise on revenue potential of England captain's Asian tour." *Independent* [London], 18 June 2003. www.independent.co.uk

BUSINESS MODEL: REVENUES

Despite Real Madrid's self-confidence in its brand, it felt it still had a long way to go to maximize earnings from marketing and merchandising. The club started attracting sponsors that recognized the global value of the Real Madrid brand. It intended to launch a number of shops and theme restaurants around the globe to capitalize on the strength of the brand.

Membership Fees

Real Madrid had more than 70,000 members, whose membership fees represented approximately 5% of the club's total ordinary revenues. Revenues from membership increased by 9.5% in the 2001/02 centenary season. (*Refer to* **Exhibit 5** *for an overview of how Real Madrid made its money.*)

Gate Receipts, Season Tickets and Competition Revenues

Real Madrid's basketball and other sporting activities accounted for less than 10% of its revenues, but as these sports were as important to the club as football, it did not break down its revenues by sports category.

With no outside investor scrutiny, the club was not obliged to provide details of its gate receipts or competition revenues. However, the club had been successful in negotiating a higher share of revenue for participation in UEFA matches and this, together with being at the top of the European list, worked in the club's favor. Season ticket sales had risen by 12.5% in the 2001/02 season and represented more than 55% of this revenue category.

VIP Boxes, Conferencing and Catering

The number of conferences and VIP boxes more than doubled in 2001/02, but they still contributed less than 5% of the club's total ordinary revenues. In its debt-ridden days, the club had sold concessions for boxes at the stadium to third parties, thus forgoing a source of recurring revenues not only for the boxes themselves but also for the catering, which the box holders arranged independently of the club. Pérez started buying these concessions back with the aim of providing the club with a new, growing and sustainable source of income. In line with this strategy, the club acquired 100% of RM Eventos, an events management company.

Exhibit 5 ● How Real Madrid Made Its Money

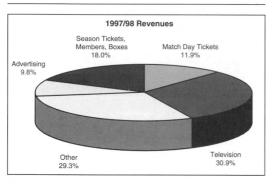

Source: Real Madrid Annual Report 1997/98

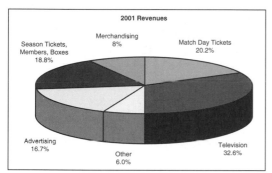

Source: Real Madrid Annual Report 2001

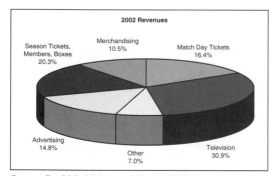

Source: Real Madrid Annual Report 2002

Television and New Media Income

Real Madrid had a history of actively managing a number of television rights contracts for maximum cash flow, and for more than a decade it had benefited from steadily rising income from the sale of television broadcasting rights to various operators. It had contracts with domestic state television company RTVE, with Sogecable SA and with pay-per-view operators. The club's aim, however, was to reduce its dependence on television rights revenues. (*Refer to* **Exhibit 6** *for details of media revenues and sponsorship.*)

Sponsorship and Royalties

Pérez attempted to bring in household names as sponsors, attracted by the Real Madrid global brand. He believed they would raise the club's status, boost its following abroad and in turn allow it to sell more replica kits and attract more sponsors and more television income. To celebrate its centenary and in a display of financial confidence, the team dropped its long-time shirt sponsor for 2002 and returned to the unblemished white-on-white kit, with not a logo in sight.

We are also trying to capitalize on the legend of the club. So you've got to be careful to keep the balance: commerce must not be allowed to sully the grass of the pitch, says Jorge Valdano, Sporting Director of Real Madrid.[9]

In a deal described at the time by a senior Real official as "possibly the biggest marketing deal made for a football player ever," Figo, the 29-year-old Portuguese star, was signed by Coca-Cola in 2001, just after he was named FIFA world player of the year. The deal was to run for three years, during which time Figo would, among other things, promote the Coca-Cola brand during the 2002 World Cup finals. The proceeds of the deal were to be split 50:50 between the player and the club. The transaction would thus help the club to recoup the transfer fee it had paid to sign the player from archrivals Barcelona.

The club had also entered into a three-season agreement with Siemens, the German multinational, as its global technology partner.

9. Keith Johnson. "Madrid's Valdano Pursues Validation." *Wall Street Journal* [Brussels], April 23, 2002

Exhibit 6 ● Real Madrid Media Revenues and Sponsorship

	Contracts duration			Income to be deferred over various years
	Utilization rights	Special options	Calculated results	
TV rights to open competition, and pay per view football, League and Cup	2002/2003	2008/2009	23,879	3,005
Audiovisual and Canal Blanco television rights	2002/2003	2010/2011	3,005	3,005
ACB League audiovisual rights	2002/2003	2007/2008	1,088	361
European football competition audiovisual rights	2001/2002	2009/2010	16,045	-
European basketball competition audiovisual rights	2005/2006	2009/2010	2,054	-
Friendly matches and Bernabéu Trophy	-	2006/2007	1,001	1,735
Total television rights			47,072	8,106
Rights for Internet sales, halls sets and external advertising	2002/2003	2010/2011	2,972	2,972
Sponsorship of sports clothing	2007/2008	-	15,484	22,100
Billboard advertising	2002/2003	2007/2008	3,131	3,005
Others	-	-	2,427	-
Calculation under the heading "other income"	-	-	(1,503)	-
Total advertising rights			22,511	29,412
Total audiovisual and sponsorship rights			69,583	37,518

Source: Real Madrid Annual Report, 2001/02

Merchandising and Other Revenues

The player gives you more than football. He gives you his image and marketing assets. Real Madrid is a pioneer club in buying the personal image rights of its players.[10]

Pérez generated more than €12 million from marketing Figo's image and trademark number 10 shirt. His key decision—one that distinguished him from the other club presidents outside the UK—had been to retain the shirt, Internet and advertising image rights of all new players, turning their on-field visibility into merchandising revenues and offsetting their annual

salaries. Pérez wanted to develop commercial revenues from merchandising and licensing globally. He felt that the availability of a sizable number of star players with different geographical backgrounds would unlock substantial new markets and enable the club to continue paying high prices for new top talent:

The acquisition of big players helps project the club's image around the world and, consequently, we will receive earnings that allow us to keep buying the best footballers. This is like a company, if you want to sell shirts, you need to have big stars" [Pérez].[11]

The club entered into a €17 million agreement with Groupo Caja Madrid and Sogecable SA to develop the merchandising, images and Internet business.

10. David Owen and Thilo Schafer. "A weight off Real shoulders: Football Real Madrid: A $180m property deal promises to relieve the club of its burdensome debt." *Financial Times* [London], 29 December 2001

11. ibid.

Groupo Caja Madrid would have a 20% share, Soge-cable 10% and Real Madrid 70% of the returns.

Real Madrid's official store selling club merchandise was in the Esquina del Bernabéu shopping center close to the stadium. It sold a whole range of goods—from items for the bathroom, kitchen or bedroom to smaller gifts such as pens, watches, lighters and pins to clothing. Garments included T-shirts sporting the name and number of players, tracksuits and sweatshirts in all sizes—right down to baby gear. It was also possible for fans to have the merchandise personalized.

BUSINESS MODEL: COSTS

Wages

The club paid high wages to its top players. In the 2000/01 season, wages were approximately 70% of ordinary revenues (excluding player transfer revenues), rising to more than 85% in the 2001/02 season. Real Madrid was one of a number of top European teams seeking to raise marketing income to help offset spiraling player wage and transfer costs.

40 per cent of income should come from sports marketing in the future, versus 20 per cent at present.[12]

12. *Financial Times* [London], 28 December 2001

Player Transfers

Jorge Valdano, Real Madrid's sporting director, was the architect of a team that was expected to win everything, every year and make money in the process. His strategy was to buy one top player every year to promote his objectives. To this end, Real Madrid used the profits from its land sales in 2001 to fully amortize the intangible assets associated with its purchases of top players on the transfer markets in previous years.

The Beckham deal with Manchester United was incentive related. Only €25 million of the €35 million transfer fee was guaranteed to the British club. The remaining €10 million was dependent on Real's performance over the next four years. Since payments were to be triggered by the club qualifying for the Champions League and reaching the quarterfinals, something it had done every year since 1998, United was confident it would be paid in full. Beckham's contract also gave him an option for a fifth year.

*(Refer to **Exhibit 7** for details of sports-related intangible fixed assets.)*

Exhibit 7 ● Sports Related Intangible Fixed Assets

	Cost	Amortization	Net
Balance as of June 30, 2001	275,625	(89,416)	186,209
Acquisition of players	81,860	-	81,860
Release of players	(23,747)	21,418	(2,329)
Annual team amortization	-	(265,740)	(265,740)
Balance as of June 30, 2002	333,738	(333,738)	-

Source: Real Madrid Annual Report, 2001/02

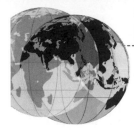

CASE 17

Football Club Ajax

Ajax was an Amsterdam-based football club with an impressive track record in both the Dutch league and European football. It was listed on the Amsterdam Stock Exchange and had a market capitalization of €66 million. (*Refer to* **Exhibit 1** *for the share price performance.*)

Since professional football began in the Netherlands in 1955/56, Ajax had won a record 19 national championships. The club had only once been ranked outside the top three in the national league since 1996, and it had qualified for European competition every single year (*refer to* **Exhibit 2** *for the club honors*).

Ajax was strongly characterized by its youth development program, which resulted in a specialized type of game and a distinctive style of play. Despite having one of the best on-pitch records in Europe, Ajax's brand remained underexploited. (It had an estimated 1.2 million domestic supporters, with 42,000 season ticket holders and a waiting list of 6,000.)

Football activities generated 48.5% of the net turnover in the financial year 2001/02, with sponsorship and advertising contributing 35.9%, the exploitation of television rights 9.8% and merchandising 5.8%.

Located as it was in one of the smaller football markets in Europe, Ajax faced the challenge of having to compete against teams from bigger markets. If Ajax wanted to keep up with the Manchester Uniteds

Research Associate Lisa (Mwezi) Schüpbach prepared this case under the supervision of Professors Robert S. Collins and Jean-Pierre Jeannet as a basis for class discussion rather than to illustrate either effective or ineffective handling of a business situation. We should like to acknowledge the support of Gerry Boon, Partner in Charge, Deloitte & Touche Sport, in the preparation of this material. We should also like to acknowledge Ernesto Mancosu for his contribution. Copyright © 2003 by IMD—International Institute for Management Development, Lausanne, Switzerland. All rights reserved. Not to be used or reproduced without written permission directly from IMD, Lausanne, Switzerland.

of the industry, the club would have to review its own business model. Could Ajax follow a similar path to Manchester United, or would it have to take a completely different approach?

CLUB HISTORY: ON THE PITCH

Foundation of AFC Ajax

On 18 March 1900 three friends, Han Dade, Carel Reeser and Floris Stempel, founded Football Club Ajax in a café in Amsterdam. The club joined the Amsterdam Football Association (Amsterdamse Voetbal Bond/AVB) and rented a playing field in the north of Amsterdam for its home games.

By the summer of 1907 the club had to leave its playing field and found space in the municipality of Watergraafsmeer. There were no stands, no dressing rooms, not even any water, but there was a good tram connection to the city and there was more room for additional pitches.

In 1909 the club took on its first paid coach, John Kirwan, who had had a long international career with UK's Tottenham Hotspur. Ajax went on to win the second league championship in 1911 and finally obtained its long-desired promotion to the first league.

The Jack Reynolds Era

In 1915 Jack Reynolds—who would go on to coach Ajax teams for 25 seasons—joined the club and built a team that won the league championship three times in a row. The club won its first national championship without losing a single game in the 1917/18 season—a feat that was to be repeated again 55 years later.

The 1930s was a Golden Age for the club, during which it won the league championship seven times, and the national championship five times. These successes prompted Ajax to build a new stadium, De Meer, at the

Exhibit 1 ● Share Price Performance since IPO (in €)

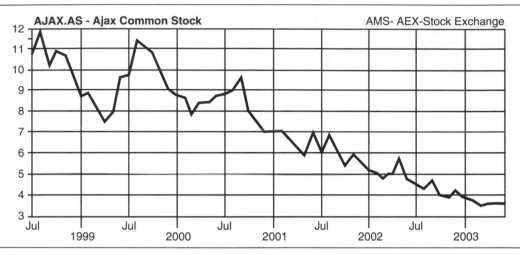

Source: Factiva

Middenweg in Watergraafsmeer in 1934 to accommodate the increasing number of spectators. Despite the international economic crisis caused by the Great Depression, the club was able to pay for most of the stadium itself.

The Ajax club magazine at the time described the type of play Reynolds had introduced: "The championship is not only a success for Ajax, but also for the type of football that is nowadays often called 'scientific' or 'technical.'"

Going European

In November 1954 the Royal Dutch Football Association (Koninklijke Nederlandse Voetbalbond/KNVB) officially allowed professional football in the Netherlands for the first time, and Ajax became an inaugural member of the Dutch professional football league. Until then, all players had been amateurs with regular jobs outside football, but since top players could now earn a great deal of money abroad, many started to leave the club.

In the new Premier League (Eredivisie) Ajax held its own and earned the right to play in the European Cup by winning its ninth national championship in 1957. In 1958/59 Ajax had slipped to sixth place, but it was nevertheless a significant season because it

was the first time ever that highlights of a football match were shown on Dutch television.

The Rinus Michels Era

When Rinus Michels was appointed as coach in 1965, he introduced professionalism to the club. He adopted Reynolds' attacking playing style and brought back experienced players and acquired some new ones. Over a six-year period Ajax won the national championship four times and the KNVB Cup three times. On the international level the club had built a reputation as a European force to be reckoned with.

In the golden years from 1971 to 1973 the club won the European Cup three times in succession. Stefán Kovács, who succeeded Michels in 1972, built on his predecessor's distinctive playing style, which came to be described as "total football." Johan Cruijff was the club's key player in the 3-4-3 system which, with its focus on speed and attack—even by midfielders and defenders—filled Ajax's national and international opponents with dread.

Loss of Players

Following the club's European Cup final successes, countries such as Spain and Italy, which had opened their borders to foreign footballers, lured Ajax players

Exhibit 2 ● Ajax Football Club Trophies

Title	Year
National champions:	*1918, 1919,* 1931, 1932, 1934, 1937, 1939, *1947,* 1957, 1960, *1966, 1967, 1968, 1970,* 1972, 1973, 1977, 1979, 1980, 1982, 1983, *1985,* 1990, *1994, 1995, 1996,* 1998, 2002
Divisional champions First Class:	*1918, 1919, 1921,* 1927, 1928, 1930, 1931, 1932, 1934, 1935, 1936, 1937, 1939, *1946, 1947,* 1950, 1952
National Cup—(K)NVB—winners:	1917, 1943, 1961, *1967, 1970, 1971, 1972,* 1979, 1983, *1986, 1987,* 1993, 1998, 1999, 2002
Intertoto:	1962
Dutch Super Cup:	*1993, 1994, 1995*
European Champions Cup/Champions League (from 1956):	*1971, 1972, 1973, 1995*
European Cup Winners' Cup:	*1987*
UEFA Cup (from 1972):	*1992*
European Super Cup (from 1972):	*1972, 1973, 1995*
World Cup (from 1930):	*1972, 1995*

Jack Reynolds, 1915–1925, 1928–1940 and 1945–1947

Rinus Michels,* 1965–1972 and 1975–1976*

Stéfan Kovács, 1972–1973

Johan Cruijff,* 1985–1988

Louis van Gaal,* 1991–1997

* as technical director

Source: Ajax website <www.ajax.nl>

to join them with offers of high salaries. Now more than ever, Ajax needed to focus on the training of new young players.

The system paid off, and between 1981 and 1987 the club won both the national championship and the KNVB Cup three times. Cruijff returned to Ajax in 1985, this time as "technical director," and spurred the team on to win its first international trophy in 14 years. Two years later, in 1987, Ajax won its only European Cup Winners Cup.

In the late 1980s the club lost more talented players. It also suffered two further setbacks when, in 1989, it was banned from European football for a season after a spectator threw an iron bar onto the pitch during a UEFA Cup match, and a year later, when it pleaded guilty to an illegal transfer payment.

The Louis van Gaal Era

Louis van Gaal was undoubtedly the most successful coach in the history of Ajax (*refer to* **Exhibit 2** *for successes during his tenure from 1991 to 1997*). By the end of his sixth season, the club had equaled the successes of top clubs like Juventus (and later Barcelona and Bayern Munich) which had won every European Cup.

After Van Gaal stepped down in 1997 a series of coaches came and went; players also left and returned. For many of the coaches, it was mission impossible to get the team going again, despite a number of victories on the pitch. In 2000 the club hired two coaches.

CLUB HISTORY: IN THE BOARDROOM

From Club to Business

With the introduction, in June 1962, of a Members' Council of the Association, the club took on a more professional aspect. Among other things, the Council appointed and supervised the management board, which consisted of five people: one managing director and four other directors responsible for marketing, professional football, training and operations. The supervisory board had three members.

Ajax and its group of four subsidiaries, held in a subholding company—Teucrus NV—had been designed to support the club's football and football-related activities (*refer to* **Exhibit 3** *for the organizational structure*).

Going Public

On 16 February 1998, the Ajax Members' Council, at the request of the board, took the decision for AFC Ajax to go public. Ajax intended to use the proceeds on: expanding its player development scheme and scouting operations internationally; equity stakes in other football clubs; and expanding its merchandising operations, first in the Netherlands and then abroad. On 11 May 1998 Ajax became the first Dutch football club to be quoted on the Amsterdam Stock Exchange. Its market capitalization on introduction was €208 million; by May 2003 it had dropped to €66 million. (*Refer to* **Exhibit 4** *for the ownership structure after the IPO.*)

Since Ajax had been run as a members' association, it had never paid a dividend. A year after flotation AFC Ajax NV paid dividends to its shareholders in cash.

Exhibit 3 ● Ajax's Organizational Structure

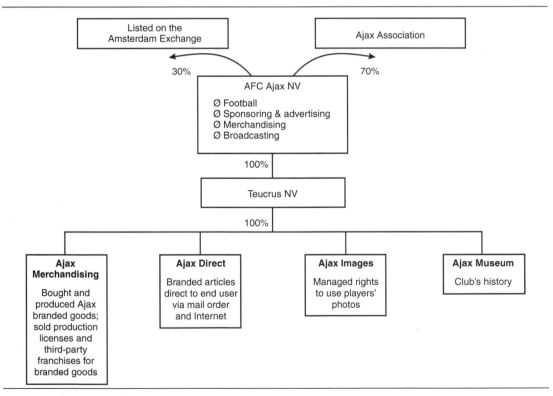

Source: Ajax Prospectus 1998

Exhibit 4 ● Ajax's Ownership Structure

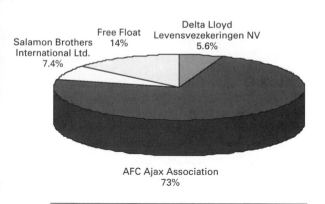

Salamon Brothers
International Ltd.
7.4%

Free Float
14%

Delta Lloyd
Levensvezekeringen NV
5.6%

AFC Ajax Association
73%

Source: Ajax Annual Report, 2002

BUILDING THE BUSINESS

Ajax's strategy was to keep the club at the top of both Dutch and European professional football with its high quality of play. Its objective was to invest only in its core area of competency and to diversify its revenue streams by operating commercial player development schemes and taking strategic stakes in other clubs internationally.

Proceeds from the IPO enabled Ajax to take equity stakes in several training centers around the world: South Africa (51% in Ajax Cape Town), Ghana (51% in Ashanti Goldfields) and Belgium (30% in Germinal Beerschot Antwerpen). An important criterion for investment was that the club in question was in a country where GDP per capita was high enough to interest European sponsors and potentially stimulate demand for Ajax goods and broadcast rights. Ajax hoped to create a truly international presence and wanted to use these centers both as a source of new talent and as profit centers in their own right. However, by 2001/02, Ajax had decided to cease its investments in Belgium and Ghana to comply with changed FIFA regulations concerning financial participation in foreign teams.

Off the pitch, Ajax aspired to strengthen the relationship with its sponsors so that both parties could maximize exploitation of the Ajax brand.

Football: Developing the Team's Assets

Stadium

During its 100 years of existence, Ajax had moved pitch five times, always to a bigger and more impressive stadium. In 1996 the club signed a long-term lease—as tenant and minority (13.1%) owner—on the new multifunctional Amsterdam ArenA stadium. Ajax was the main tenant of the ArenA stadium with a rental agreement for a 30-year term and an option to extend. The club paid the ArenA 30% of its first NLG 15 million of gate revenue, and then 25% of any gate revenue over NLG 17 million, subject to a minimum NLG 6.9 million.[1]

The ArenA was an all-seater stadium. This was to comply with the UEFA ruling—in response to increasing hooliganism during matches in the Netherlands in the late 1980s—that by 2000 all stadiums would have to be all-seater stadiums. Apart from the regular seats, the ArenA had 1,535 business seats and 540 sky box (enclosed) seats. The retractable roof eliminated disruption to fixtures due to weather and created a more comfortable environment for spectators.

Other facilities included several restaurants, offices and conference rooms, as well as players' changing rooms, medical treatment rooms, a power training center and a relaxation room. There was also an indoor sports arena and two outside pitches for training. In 1998 Ajax opened a museum of the club's history in the ArenA.

The move increased capacity to about 51,000, from just over 18,000 in the De Meer stadium, and revenues had gone up 60%. But still the stadium was losing money.

The Squad

Ajax's first team played in the Dutch Premier Division and the national cup competition, and, with the exception of the 1990/91 season, had played in one of the European Cup competitions for the past 38 years. It also played in international cup competitions and friendly matches.

The squad generally consisted of players under 21. The first team had 25 players. The second team, with about 16 players, played in competitions for

1. Exchange rate 1996 NLG 1 = US$0.59

reserve teams and acted as a springboard for young talents to the top.

Talent

The youth program was the main pillar of Ajax's success. In the selection and training process, the TIPS model of assessment was used: **T**echnique (ball skills), **I**ntelligence (reading the game, tactical skills), **P**ersonality and **S**peed (both physical and handling speed). Ajax had an extensive network of scouts, including two full-time scouts, who assessed young players using the TIPS model. Every year, between 30 and 45 young players, as well as an average of 15 older players (aged 14 and above), were invited to enter the Ajax youth training program.

Ajax trained players to follow its preferred system and had the strongest player development brand in the world. Both first and second team players commanded high prices from other clubs, which valued them for their exceptional technique and fitness. (*Refer to **Exhibit 5** for famous players from the youth development scheme.*) The sale of a player minus the initial investment covered the salaries of two coaches as well as pitch and training facilities at the modern sports park De Toekomst. If young players were taken on (at no cost) aged 11 to 16, Ajax assumed that it took three years to train them to a level at which they could be sold internationally. (*Refer to **Exhibit 6** for the training center analysis.*)

Four Ajax amateur teams played in the Saturday league organized by the Dutch Football Association. The players—a number of whom were former first team players—were also club members.

Exhibit 5 ● Famous Players from the Ajax Youth Development Scheme

Johan Cruijff
Sjaak Swart
Piet Keizer
Rinus Michels
Frank Rijkaard
Wim Suurbier
Dennis Bergkamp
Patrick Kluivert

Source: Ajax Prospectus, 1998

Fans: Developing the Fan Base

The club estimated that it had about 1.2 million Dutch fans, 42,000 of whom were season ticket holders. Members of the Supporters Association numbered about 75,000, and there were more than 28,000 Club Card holders.

Ajax's aim was not only to increase the number of supporters but also to make sure that it met their justified expectations, wishes and demands, and guaranteed their safety. Together with the city of Amsterdam, Ajax financed the Axios foundation, which aimed to prevent vandalism by Ajax supporters through creating a strong bond between the club and its fan base.

Ajax did not want to risk alienating its supporters after flotation—for example, if the expansion of club

Exhibit 6 ● Ajax International Training Center Analysis

(NLG '000) Year	0	1	2	3	4	5
Initial investment	2,500					
Operating costs (+3% per annum)		500	515	530	546	563
Accumulated investment		3,000	3,515	4,045	4,592	5,155
Proceeds for players sold (NLG '000)				**Sell first player in year:**		
				3	4	5
Required return is 10%				935	1,006	1,078
Required return is 15%				1,137	1,235	1,336

Source: Ajax Prospectus, 1998

merchandising activities was seen to divert funds away from investment in on-pitch activities—and therefore made sure that supporters had access to all club information, and that they could communicate their ideas, complaints and suggestions to the club.

Media: Bringing Fans and Football Together

The club communicated with its supporters through the Club Card, via teletext on RTL and with *Ajax Life,* the official fan club magazine, and *Ajax Magazine,* free to all season ticket holders. It also published "Kick-Off," a complimentary program for each game. Ajax had its own official website (www.ajax.nl), available in Dutch and English, and fans had also created a large number of unofficial club sites. The increase in broadcasts of live matches over the Internet allowed the club to reach out to fans all over the world, as well as offering new advertising and sponsorship opportunities.

Building the Brand

Excellent on-pitch performances meant that Ajax had the largest number of supporters of any Dutch club. Its high profile reinforced supporter loyalty, and the club could hence afford temporarily lower gate receipts if there was a period of poor on-pitch performance.

To protect and develop its existing brand Ajax's key objectives were to develop or import star talent, build on differentiating its playing style and influence media coverage. It also aimed to maximize merchandising revenue by growing brand awareness through expanding its product range and stores.

Although Ajax wanted to concentrate its efforts on the domestic market, it also intended to market its brand internationally through the Internet, and possibly by establishing retail outlets abroad.

BUSINESS MODEL: REVENUES

During the football season Ajax received income mainly from TV rights, gate receipts and—if the club qualified—premiums from the Champions League. Ajax's outgoings, apart from the costs related to signing new players, were relatively stable. Ajax's future profitability depended on the club's performance in the Champions League and its ability to capitalize on its development program. (*Refer to* **Exhibit 7** *for an overview of how Ajax made its money.*)

Exhibit 7 ● How Ajax Made Its Money

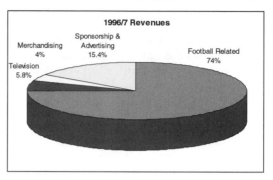

Source: Ajax Prospectus, 1998

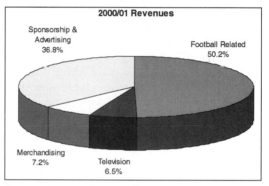

Source: Ajax Annual Report 2000/01

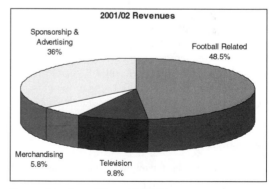

Source: Ajax Annual Report 2001/02

Ajax's main financing needs were: transfer and signing fees, personnel costs, the youth training program, direct match costs and housing costs. The cash flow was mainly characterized by high income at the start of a season from the sale of season tickets and business and sky box seats (fully paid in advance) and from sponsor contracts (partially paid in advance). In the summer, as part of the preparations for the new season, players' contracts were typically negotiated. Ajax aimed to finance the costs related to the signing of new players' contracts from the operational cash flow and the sale of players.

Gate Receipts

After its move to the ArenA from De Meer, Ajax continued to play to a packed stadium. There were two categories of tickets: those that were prepaid for the whole season—including season tickets, executive (sky) boxes and business seats—and those that were sold on match days. Season ticket holders could attend all 17 home league matches in the Premier Division and received priority for European Cup and Amstel Cup (domestic) matches. Business seats and boxes were valid for all matches played at the stadium, without the need to purchase additional tickets.

Gate receipts from matches played at the ArenA stadium made up the largest part (40.7%) of Ajax's revenues. There were 42,000 seats for season ticket, business and box holders (up from 15,000 in the old stadium), with a waiting list of 6,000. Business seats and boxes accounted for only 6% of the prepaid seats, yet they generated 50% of the total revenue from this category. Although the club could probably increase prices in all ticket categories and still operate at near capacity, the tickets, at NLG 15, were the most expensive in the Netherlands (even though supporters considered them to be reasonably priced).

Competition Revenues

Participation in the Champions League was a vital source of revenue for Ajax. The competition paid a fixed fee for entering, guaranteed a minimum number of home games and provided the opportunity to secure merit payments and further home matches—thus gate receipts—if successful.

Given the small Dutch market, Ajax will stay very dependent on revenues from the [European] Champions League. We expect the club to make a loss (before net transfer fee income) in the years ahead, except for the years when the club is successful in the European Champions League.[2]

Revenues from other European competitions were lower as they were wholly dependent on field success and lacked a fixed income element.

The club had the right to almost all revenue generated from ticket and merchandise sales at its home games in the domestic league and in European competitions, but it paid 7.4% of ticket receipts for domestic games to the KNVB, and for games in the UEFA and Cup Winners Cups, it paid 10% of television revenues and 4% of gate receipts less stadium rental to UEFA. Revenue from the Amstel Cup matches was split 50:50 with the away side. (*Refer to **Exhibit 8** for the consolidated P&L report and details of the operating results and net turnover of football activities.*)

Conferences and Catering

Despite Ajax's 13.1% equity stake in the Amsterdam ArenA, the club took no share of the catering revenues and it had little incentive to persuade people to come to the stadium early, by showing, for example, the previous away match on a big screen, to increase consumer spending.

Television and New Media Income

Live football matches were the most watched television programs in the Netherlands, with an average 3 million viewers. The KNVB, on behalf of the Dutch Football Clubs, collected the monies from television rights and distributed them to the clubs according to their position on the promotion and relegation table. There was a distribution ratio between the highest-placed club and the lowest-placed club of approximately 3:1. Domestic pre-eminence secured Ajax a high proportion of pay and free-to-air television rights revenues.

2. Fortis Bank Equity Research, 2 May 2003

Exhibit 8 ● Consolidated P&L Report

NLG'000	2001/02	2000/01	1996/97
Revenues			
Match day gate revenue	5,130.00	4,444.00	
Gate receipts Europe & Africa Cups	2,120.00	813.00	Comparable
Season tickets	7,975.00	7,944.00	breakdown
Business seats and sky boxes	9,443.00	9,608.00	not available
Indirect competition revenues	2,169.00	2,005.00	
Total match revenues	**26,837.00**	**24,814.00**	
Sponsoring	19,911.00	17,839.00	Comparable
Television	5,419.00	3,250.00	breakdown
Merchandising	3,216.00	3,546.00	not available
Total net revenues	**55,383.00**	**49,449.00**	
Net Turnover	**55,383.00**	**49,449.00**	**41,211.36**
Operating Costs			
Cost of Sales	1,366.00	1,980.00	52.27
Wages, salaries, social security	35,001.00	30,098.00	15,402.27
Depreciation of tangible fixed assets and goodwill	3,659.00	4,211.00	933.64
Other operating costs	24,327.00	24,188.00	18,045.45
Total operating costs	**64,353.00**	**60,477.00**	**34,433.64**
Operating results before depreciation transfer and signing fees and players' result	-8,970.00	-11,028.00	6,777.73
Depreciation transfer and signing-on fees	-19,933.00	-15,065.00	-4,837.73
Capital gain on players	3,935.00	11,774.00	5,153.18
Operating result after depreciation transfer and signing on fees and players' result	-24,968.00	-14,319.00	7,093.18
Interest received and similar income	489.00	1,070.00	2,193.64
Change in value of securities	0.00	-141.00	0.00
Result from ordinary activities before taxation	-24,479.00	-13,390.00	9,286.82
Taxation on result on ordinary activities	5,994.00	2,436.00	-3,428.18
Result from ordinary activities after tax	-18,485.00	-10,954.00	5,858.64
Extrordinary income	-10,660.00	0.00	0.00
Tax on extraordinary results	1,292.00	0.00	0.00
Extraordinary results after tax	-9,368.00	0.00	0.00
Net result after tax	-27,853.00	-10,954.00	5,858.64
Minority interests	2,066.00	2,734.00	0.00
Net result	**-25,787.00**	**-8,220.00**	**5,858.64**

Source: Ajax Prospectus 1998, and Annual Reports 2001, 2002

Pay-television operator Nethold (later acquired by Canal+) held the exclusive rights to live and integral broadcasts of the Premier League (Eredivisie) matches via cable and satellite. The deal for up to 70 matches a year ran from the 1997/98 season to 2001/02 and was worth NLG 16.5 million in the first year rising to NLG 40 million in the final year. The Dutch national broadcast organization, NOS, paid the KNVB NLG 35.3 million a year for the rights to the highlights of every Eredivisie match. International distribution rights for these matches were sold via the ISC rights agency for NLG 5 million per annum. The KNVB also had a contract with SBS to broadcast Amstel Cup matches and their highlights.

For European Cup Winners Cup and UEFA Cup matches, the clubs themselves sold the television rights. For these matches, Ajax had entered into an agreement with the NOS, which expired in July 2003. The television rights for the Champions League were collectively exploited by UEFA, and this was a condition for participation in this competition.

Ajax was watching the "pay-per-view" and "video-on-demand" market closely. At the time of the 1997 KNVB/Canal+ deal, the TV channel had about 160,000 subscribers, which in 1998 went up to an estimated 240,000—just 3.7% of the total 6.5 million Dutch households with television. Because of the high demand for tickets and the dispersed fan base (only 5% of the total population lived in Amsterdam), Ajax wanted to reach out to the pay television market, but there was cultural resistance to it as almost 94% of Dutch households received cable. Although Dutch football had experienced significant growth in the total value of its television contracts, in absolute terms it was still low compared with Europe. (*Refer to Exhibits 9 and 10 for comparison of Dutch television rights and domestic television contracts.*)

Ajax explored other broadcasting opportunities in themed television channels, radio and Internet broadcasting. For Ajax to establish its own television channel, like Manchester United's, for example, would be a challenge without a larger supporter base. NOS held radio rights for NLG 1 million per annum. Like digital television, digital audio broadcasting enabled simultaneous broadcasts of a number of matches, but supporters were unlikely to pay for the service. Ajax also had a cooperation agreement for its audio-visual activities with TV producer IDTV for the development of the "Stadium Journal" and television programs, mainly for foreign broadcasters.

Sponsorship and Advertising

In 2002 Ajax had 17 sponsors, including a shirt sponsor (ABN AMRO) and a clothing sponsor (Adidas). Sponsors received a basic package of benefits at a standard rate, which included exposure, hospitality and display of name and logo. These benefits applied to all matches with the exception of the Champions League, which had its own sponsorship arrangements organized through UEFA.

Ajax Images, one of the company's subsidiaries, was a marketing and service organization whose main function was to generate extra income for the club and the players by exploiting their advertising value in a more organized way. Ajax Images would enter into contracts with Ajax players enabling them to exploit portrait rights and link individual players to brands for advertising purposes or use individual players for promotional activities for various companies.

Merchandising and Other Revenue

In January 1997 merchandising at Ajax was brought back into the company. However, by the 2001/02 season, Ajax had reassessed its approach and outsourced a sizable part of the merchandising.

Ajax had more than 400 products for sale, varying from souvenirs and gadgets to clothing, cosmetics and household articles. Ajax estimated that about 50% of its total merchandise revenue came from sales of leisure goods and that 70,000 club shirts were sold a year.

In addition to the fan shop in the ArenA, the club had set up "shops-in-shops" in various chain stores across the country that sold Ajax articles exclusively. The club had comparatively little control over the number of points of sale at which its branded products could be sold within the ArenA, or over the degree to which it could expose fans to advertising its merchandise. On match days, Ajax generated about 3% of its merchandise revenues.

Through its mail order catalogue and its Dutch and international website offering merchandising products, the company aimed to gain more control over sales of its fast-moving products—the "real fan" articles such as shirts, scarves, caps and flags.

Exhibit 9 ● Dutch Television Rights

NLG m	Actual		Estimated			CAGR
	1997/98 NLG m	1998/99 NLG m	1999/00 NLG m	2000/01 NLG m	2001/02 NLG m	
NOS	35.3	35.3	50	50	50	9.2%
Canal Plus (assuming new contract)	16.5	22.4	28.3	34.1	40.0	24.8%
SBS	5.3	5.3	10	10	10	17.2%
International rights	5.0	5.0	10	10	10	18.9%
Total	**62.0**	**67.9**	**98.3**	**104.1**	**110.0**	*15.4%*
PTT Telecompetitie percentage	55%	55%	82%	83%	84%	
PTT Telecompetitie total payments	34.1	37.3	80.8	86.6	92.5	28.3%
Toto divisie total payments	27.9	30.5	17.5	17.5	17.5	
Proportion split equally between PTT Telecompetitie teams	80%	80%	50%	50%	50%	
Total fixed payment pot	27.3	29.9	40.4	43.3	46.3	*14.1%*
Number of PTT Telecompetitie clubs	18	18	18	18	18	
Fixed payment per club	1.5	1.7	2.2	2.4	2.6	*14.1%*
Pot available for performance related payments	6.8	7.5	40.4	43.3	46.3	*61.4%*
Payment to first placed team	0.6	0.6	3.4	3.6	3.9	*61.5%*
Payment to bottom placed team	0.2	0.2	1.1	1.2	1.3	*61.5%*
Maximum available payment per club	2.1	2.2	5.6	6.0	6.4	*32.5%*
Minimum available payment per club	1.7	1.8	3.4	3.6	3.9	*22.6%*
Ranking						
1	0.6	0.6	3.4	3.6	3.9	*61.5%*
18	0.2	0.2	1.1	1.2	1.3	*61.5%*
Total	**6.8**	**6.8**	**40.4**	**43.3**	**46.3**	*61.5%*

Source: ABN AMRO

BUSINESS MODEL: COSTS

Operating costs were broken down into fixed wages and social security contributions, bonuses, transfer fees and the costs of youth development. (*Refer back to Exhibit 8 for a breakdown of Ajax's costs.*)

Wages

In the 2001/02 season, Ajax paid 63.2% of its revenues in wages, up from 37.4% in 1996/97. The total cost covered the players in the first and second teams and the (usually younger) players in the reserves. The high Dutch upper income tax rate of 60% meant that Ajax had to pay more in absolute terms to allow a player to receive the same amount as he would receive in countries with lower tax rates.

Players also received bonuses for success in all of the major competitions in which the club participated.

Player Transfers

In December 1995 the Bosman ruling allowed out-of-contract players from European Union states to move freely to other clubs without payment of a transfer fee. Ajax was affected in two main ways. First, it had to pay substantially increased wages to persuade players to sign longer-term contracts so that it could ensure it had an opportunity to secure payment for them before their contracts expired. Second, Ajax lost five valuable players at the end of the 1994/95 season without receiving compensation and it had to spend heavily in the transfer market for the next two seasons to regain a full squad of high caliber players.

Ajax capitalized the total of transfer fees and other player costs and depreciated them in a straight line over the player's contract period. Transfer income was defined by the difference between a player's transfer fee and his book value.

Traditionally, Ajax was more of a net exporter of players as a result of its excellent youth training programs and its extensive scouting.

Exhibit 10 ● European Domestic Television Contracts

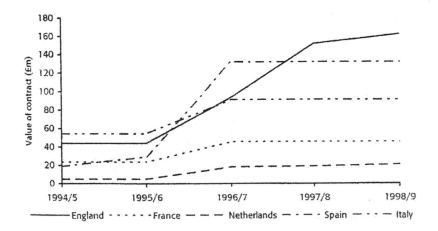

Total domestic television contracts

Source: Ajax Prospectus, 1998